Writing Plague

JEWISH CULTURE AND CONTEXTS

Published in association with the Herbert D. Katz Center for
Advanced Judaic Studies of the University of Pennsylvania

Series Editors:

Shaul Magid,

Francesca Trivellato,

Steven Weitzman

A complete list of books in the series
is available from the publisher.

WRITING PLAGUE

Jewish Responses to the
Great Italian Plague

Susan L. Einbinder

PENN

UNIVERSITY OF PENNSYLVANIA PRESS

PHILADELPHIA

Published by
University of Pennsylvania Press
Philadelphia, Pennsylvania 19104-4112
www.upenn.edu/pennpress

Printed in the United States of America on acid-free paper
10 9 8 7 6 5 4 3 2 1

Hardcover ISBN 9781512822878
Ebook ISBN 9781512822885

A Cataloging-in-Publication record is available from the
Library of Congress.

To Jerry Singerman
Unparalleled maker of books and friends
With deep gratitude and love

Contents

Figure 1. Map of Northern Italy, c. 1630. Created by Gordon Thompson, 2021.

Introduction

I was completing a book about the Black Death and Iberian Jews when Michelle Chesner, curator of Hebrew manuscripts at Columbia University, mentioned that library's copy of Abraham Catalano's account of the 1630–31 plague in the Paduan ghetto.[1] As I am not an early modernist, nor has my work specialized in Italian Jews, I was tempted to dismiss her suggestion that I take a look at it. As it turned out, Columbia's copy of this extraordinary narrative is probably the oldest; it was made by Isaac Hayim Cantarini (1644–1723), like Catalano a physician, who painstakingly inserted marginal descriptions of the kinship ties that bound him to some of the individuals mentioned in the narrative.[2] Catalano's extraordinary narrative was riveting, and so was the persona of the author. I began to look for more Jewish sources for this plague, and so began this book.

The immediate subject of this book is the Jewish experience in northern Italy during the Great Italian Plague of 1630–31, explored in a series of case studies focused on Hebrew textual witnesses to this event. Jewish sources on the Great Italian Plague of 1630–31 have not been collected before, nor assessed for what they contribute to a bigger picture of this major plague outbreak and how it affected people, institutions, and beliefs; how individuals and institutions responded to it; how they did or did not try to remember it. Many of the sources I bring together are new to scholars, and it has been necessary to devise new ways to work with them; thus my methods of reading these texts as well as the text themselves expand the kinds of writing we might use to shed light on historical questions.

One point I can underline is that genre—Jewish or Christian—matters. Early modern Italian Jews drew on their own classical and postclassical traditions, but also on the flourishing literary forms and trends around them. Some of the texts treated in this book are poetic, some are liturgical or homiletical, and some are narrative; each genre enlists its own conventions for representing collective catastrophe and harmonizing the potential dissonance between collective and individual trauma, memory, and loss.[3] With the exception of Chapter 4, the following chapters all explore unknown or nearly unknown Hebrew testimonies to the 1630–31 plague with an eye to strategies of authorial self-representation, and how these strategies shape and are shaped by plague. Joseph Concio's two-part lament, the topic of Chapter 1, commemorated plague victims in his own community in Chieri and the neighboring community in Turin, alternating biographical vignettes with penitential appeals for divine mercy and forgiveness. Many of the vignettes read like the poetic epitaphs they were undoubtedly intended to be and whose forms Concio had mastered as an occasional poet. In this memorial work Concio restores individuality to loved ones consigned for eternity to nameless mass graves; to do so he experimented with a fusion of old and new, vernacular and Hebrew associations. In particular he made a remarkable choice to compose these poems in the hendecasyllabic *terza rima* associated with Dante. Joseph's heart-wrenching description of his own son's death permits us also to raise questions of authorial voice and the relationship between private and public grief.

Chieri and Turin counterpoint the experience of Jews elsewhere in northern and central Italy, reminding us that Joseph Concio lived and wrote under conditions that did not characterize those of the other authors represented in these studies. Their singularity does not merely lie in plague, which ravaged the entire region in 1631, and which cities and health boards struggled ubiquitously to contain.[4] Rather, it is the fact that the Jewish Piedmontese communities were not yet in ghettoes: These were the last Italian Jewish communities to be enclosed. Although plans to construct a ghetto in Turin had been considered since the 1620s, they were not realized until 1679, and then not as originally conceived. For the remaining Piedmontese communities, walls did not rise until the 1720s and into the mid-eighteenth century.[5] In 1630 the distinction might be expected to have epidemiological consequences. As a rule, the physical footprint of a ghetto was small, far smaller than the community wished, and living conditions were cramped. One solution was to build upward, resulting in greater fire hazards and loss of light. Often, as in Venice, the ghetto was situated in a less than desirable location, susceptible to flooding and rarely graced with adequate drainage or sanitation. Nineteenth- and twentieth-century historians liked to imagine that superior hygiene practices among the Jews granted them some immunity to ravaging epidemics, but if anything conditions in the ghetto were stacked against such an outcome.[6] Enclosure concentrated a population that had previously been dispersed more widely, inside and outside of the city, albeit with predictable clustering around a synagogue, ritual bath, bakery, and slaughterer. The closure of the ghetto might win the community a temporary advantage in delaying the appearance of plague, but inevitably disease would breach the walls to devastating effect. By comparison, we might expect that the impact of a plague outbreak would be less severe in a setting of lower density, better air, and possibly cleaner water. That does not seem to have played out in 1630–31, for several reasons, beginning with the sustained droughts and warfare that had battered the region in recent years.

Directly or indirectly, four of the remaining five chapters circle the captivating figure of Abraham Catalano, the physician, civic leader, and author who survived to record the terrible plague of 1630–31 in Padua. Chapter 2 treats two Hebrew narrative accounts of the plague from Padua and Mantua. Abraham Catalano's 'Olam Hafukh (World Upside-down) has deservedly found some attention recently, and one can only hope that the entire text will soon find an able translator. In fact we must hope for two translators, as an Italian vernacular version of the text that seems to have preceded the Hebrew came to my attention only as this book reached completion. I have inserted brief references to this important manuscript where appropriate, but it warrants a full and detailed comparative study.[7] Catalano, a trained but not practicing physician, served on the Committee of Four that oversaw plague arrangements in the Paduan ghetto in 1630–31; his narrative is an extraordinary piece of writing by a literate, learned, and thoughtful man. Of all the authors I have met in assembling this work, he is by far my favorite, and he has to a large extent been the catalyst for this book's questions of self-representation and meaning. In contrast, Abraham Massarani of Mantua was not an eyewitness to the brutal war of succession and plague that culminated in the expulsion of Mantuan Jews. He assembled his account from survivors upon his return to the ghetto the following year, where he also played a role in negotiating the return of the remnants of the community. The plague is a peripheral player in his narrative, but a meaningful one. Shlomo Simonsohn's account of the Mantuan expulsion in his magisterial history of Mantuan Jews relied closely on Massarani's, which he excerpted in translation; Catalano has not received real attention otherwise and certainly not as a literary witness.[8] Massarani's chronicle serves as a foil to Catalano's, on the one hand demonstrating that the narrative techniques enlisted by the latter were not unique to his writing, and on the other rejecting plague as a narrative brace.[9]

I am interested in the way Catalano and Massarani construct their narratives to convey both their understanding of events and their role in them; in other words, I am interested not just in how these authors narrate plague but how plague, in some sense, narrates them as well.[10]

Chapter 3 turns to poetry, specifically the interpolation of poetry in the two prose accounts discussed in Chapter 2. Catalano's brief Aramaic lament for his wife is embedded midway through his Hebrew narrative, and a series of didactic poems by his son offering advice in times of plague is appended to its end. (Strikingly, both inserts are lacking in the earlier vernacular narrative.) Massarani's lament for the Jewish community of Mantua is inserted strategically between his account of their travails in expulsion and their return to the ghetto. To my knowledge interpolated poetry is not a feature of Christian plague narratives, and it merits attention as a genre adaptation unique to the Hebrew. Chapter 3 asks what purpose these poetic inserts serve, what they add to the prose, and how they change it. I claim that the interpolation of poetry does not just complement prose narration; it augments it, breaching the temporal and spatial constraints of the prose. In some cases, poetry suspends the chronological thrust and public emphasis of the narrative to permit the exposure of private grief and space; in others, it shifts the tenor of the overall narrative from trauma and loss to an assurance that providential design or civic institutions shall prevail over chaos. Massarani's poetic lament, for example, swerves his narrative arc away from the destitute, traumatized survivors to emphasize the providential redemption of restoration. Analogously, Moses Catalano's didactic verses transpose the weary pessimism of his father's narrative to a brighter key, emphasizing pragmatic agency with no-nonsense advice for future outbreaks.

Like Joseph Concio's laments, the liturgical compositions discussed in Chapter 4 also reach back into the past as well as out into the contemporary world around them, recycling and emending familiar *piyyutim* (hymns), occasionally composing new ones. The traditional liturgical recitation of the *Pitum haKetoret*, an assemblage of biblical and Talmudic passages describing the preparation of the incense used in the biblical cult, was generously embraced for plague liturgies, and Italian Jewish intellectuals, many with medical training, enthusiastically identified the biblical incense with the plague fumigation practices of their day. Although in certain respects an "outlier," this chapter moves steadily to the center of concerns raised in the preceding and following chapters. Ongoing recourse to the *Pitum haKetoret* and other liturgical favorites illustrates the pluralism of Jewish responses to plague in 1630–31: Liturgy, drawing on ancient topoi and sources, flourished alongside the more secularized genres of medical and historical writing, laments, sermons, and recipes. At the same time liturgy itself was a hybrid construct, plaiting traditional forms and texts with more recent compositions associated with local events and their pious authors, as well as contemporary practices imported from medicine and occult sciences. The sturdy survival of this liturgy into our own COVID times suggests also that the time-and-space-specific crafting of individual authors did not prove as durable as generic, recyclable prayer.

Chapter 5 turns to another of Catalano's cohort, the rabbi-physician Solomon Marini, the only one of Padua's two dozen rabbis to survive the 1630–31 plague. Two extant manuscripts preserve notations or outlines of sermons Marini delivered in Padua over the course of a long career and including the plague years of 1630–31. Hastily scrawled, they consist mostly of strings of prooftexts with minimal prose ligature. Nonetheless, they are important sources for a fuller picture of Jewish responses to the plague, and I have devised a way of reconstituting them for use to this end. In a homiletical medium, Marini as a preacher also exhibits some of the same concern for self-presentation and public identity that characterizes Catalano's and Massarani's narratives, and this aspect of his preaching sparked my interest. Finally, Chapter 6 takes the opportunity to ask how well all this self-fashioning worked. This chapter gathers a handful of texts composed to commemorate the death of the physician (and my hero) Abraham Catalano in 1641. The lengthy epitaph on Catalano's tombstone, which still stands, was published by David Malkiel in his study of Paduan Jewish gravestones.[11] In addition, two sermon outlines by Marini and a bilingual Hebrew-Aramaic lament by Abraham's son, Moses (the author of the didactic poems), survive. How they saw Abraham—or how they thought he would have wished to be seen—can therefore be juxtaposed with how he wished us to see him. Ironically, plague figures only in one of these witnesses— the epitaph—leaving us also with questions about how plague shaped Jewish memory and how Jewish memory reshaped plague.

Writing Plague hovers over the period from the summer of 1630 to a little more than a year later, the period roughly corresponding to the plague outbreak in the north. The commemorative texts composed following Abraham Catalano's death in 1641, and Rabbi Marini's 1656 sermon on behalf of the plague-stricken Jews of Rome, permit some insight into the lingering impact and memory of the epidemic. Certainly both Catalano's Hebrew account and Massarani's chronicle were composed at some distance from the event; future comparison of Catalano's Hebrew and Italian narratives may clarify some of the ways that retrospection mattered. So, too, the survival or disappearance of texts, rituals, and personages from subsequent history conveys useful information. The liturgical chapter reminds us that traditional framing and language continued to function alongside newer genres, and in fact showed greater durability over time. The literary pluralism that characterizes early modern plague response is a theme I invoke repeatedly in this book. Implicitly, Jewish sources remind us that plague experience exceeded the meaning capacity of any single genre. The dance of multiple options for making meaning equally reflects a normative feature of early modern Jewish life, a feature strained by plague but not extinguished.

Likewise, questions of subsequent memory are intrinsic to these texts. To some degree the survival of Jewish writing is always a matter of historical caprice. That is not a novel observation. However, I claim also that the survival or disappearance of this catastrophic epidemic in Jewish memory is also inextricable from the choices made by our authors. A major theme of this book is the importance of narrative voice and the use of that voice as a vehicle for authorial self-fashioning. The sophisticated and deliberate ways these authors represented themselves reveal a complex process of self-fashioning that equally contours the representation and meaning of plague; conversely, it is under the strain of plague that conventions of self-fashioning come to the fore. The idea of "self-fashioning," which we associate with the hallmark studies of Stephen Greenblatt, is deepened in my usage by readings in anthropology, sociology, and the social sciences.[12] I also push the concept further than the familiar distinction between author and narrator that we have recognized for decades. I am arguing in this book for a reciprocal relationship between the forms of self-representation in writing—the techniques, the selective vignettes, the type-scenes of conflict (failed or surmounted) the narrators encounter—and the way these authors saw themselves. All of them were public figures with responsibilities for their communities. Sometimes, as in Joseph Concio's case, those responsibilities fell to them as a consequence of the plague, with the request to commemorate the victims. In Abraham Massarani's case, the expulsion that accompanied the plague in Mantua involved him in negotiations for the community's return. Abraham Catalano and Solomon Marini in Padua, on the other hand, had roles as communal leaders before the plague and continued to exercise them afterward. How they were seen by their communities was important to them, and their writings expose self-conscious strategies for representing themselves in ways that their coevals understood and admired. Conversely, public image pointed inward as well as out; it played a role in how these writers saw themselves as "private" men, extending a vocabulary for self-expression into domestic and personal terrain.[13]

The early modern distinction between public and private, therefore, is not as sharply drawn as it might be in our own time. The authors depict themselves in their families and communities at moments of personal stress that electrify the boundaries between individuals and collectives. Over the span of a narrative, these charged lines illumine a self-portrait; they are complemented by the use of type-scenes that constitute their own idiom of self-fashioning. The following chapters permit us to identify this language of self-construction and analyze specific examples of its use. This should be a desideratum for analysis of other texts responding to premodern epidemics or other forms of collective catastrophe. I focus on representations of anxiety, family, and domestic or public conflict, but other elements of affective or social behavior might equally be pursued. Anxiety, for instance, characterizes the narrator's voice in Massarani's and Catalano's accounts—but anxiety is a strategically enlisted emotion that captures a specific kind of tension between the exercise of public duty and private life.[14] It is not that the narrators are falsely representing themselves; it would be very strange if they did not feel anxious given the circumstances. But the invocation of anxiety articulates a value, projecting concern and dedication to the public good—and a desire to be seen embodying that value.

Similarly, in these plague settings, questions of family (and communal) loyalty and obligation emerge repeatedly. Families conceal illness from the authorities or nurse loved ones at certain risk to their own lives; at the other extreme, family members abandon parents, spouses, or children, hoard or sell scarce goods, report neighbors for violations of quarantine or flight. Italian Jewish sources document the significance of family ties in the dynastic strength of banking, rabbinic, and physicians' families, but they also permit glimpses of the durability of poor or broken families that staggered along on the social periphery. In plague chronicles and poetry, the motif of the dissolution of family ties highlights how critical relationships of kinship were to an individual and social sense of mooring and meaning. As Shona Wray and James Amelang have both underlined, this recurring thematic strand in plague literature also underlines an implicitly or explicitly articulated concern for the common good.[15]

Intriguingly, the Jewish plague texts from early modern Italy enlist family imagery selectively and deliberately. Liturgical and medical genres largely elide mention of families. Synagogue poetry, illustrated in several laments treated in this book, invokes individual human beings as types or metonyms for a collective. A Jew represents all Jews, and a Christian represents generic Christians. Women and children cannot serve this end in the patriarchal models governing the genre. In contrast, the *'Olam Hafukh*, Abraham Catalano's plague narrative from the Paduan ghetto, is full of references to children, mothers, nursemaids, siblings, widows, and orphans. As I will argue, his narrative also artfully maneuvers between depictions of his personal family crises and those that unfold on a communal scale and for which he bears administrative responsibility; the tension between private and public duty is central to his account. Abraham Catalano has deep ties of affection not only to his wife and children but to his in-laws and their family, and to household servants as well. The relationships captured in his prose narrative, or in Joseph Concio's double commemorative lament, also disclose non–nuclear family ties to nursemaids and servants, student boarders, business partners and guests. Extended dynastic relationships bind these elite authors and their families to wider affective networks. Indeed, while Solomon Marini's sermons in Padua during and immediately after the 1630–31 plague do not invoke family, they emphasize Jewish ties and mutual obligation that extend to a wider network of Italian Jewish settlements, as is vividly illustrated in his 1656 sermon urging Paduan Jews to provide aid for Jews in Rome suffering from famine and plague.

These Jewish authors were without exception educated, privileged, and male; most if not all of them were linked by birth to dynastic networks that spanned communities in northern Italy and sometimes beyond. Catalano and Marini were graduates of the University of Padua; Massarani's father—a musician, composer, and dancer—was an intimate in the Gonzaga court. Their perspectives reflect their stations in life, as do their reactions to hardship and expectations of redress. Personal and professional relationships with Christian peers are common, but analogous crossing of class lines is hard to find. Compassion across class lines, even rarer, finds expression in the language of collective responsibility, as when Abraham Catalano resists withholding aid to the poor to coerce them into serving the sick and dead. In a more intimate setting, Abraham poignantly depicts his wife's attempt to shield their Christian servant from sickness, a decision that leads to her own sickness and death.

What proves ultimately most striking about all these accounts, however, is that, with the exception of the (generic) *Pitum haKetoret* liturgy, they do not last. As collective memory, the 1630–31 pandemic in Jewish sources, at least, went the way of other natural disasters, earthquakes, floods, and fires. That, too, is worth pondering, and this book concludes on this note. Why was this plague pandemic, according to historians the most documented of all outbreaks since the Black Death, consigned to such silence in collective Jewish memory? Or did collective memory take shape outside the written or material remains we typically consult, in ephemeral forms that were lost or suppressed over time? Indeed, how much were the official genres of commemoration *responsible* for the erosion of local historical memory? Did they help individuals find language for private experience, and how did they enlist private experience to signify public grief? How do we disentangle the constructs of public and private speech, or public and private fashioning, to make plausible our claims about what people felt or did at all?

The prose narratives of Abraham Catalano and Abraham Massarani provide two of the most gripping testimonies of the Great Italian Plague among Jewish communities, and they also emblematize challenges that arise when dealing with narrative sources. There are two reasons that narrative prose continues to dominate questions (and studies) of history and meaning. The first is the assumption that narrative, more than other types of writing or speech, looks most like "real life." The idea that narrative mimics life boosts it considerably in historical studies, but also among scholars of literature who privilege the kinds of meaning that emerge from prose exposition. The second is the equally popular but inverse assumption that life mimics narrative, meaning that narrative discourse offers its users a way to make meaning of their own experiences (to construct a "self") and what they perceive occurring outside them in the world. Each of these assumptions is problematic.

Our attachment to narrative, whether in the belief that it mirrors or constructs reality, is a culturally bound conviction. The idea that narrative mimics life more than other types of language emerges from the modern belief that prose looks more "real" than, say, verse. In fact, those who claim realism as a property of narrative prose often have poetry in mind as its antithesis. This idea is very old. Skimping on poetry's affinity for aural and rhythmic effects (which target emotional rather than rational faculties), prose seemed more "factual" and trustworthy, of course assuming that "factual" better represented our experience of reality. Similarly, the argument that poetry and prose might be expressing different *kinds* of truth or reality was often limited to the notion that poetry better expressed affect in ways that logical narrative could not.

Another aspect of prose narrative that privileged it in modern Western eyes was its attraction to linearity. Real life was linear, this argument assumed, and so was narrative; an attachment to chronological exposition was therefore intrinsic to narrative's superior "realness." This claim that narrative authentically mimics biological or mental process is something I do not think experience affirms. We live life in biological progression from birth to death, but that is not necessarily how we experience it. As for the plague accounts that Samuel Cohn has called *successo dalla peste* narratives, convention demands that they track plague chronologically from its first known manifestation through its spread and mounting toll, frequently followed by a winter lull and renewed outbreak in the spring, then a denouement.[16] Yet, although Catalano's and Concio's accounts of the plague nominally adhere to this format, they also resist linearity as a determinant of meaning. The day-by-day iteration of death, up and down, makes for boring literature.[17] What animates the narrative chronology of outbreak to epidemic to recovery are the moments when the narrative veers away from clockwork chronology, doubling back or slowing down to describe conflict or time-stopping moments of shock and dismay. Haunting vignettes linger as we read on— the wagons carrying the dead through the nighttime streets of Padua, a child trapped under a dead sibling, a menacing official, an orphaned infant unsuccessfully nursed by a goat. Narratives also end, and an author shapes them toward that culmination. Abraham Massarani's narrative ends triumphantly with the departure of imperial troops from the city and the return of the duke of Gonzaga. The debilitated state of the Jewish remnant that returned to the ghetto is downplayed, as are their subsequent woes. For Abraham Catalano in Padua, the "end" is a somber checklist for future epidemics, most of them inspired by inadequate or failed planning in 1630. Certainly, these narratives capture a human need to look back on catastrophe and try to make sense of what it meant. But their conclusions are foreordained— the plague has ended, permitting the narrator to narrate from a safe "afterward" beyond his story, which acquires its beginning and middle in hindsight as well.

Narrative is also characterized by omission. Someone's reality speaks at the expense of others. That is why it is so important in Catalano's and Massarani's accounts when other voices disrupt the narrator's, or when desperate people defy the regulations, policies, and interpretations imposed on them by institutions and authorities. These scenes remind us that we cannot identify policies and regulations with what people actually did, but they also beg us to ask why men with responsibility for implementing them were invested in describing their failure. So, too, something is afoot when poetry disrupts prose, intruding a competing temporality and priorities. How these competing representations of "reality" work with and against each other is the subject of Chapter 3.

The assumption that life mimics narrative is equally problematic. Across disciplines we encounter the argument that human beings are attracted "naturally" to narrative in order to organize reality; it is the brain's natural way for people to make sense of their lives and who they (think they) are. Narrative in this context is synonymous with storytelling; it is key to self-fashioning, but also to self-knowledge. This belief is core to Western trauma theory, which links healing to the victim's ability to narrate traumatic experience that has been erased or displaced, escaping verbal memory. Narratologists (understandably) also express conviction in the centrality of narrative as a tool for organizing experience and a sense of self.[18] Other psychological and anthropological studies have pushed back against this desire to privilege narrative modes of thinking.[19] Postmodern cultural theory has also favored nonlinearity and rupture as generators of meaning. But my point here is really that plague, like other catastrophes, can be processed in more than one way, and most likely was. Narrative offered one way to make sense of plague, but narrative did not perform unaccompanied by other ways of making meaning. To cite Mark Jenner, we must "move beyond the concentration on 'narrative' predominant in cultural histories of epidemic disease."[20] Jenner's work points to the coexistence of visual and graphic representation; this book emphasizes liturgical, homiletical, and poetic discourses that coexisted with narrative prose.

Very few early modern people would have relied exclusively on narrative prose to understand their world. A multiplicity of narrative and non-narrative options for organizing experience, emotion, subjectivity, and history existed in 1630 as they do now. In fact, we move easily among them, shifting paradigms instinctively when a change of gears is called for. A seventeenth-century Italian Jew could pray in the morning and then turn to commerce, medicine, or Kabbalah, just as today it is possible to pray or meditate, read the news over coffee, then turn to work, pick up a cello or teach poetry, sell software, study genetics, grow soybeans, or fly a plane. Among extant Jewish manuscripts and codices, the abundance of liturgical manuscripts and codices testifies to the ongoing durability of liturgical ways of ordering experience for individuals and communities. Liturgical texts, though choreographed according to predictable sequences, are inherently nonlinear, enclosing present catastrophes in the tropes of sacred history. Jewish plague liturgies, like individual plague hymns, also cast their sights far past human history to anchor in eternity. That is a narrative arc, to be sure, but one that is quite different from the earthly conclusion of the plague narratives or medical tracts. Music and visual art do this work of making meaning, too, as do amulets, scents, tactile artifacts; so did the spatial organization of the city, the choreographed movement between city and countryside, or between city and ghetto. To single out narrative prose as a precocious forerunner to our own kind of consciousness and cultural condition lets familiarity overshadow the presence of active alternatives.

These observations, like others that emerge from the close readings informing this book, underline the importance of recognizing the genre conventions and related cultural idioms that undergird writing plague, but also what is recognizably familiar and human in their witness. Precisely because plague strained domestic and public domains so severely, the attempt to put its effects in writing bares the ever-shifting dialectic that defines us as individuals (and writers) in relationship to overlapping private and public collectives. The ways we relate ourselves to the communities, institutions, national or transnational bodies around us surely leave their traces in the flood of literary activity during COVID-19's emergence and spread; some future study may probe these themes valuably. The present study of an early modern epidemic emphasizes the inextricability of the authorial "self" from a plague account, with the awareness that plague acted reciprocally on what that "self" was expected to be and where it was doomed to fall short of an ideal. How much the same dialectic of interdependence and strain characterizes Christian (or Muslim) accounts is a question that other scholars may wish to pursue. Minimally, the Hebrew sources enrich the Italian Christian records that voluminously document the devastation of the Great Italian Plague and shed light on aspects of plague experience not highlighted by previous studies. The pluralism of plague responses, the strained boundaries of self and family or community, the stress on belief systems and on the civic or religious institutions responsible for disciplining and producing meaning, also come to the fore. So, too, does the tension between erasure and commemoration, memory as simultaneously an impediment to and foundation stone of recovery. Future studies will tell us more.

A brief historical overview follows, with a return to our Jewish sources, and some of the challenges of writing plague, then and now.

*   *   *

Although most studies of the 1630–31 plague focus on specific city-states or regions, they echo each other in pronouncing this outbreak the worst to reach northern Italy since the Black Death.[21] Synthesizing contemporary accounts and the evidence of death registers and administrative records, historians note the coincidence of plague and war, in this case the Thirty Years' War that spilled into northern Italy in 1629 with the death of the duke of Mantua and the battle over his successor. German armies entering northern Italy in 1629 were blamed by contemporary chroniclers for bringing plague. This is possible: Henderson notes that the first cases were seen in October 1629, west of Turin in the Piedmont, with the arrival of German troops, and soon after in Milan.[22] Suppressed by the onset of winter, the outbreak gained new force in the spring of 1630, erupting in Milan in March, reaching Bologna by May and Florence and Tuscany by summer. Mantua was also struck in the summer of 1630, and Padua by summer's end. The Mantuan ghetto seems to have been hit by disease around the same time as the Christian city; Massarani describes the plight of the sick and dying when the Germans entered the city in August and, soon after, expelled the Jews. In contrast, the outbreak in the Paduan ghetto lagged considerably behind that of the Christian city, where plague was active by late summer or September, perhaps because the ghetto was quickly put under closure.[23] One of Solomon Marini's sermons responds to the initial sparing of the ghetto, which at the time seemed an act of divinely ordained mercy. God would change His mind by winter, as was clear to all. In Venice, where the plague struck during the High Holy Days of 1630, it slackened during the winter; in the early spring, the enclosure of the Jews delayed the resurgence experienced in the Christian city, sparing the Jews in what Judah Modena also described as an act of God.[24] These epidemiological details suggest the ways that variability in topography, enclosure, human activity, and Christian-Jewish and human-animal relationships influenced the trajectory of plague as well as its uneven ferocity. Ecological and environmental factors mattered also, and scholars today still struggle to understand them. The complex interrelationships of wild and commensal rodents, cultivated and uncultivated land, comorbidity and traffic between country and city, add to the impact of social inequity, violence, and ignorance.[25]

The statistics of loss are staggering. Although mortality varied from city to city, and between urban and rural spaces, an estimated 27 percent mortality for northern Italy remains credible. In some locations it was far worse. In Milan—whose outbreak was immortalized by Alessandro Manzoni in his epic novel, *I Promessi Sposi*—a pre-plague population of approximately 130,000 was reduced to 70,000 by August 1630.[26] In Parma, with a pre-plague population of approximately 30,000, fatalities of 16,000 to 18,000 were tallied between April and June 1630.[27] In Verona approximately 30,000 of a total population of 53,000 were lost to plague, and Venice, with roughly 45,000 dead, lost one third of its population.[28] Battered by plague and expulsion, Mantua's pre-plague Jewish population of two thousand was halved by the fall of 1631.[29] In Padua an estimated 30,000 inhabitants died of plague out of an urban population of approximately 100,000; in the ghetto more than half of the Jews perished.[30] A census taken at the start of the epidemic recorded 721 inhabitants in the Paduan ghetto; when the city's chief health officer (*provveditore*) officially declared the epidemic over in the fall of 1631, 421 were dead.[31] With the exception of Milan, which had expelled its Jews in 1597, these cities all had ghettos.

And yet: When compared to mid-fourteenth-century options, the range of early modern institutional responses to plague, and their hefty bureaucratic weight, remain terrifically impressive. The Black Death caught European cities and villages unprepared; nothing on this scale of mortality or indiscriminate devastation persisted in historical memory, and what forces might be mobilized to stop or treat it, while drawing on preexisting practices, were largely improvised.[32] As Ann Carmichael has noted, early experiments in quarantine and other containment measures were so visibly ineffectual that they were largely abandoned for the next hundred years.[33] But by the mid-fifteenth century, plague was a regular visitor—not, however, in the indiscriminate, highly virulent form it had taken in 1348 but as a continuous series of localized outbreaks, lower in mortality, that landed more heavily on the poor. Bureaucratic responses did not take long to emerge.[34]

The vulnerability of northern Italy to pandemic catastrophe in 1629 is a topos of the studies. War, with its endless streams of armies, brought misery to a region that was already suffering from successive droughts, famine, and severe economic depression. Among contemporary accounts that are hardly notable for pro-Habsburg sympathy, a sense of the soldiers' misery is palpable. The physician A. Tadino in Milan reported the "wantonness and . . . dirtiness" of the plague-stricken soldiers, describing the "unbearable odors due to the rotting straw where they sleep and die."[35] The Venetian forces sent to counter the Habsburg incursion were heavily composed of mercenaries, who dispersed with defeat to range the countryside, starving, filthy, and desperate. Typhus accompanied them as well as plague, and most likely a variety of other ailments: Edgardo Morpurgo's comprehensive account refers to waves of smallpox and measles in 1629, as well as some kind of bovine/ovine epidemic, perhaps rinderpest, as he describes "una infezione general fra gli ovine e bovini nel Padovano della flacidezza."[36] He believed that typhus preceded plague in 1630.[37] Early modern accounts hew rigidly to a conviction that outbreaks were traceable to a single "Patient Zero," and most of the Hebrew records follow this pattern, which becomes a genre convention. Nonetheless, the truth is that plague and its companion diseases had many points of emergence, and logically so. Indeed, as Ann Carmichael and others who have shifted our attention to enzootic models for regional plague persistence point out, *Yersinia pestis* had found a home in northern Italy for centuries following the Black Death; war arrived to tip the balance fatally on the heels of longer trends of ecological disruption, land clearing, commercial traffic, and climate change, making plague a story about humans again. Scholars today struggle to convey the complexity of these factors, whose relevance is critical to understanding the emergence of pandemic conditions and their outcome.

The Patient Zero model is both an epidemiological and narrative device: as epidemiology, it is linked to contagion models that should have competed with causation models that focused on corrupted air (miasma); in fact, both explanations often traveled together.[38] As narrative technique, it marks the moment when conditions of equilibrium begin their deadly transition into a human-centric story. In 1630 that story was one of stunning mortality that unfolded swiftly and inexorably, pausing briefly in some regions during the colder months and resuming at an even more frantic pace in the spring. The Paduan ghetto did not mark the end of the outbreak until August 1631, and as John Henderson notes of Florence, sputtering recurrences startled weary communities into the following year.[39] The Jewish sources discussed in this book capture the shock and panic of the initial phase as well as the weary numbness that concluded it. Abraham Catalano vividly preserves the frantic efforts of ghetto officials to prepare for an outbreak whose force would soon surpass all estimates, an impact echoed in Joseph Concio's verse vignettes and Solomon Marini's homiletical emphasis on the inscrutability of divine will and the inadequacy of human knowledge. So, too, the pessimistic counsel that concludes Catalano's essay testifies to the cumulative effects of this outbreak, and the foundering steps a community might take to rebuild and prepare for future disaster. Abraham Massarani, who attempted to conclude his chronicle on a brighter note, was nonetheless stupefied to return to Mantua to find his mother dead and his family home usurped by occupying officers. He, too, describes a period of helpless paralysis. In his expulsion narrative plague is collateral to other kinds of catastrophe whose solution is ultimately political, not medical, and manifested in the Gonzaga return to rule. Even so his chronicle repeatedly notes the degree of hospitality or rejection offered the disease-ridden exiles, implicitly linking plague policy to the durability of social and urban ties. It was a standard most rulers failed to meet. Even the indefatigable Marini implicitly acknowledges the lingering emotional and financial depletion of his flock when, twenty-five years later, he must exhort them to come to the aid of fellow Jews in plague-stricken Rome.

Genetic studies have identified the *Y. pestis* strain that characterized this outbreak in the aDNA (ancient DNA) of dental pulp from seventeenth-century soldiers' remains in Germany; it is a direct descendant of the Black Death genotype.[40] Whether German soldiers imported *Y. pestis* into Italy or added it to an existing reservoir is less clear; in the late 1620s plague was also active in Lyon and other French regions, which could have supplied a second route of importation. From the perspective of *Yersinia pestis,* the flea or louse that was fated to carry it, or the rodent that carried the flea, war, like changing patterns of land use, travel, and climate, offered opportunities as well as challenges. Pathogens, rodents, and ectoparasites adapted. Their side of the story remains to be told. This book focuses chiefly on the period when arthropods, insects, and rodents crossed paths with vulnerable humans.[41]

*   *   *

How *we* read, how we write, and where we hide in our writing also have preoccupied me in writing this book. Our own witting and unwitting alignment with certain narratives, character types, and displays of value, feeling, or experience influence both our reading of the past and the way we direct others to read it with us. Our desire to find meaning in past events and their testimonies to struggle exerts another kind of pressure on the textual record and how we use it.[42] The narrators of past catastrophes, like the men who wrote commemorative verses, epitaphs, or drug recipes, earn our recognition; we come to see them as people we might have known and whose choices, conflicts, and suffering can evoke identification and empathy. And yet, whereas cultural anthropologists have grappled for decades with the awareness that their presence as observers among their subjects alters the picture they draw, we as literary and historical scholars have not said much about the ways our own presence changes the world of our texts, or how they might resist us.

(They can!) On the simplest level, we select what we are studying, whether it is a topic among myriad topics or an author, event, or text among a set of possible others. We are drawn to scholarly projects for whatever personal, professional, or historical reasons, which we want to make appealing to others. By the same token we want our topics to make us look appealing also.

We are selective, too, in the questions we ask. Scholars of the past pursue questions we care about in the present. Pandemic history now has tragic relevance, but also cachet; the coronavirus has done wonders for plague historians' careers, although this richly interdisciplinary meeting ground of scholars has been thriving for some time. For me, personally, an interest in past pandemics emerged from a career devoted to medieval European Jewish communities and their responses to violence, persecution, and catastrophe—topics that have meaning to me for reasons of which I may only partially be aware. The same is true for questions about family bonds, gender, class, and power, or about the ways human beings understand each other and themselves, or the place of sacred meaning in their lives. These questions rise and fall because social history brings them to the surface or submerges them, but they also reflect our own sense of personal and institutional identity, insider- or outsiderness, solved and unsolved problems, pleasures and pains.

It is hard to avoid the tendency to point the past to us, and too often we align our texts or artifacts to conform to a narrative we wish to find. Likewise, we privilege the expression of behaviors or values that speak to us now, elevating virtues because they are our virtues, bracketing behaviors we find immoral or inhumane. "History from below" has powerfully revised our picture of the past, and I am all for it. I am, nonetheless, observing that we as scholars stand inside our own history, and questions of power versus powerlessness, subjectivity versus agency, individuality versus solidarity, are stamped with our address. The social sciences have an edge on us right now in exposing this emic nerve.

By extension, the valorization of history from below offers a way of valorizing our own role as writers of this history; our heightened sensitivity to experiences of suffering and past injustice presents us as advocates on behalf of the victims of history. I am not condemning this practice. Rather, I am saying we need to be more aware of how we stand with respect to our subject matter. Advocacy is a tricky business. Without intending to do so, our need to identify with those we deem innocent and vulnerable may occlude experiences and dynamics that are ill-suited to our subject in favor of those that register marginality or distress. The richness of Jewish life in medieval and early modern Europe, for example, survives in an astonishing polyphony of texts and material witnesses; it deserves more than this reductionism. Yes, we are desperate for a "usable past." But the past, like its authors, is not passive; it tolerates homiletic bending but ultimately resists advocacy dressed as history. So, too, we cannot assume a facile equivalency of categories across history. What it meant in another time and place to be a "self," or how social, cultural, religious, and other idioms contoured the interplay of individual and communal identities; what it meant to see the "other"; what role affective ties played in self-definition and how one viewed those less fortunate or powerful, or conversely, more fortunate and powerful; how Jews saw themselves in expanding networks of kinship and obligation beyond the boundaries of daily existence—all these things are moving, not stable, and they must be defined and redefined again and again. Plague, and especially a terrible plague like the 1630–31 outbreak, can be a fruitful lens through which to ask how these connections were understood in early modern northern Italy. What we find may contrast with our own experience as much as it echoes it.

And finally, our writing. Writing is a sly medium. We are not anthropologists or clinical therapists. The people I write about are long dead, and I, like others who study the past, have a relationship to them that is articulated in teaching and writing. The premodern authors I treat in this book can be credited with writing smartly, aware that language communicated not just content but a portrait of themselves. So, too, do we ply words to communicate findings and insights but also identity—not just theirs but ours. How we write and speak is also something we learn, either by imitating those we admire or what the system rewards. We perch our sentences on mountains of footnotes. We cite sources in multiple languages. We imbibe trending terms. We may write dense, impenetrable prose, strutting contorted syntax and jargon.[43] Alternatively, we may write clearly, but invoking the language of morality and witness, to steer other sympathies. Or we may write some other way altogether. No matter how we choose, we stage ourselves as privileged witnesses to the past who seek to impress, persuade, and move. But who is it we are moving? And where? And here I have no real answer. Even to write the questions is to acknowledge that the house is burning, and academic words burn cheaply in its flames. I can only leave the question, and a half-consolation: We write for ourselves, assuredly, because we are that kind of people. But we also write for each other, the way that Abraham Catalano wrote for us, reaching beyond what is burning to remember what can be built.

Chapter 1

Poetry, Prose, and Pestilence
Joseph Concio and Jewish Responses to the 1630–31
Italian Plague

Jewish writings about the Great Italian Plague of 1630–31 respond to the same event, but they do so in different ways. Nevertheless, there are a few things we can say about all of them. Whether they are poems of mourning and commemoration, didactic verse, historical chronicles, or medical tracts, Jewish plague writing is shaped by the evocative range of classical Hebrew, the conventions and constraints of Jewish genres, and an acute awareness of cognate writing by Christian authors. Many of the attitudes and everyday beliefs of their Christian neighbors and sources permeated Jewish circles, too. The Jewish authors are also familiar—sometimes personally—with each other and their respective literary efforts. The tussle of old and new, outside and inside, resolves distinctively in each exemplar; yet each of the literary efforts treated in this book struggles with the limits of conventional genres to express the enormity of what its author wanted to convey. As we shall see, the writers' frustration rarely if ever led them to jettison convention completely, but more often to press its limits formally and thematically in ways that illuminate their sense of themselves, and their relationship to a wider community and to what had befallen them.

I begin with what is perhaps the most unusual of these Hebrew testimonies, Joseph Concio's two-part lament, *Zokher haNeshamot* ("In Memoriam"). One other extant lament in Hebrew, by Abraham Massarani, documents this outbreak and will be treated later as a more conventional composition. In contrast, Joseph's lament illustrates what may have been a unique solution to the challenge of adapting a traditional genre to new needs. Those needs were not merely literary; they were social, theological, and spiritual, and arose from the immediate challenges of rebuilding a community of grieving and impoverished survivors. And yet, because it is poetry, the *Zokher haNeshamot* is more than a sociological artifact. It makes meaning by making literary choices and using language, sound, allusions, and imagery in literary ways. It is only by reading it through this lens that we discover its potential to fill historical gaps as well. In other words, even when the *Zokher haNeshamot* tells us something about history, it does so as poetry: what Joseph Concio wished us to know and to remember is inseparable from the way he chose to write it down.

Joseph's compelling poem launches this study for several reasons. It is unique as a formal experiment, at least to judge by what has survived, and yet points to preoccupations reflected in the other genres we shall examine. It is commemorative, like some of the other texts treated in this book, and underscores the challenge of memorializing individual members of a community in the wake of mass death. Behind the struggle to remember each man, woman, and child who fell victim to the plague over the late summer into the winter of 1630–31, we sense the lingering trauma of mass burial minus the comfort of ritual and mourners, the dead whose final departure from the living held no dignity and left no stone. Joseph's lament, like the lament embedded by Abraham Massarani in his chronicle for the Jews of Mantua, also stands at one end of the spectrum of public voices an author might adopt in a text of public commemoration. Other authors positioned themselves differently along that spectrum, and I treat them in later chapters.

Whether intentionally or not, the Hebrew testimonies to the 1630–31 plague preserve information about social institutions and practices that governed Jewish life in northern Italy in times of crisis. In this regard, the *Zokher haNeshamot* is unique in being the only composition treated in this book that comes to us from an Italian community that had yet to be enclosed in a ghetto. How that may have shaped its content and concerns, the poet's voice, and his sense of his role in his community are questions that open the door to considering the ways other authors and works responded to similar pressures within ghetto walls. For plague historians, the unenclosed communities of Turin and Chieri have epidemiological interest, too, and may be compared to the experience of plague within the crowded confines of the ghetto. Curiously, fatality rates do not seem to have differed greatly—worth noting in itself—but other aspects of this pandemic did. If the ghetto communities suffered from cramped housing and lack of hygiene, they nonetheless had their own physicians and lazarettos, with considerable autonomy for managing internal Jewish affairs. While the Jews of Turin and Chieri memorialized by Joseph Concio were undoubtedly concentrated in "Jewish neighborhoods" or streets, he does not mention physicians attending specifically to their needs; if I read the lament correctly, the sick and dying often met their ends in the Christian lazaretto.

And yet, whether their authors and communities were enclosed or not, all the texts treated in the following pages share certain goals. Like plague writing in general, each seeks to shape the memory and meaning of historical experience for future readers. In doing so, each blends images of private and public life in distinctive ways. How and when each author weaves his own experience into his writing, and what this tells us about the uses of private grief and trauma as vehicles for expressing collective experience and cohering public memory can illuminate other aspects of early modern Jewish life in Italy and perhaps beyond. Scholars of Christian or Islamic plague accounts may wish to ask whether my conclusions characterize their texts as well.

Hebrew sources on the Great Italian Plague of 1630–31 have only recently begun to interest scholars, but they have been there all along for us to find. Like the abundant plague writings in Latin and Italian to which they add, Hebrew sources constitute a corpus, which will undoubtedly expand as new examples join those treated or mentioned in this book. Already the wealth of this collection tells us much about the importance of literature as a way of responding to catastrophic events. The range of perspectives and genres represented also signals that, for these seventeenth-century Jews, it was possible and even necessary to view catastrophe through multiple lenses. In this sense they mark a long distance from the medieval world and authors who preceded them. The assertive hybridity that characterizes all these works is reflected in their literary strategies, but also in the self-representation of the authors and their sense of themselves as voices of authority and witness for their communities. So, too, it is important to remember that these works and genres coexisted with each other, offering a multiplicity of options for making sense of a pandemic and for moving effortlessly among them.

It is one of my claims in this book that, varied though their forms and voices may be, the Jewish authors strove to depict themselves as idealized public men with responsibilities for their communities which they did not shirk in a time of great crisis. Their personal losses during the plague legitimate their accounts of wider suffering while testifying to the relentless pressure of juggling private and public roles. The authorial voice that characterizes different genres and texts will vary but in each case documents the ways private experience could be harnessed in the construction of public memory; movingly, each case equally suggests how much the resulting projection of "self" into public space reverberated in how the authors understood themselves. What we would anachronistically label "identity" is something worked out not in retreat from public scrutiny but in an unceasing dialectic of public and private worlds and their representations. The Jewish authors, all men learned in Jewish texts and traditions, were also deeply immersed in vernacular Italian literature and culture, and their writings offer a deliberate synthesis of Italian form and aesthetics with Hebrew language and its own legacy of literary elegance. If their accounts assimilate vernacular techniques of self-representation, they equally testify to similar social and cultural pressures to represent, and be represented, in certain ways, modeling attributes that shaped public and private identity. With these observations in mind, we can begin to look at our first example, the two-part lament known as the *Zokher haNeshamot* by Joseph Concio in Chieri.

Joseph Concio and His Laments

The *Zokher haNeshamot* is a two-part poem, or two conjoined poems, extant today in two unpublished copies, one complete copy in Paris at the Alliance Israelite Universelle and one partial copy in New York City at the Jewish Theological Seminary.[1] Both copies include a title page that clearly demarcates the two parts to follow: "The First Story" commemorates the Jewish plague victims in the city of Turin, and "The Second Story" performs this task for the Jewish victims in Chieri. They are of approximately equal length, and each is comprised of three-line stanzas. Each lament contains a brief introduction, a long commemorative sequence that eulogizes victims by name and frequently by kinship, and a long penitential conclusion that taps familiar liturgical conventions (for instance, "Our Father, our King, we have sinned etc.") and petitions God for forgiveness and relief. At first glance the laments are unexceptional to an eye trained on medieval tropes. Indeed, unlike the ghetto writers who emphasize their modernity, Joseph builds on medieval foundations—but they are not the foundations we expect. While there is little new in Joseph's puns or prooftexts, and nothing new in his emphasis on sin and repentance, his prosodic scaffolding is a surprise: a decasyllabic line arranged in *terza rima*, exclusively associated with Dante.[2] Therefore, at a moment when his contemporaries

in Padua, Mantua, and Venice were experimenting with new and trendy literary forms, Joseph took a different tack and looked backward to the medieval,
vernacular legacy of Dante.

To understand why he might have done so, we must look at the twinned
poems, a blend of idealized encomia and biographical detail, social history,
and penitential themes. Following some general comments, I want to focus
on specific features of the double lament. I begin with the passages in which
Joseph describes the initial outbreak of plague in each city, which reproduce
contemporary medical assumptions about plague and contagion while preparing for a sequential rollout of cases in literary form. The Chieri half of
Joseph's composition suspends this sequential format midway to interpolate
an extended description of his own son's sickness and death. I consider this
passage closely in terms of its biblical allusions and composition; as an amplified instance of Joseph's emphasis on family loss and suffering; and as a
strategic use of personal experience to validate the narrator as the voice of
communal trauma. These are themes that will recur in subsequent chapters,
and they point to a certain commonality in the ways these writers—educated
Jewish men with family pedigree and a range of public responsibilities in their
communities—experienced and represented themselves.

As noted earlier, the Jews of the Piedmont did not live in ghettos until
long after the 1630–31 pandemic. This may or may not have had an impact
on plague mortality, which was painfully high in both walled and unwalled
communities. The lack of enclosure more likely did contribute to a different
experience of space and boundary between Christian and Jew, and arguably a
different sense of belonging. For Joseph Concio and his neighbors, "Chieri"
referred to an undivided landscape he could call home.[3] The son of a rabbinic
scholar and banker, Joseph spent some time in Asti before returning to Chieri, where he made a living composing epitaphs, writing occasional poetry,
and running a small printing press.[4] Joseph was a favorite of the duke's, who
licensed his press, and his 1630 lament makes only a glancing reference to
Christian suspicion, harassment, or restrictive policies that landed harshly
on the Jews.[5] Correspondingly, the description of Chieri in his lament depicts a thriving Jewish community with a synagogue, scholars, kabbalists,
musicians, and a confraternity dedicated to pious works. Chieri was a place
whose Jews dwelled in tranquility, "a holy community [that] lived and was
secure there" (II:3).

Many of the individual vignettes or depictions in the *Zokher haNeshamot*
read like epitaphs, and that should not surprise us; it is probably one of the

functions this work served. From the moment of diagnosis until burial, the gift of a personal and dignified death—so reverenced and so public in medieval and early modern times—was violently upended by plague.[6] Joseph's lament serves as a virtual cemetery, gently guiding us among its headstones. At once eulogy and record, it is an attempt to restore individuality in a time of mass death. Scholars today have some idea of the poetic abundance that someone like Joseph Concio would have breathed and assimilated from his youth. But in 1631, even that ample repertoire did not preserve a ready model for commemoration of human loss on such a huge scale. Joseph's solution drew in part on Dante, but also on traditional penitential motifs and the conventions of occasional and epitaph verse. What could no longer be inscribed in stone could be remembered and recited in language—and not any language, but in Hebrew that echoed its biblical moorings and unfolded as sacred song. If it was wed to Dante also, well, so were its readers.

Many of the formulations found in Joseph's poetic tributes could have—and did—grace Jewish tombstones from earlier times.[7] In this universe, plague is a judgment from God for the collective transgressions of the community, experienced in the suffering of individuals whose virtues, not defects, characterize their final commemorations. At the same time, even a series of commemorative verse epitaphs like the *Zokher haNeshamot* betrays how much current epidemiological and social details might tug against this view. Each victim is listed, including wives, children, and visitors whose names he does not know. Full names and patronymics identify other figures in the margins, a very un-medieval gesture and one that speaks to local readers with an interest in dynastic history. Indeed, many of the men and women named in the *Zokher haNeshamot* can be identified from external documentary sources such as the tax and census registers published by Renate Segre in 1986.[8] For Turin those archival sources account for about half of the victims whose names Joseph records, confirming the sense of historians that a large percentage of the Jews living in the city chose to reside without belonging officially to the *università*; they represented a rising class of artisans and merchants who joined long-established networks of banking dynasties extending through and beyond the Piedmont.[9] For Chieri, in contrast, most of the named victims appear in tax or census registers; the population must have been more stable, and its banking elite still dominated local affairs.

What makes Joseph's laments poetry—their allusions, imagery, affect, and prosody—is inextricable from their historical meaning. The choices to use one phrase, allusion, or rhyme over another, one poetic form over another, even what deaths to commemorate and in what order, locate him in a specific cultural milieu (Baroque, north Italian, familiar with Hebrew and vernacular sources). Skilled in the composition of epitaphs and occasional poetry, Joseph could draw on models and techniques he had polished over time. Even so, the challenge of applying available models for so many victims must have been formidable. He solved this problem in slightly different ways in each of the twinned laments. In the case of Chieri, a relatively small community and his home, most of the victims are clustered in family groups; these were men and women Joseph knew personally and well. In the case of Turin, a much larger city, he made some attempt to cluster victims, but the number of isolated male names, or unnamed wives and children, is striking. (I shall return to this phenomenon a bit later.) An informant or informants must have supplied him with the Turin victims' names and some biographical detail; even so the total number of victims commemorated in the Turin lament is only 130, far below what would be expected from a greater than 50 percent mortality rate in the region. For Chieri, Joseph lists 41 victims, which may be closer to the actual total—or not: Without actual population figures, we cannot truly know. Segre claims that in 1638 the Jewish population in Chieri was only one-third of what it had been a decade previously; some of that attrition was due to migration, but the drop confirms that the community was hit hard.[10]

Both poetic "stories" introduce the respective communities with topoi of excellence and prestige. Turin, where the duke was resident, was the glory of the Piedmont (I:8). Chieri, "precious and beautiful," is praised at greater length for its illustrious scholars and great piety, neither of which blunted the deadly force of the plague (II:1–8). Each account emphasizes the first known case of plague in the community, testifying to a widespread belief among Jews and Christians that plague was contagious and originated with a single case.[11] Simultaneously, as befits a liturgical genre, Joseph also attributes the devastation of the epidemic to God. The coexistence of both plague etiologies is an inevitable consequence of the liturgical genre, which must acknowledge God as the ultimate cause of all things; it also illustrates how easily two causation models might coexist. Similarly, Joseph's miniature eulogies allude to actual symptoms—burning fever and chills, wandering delirium, shaking, weakness, and pain—another indication that a desire for historical (even clinical) detail was part of what he wished to convey. Nonetheless, nosological detail does not undermine the poems' theological framing, which remains intact.

A close reading of the two passages that describe the initial outbreak in each city illustrates how much Joseph could pack into his compact vignettes, underlining the importance of treating these texts as poetry—not just as evidence of medical attitudes or demographic data patched to familiar themes of repentance and consolation. Historical data are there, but in service to a greater goal: the attempt to provide a lasting and dignified account of extraordinary loss in a framework that rendered death—and survival—meaningful.

"The First Story" of Joseph Concio's double lament details the outbreak in Turin. Joseph tells us that celestial forces instigated the disaster. A cascade of puns on the root ts-w-r (narrow, hostile, constraining) culminates with the expression שנת המצורים (the year of the embargos or siege). The phrase may allude to the embargo on travelers and goods from Turin imposed by panicky health officials in Milan, Venice, and Verona upon learning that Turin, the capital of the Piedmont, the splendored residence of "lords and princes," had been struck by plague.[12] The first Jewish victim was Joseph Kazigin, who fell ill at the end of Tammuz (June–July 1630), the "first in the bitter storm " (I:8.i); his strength failed, and he died.[13] The expression תם כחו echoes Leviticus 26:20, where it appears as part of a curse that includes disastrous weather, famine, and plague(Lev. 26:25). שאון, the word Joseph uses for "storm," had specifically medieval echoes of pain and disease; the term is attested among several of the great Andalusian Hebrew poets—Samuel haNagid, Solomon Ibn Gabirol and Moses Ibn Ezra—in contexts of fever, sickness, and anguish. The Iberian weight of the prooftexts tells us also that Joseph was familiar with this corpus. In three stanzas he eulogizes Joseph Kazigin as a בן פורת ובחור כארזים—the first phrase ("a fruitful tree") alluding to the biblical Joseph and the second ("strong as the cedars") to physical strength, a quality matched in the following stanza by his spiritual powers as someone adept in esoteric knowledge. Although young, Joseph Kazigin was wiser than his years. The final verse sounds the young Kazigin's "praise and glory" in a familiar dyad whose first term appears in Psalms 65:8 with the less common word for "storm" that opened Joseph's eulogy, neatly tying the conclusion of the miniature eulogy to its opening.

For Joseph Concio, this first victim was hardly a stranger. During his brief sojourn in Asti, Joseph had married into the Kazigin family, where Gershon Kazigin, his wife's father, had a base as a banker. Another Turin victim is recalled as the widow of the learned Elisha Kazigin (I:46.ii), documenting the greater presence of this family in Turin. Since the name does not appear in any of Segre's published tax or census registers of Turin Jews, they were most likely "temporary" residents with banking connections. Thus Joseph begins the tally of deaths in Turin with a personage he likely knew and who represented one of the dynastic banking families of the region. Why did the plague originate in Joseph Kazigin's household? Had he been traveling abroad, or housed colleagues or travelers, servants or scholars, textiles or infested goods? We do not know, although other accounts often tie an outbreak to something of this sort. Joseph clears his kinsman of any taint of guilt, emphasizing also his physical and spiritual strength. From his household, though, plague now ripples outward, striking the Falco household and expanding.

The Chieri lament opens with an evocation of walls or cordons and disease. Joseph tells us it was the year נע קצף, the year (God's) wrath "moved" (or "awakened"). The expression is a numerical pun on the calendar year: in Gematria, the numerical equivalent to "wrath awakened" is 390, signifying the Jewish year 5390, or 1630 by the Christian calendar. It was "close to the month of Av" (בירח הקרוב אל מנחם), presumably the preceding month of Tammuz, in June–July of the Julian calendar. Since he has already indicated that plague struck the Turin Jewish community in Tammuz, Chieri was affected a little later. Joseph continues, קול חיל התחיל—a great din broke out—alluding to 2 Kings 7:6 and the lepers quarantined outside the walls of biblical Samaria. In the biblical passage Samaria is under siege by the Arameans, and the lepers defect to the enemy camp, which they will discover has been deserted by panic-stricken soldiers. But the word חיל can also refer to a wall or rampart, as it does in Lamentations 2:8, Isaiah 26:1, and elsewhere. I think Joseph is letting both associations echo to evoke Chieri's quarantine. By July the plague was peaking in Turin. Wealthier residents had been fleeing the city for Chieri and elsewhere, so that Chieri was closed to outsiders without permits in late May. Nonetheless, according to the chronicler Giaochino da Montù, there were plenty of Torinese in the city, and by June, Chieri was seeing cases of plague.[14] In both cities, then, a quarantine or cordon around the city has been erected before the Jews count their first victims; Joseph Concio's images of enclosure refer not to a ghetto but to the closure of the city.

In contrast to the description of Joseph Kazigin in Turin, however, the first two victims to appear in "The Second Story," dedicated to the victims in Chieri, are a husband and wife who are recalled almost exclusively in conventional terms of piety. Menahem Verona (or de Verona) headed a kosher home. His pure wife, Rosa, drew strength from her fear of God; Rosa was "beautiful in her deeds, and pleasant" (יפה במעשיה ונעימה) (II:11:ii–iii).

Did Joseph intend this praise to complement Rosa's physical beauty or as a compensation for its lack? The echo of Canticles 1:16—"behold you are beautiful, my beloved, and pleasant"—also highlights the poet's omission of "beautiful," a curious decision. We also learn that in addition to his devout character, Menahem was versed in "wisdom," perhaps science or philosophy. From the Verona household, the plague moved on to Moses Falco's home, striking Moses, his wife, Contessa, their four sons (Tuvia, Jacob, Menahem, and Samuel), and three daughters (Stellina, Ottavia, and Leah). Each member of the family is eulogized individually, so that even the daughters are distinguished from each other:

סטילינה שם הבת הגדולה
אוטאביה שניה בת שעשועים
השלישית לאה נגעה נגלה

> Stellina was the eldest daughter's name
> Ottavia was the second, the favorite child
> The third was Leah, whose infection was uncovered. (II:16:i–iii)

Was Leah's sickness "uncovered" by a medical examiner? If so, was she the last of Moses and Contessa's children to fall ill, and without adult or older sibling protection? Or are the girls listed in order of their age but not necessarily in order of sickness, so that Leah may even have been the first child to show signs of plague, leading to the closure of the Falco house and the subsequent deaths of all its members? The language of the stanza does not anwer these questions. What mattered, from Joseph's perspective, was that the "Destroyer's hand cut [them] off in anger" (II:13:i), annihilating an entire family.

There are other tantalizing details in these laments. In Turin, Joseph tells us that "Todros Segre was separated from the community" (I:30:i); that Esther Levi and her son were "separated" while three young brothers "wandered off" from their father Jacob (I:44); and that Eleazar Pescarolo "helped himself" while "his son and daughter went with their mother" (I:63:i–ii). In other descriptions, men, women, and children "depart" or "wander from their place" or "were uprooted." Similarly, in the Chieri lament, a five-tercet eulogy for the teacher Jacob Yarach concludes with Jacob and his wife, Esther, "departing joyously from their tent" (II:29:iii); surely they have died, but it is not clear if their "departure," like those of the Turin victims, is simply from this world to the next, or from their home to a hospital or lazaretto, and then to their heavenly resting place. Jacob Segre, a leader and sage steeped in "musar," had two daughters, Rachel and Miriam, who "were taken from him" (II:36:ii–iii), and Abraham Cohen lost his son of old age, Nathaniel, while a "small daughter was taken from his house"; the old man was so devastated that he took to his bed and died (II:72–73).

In some of these cases, Joseph may be referring to attempts to flee the city for imagined safety elsewhere, or to the forced removal of the afflicted to confinement. Since Turin was struck by plague first, sending a flood of (aristocratic) refugees into Chieri, the sick and well were both on the move. As for local lazarettos, the Piedmontese region favored "tiny confinement areas" over large lazarettos; in Chieri chapels were used to confine the sick, as were locations outside the city like farms, vineyards, or meadows.[15] Chieri's Jewish population was small, even with an influx of refugees, and must have relied (or been forced to rely) on Christian facilities, where a Capuchin presence would have been daunting.[16] The conflated language of "departure" as removal and "departure" as death preserves the horror of enforced separation from family and community to what was almost certainly a place of no return. The omission of specific references to gentile officials may also reflect a lesser presence of the Health Office (Sanità) and its surveillance mechanisms.[17]

Likewise, both laments enlist the language of nets, snares, or traps in describing some victims' fates. In Turin, Samuel Nizza "fled to the dust" with his wife and son "with him in his trap" (אתו במלכודתו), suggesting the family had been enclosed in their home. But when Menahem Pescarolo died, his wife and son "departed from their dwelling place / for they were caught in the evil of the snares" (נלכדו ברוע הפחים, I:24.iii). Similarly, the mother, son, and daughter of Samuel Calanis (sp?) "were caught in the smiter's net" (ברשת הנוגף אז נלכדו, I:44.iii). In the first case, Joseph lightly alludes to Job 22:4–10, a nightmarish scenario in which desperate men strip the dead for their clothing and deny water and food to those in need—scenes that might equally have been seen in plague-stricken Turin. In the second case, the Hebrew word for "smiter" reminds us not just of the biblical plagues (Ex. 7:27) but of God's promise to punish King Jehoram of Judah with a plague on his people, wives, and property, to be followed by a wretched sickness in the king's bowels (2 Chronicles 21:14). In Chieri, another Menahem is trapped with two sons by the one "who spreads the cords of its net" (קוטי רשתו, II:33.i),[18] while Joseph's own son, whose death I treat later, is described by his horrified father in a long passage that includes the phrase "how your leg was caught in a time of grief" (איך נלכדה רגליך, II:61.iii).

The imagery of nets, snares, and traps appears a half-dozen times across both laments, and in contexts that cannot uniformly refer to the same thing. In some instances Joseph anthropomorphizes pestilence, which casts its net over one and all. In other examples he seems to be describing confinement to a house or apartment, while still other verses may refer to border-control policies that "ensnare" anyone trying to leave the infected cities.[19] As for the younger Concio's leg, Joseph may mean only to say that his son was trapped by "fate" (an evil time) that cost him his life. The verse preceding the description of his "snared" leg refers also to binding—in this case, of the young man's hands, which "seemed bound." Joseph may be alluding to the physical restraint of a delirious patient or to the crossed hands (and shrouded feet) of his son in death. Whatever the range of meanings we could assign these figures of entrapment, they tell us that the experience of plague in 1630 was inseparable from a sense of isolation and involuntary confinement, a real consequence of roadblocks, house closures, quarantines, and perhaps forcible removal to a lazaretto.

Noteworthy also are the poet's efforts to preserve family integrity by grouping victims in family clusters. We have seen several instances of this already in the Chieri account, where Joseph meticulously records the names and relationships of parents and children as well as other kin or visitors within a given household. Among the Chieri victims, for instance, the three daughters of Menahem Verona mentioned earlier comprise only one part of the full family unit. Recall that Menahem Verona was the first known Jewish victim in Chieri; his entire household apparently succumbed: "In wrath, the Destroyer's hand cut him down," followed by his wife, Contessa, three daughters, and four sons (II:10–16); brief descriptions of each child follow. The next four stanzas describe the three sons of a widowed mother, one of whom was married with three children of his own and another on the way. The predeceased patriarch of the family was Yequtiel, leaving behind his wife Simha. The eldest son, Zerah, was married to Shoshana, who was pregnant; Zerah and Shoshana had three other children, Yequtiel, Yosef, and Viola (II:19–23). The other two brothers, Samuel and Reshef, and their sister Tovah, must not have been married. Other household groups follow in careful groupings. Most are nuclear family units, but occasionally other arrangements appear. Samuel Pescarol died along with his wife, two daughters (Brevelis[?] and Fiorta), and a son, David Samuel. With them went the "darling" young Hanoch Nieti, the son of Samuel's wife, Esther, by a former marriage (II:27–32). Jacob Segre's wife also had children from a first marriage living with them, all victims, as was his kinswoman, Jocheved Todros (II:35–37). In Turin, Moses Falco was housing a guest named Benjamin Fontanel, who was included among the household's dead (I:13); Baruch Sinai died of plague along with his wife, son, daughter, and a nephew (I:36–38); Judah Sinai and his wife and daughter all died, as did his wife's uncle, David Milano, and his three daughters and son (I:48–54). Widows and widowers dot the list as well.[20]

As a rule Joseph was able to fill in the names and relationships of his Chieri neighbors with greater precision than he managed for the Turin dead. As I have already observed, the list of the Jewish Turin victims must be partial, but it is also less specific, especially when it comes to naming wives and children (and among the children, girls). This makes sense, as it was not Joseph's community, and he was relying on testimony from others that was supplied after the plague had come and gone. What remains, even so, is the cultural significance of family units, which are depicted as microcosms of patriarchal order and pride. Families not only formed the economic backbone of these communities, from the wealthy banking and physicians' dynasties to the merchants and artisans who had begun to challenge them. Families also reflected a way of seeing oneself: For men, the family was a microcosm in which patriarchy mirrored the performance of authority in the public sphere; for women, the nuclear family was an arena for negotiating extended family loyalties; for children, how one internalized and navigated family expectations shaped one's future. That families were also affective units is clear from the vignettes Joseph weaves throughout the Turin and Chieri laments. Small daughters are "charming" or "refreshing"; sons are students and devoted to prayer, singing in the synagogue, helping with family trade; wives are sweet and pious, loyal to their nuclear family but with residual ties to their brothers and nephews. The degree to which family—or more to the point, representations of family—plays an important role in the commemorative writing about plague will surface repeatedly in the following chapters, too. For the *Zokher haNeshamot*, grouping the dead in families is one of the most prominent techniques Joseph enlists in constructing his verbal memorial. It is also a strategy that assumes centrality in the Chieri lament with his description of the death of his son.

Joseph's lament embeds a twenty-five-stanza sequence—a lament within a lament—that recounts the death of his son Abraham. Joseph's eldest son (בחור) was chosen (נבחר), and he had himself chosen (בחר) a life of study. The "Father on High" (אב רם) favored Joseph with *Avraham* (אברהם), who was not quite twenty when he died on the ninth of Heshvan (II:48:ii–iii). He was a source of pleasure and support to his father, restrained of tongue and wise. Pious and learned, he composed literary works. He sang in the congregation—perhaps in a choir, as music played a huge role in the Italian Jewish communities[21]—and to help his father, he learned the printer's trade. The father describes his grief:

אוי כי בזכרי זאת עצמי נרפה
מידי דברי בו רעד בא בי
מעי המו איפוא אמצא מרפא

לבי לבי יחיל בתוך קרבי
יען כי מכאובי תמיד נגדי[22]
כבדה אנחתי כמו חובי[23]

עיני עיני על שבר מחמדי
יורדה מים אצעק בקולי[24]
אוי אוי בני רבי ותלמידי

בני בני אשר נעמת לי[25]
אנה פנה הודך וקנייניך
אה הלך אורך מאהלי[26]

מה זה מהרת צאת ממכונך
למצוא בני בשחק מנוחה[27]
מה זה ועל מה זה זז זיו עינך

מה אחשוב נא להשיג הנחה[28]
מה מדבר להסיר דאגה
מה אעשה להקים מנוחה[29]

איך זוהרך חדל ביום תוגה
איך ידיך היו כאסורות
איך נלכדה רגלך בזמן תוגה

למי אלך לעזרה בצרות[30]
למי אברח לערות מענה רך[31]
למי אקרא ביושר אמרות[32]

אמנם ידעתי כי כן דין ערך[33]
דיין אמת נורא הוא אל שדי
הוא נתן הוא לקח הוא יבורך[34]

Alas, when I recall this, my bones grow weak
When I speak of him, I tremble,
My innards groan. Where shall I find healing?

My heart, my heart writhes inside me
For my pain is always present
My sighs are heavy as my debt.

My eyes, my eyes—for the destruction of my delight—
Spill water, I cry aloud.
Alas, alas, my son! My teacher and my student!

My son, my son who pleased me so,
Where have your splendor and accomplishments gone?
Ah, your light has left my tent.

Why did you hasten to leave your home
To rest among celestial beings?
Why and for what did the light of your eyes depart?

What can I think to pay [him] tribute?
What can I say to relieve the worry,
What can I do to bring peace?

How your radiance ceased on a day of mourning
How your hands seemed bound
How your leg was caught in a time of grief!

To whom shall I go for help in trouble?
To whom shall I flee for a gentle reply?
To whom shall I call for an honest answer?

Surely I know that the True Judge
Passed judgment. He is El Shaddai.
He has given, He has taken, and may He be blessed. (II: 55:ii–63)

Sixteenth- and seventeenth-century Italian Jewish poets have left us many
elegies for dead relatives, rabbis, and dignitaries. Joseph's "lament within a lament" belongs to this genre and is a product of contemporary tastes.[35] Some of
his prooftexts maintain faith with earlier exegetical and poetic conventions—
for instance, the abundant echoes of Job and Psalms. Medieval plague authors
invoked certain verses, like the curses of Deuteronomy 28, to imply that the
plague came from God. Joseph ignores Deuteronomy 28 but taps other plague-
themed verses. Here, too, he conforms to convention. "What can I do to bring
peace?" comes from 2 Chronicles 6:28–30, a plea for God in time of famine
and plague. Likewise, Joseph's decision to pray for God's mercy echoes Job's
plaintive cry (Job 19:16) when he is stinking and disfigured by disease. Some
subtexts testify to the father's pain-racked guilt. The unanswerable "why did
you hasten to leave?" (or perhaps to be translated "how you have hastened to
leave!") quotes the biblical Isaac, confused in his blindness and unable to perceive Jacob disguised as Esau. Genesis 27 presents a father dying (of old age)
and a son pretending to be the eldest, a scenario Joseph reverses doubly—
father for son and natural for unnatural death.

Joseph's long, interpolated eulogy for his son transitions to his personal
prayers for God's favor and clemency. "I will plead and pray / that He shine His
countenance upon me and have mercy / and say in His pity I have suffered
enough" (II:64). Joseph continues, beseeching God to quiet his thoughts and
remove his sins. "Heal my body and soul," he asks, and he pleads with God to
guide him on the right path. Praying to God for healing and relief from sorrow,
Joseph asks God to please listen to him and accept his "song," to grant him
strength and do wonders for him: His entreaty twice taps Psalm 38, which describes God's wrath striking the psalmist like arrows, leaving him with fester-
ing wounds and sickness that cause his family and friends to "stand back" from
his affliction (Ps. 38:1–12). Joseph emphasizes that sin has brought God's wrath
upon him, and he begs God not to abandon him in his need. The heavy reliance on Psalms throughout these stanzas heightens their liturgical resonance:

אדוני נגדך כל תאותי[36]
מצער ויגון פדה עצמי[37]
חושה לעזרתי וישועתי[38]

שמע קולי רצה את זמרי[39]
ותסמכני רוח נדיבה[40]
תנה עוזך לי היה עמי

הראני צדקתך הנשגבה[41]
חנני הצילני בחמלה[42]
עשה עמי אותות לרוב טובה

O Lord, all my desire is before You[43]
Redeem me from sorrow and grief
Hurry to my aid and salvation.

Hear my voice, find favor with my song
Sustain me with a generous spirit
Grant me Your strength; be with me.

Show me Your exalted righteousness
Have pity on me and save me[44]
Make me wondrous signs of good. (II: 67–69)

At the conclusion of this peroration, the speaker returns to his plague
account: Pestilence moves on to the home of Abraham Cohen, killing him,
his only son, Nathaniel, and his sister's little daughter, Rosa (II:70–73), then
to Judah Segre, who "tried to escape" and "fell, robbed, and forfeited eternity" (II:77:ii–iii)—perhaps Segre fled, was accosted on the road, and con-
verted under duress. The litany of loss, like Joseph's personal interjection,
concludes with a prayer for divine mercy. This time the speaker's voice is
more restrained, addressing God respectfully in the third person as the One
who brings forgiveness and healing. Almost tentatively, the speaker slips
into the first-person plural, joining his grieving kinsmen to ask God to take
note of their pain. The shift is signaled with two tercets, each containing
one word evoking a new, plural speaker (underlined in the Hebrew). The next
tercet enlists the plural "us" twice, and the following tercet does this three
times, crescendoing to a full-voiced choral prayer:

יסיר צרות ישקיט נאנחים
יהפוך קול ציר לשיר חיל במחולו
יַנְחֵנוּ בדרכים משובחים

כל דבר פשע יכפר ימחול
וימחה כל דמעה מכל פנים
זַרְעֵנוּ בשלוה ירבה כחול

יאר <u>עינינו</u> בפאר? עניינים
<u>יחדש בנו</u> לבות נקיים
וישיב לב אבות עלי בנים

הנה אורך ימים ושנות חיים
<u>ישביענו יראנו</u> חסדיו
<u>ויקבצנו</u> מארצות גוים

May He who removes sorrows and quiets the sighing
Turn a voice of pain to a song of might with His pardon.
May He *lead us* on praiseworthy paths.

May He forgive and pardon every transgression,
And wipe every tear from every face.
May He multiply *our seed* like sand [to live] in peace.

Enlighten *our eyes* to the splendid meanings [?]
Purify *our hearts anew*
Turn the hearts of fathers to their sons again.

May He *satisfy us* and *show us* His mercies
With long days and years of life
And *gather us* in from gentile lands. (II: 82–85)

These requests are not unusual, and not necessarily evocative of plague.
Only the plea to "multiply our seed" (children) hauntingly reminds us of the
heavy child mortality of this outbreak.[45] Similarly, the need for renewed pa-
rental affection uneasily hints at the strain on families wrought by plague.
Despite the familiar platitudes, Joseph turns his theme to healing with a note
of weariness: "Who will give us healing?" he asks, hoping that God grant
healing willingly, as a parent would grant the request of a child. The movement from Joseph's extraordinary outburst to these conventional tropes is
striking. It is as if a curtain had closed on a scene of personal pain and a more
formal public voice resumed its task. But that is of course the point. By embedding a searing record of private anguish directly into a formal account of
communal loss, Joseph legitimizes his right to speak on behalf of the collective. Among his listeners, survivors might cling to the tiny eulogies and generic expressions of mourning while recalling their own bereavement, which

had no record in writing just as their dead lacked marked graves. The intensely personal grief Joseph describes thus also serves to cohere the unrulier emotions of grief-stricken survivors; perhaps for some of them platitudes of repentance and anticipated redemption were inadequate balms. From this perspective the insertion of Abraham Concio's death and his father's mourning, midway through the Chieri lament, is both strategic and therapeutic; it anticipates the transition to the first-person plural in the closing section of the text and permits the speaker to speak on others' behalf.

The tension between personal and public voice, less evident in the Turin lament than in the lament for his own community, is intrinsic to this composition. In subsequent chapters we will see that it was a major preoccupation for other Jewish (and non-Jewish) authors as well, all of them men of learning and social privilege who found themselves shouldering communal responsibilities during the 1630–31 outbreak and trying to write about it. In Joseph Concio's case, the *Zokher haNeshamot* suggests aspects of this challenge that we shall also encounter again. One is the enlistment of private grief depicted as the loss of an intimate family member or members, or perhaps also of a home and possessions—as a means of legitimating the author's right to speak on behalf of a grieving collective whose unvoiced experiences are now emblematized in his own. The record of Joseph's inconsolable reaction to his son's death not only turns a larger and public narrative to the most intimate of spaces and experience; it validates the narrator as witness to the wider landscape of loss. At the same time, the inevitable shift in register from personal despair to public mourning also mimetically performs the author's suppression of private emotion in resumption of public duty. The dialectic of private and public is thus more than a solution to a literary problem (how to describe so much individual suffering); it is also a vehicle for constructing a sense of personhood with private and public dimensions. That this kind of hypersensitivity to how one was perceived in public life reverberated in private identity is a recurring aspect of the general corpus of Hebrew plague writing from 1630, whether the writer lived in a ghetto community or not.

Nonetheless, Joseph made some unique choices, among them the decision to relocate Jewish tropes and language to the realm of Dante. Both the Turin and Chieri laments are built on a decasyllabic line arranged in *terza rima*, with its powerful associations with Dante.[46] The adoption of Italian meters was not unique to Joseph, but his choice here seems deliberate. Formally echoing the *Divina Commedia*, Joseph consciously realigned his verbal memorial with another journey among the dead. It was not necessary to

invoke specific verses or passages from this model; the overarching theme
and trajectory of Dante's epic of descent to the realm of the dead was enough.
From this perspective even the inserted lament for his son acquires new
meaning: Joseph's son Abraham is both Virgil—the guide who will ultimately
abandon the poet—and Beatrice, the beloved whose death and example drive
him through grief to prayer. In this reading, too, the "lament within a lament" devoted to Joseph's private loss becomes core to the entire composition,
a record of personal agony that empathically bears witness to the losses of a
community, rendered household by household, and death by death.

Other records tell us that, in the summer of 1630, Joseph's Christian
neighbors also gathered in public prayer, pleading with God to relieve them
of pestilence. According to Giaochino da Montù, who exhaustively documented this outbreak two hundred years later, some of their prayers were
directed to Saint Sebastian and other plague saints, but the lion's share addressed the Blessed Virgin, whose power, as Health Office and government
councilors agreed, "exceeds that of the saints."[47] The city decreed that an
altar and special prayers to the Blessed Virgin be instituted in the summer
of 1630, when mortality was severe. Writing in 1830, da Montù honors their
faith in the Virgin's intercessionary powers by invoking Dante—not his *In-
ferno*, however, but the *Paradiso*, with its glorious praise of the Virgin:

Donna, se' tanto grande e tanto vali
Che qual vol grazia e te non ricorre
Sua disianza vuol volar sanz' ali.

In te misericordia, in te pietate,
In te magnificenza, in te s'aduna
Quantunque in creatura è di bontate.[48]

Of course we have no idea whether these verses echoed in the minds of
those frightened men and women in Chieri—but if they did for Joseph, their
Jewish neighbor, why not for them also? For Joseph, the mantle of Dante also
reminds us that the dead still inhabit a divinely ordered cosmos: They have
been removed from the land of the living but not from the reach of God's
mercy or justice. Among the varied literary forms that preserve Jewish accounts of this plague, only poetry could offer its readers or listeners this
consolation; the narrative chronicles and plague accounts must remain within
the boundaries of human time and space, constraints they try to breach by

various means but that cannot promise eternity. Medical genres find their
own ways to relieve the claustrophobic reality of epidemic grief with reas-
suring guidelines and recipes for future outbreaks. From this vantage alone,
Hebrew poetry, whether it adhered to its own commemorative traditions
or experimented with vernacular exemplars, may have been better suited to
console than anything the men of history or medicine had to offer. Ironically,
the poets, chroniclers, and physicians were sometimes the same men, reminding us also that in real life we can tolerate a multiplicity of meanings that may
be packaged separately in books.

Like the evidence of funeral elegies, charitable bequests, lavish epitaphs
and tombstones, public memorials and ceremonies, even intimate ascetic
practices or mystical devotions, Joseph's double lament documents a fascination with funerary genres and mortality that was a direct legacy of the Black
Death. Thus even where Joseph seems to diverge most from the commemorative conventions of the medieval past, and even where his contemporaries—
men like Abraham Catalano in Padua, Abraham Massarani in Mantua, or
Judah Modena in Venice—seem most to reject medieval models, these writers share a preoccupation with the depiction of mass death that roots them
securely in medieval experience. At the same time each writer grapples with
a very un-medieval pressure to locate himself in his account and in so doing
to navigate cultural boundaries of public and private "self" that medieval
authors did not recognize or find relevant.

Thus the Jewish authors of 1630 plague accounts also construct a portrait of themselves. In Abraham Catalano's 'Olam Hafukh, which we will
examine in the next two chapters, his first-person voice sustains the narrative from beginning to end, so that we follow the unfolding events through
his perspective. Catalano's account shifts spatially from the interior of his
own apartment to range the ghetto and beyond, into the villa he and his
family temporarily inhabit in the Christian city, to the proposed sites for
a Jewish lazaretto, an expanded cemetery area, and a site for warehousing
"protected" textiles and property. The expansion or contraction of his lens
also lets Abraham depict himself as an honorable, dedicated public man;
even the narrative's most intimate moments, describing the deaths of his
wife and children, underline his roles as a husband and father whose dedication to family is reflected in the other accounts as well.

Abraham Massarani's chronicle is another text I treat in the next two
chapters. The Sefer haGalut vehaPedut ("The Book of Exile and Redemption")
covers a wider geographical and temporal terrain than Catalano's plague

narrative, and plague serves as a backdrop to a story of expulsion and wandering. Massarani enlists family scenes only once, describing the shock he and his brothers experienced upon returning to their ransacked home to discover that their mother had died on the road, while the home itself was occupied by German soldiers. Why he suppresses the family motif ubiquitously used elsewhere will be considered in the pages ahead. In his double lament for the Jewish plague victims in Turin and Chieri, Joseph Concio also constructed an authorial persona: Like the composers of Hebrew laments long before him, he assumes the voice of a community and gives shape to an experience and memory of collective disaster. By harnessing the schematic form of Dante's *Commedia*, he subtly highlights his own role as a guide through the realm of the dead, and by inserting an account of his personal loss, he renders a most private pain as an authenticating witness of grief that speaks on behalf of other mourners.

These early modern Jewish writers further testify to the multiplicity of genres available for commemorating the epidemic that they had the good fortune to survive, and by extension to the multiple temperaments, settings, and needs that permitted such variety to coexist. The stylistic and genre choices represented by these authors also committed them to a particular chronotope, defined as the temporal and spatial dimensions represented in a work. Genre partly set its limits, but so did local and individual taste. Each work constructs a special kind and depth of past, just as it projects a specific kind of future, and each limns a geographical scope for disaster that is likewise variable in range. All these works root themselves in local experience: Whether the communities they describe were ghetto-enclosed or not, the writings trace a bounded world of neighbors and landmarks, along with the fellow Jews whom fate had drawn into the community as visitors or temporary residents. From this social core the texts gesture further outward to networks of communication, commerce, and kinship that stretched to other Italian Jewish settlements, and the continuous interplay of Jewish and Christian institutions and authorities in times of calm or crisis. Strikingly, both ghetto and non-ghetto communities describe a lag in the appearance of sickness among the Jews, suggesting a degree of insularity even among communities, like Chieri's, that were not enclosed by walls. Although ghetto closures were usually motivated by a gentile desire to halt traffic in items associated with Jews, such as secondhand clothing or grain, they brought temporary benefit to the Jewish inhabitants. Why a similar benefit extended to unenclosed communities remains to be explored.

Finally, among all the authors considered in the following pages, it is Joseph Concio whose double lament most freely taps the forms of medieval Hebrew and vernacular commemoration, and fuses them in a single voice. And it is Joseph Concio whose blend of epitaph and epic most eloquently bridges the chasm between the memory of disease, indignity, suffering, and death, and the promise of healing in the world to come. Massarani will also strive to do this in the poetic lament that bridges the two halves of his chronicle, but his effort, I think, is far less successful. In a sense, Joseph's memorial poetry represents a more conservative solution to the novel challenge of mourning mass death. Even the prosodic gesture to Dante is a nod to a medieval poet and a long-ago past. Beyond that gesture no radical theological or poetic expression breaks step with Hebrew commemorative or penitential conventions: Joseph's laments ask the Jewish survivors in Turin and Chieri, ravaged by a vicious epidemic, to find solace in age-old tropes of sin and forgiveness, punishment, and redemption. Jewish authors in the ghettos also retrofit traditional genres, motifs, and even texts, sometimes aligning new needs to received forms and ideas. Alternatively, they looked to more contemporary, Christian models, penning secular chronicles, plague narratives, medical recipes, and tracts.[49] The beauty of this seeming divergence is that it was not a divergence at all. Both types of seeing and self-fashioning coexisted, and so did the meaning they offered. A man might rise early to pray and lament in the morning, then arrange for storage for his brocades and mattresses, and myrrh and cedar for his hearth. He could hire a notary to record his last will and testament, and hope a generous gift to charity did not escape God's eye. He could tell his wife and children that he loved them. If he was lucky, his community officers had hired a surgeon in advance and stockpiled food and other supplies. If he was very lucky, the surgeon would live long enough to ease some suffering, and the food and bedding would suffice. Today, as we have discovered, we cannot do much more.

Let us turn, then, to the Jewish prose accounts of this outbreak from Padua and Mantua, and see if we can understand how they served different needs while testifying to similar preoccupations as those so hauntingly conveyed by Joseph Concio in the *Zokher haNeshamot*.

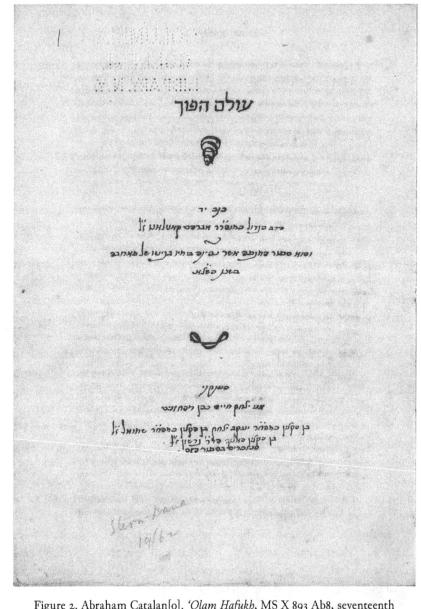

Figure 2. Abraham Catalan[o]. *'Olam Hafukh*, MS X 893 Ab8, seventeenth century. Rare Book and Manuscript Library, Columbia University, New York City.

Chapter 2

Narrating Plague
Abraham Catalano and Abraham Massarani

The storyteller is the figure in which the righteous man encounters himself.

—Walter Benjamin, *The Storyteller Essays*

A terse, unadorned account of the plague that ravaged the Paduan ghetto in 1630–31 served as the scaffolding for an embellished and highly literary version produced in Hebrew not long afterward. Both versions were by the same author: the physician, scholar, and civic leader Abraham Catalano. The Italian version came to my attention as this book neared completion, so I have not been able to give it the attention it truly deserves. According to a dealer's assessment, it was written for circulation within a regional Jewish community: Hebrew words are embedded throughout, and the dialect is a blend of Judeo-Italian and Tuscan forms.[1] Under the press of time, I have tried, for some of the following examples, to check the wording in the Italian version. Even a cursory comparison confirms the claims this and the following chapters make for the Hebrew reworking and for the importance of recognizing the degree to which these narratives could be and were shaped by their authors.

Certainly, when Abraham Catalano composed his Hebrew account, he knew what a plague narrative looked like. According to Samuel Cohn, this new genre of plague literature arose with the severe epidemic that swept northern and central Italy more than a half-century earlier (1575–78). Many of the compositions recalling that epidemic were written in the vernacular, by men who were not necessarily physicians;[2] some of these works, like a fifteenth-century predecessor, Giovanni Savonarola's *I trattati in volgare della peste e dll'accqua ardente*, were widely read and consulted, according to Cohn achieving something close to the status of "popular literature."[3] Certainly many features of these late sixteenth-century *successo della peste* narratives are recognizable in Catalano's work: the chronological organization of the narrative; the careful inclusion of daily sickness, mortality, and convalescent statistics; detailed accounts of financial outlays and administrative rulings; the insertion of poignant vignettes; and testimony to the author's shock and fear. Thus, minimally, Catalano's account documents this genre in Hebrew, and illustrates an elite sensibility that straddles Jewish and Christian ways of seeing while refracting the world of the ghetto through the lens of its author. This chapter claims that it did more than that, too. Indeed, even a cursory comparison of the Hebrew to its Italian precursor evidences the author's conscious efforts to compose a literary narrative in Hebrew that reached far beyond the journal record he had kept in the vernacular. How the Hebrew text was written suggests what he was trying to do.

Like the authors who preceded him, and the many who composed contemporary accounts of the Great Italian Plague, Catalano turned to narrative as a way of imposing coherence on a fraught personal and collective experience. The pandemic of 1630–31 was traumatic as an epidemiological event, but also for its power to unravel social ties and disrupt familiar networks, institutions, beliefs and theories, even ways of ordering the physical landscape. Plague threatened social, civic, and religious order, especially when, as in 1630, it came on the heels of famine and accompanied by war. And while *Yersinia pestis*, and the fleas or lice that carried it, were not discriminating, human society was marked by all sorts of difference, ensuring that the same bacterial catastrophe might be experienced variably by the men, women, and children it affected. In 1630–31 many of them died, and not every survivor felt like writing. When, like Abraham Catalano, they did write, the result can tell us as much about how they saw themselves as about how they saw the plague. The following pages focus on Catalano's Hebrew chronicle and its construction of the narrator. I claim that even when Catalano permits us glimpses of his personal losses and frustrations, these glimpses serve to bolster an ideal of public service; what Catalano's narrative projects is ultimately a representation of the author as a devoted public servant, a communal leader and family man who is unflagging in his dedication to others. This construct of a public persona relies on narrative techniques and conventions this chapter explores. At the same time, as I also emphasize, the contours of public identity are reabsorbed into domestic and private terrain, where they contribute to the formation of personal identity. In today's language we might describe this as enlisting the language of "inner" life as a critical component of public or "outer" life (for instance, the politician as family man), while simultaneously exploiting the language of "outer" life to depict an "inner" world (a conflict of conscience as a war or battle of competing interests).

To invoke the language of techniques and conventions, as I am doing, is to imply that Catalano's construct of public self was recognized and implicitly or explicitly tapped by other men—Jewish and Christian—of similar standing in their respective societies. Accordingly, the first part of this chapter analyzes aspects of Catalano's plague narrative that shape his literary persona; for contrast and comparison, the second part turns to a contemporary Jewish author, Abraham Massarani, who is not primarily concerned with plague but incorporates details of this outbreak into a wider-ranging chronicle. Both authors—from Padua and Mantua—narrate accounts in which they themselves play a role. This chapter assumes, as literary scholars have long observed, that their narrative personae should not be conflated with the person of the author but understood as a constructed voice that contributes to the author's literary goals. Nor should the narrative personae of these seventeenth-century narratives be confused with the personal voice and subjectivity invoked in twenty-first-century narratives, or generalized to represent the totality of a seventeenth-century community. Catalano's self-representation engages conventions that emphasize values and demonstrations of "character" that the author believed a communal leader should embody. Massarani's chronicle confirms that the forms and meanings of these conventions constituted an available idiom for representing the symbiotic interrelationship of private and public lives in constructing a sense of "self" (at least among a male Jewish elite). The following pages try to identify and understand some of these conventions as part of a shared cultural idiom for expressing ideals of communal leadership and public identity. We are free to speculate about what kind of man was drawn to those ideals, and why they mattered to him. But if we do wish to make such speculation, we need to understand the language these men used to describe themselves.[4]

Abraham Catalano refers to himself modestly as "the young one" in comparison to his fellow administrators, but in 1630 he was already a man of

importance in the Padua ghetto. He is a figure who comes installed with
what Marshall Sahlins and other anthropologists have described as "systemic" or structural power that derives in Catalano's case from family, wealth,
education, and a history of engagement inside and outside the ghetto.[5] A
graduate of the University of Padua's medical school, he does not seem to
have been a practicing physician. In 1630 he was already serving as one of
the three judges of the *beit din* (Jewish court) in the ghetto, and he refers
twice to the community *parnassim* (financial officers) as his "colleagues."
The same year, he was elected by the ghetto council to a "Committee of
Four" created to oversee plague response within the ghetto.[6] By his own account he emerged as a prominent negotiator with Paduan and Venetian officials before, during, and after the outbreak (in part, he demurred, because
more suitable candidates had succumbed to plague).[7] As the fluent and
learned Hebrew of his chronicle attests, Catalano was a cultured man, at
ease with traditional Jewish texts as well as secular and medical writings
circulating in northern Italy.

The complexity of the narrator's persona as Catalano constructs it unfolds gradually in his narrative, a self-conscious product of craft and strategy.[8]
What we can know about Abraham Catalano derives from this self-portrait,
augmented by scraps of archival testimony and the commemorative homages
he received after his death (which are treated in Chapter 6). The narrator "Catalano" of the *'Olam Hafukh* is a literary construct that is rooted in a social one,
exploiting a shared Jewish and Christian idiom for representing a public figure with responsibilities for the welfare of his community in a time of great
crisis. Abraham and his contemporaries present themselves through a template
that highlights specific traits and airbrushes others; we learn about the person
by understanding that these features had meaning to him, not by assuming
that the portrait equals the man. This is not something scholars have noted
about plague narratives to date. Yet understanding that these narratives are
neither naïve nor transparent reflections of events tells us a great deal about
their authors and the world as they saw it.

The *'Olam Hafukh*

As the plague took root in Christian Padua, the city's chief health officer
(*provveditore*) asked the ghetto to conduct a census; when he officially declared the epidemic had ended in the fall of 1631, he seems to have demanded

a new accounting. Of the 721 inhabitants tallied at the outbreak's beginning, 421 were dead, 213 had fallen ill and recovered, 75 had escaped illness,
and 12 had fled the city. The statistics appear near the end of Abraham
Catalano's Hebrew plague narrative, which circulated unpublished for several centuries under the title he had given it: 'Olam Hafukh (World Upside-
down).[9] The 'Olam Hafukh survives in several manuscript copies; based on
one of them, a transcription of the Hebrew was published in 1946 by Cecil
Roth. Over the years Catalano's narrative has been partially translated into
French and English and received sporadic if glancing attention; during our
own pandemic year and more, it has been invoked increasingly, and hopefully someone will undertake a full English translation.[10] It is a remarkable
document.

As a historical record, the 'Olam Hafukh offers a rich account of institutional Jewish responses to plague and the ways ghetto officials and lay folk
negotiated the complex regulations, politics, and personalities that connected
the Jewish ghetto and the gentile city.[11] The ghetto itself was a fairly recent
reality; plans had been discussed for enclosing Padua's Jews since the late sixteenth century, but the torturous negotiations over location and boundaries,
compensation for displaced tenants, expenses, and rental arrangements delayed the actual move to a ghetto until 1612. Abraham Catalano, like many of
his coreligionists in the ghetto, and Paduan citizens on the other side of the
ghetto walls, could thus remember another landscape and other kinds of spatial relationships to the city and its Christian inhabitants.[12]

Catalano introduces the Hebrew narrative with a statement of purpose
that is absent from the Italian account he apparently logged during the epidemic and used as a foundation for the literary, Hebrew, version. He cites
three reasons for producing this work: (1) to emphasize that this plague
befell Padua and its Jews as an act of divine chastisement, and to exhort his
readers to repent for their sins; (2) to counsel future generations, ostensibly
those in positions of authority, on how to prepare for future epidemics—
"not just what was done [by us] but what should have been done"; and (3) to
provide guidance for ordinary householders who wish to preserve their families and possessions. Laudable and unexceptional goals, they unfold in a
mix of direct advice, gripping narrative, and bitter hindsight. Nonetheless,
the tutelary aspirations of the 'Olam Hafukh are not its only achievements,
which are dominated for a modern reader by its harrowing account of the epidemic and by the striking complexity of the arrangements and institutions—
failed or not—enlisted in urban settings in times of plague.

The *'Olam Hafukh* is equally remarkable for the ways its author permits us to glimpse his sense of himself as a public man, and how what we call private life contributes to that portrayal. Catalano's insertion of himself in his account exploits narrative techniques and conventions that highlight aspects of the persona he wishes to project. I wish to focus on four examples, two technical and two more thematic: (1) chronological sequencing; (2) statements of anticipatory knowledge; (3) episodes depicting opposition or dissent; and (4) expressions of emotion. For comparison I then turn to Abraham Massarani's chronicle of the expulsion and tribulations of Mantuan Jewry, which incorporates this plague outbreak as a corollary disaster to expulsion. My intent here is to illustrate that the idiom enlisted by Abraham Catalano as a means of self-fashioning was recognizable and utilized by contemporary Jewish writers, who likewise exploited it in their own works.

I begin with Abraham Catalano, the *'Olam Hafukh*, and some of its narrative techniques.

Chronology in the *'Olam Hafukh*

The chronological format of Catalano's narrative justifies the juxtaposition of private moments and communal events. Since the narrative unfolds in linear time, that is what apparently determines what precedes and what follows, in a semblance of editorial impartiality. Yet, as chronological sequence weaves Catalano's domestic struggles and losses into the fabric of communal grief, the author underscores that private anguish does not sway the public man from his duty. Thus a description of procedures instituted for locking away valuables under seal of the Health Office concludes with the narrator signaling his presence on the scene, as he notes that he and two of his fellow committee members "were the first" to comply with the Health Office protocol.[13] The narrative moves immediately to Catalano's account of an additional room he has rented to secure his family's large household possessions, and where he graciously allowed "others to store trunks full of possessions to save them from the plague," segueing next to a *parte* (proposal) for augmenting a loan submitted to the ghetto council.[14] The weave of personal and communal activity shows us Catalano operating energetically in two spheres, protecting his personal property while simultaneously securing the property of his neighbors. The two spheres overlap when he generously offers his supplemental storage space to others (generosity that demands no additional sacrifice of his personal resources). In other words, although the narrative sequence appears to be motivated purely by chronology, the deft interlacing of these particular narrative details emphasizes Catalano's personal responsibility and largesse to his community.

The overlap of public and private is more problematic when it discloses Catalano losing control of its staging. Soon after the eleventh of Sivan, when his servant girl falls sick, Catalano confines her to an upstairs room, then himself to his house. From confinement, he consults with colleagues through his window. This passage spills into committee business with the reluctant hiring of an unsavory gravedigger, a charlatan who has been offering "treatment" to plague victims while stealing and abusing them; the need for gravediggers is so urgent that they have no alternative. Throughout the *'Olam Hafukh*, Catalano lightly weaves biblical allusion and phrases into a fluent prose style, and this passage flits from Genesis to Exodus, Chronicles, and Job. When he argues from his window on behalf of the needy, Job 16:19 animates Catalano's anguished "as the heavens are my witness"; Job echoes once more when he describes the sinister charlatan who "wanders the land to and fro" like the troublemaking angel in Job 1:7. The greater sweep of the passage does not sustain or link these allusions, which add depth to their immediate context only; the passage of chronological time is not disrupted by the subterranean rumbles of competing temporalities.

On the sixteenth of Sivan, Catalano notes that objections from the nuns near the Jewish cemetery have forced the Jews to use the old Jewish cemetery outside the city walls, which in turn requires the acquisition of a donkey, then two donkeys, and wagons. As the deaths mount, the ghetto has desperate recourse to prayer. On the nineteenth of Sivan, Catalano tells us that his servant girl has recovered, precipitating a conflict over when to release her (and himself) from confinement; pressured by his colleagues to return to work, he releases the girl earlier than he feels is right, and when his daughter sickens two days later, he is stricken with guilt.[15] Once again the threads of public and private events are closely intertwined, and it is easy to forget that they are deliberately selected for inclusion from a myriad other happenings.[16] This time, too, the effect is to enhance the portrait of Catalano's frantic but unflagging devotion to responsibilities at home and in the ghetto. In this example, the communal crises he describes, like the conflict with the charlatan or with the nuns of Maria Mater Domini, or the recurring shortage of gravediggers, resist ideal solutions. Analogously, the crises in his personal and family life also highlight the limits of his foresight and authority, so that in neither realm does he invariably emerge victorious. (This is one trait that makes Catalano so admirable.) The same overlap of public and private that creates opportunities for Catalano to demonstrate leadership and largesse can equally disclose his impotence. At both extremes, the selection of episodes captures critical aspects of Catalano's persona—benevolence toward fellow Jews, responsibility toward his family, and anxiety when they conflict.

Anticipatory Knowledge

Catalano occasionally inserts statements that anticipate developments he could not have foreseen at the point in the narrative where they appear. These interjections further shape our sense of his character. By my count, this happens seven times in the *'Olam Hafukh*. Significantly, four of those instances are clustered in the early days of the outbreak, two in the middle, and one near the end. It is also noteworthy that the first four examples concern the committee's decisions preceding the plague's arrival. The fifth and sixth refer to a period when the outbreak is underway, and Catalano overcomes opposition to take lifesaving action; in the seventh example, he bitterly comments on the futility of his plans to save his own family. These moments of *post hoc* commentary can be summarized as follows, in order of appearance. Significantly, although I have not had an opportunity to check each instance, they do not seem to appear in the Italian version.[17] Between the twenty-ninth of Heshvan (November, approximately) and the first days of Kislev (a little over a month later), the ghetto launched preparations for closure and pestilence. The committee ordered a large quantity of milled flour, some to set aside in the event the ghetto were still under closure during Passover; they also paid two representatives to invest in foodstuffs, oil, and wine. "But we trusted in vain," Catalano interjects in hindsight, for both men would later die of plague. Invoking his powers, Catalano increased the authority of the Committee of Four, on which he served, to buy and store more wheat, "but our power went untapped, for we didn't buy the wheat—and if only we had! Because it became expensive." The next day, on the first of Kislev, the Health Office decreed that any sign of illness should be reported to one of their notaries, and the four considered renting space to house family members of the sick, as contacts were also sequestered. They discuss renting a residence in the nearby village of Brentelle. "And if only we had not done so," Catalano comments, "for it became the source of many troubles, as written here." Indeed, the Christians also had their eye on Brentelle, and when the Christian lazaretto overflowed, they built pest huts in Brentelle without informing the Jews. (Later, another battle would erupt over Jewish plans to use Brentelle for decontamination of goods, which the Christians also opposed.) Two months later, at the beginning of Adar, the stored flour was sent to be made into matzah, but the committee failed to buy oil. "And if only we had done as I wished," Catalano again mourns, "for it became very expensive afterward."[18] Anticipating failures of planning, these examples all consist of retrospective judgments. In the *'Olam Hafukh*'s concluding paragraphs, Catalano will return to their lessons to warn future readers to avoid these mistakes, confirming that they weighed on him heavily. The didactic poems by his son that are appended to most copies of the text also incorporate instructions for stocking provisions, buying spare utensils, hiring servants, and protecting possessions by securing them under Health Office seal.[19]

The fourth example pointedly underlines that Catalano personally foresaw the possibility of an oil shortage, but no one heeded him. The fifth example also involves a situation in which Catalano locks horns with his colleagues, this time over loan terms offered by a Christian nobleman named Zuane (or Giovanni) Michel. Two of the Committee of Four opposed the loan. Catalano tells us that he argued bitterly with them, "for need would increase daily, and there was no money to lend to those in need." He continues, "In vain I pleaded with them to agree with me! And God in Heaven was with me, for had we not taken that money . . . many would have died of hunger and want, but God remembered me favorably."[20] The sixth example also highlights Abraham's exertions to protect the possessions of ghetto residents, in the episode described earlier, where household goods were inventoried and locked under seal by a Health Office representative. According to Catalano, ghetto residents hastened to comply: "and had we not done so, nothing would have remained of our community's possessions with all the trouble that followed." This time, too, Catalano intervened personally, making available space in a large attic room he had rented for his own property.[21]

The final example of anticipatory knowledge comes when the plague was well under way, early in Tammuz (approximately July). Using his friendly connections with the first *provveditore*, Ettore Sala, Catalano rented a large apartment outside the ghetto, "with gardens and orchards, in the Savonarola neighborhood, a building called the Accademia."[22] In detail, he describes his plans to divide the house in two, half for his family and half for his father-in-law's. Each half had its own exit, and each household would likewise dedicate a room for someone to tend to the sick; his half included a room designated for Catalano's wife and their Christian servants, and his in-laws' half had a room for his mother-in-law and sister-in-law, who had cared for children of the dead. *"But all these precautions were worthless for us, as I shall relate."* Catalano's meaning becomes clear two months later, in early Av (July), when he and his relatives were evicted from the Accademia following complaints from Jews confined to the ghetto. The attenuated wait for an explanation creates a sense of narrative delay; the litany of deaths and crises that separate prediction from fulfilment track the ongoing epidemic but also the clock silently ticking on his foes' resentment, which will shock Catalano completely.

This incident touches Catalano personally and strikes deeply at his sense of dedication to the very Jews whose meddling interferes with his concern for his family. That he tells the story reminds us that he wants us to see his selflessness, even—or especially—when it goes unappreciated. The seven incidents form a progression, moving from negotiations with merchants, brokers, and Christian landowners, to resistance on the Committee of Four, to an instance of successful planning and his own benevolence, to a bruising account of communal ingratitude that thwarts his plans to protect his family. Together the examples trace an evolution in the narrator's recourse to retrospection. As they steadily become more personal, the emphasis on his foresight, prudence, and selflessness is likewise amplified. Here is Catalano as he wishes us to see him, but also as he wishes to see himself: The wound to his ego that follows the shock of eviction from the Accademia is palpable in his prose. Is this the real person Catalano? Or is this depiction of wounded pride also a convention that signals a trait of the public man? Perhaps, at certain moments, the public and private man converge. Perhaps, indeed, the public man told the private man how to feel what he was feeling.

Defiance and Dissent

In addition to technical devices like sequencing and anticipatory knowledge, Catalano's account of the plague enlists thematic motifs or scenarios of opposition and boundary-testing conflict. These scenes are intrinsic to Catalano's self-representation.[23] We might even say that his sense of self is erected on counterpoints of resistance from people and forces with competing perspectives and agendas; the 'Olam Hafukh discloses its author most vividly in moments of conflict with family members, Jews, Christians, officials, laborers, envoys, medical personnel, poor people, servants, nuns, and rogues. The contest of forces does not invariably conclude in the narrator's victory, either, which has the result of rendering him as very human. In general Catalano bequeaths his unknown readers an account of not just what the Paduan ghetto officials did, or what government or health office officials did, but also what they failed to do, or what they did that failed. At the same time he is neither a radical nor a visionary: He does not imagine life without these institutions. Like the spatial, confessional, professional, class, and gendered hierarchies they inscribe, bureaucracies and institutions have acquired the status of naturalized features of the social landscape; their hierarchies are not contested.[24] Civic order and social hierarchy are values he consistently upholds.

These scenes of defiance and dissent also articulate the public subjectivity that characterizes Catalano's representation of himself. They stage the moments when the narrator defines himself *against* his family and community and highlight character traits that he wishes to project. Certainly these scenes of contest are of historical interest, but they play literary and psychological roles, too. They propel the narrative as much as the plague does and continue after the plague dies out. As is evident from the examples that follow, they are not formulaic type-scenes, although some of their elements appear in more than one episode. Nonetheless, they function similarly to type-scenes, and their subtle variations are meaningful. Catalano's inclusion of these episodes tells us that they were important to him, but also that they can be used to convey meaning or instruction.

These episodes also testify to voices and perspectives that differ from his own, reminding us that Catalano's is only one version of what it was like to live through the Great Italian Plague—a privileged, literate, male, and Jewish version at that. The residue of these dissenting voices is another of the narrative's striking features, suggesting that the assumption of responsibility for others—at home, in the ghetto or city—might be prized not just as a privilege but precisely because it was a burden: The wear and tear of politics, the scars of public battle, were worn as badges of honor. They constituted an integral feature of what it meant to be a public man, and they reverberated in private identity.

The contexts where dissent is voiced in the *'Olam Hafukh* vary considerably. Sometimes Catalano laments shortsighted planning, sometimes botched execution. Frequently, though, trouble erupts in seemingly spontaneous objections, sometimes from individuals, sometimes from larger classes, groups, or factions. In some cases, he can and does name their protagonists—his daughter Hannah who refuses to relinquish her mother to go to the lazaretto;[25] or the widow Sarah Romano, who may have set her home on fire in revenge for *not* being taken to the lazaretto (where she imagines she will receive better care);[26] the Alatrini brothers, who serve as gravediggers but refuse to enter households to remove the dead;[27] or the difficult *provveditore* Alvise Valaresso, who was appointed after the death of the pro-Jewish Ettore Sala.[28] In contrast to the harmonious decision-making Catalano imagined would characterize the Committee of Four, conflict among the committee members also surfaces rapidly. Catalano describes his disputes with his three colleagues, as when he berates them from house confinement. Here, as in several other examples, his criticism of his colleagues indirectly testifies to his own compassion, defining the idealized balance of justice and empathy in the cause of common good:

> Then I myself was enclosed in my home, and my colleagues would come from the Ashkenazi synagogue while I was at my study window across from the synagogue, so I could consult with them on plague matters. May Heaven be my witness that I would cry bitterly from my window to bring men and women servants from Venice or wherever, and skilled empirics who knew how to prepare medications and open abscesses, for I was moved to compassion for the many who were dying without medicine or skilled help.[29]

In other cases, the dissenters are nameless. Twenty-three poor Jews (men and women) refuse to serve as gravediggers and caretakers of the sick;[30] other disgruntled Jews complain to Christian officials when Catalano moves into a villa outside the ghetto.[31] Townspeople object to the ghetto housing its gravediggers in an apartment whose windows open onto a city street;[32] nuns do not want the Jewish cemetery inside the city walls;[33] and city officials refuse Catalano's committee permission to build a Jewish convalescent house or *sabore* (decontamination area) on land the Jews have already rented.[34] In one case Catalano flatly refuses to name his opponents other than to identify them as "two of my colleagues" (of the Committee of Four?).

Tellingly, this instance touches his personal life—a collision of personal and public identities that has proven volatile before. When his sick daughter, Hannah, refuses to be separated from her mother, Catalano tries to protect his wife by hiring a nurse who has already been taken to the section of the lazaretto for family members exposed to plague (the so-called *sospetti*). The young nurse is the daughter of Sarah Romano (the suspected arsonist); both mother and daughter subsequently die in the lazaretto. At first Catalano exploits his personal connections with the first *provveditore*, Ettore Sala, to remove the Romano daughter from the contact ward of the lazaretto. The girl is brought to his rental villa to care for his daughter in a quarantine room, but things do not work out as he intended:

> Then two of my colleagues, whose names I shall not utter, refused to grant me permission to bring that woman from the lazaretto to my home, apologetically saying that they feared for their lives if the matter angered the *provveditore*. . . . [But] the minister, Signor Ettore Sala, ordered the lazaretto official to bring her to me, and he did. [Then] the young woman came to my house, but my little girl cried so bitterly when her mother left [the room that] she could not refrain from going in to see her. The next morning, the young woman changed her mind. Weeping, she said, "I will go back to my mother in the lazaretto," so my wife made me return her there.[35]

Both his wife and daughter will die of plague, devastating Catalano. The description of Catalano's personal grief suspending the Hebrew narrative is notably absent from the Italian journal on which he based his account, reinforcing my claim that the construction of this episode was carefully crafted in the Hebrew revision. The Italian account records Sarah's initial illness ("in q[ue]sto temp si tocho' mia moglie") and her death shortly afterward amid a flood of fatalities ("et anco mia moglie").[36] In contrast, the Hebrew version painstakingly distinguishes this loss from all others: "The pious and humble" Sarah Catalano, "Sarah my wife, the wife of my youth, my wedded love," falls ill on the tenth of Tammuz (the end of June or early July 1631). A terse record of the mortality statistics for the eleventh, twelfth, and thirteenth of the month follows. "Then on the fourteenth, three died in the ghetto and one in the lazaretto, and my righteous wife in that aforementioned house, after twenty-one years we had been together." The narrative halts with a brief eulogy in verse, then resumes with the death of Ettore

Sala, the friendly *provveditore,* "and from that moment on, we knew no peace."[37] The interjected glimpses of private grief illuminate a numbing litany of collective loss; like a veil ripped open briefly, the passage exposes then quickly falls shut. But the tableau of the bereaved husband and father lingers as the public Catalano resumes lobbying to counteract the burghers who seek to sway the new *provveditore* against the Jews. Like her husband, the saintly Sarah who would not leave her children exemplifies an ideal that contrasts sharply and intentionally with scenes of family ties rent, and abandoned women and children.

The intersection of private and public can also go awry. When the grumbling of Jews within the ghetto forces him to leave the spacious villa in the Accademia, Catalano is both stunned and deeply offended. A Christian official shows up at his door unexpectedly:

> On Saturday, one of the ministers, Davilo [or Avolo] Dotto, stood at the entrance to the Accademia's gate and asked me, are you Doctor Catalano? I said, yes, I am he. He said, this is by order of the *provveditore*: You and your family must leave this house and go to the ghetto within three days; if you do not, everything you have here will be burned. He said the same thing to my father-in-law. Some Jews were behind this, as they had been grumbling about us and about me especially, why didn't we stay in the ghetto to oversee the ghetto and God's people? God knows that even though I was enclosed in the Accademia, I would go occasionally to the ghetto with the *fante* from the health office to see what was going on.[38]

Later, Catalano is uneasy when a proposal by other ghetto leaders for compensating the Jews for mattresses, linens, and goods sent for decontamination (which invariably ruined them) spurs the ghetto residents to complain. Even Azriel Katz, he notes, one of the Committee of Four, had preferred to burn all his contaminated possessions, estimating that the cost of decontamination and restoring them would outstrip that of total loss.[39] "I didn't want to say anything pro or con," Catalano writes, "because decontamination of my contaminated possessions, and those of my father-in-law's, had taken place at the Accademia under the officials' supervision, and as for our contaminated property in the ghetto, it had been shipped out by hiding it on a wagon carrying goods for burning—so how could I judge whether others' property should be burned?"[40] Even as he sidesteps the wrath of " everyone" in the ghetto, Catalano is fighting bitterly with the *provveditore* over terms for releasing Jewish convalescents and reopening the ghetto gates.

Poor Catalano, who means so well and is rewarded with ingratitude![41] Defiance meets him at every step, from high and low, Jew and Christian, men, women, and even small children, each motivated by his or her own blend of fear, desperation, and sometimes greed and meanness. What purpose does the inclusion of all these incidents serve? In addition to documenting the thankless work of the ghetto officials, these episodes burnish Catalano's image as a civic leader and family patriarch challenged by resistance from within and without. Competing, incompletely suppressed, voices test the boundaries where "Catalano" begins and ends, limning a figure of prudence and integrity, a family man and community leader dedicated to the common good. That the community does not always respond with appreciation is a defining element of his role and of his self-representation. Ironically, the dissonant perspectives that are inscribed in the *'Olam Hafukh* permit us to glimpse the traces of a world outside the author's narrative control, where multiple actors live their own version of events: women, children, and poor folk, gravediggers, burghers, and nuns, colleagues, servants, and urban bureaucrats. The narrator's projection strives to stay aloft despite constant puncturing from below, but the puncture points also locate the defining features of what it means in this setting to be a public "self."

Private and Public Emotion

As historians of emotion remind us, the expression of emotional states is culturally conditioned, whether this refers to how we permit their display in public or how we learn to identify and experience emotional states as private and subjective.[42] The *'Olam Hafukh* marshals a variety of techniques for conveying the narrator's or others' emotional responses to situations of stress, conflict, or grief. I have singled out a few examples, some of them cued by linguistic usages and some by scenario.

Repeatedly, Catalano has recourse to the expression צעק מרה, to cry out bitterly, variations of which appear multiple times in the narrative. He himself "cries out bitterly" when his three colleagues reject loan terms that would have permitted them to purchase urgently needed supplies,[43] and when he pleads with them to bring medicine and medical practitioners from Venice.[44] His use of this idiom is clarified when we review its other appearances. When Catalano's daughter Hannah sickens, he initially planned to "pay four or five times the [accepted] salary" for a nursemaid in the lazaretto. But his wife was distressed by the agitated child who "cries out bitterly," and then "cried out bitterly" again when a nurse was brought in and her mother was removed from her.[45] The mother of Sarah, wife of Joseph the *shamash*, also "cries out bitterly" from the window when no one in the household will go near her dying daughter or bring her down for burial after she dies.[46] Bona, the wife of Shlomo Turchetti in the ghetto, "cries out bitterly and dies" after miscarrying..[47] Finally, Catalano and his fellow negotiators from the ghetto also "cry out bitterly" over the discriminatory conditions they must meet for decontamination, demanding to know why the same conditions do not apply to the Christians.[48] The Christians "cry out" too, but not with the appended "bitterly": The nuns "cry out" to protest the Jews' use of a burial ground within the city,[49] and the burghers make an outcry over the proposed Jewish site for their lazaretto.[50] In both cases the Christians צעקו (cried out), or צעקו יחדיו (cried out together). In one case, near the end of the narrative, the convalescent Jews remain in the lazaretto while Catalano and his friends negotiate with the Health Office for their reentry, and צעקת האומללים ההם [the outcry of those wretches] begged us to bring them back to the ghetto."[51] Thus Catalano describes an emotional state but also colors the phrase slightly differently from the way we might otherwise read it. As the examples demonstrate, the full expression implies distress but also a plea for justice and redress. In fact, that hue already colors the unique biblical use of the full term, in Genesis 27:34, where Esau, defrauded of his birthright, "cried out mightily and bitterly."[52] No wonder, then, that the Christians, whose outcry is unjust, do not merit the full expression. In the case of the convalescents, Catalano and his colleagues were also ambivalent about their return, out of fear that any new illness would prolong closure of the ghetto. The justice of their cry is also qualified.

Other expressions of emotion describe moments where Catalano is touched by compassion. These episodes should be read in concert with descriptions of communal compassion; taken together, the range of meaning grows clearer. Notably, with one exception, compassion is reserved exclusively for other Jews. Three times Catalano uses the phrase נכמרו רחמים (to feel compassion or pity). The biblical expression appears twice: in Genesis 43.30, where it refers to Joseph's pity for his brothers, and in 1 Kings 3.26, in the tale of King Solomon's judgment between two women who each claim to be the mother of a child; when Solomon proposes slicing the child in half, the biological mother is overwhelmed by pity for her son. In the *'Olam*

Hafukh, this kind of compassion is almost entirely restricted to family members or other Jews. Thus, for instance, the beleaguered community votes despite its woes to send charity to the plague-struck ghetto of Florence: "when we heard of their affliction, נכמרו רחמים עליהם [we felt pity for them], and even wrapped in the coils of death, we imposed [a tithe] on each member of the community . . . to help." So, too, when Catalano is confined to his home and arguing through the window with his fellow committee members, he pleads with them to hire empirics who can open buboes and treat the sick, "for נכמרו רחמי [I felt pity] for the many who were dying without medicine or trained help."[53] The final instance is also dramatic, and underlines how much the breakdown of family, communal, and religious order in the ghetto shook the author: "When I heard the wagon's bell ringing, I looked up and saw the healthy were being brought on the wagon, weeping for their families, together with the afflicted so helpless they were brought like lambs to slaughter. נכמרו רחמי עליהם [I felt pity for them], and I couldn't breathe. Sometimes I would see the wagon carrying the pallets of the dead, people whom I knew by name, and it was as if I had lost all my strength. The infected also wandered here and there against all order and law."[54] When the ghetto's *parnassim* force the Committee of Four to withhold the charity stipends of the poor in order to compel them to serve as gravediggers and attendants for the sick, Catalano also expresses pity, or compassion, for their plight. "Then a few of us, including myself, wanted to revoke [that decision] and resume their stipends as before, for we said, money means nothing to a man compared to his life, and how can we ask them to die?"[55] He votes to repeal the decision but loses (the vote is two against two), upon which many in the community assist the poor despite the ruling. And finally, after the Romano girl returns to the lazaretto, Catalano describes going to great lengths—in fact, breaking the law—to hire a Christian servant to nurse his sick daughter. He does this to spare his wife, whose devotion to the little girl puts her at risk. But his wife refuses to let the Christian girl expose herself to plague: "Through various means, a Christian servant girl was found—though the *provveditore*'s decree was still in force—who came to work for six litres a day for as long as the plague lasted. She arrived when my little girl was dying, but my wife did not wish the gentile to be infected because of a momentary crisis."[56] In all four examples, evincing compassion is noble, but mapped against boundaries of class and religion. In the unique case where it applies across faith boundaries, compassion is exercised by a woman. In the other examples, Catalano describes compassion for (nameless) fellow Jews, for the dead and their grieving companions on the wagons, and for the ghetto poor. Each instance adds to his moral capital, and the final instance, manifested by his saintly wife, also adds luster to his name.

Worry is another emotional state that makes multiple appearances in the *'Olam Hafukh*. This feeling, too, is displayed most often with respect to communal concerns. Plague struck the Christian city before the ghetto, and for a while the Jews hoped they would escape it. Christians saw this differently, and Catalano describes mounting resentment ("envy") among the Christian populace: "We feared them, because they sought to libel us, accusing us of disposing [secretly] of the dead." The Health Office orders the ghetto to take a census, which causes the Jews greater unease: census-taking had been associated with divine displeasure and plague since biblical times, and head counts among Jews are still considered to bring bad luck.[57] With no cases of illness in the ghetto, Catalano and his Committee of Four worry also when the wife of their Christian gatekeeper falls sick, with a bubo behind her knee. After a twenty-day confinement, the Health Office clears the gatekeeper and his family, but the anxious committee refuses to allow the gatekeeper to enter the ghetto, paying his salary to stay home. Despite their efforts, the gatekeeper's little boy returned to the ghetto to play with the Jewish children, and the father also ignored their pleas. Soon afterward, the gatekeeper fell ill, and plague appeared among the Jews.[58] The committee's worry was, in their view, well founded.

Similarly, as the outbreak ends, Catalano and his committee agonize over the fate of the convalescent Jews housed outside the ghetto, whose return must be weighed against the desperate need to reopen the ghetto. The committee (with Catalano as their mediator) had already negotiated with the Health Office and *provveditore* over which Jewish property had to be burned and which could be sent for decontamination, where they could decontaminate, and who would appraise condemned goods for reimbursement. With communal funds they fumigated and cleaned the ghetto, then painted the houses with lime and aired them. At this point the convalescents could return to an eight-day confinement, but the *provveditore* announced that even a single death would close down the ghetto again: "So, we feared greatly to bring the convalescents back into the ghetto in case of sickness that would cause the ministers to confine the whole Ghetto."[59]

Worry and dread can also be personal, illustrating again how the magnified representation of Catalano's domestic world counterpoints the more restrained expression of public emotion. When his Jewish servant girl falls sick, Catalano writes that "my heart dissolved inside me" (ויפג לבי בקרבי).[60] The expression echoes the biblical Jacob's reaction to hearing that his long-lost son Joseph is still alive; Catalano inverts the biblical scenario, subtly anticipating his own child's death.[61] Indeed, the servant girl recovers three days later, but his daughter Bona sickens then dies, the servant girl falls sick again, and then, as we know, so does his daughter Hannah, leading her desperate father to bring the Romano girl from the lazaretto. When the Romano girl refuses to stay, Catalano returns her to the lazaretto, "in anxious sorrow for my wife who went back to tending the little girl, who died soon after."[62]

Once again public and private emotional states deliberately refract each other. Catalano invokes anxiety to reflect a range of feelings, from premonition of disaster to worry about inadequate planning or unmanageable political situations. Dread and anxiety ricochet between the privacy of his home and the public arena, as we have seen with the expression of other emotional states. Worry is part of the job in both realms, where it is also carefully disciplined to prevent emotional collapse or paralysis. Perhaps unsurprisingly, Carlo Cipolla identified this same anxiety in his study of Cristofano di Ceffini, Catalano's contemporary in the Health Office in Prato. Sketching the challenges facing the health officers during the 1630 epidemic, Cipolla asked what these men felt "deep in their hearts." His answer: "a sense of intolerable fatigue and constant worry."[63] That emotional condition was shared by their Jewish counterparts. And they considered it a privilege.

Abraham Massarani's *Sefer haGalut vehaPedut*: The Case for Comparison

My reading of Abraham Catalano's plague narrative has illustrated some of the ways in which rhetorical and literary features of that work were enlisted to shape the author's self-image, both as a public figure marshaled through the voice of his first-person narrator and as a private person, a husband and father whose personal experiences are embedded in the larger story. I have tried to show that these two realms of self-representation—public and private—are also reciprocal constructions: They exist (or coexist) in tandem, one drawing articulation and meaning from the other. This argument makes sense only if Abraham Catalano's peers spoke the same language. How do we know that Catalano was really tapping what I have called an "idiom" of self-fashioning shared by members of a community? Who constituted that community, and how do we identify them?

The second (two-part) question is easier to answer than the first, although the community surely was constituted by a core circle with concentric rings of diminishing participation. The preceding and following chapters track the writing activity of a small circle of educated Jewish men, all but Joseph Concio situated in Mantua and Padua but with ties to other major Jewish and urban centers in Modena, Venice, Verona, Florence, Bologna, Vicenza and elsewhere. Some, like Abraham Massarani in Mantua, had ties to the banking elite in the region. Others, like Abraham Catalano and Solomon Marini, had ties to fellow students from the University of Padua. As Joseph Concio's example illustrates, even when they functioned on a local level, they were avid consumers of print as well as manuscripts; they were also correspondents, travelers, and prominently engaged in ghetto affairs as well as the cultural and political traffic between the ghetto and Christian city. They had disciples and friends, men from similar backgrounds to their own, whose names appear and reappear in community *pinkasim, ketubbot,* contracts, lawsuits, loan records, and cemeteries. They played important roles in their synagogues and possibly in synagogue-based confraternities: Joseph Concio composed epitaphs and wedding poems, and his son sang in a synagogue choir; Abraham Catalano served on the local *beit din* and was a personal friend of the rabbi Solomon Marini. Marini represented the Ashkenazi congregation but preached in the smaller synagogues also and had no qualms about issuing dictates for the entire ghetto community; Abraham Massarani describes his connections to the synagogue and banking princes of the Norsa family.

These men also had families, meaning that their values and interests reverberated in a domestic setting that often escapes printed memory but points us to a shadowy world where we dimly perceive household arrangements, aesthetic tastes—including music, a striking feature of Jewish interest in this period and region—religious practices, ethical and affective behaviors, female literacy and agency, and the presence of household servants and guests. Together these relationships define the concentric circles of what Brian Stock has termed a "textual community," and what, based on that coinage, Barbara Rosenwein later called an "emotional community."[64] These overlapping identities were forged through a shared vocabulary supplied by Jewish and secular learning, and immersion in the cultural and intellectual currents of the

day. These affective and intellectual networks have been studied fruitfully for
some time now, and I am not claiming anything new.

My first question, however, demands closer scrutiny and proof. How do
I know that Abraham Catalano's colleagues and peers would have recognized his cues as conventions of representation that drew on an available
repertoire? If these conventions really did constitute a cultural idiom for
representing a certain kind of public identity, then they had to be legible to
a contemporary audience that could understand their association with a
convergence of public and private responsibilities, anxieties, and identities.
One way to answer this question is to demonstrate that the same vocabulary
or idiom is found elsewhere in contemporary Jewish writing. To do so, I
want to turn to another Hebrew prose narrative composed in the wake of
the 1630–31 plague in Mantua. The author, Abraham Massarani, was not
especially interested in the plague but instead focused on recounting the
travails of Mantuan Jews expelled in the late summer of 1630. His account,
therefore, is not a *successo della peste* exemplar at all. Massarani has his literary sights set on a different kind of historical narrative, a standard historical
chronicle that emphasizes political and collective events over individual stories. Individual stories play a role, however, in the form of exemplary vignettes,
and so does the narrator, who moves in and out of view as he narrates. Does
Abraham Massarani's *Sefer haGalut vehaPedut* (Book of Exile and Redemption)
exploit the same idioms of "self" that we find in the *'Olam Hafukh*? The next
section of this chapter says yes.

*   *   *

Like Abraham Catalano, Abraham Massarani was a man who came endowed
with systemic agency and status. In addition to his own wealth and family
ties to banking activity, his wife was a Sulam, another prosperous banking
family with ties in Venice.[65] Massarani's father, a gifted musician and dancer,
was a favorite of the Gonzaga court, and Abraham Massarani would have
been raised with the music, culture, and literature of Christian aristocrats
and literati to complement his education as a Jew.[66] Abraham Massarani's
chronicle of the expulsion from the Mantuan ghetto incorporates plague as
a supplementary catastrophe that befell the Mantuan Jews. The *Sefer haGalut
vehaPedut* chronicles the famous sack of Mantua, focusing on the fate of the
ghetto under siege, the arrival of the plague, and the subsequent expulsion

and return of the Jews. It therefore covers a wider geographical terrain and longer chronological span than Catalano's plague narrative; beginning in 1625, under the reign of Duke Ferdinand Gonzaga, the account ends in 1631 with the departure of imperial troops and the reentry of Duke Carlo Gonzaga of Nevers to the city.[67]

Massarani does not write as an eyewitness to most of the events he details. From Vienna, business had taken him to an uncle's home in nearby Regensburg, where he learned of the travails of the Mantuan community from a handful of Jewish emissaries who arrived many months later. Upon his return, Massarani relied on survivors and witnesses to reconstruct events, including some details and omitting others. Most of the chronicle is aerial in perspective and treats the Jews as a collective facing armies and rulers, the siege and sack of the city and ghetto. After their expulsion, Massarani traces the Jews' two routes into exile and the eventual return of survivors to the ravaged ghetto.

Massarani's narrator keeps his distance for most of the text, with occasional reminders of his presence with phrases like "as we shall explain," "as we shall see," or the theological idiom, "on account of our many sins," intended to explain dire misfortune. When, for instance, the Germans first entered Mantua, the Jews frantically buried their valuables, thinking that if the city were captured, they would be able to flee with some wealth. It is impossible to thwart God's will, the narrator interjects darkly (in other words, "no such luck"): God intends to punish the Jews for their sins. Foolishly, the Jews conclude that the Germans have retreated, and they dig up their "silver and gold and sacks of precious things and commodities."[68] The Germans return to sack the city. In this case, an allusion to Proverbs 19:21 ("Many are the plans devised by man's mind, but the Lord's purpose will be established") anticipates disaster. Throughout the body of the chronicle, the community moves as a single character. It is not anyone's individual sins that bring disaster on them all but a generic and unspecified moral condition. This corporate perspective is strengthened by the frequent erasure of individual names and identities, and attributions of unified emotional responses to the community, which can be frightened or misguided, famished, thirsty and tired, and even occasionally defiant.

In contrast, when Massarani figures personally in his account, he enlists some of the same techniques of representation that characterized Catalano's 'Olam Hafukh. This occurs in his preface, describing the return of the expelled Mantuan Jews, and again in a dramatic episode toward the chronicle's conclusion. Both examples illustrate a manipulation of temporal sequencing and scenes of contested authority that demonstrate personal character enlisted for the public good. Let us look first at the chronological manipulation, and then at the scenes of challenge.

The preface of the *Sefer haGalut vehaPedut* opens with a highly stylized effusion evoking communal ruin and mourning, enriched by rhymed prose. Massarani describes his return to the ravaged ghetto, where he discovers that his mother has died on the road and the family house has been taken over by German soldiers. He is overwhelmed by the magnitude of personal and communal loss. "I will never be consoled," Massarani says, "for I was not with them to mourn and eulogize them as befitted their glory and honor." This is one of his stated motives for composing his chronicle.

> [Upon returning] I did not find my mother, my beloved parent, whose pure soul had departed in a foreign land. Alone I sat stunned and silent; I could not gather [my] strength. I had thought to dwell at home with my household, in the dwelling of my א"א [beloved mother?] may her memory be blessed. But I discovered that it was inhabited by the Germans, and my brothers and I were treated like strangers. I was stunned: "naked I went out as naked I began." And I discovered my people steeped in sorrow and the tribulations of the wars and upheavals.[69]

Massarani suspends chronology again to account for his own late entry into the narrative. For the first time we learn that the Jewish hostages held in Mantua when the community was expelled had managed to contact their colleague in Venice, who wrote to two prominent Mantuan Jews in Bolsano, who recommended in turn that they petition the emperor for help. Joined by a third Jew, the men set off for Innsbruck, where they decided to appeal to Archduke Leopold of Austria, the emperor's brother, to write to the emperor on their behalf. Unfortunately, the archduke was not in Innsbruck, but in Rieti, so they continued onward, obtaining the desired letter. Their next stop was in Regensburg, where the emperor was hosting the Reichstag. The Jewish delegation arrived in August 1631, "And I, the writer, had been there about a month before their arrival, along with my exalted uncle, Eleazar Hayyim Kazim, may his name be remembered for a blessing—and we had not known a thing about all these tribulations."[70] The narrative resumes, carrying along our narrator until its conclusion. Notably, the authorial insertion efficiently

links private and public spheres while exonerating Massarani from any ac-
cusation of inaction.

When Massarani is a live participant in his story, the narrative is also re-
plete with names, dates, and details. As he enters the public sphere, we also see
him confronting the kind of opposition and defiance that characterized Catalano's narrator. The return of the refugees was a ragged process complicated by
the transfers of power between imperial and French forces, the departure from
Mantua of the German occupiers, and the entry of Duke Carlo of Nevers.
Several months prior to the final departure of imperial troops in September 1631, the Germans imposed a crushing tax on the returning Jews (ostensibly for military expenses). Importuned by a Jewish delegation, the duke sent a
French officer to Mantua to demand that the Germans cease harassing the
Jews. Massarani accompanied this group. He was leaving the Great Synagogue
in Mantua on the twelfth of Elul (late July), a Sabbath morning, when a
German officer with three men appeared at the entrance. The officer stopped
Massarani and asked him to identify the wealthy members of the community
among the emerging worshippers.[71] Massarani stalled, exploiting his own recent arrival to claim that he had no idea which Jew was rich or poor, but that
"my lord knows that all of them are poor and debased now." The officer detained him, with three other Jews,[72] demanding that Massarani identify the
owner of "this house near the synagogue." Massarani knew the building belonged to Ben Zion Norsa, but again pretended ignorance; undeterred, the
officer ordered him to go into the synagogue and find him.[73]

> I went up into the synagogue and told these things to that afore-
> mentioned Norsa, who was terrified. He told me, go tell him that I
> am coming. So, I went down and told the officer what he said, and he
> waited until he saw no one was coming, for Norsa had fled for his life
> through the windows and openings in the synagogue attic. I went
> down to tell the officer. Then he became very angry with me and
> struck me, saying, "Tell these men to stay put and not move from
> here until I speak to them! And you come with me." He went up to
> [the synagogue] and searched everywhere without finding him. Then
> he grew angry with me, saying I had helped him flee. He went to
> Norsa's house and searched the whole house but didn't find him.[74]

The furious officer then arrests the three Jews he has detained and gives
them eight days to come up with the sum owed in debts accrued by locals

during the Germans' stay. The Jews protest that they have nothing to do with these debts, but to no avail; shortly after, they are taken in chains to Cremona with the departing army.

Massarani depicts a double challenge in this scene, first in Norsa's defiance and then in the threatening officer. Nonetheless, the dramatic episode highlights Massarani's sense of communal responsibility. Like Catalano, he must accept defeat (deceived by Norsa, cowed by the officer), but his struggle to protect fellow Jews contrasts vividly with Norsa's self-serving defection, illustrating "character" in service to the Jewish collective. This is a model for real behavior, and how the narrator wishes to be seen. Failure is also essential to self-construction. Failure advantageously displays the narrator's persistence, commitment, integrity, and refusal to shirk responsibility. This is exactly what characterizes Catalano's frustrated record of his defeats. In other words, Catalano was not inventing this idiom. He was expertly using it, and he could expect his readers to recognize the competing pressures and psychological tensions that defined the public man—and perhaps, the insurmountable challenges of being one.

Conclusion

Abraham Catalano depicts himself in *'Olam Hafukh* as a public figure in the Paduan ghetto in a time of plague. Insofar as good leaders are stewards of order and orderly rule, they are also conscious of the burdens of leadership and the multiple constituencies they govern. Catalano's domestic world is a microcosm of the larger social order, where he strives to rule as a loving, responsible patriarch. Navigating the forces of disorder, whether external (plague, war, urban foes, or ill-disposed officials) or internal (family, servants, ghetto and city residents), is a mark of the man Catalano projects to others and presumably how he wished to see himself. A model that balances privilege with selfless dedication, it is strikingly dependent on the experience of frustration and defeat.

And yet the *'Olam Hafukh* is not political commentary, except insofar as it treats the failure of institutions designed to serve the common good. At the conclusion of his narrative, Catalano, a man with medical training and political connections, rejects medical knowledge as useless and cautions against reliance on public institutions. "Even though I have been crowned as a physician," he comments, "and I know what physicians say on this matter, I did not see fit to write a thing about the preservative techniques written in their books; rather, I write a chronicle that is suitable for future generations in whatever catastrophe, may it not happen!"[75] So, too, he counsels, "prepare many days' worth of supplies for yourself, whatever grain, drink, and oil you desire, anything you and your household will require from 'pins to laces,' so that you will not need to go seeking sustenance when plague arrives."[76] As for trusting in civic authorities, he concludes pessimistically: "As for you, my community members, remember—do not forget!—before the plague strikes, to send a community representative, a faithful servant, to Venice! Pay his salary [in advance] so that he will stay there to help in times of trouble. Then, if the ministers here denounce us without justification, to impose closure on the ghetto or something of the sort, he will be there to stand in the breach."[77]

Notably, all but one of Catalano's final recommendations are directed to heads of household rather than institutions or communal authorities; they concern provisions and funds, finding a safe space to live, and strategies for protecting one's property and possessions. Although he believes that plague is contagious, he spurns popular electuaries and medicines. As for the practice of sniffing citrus, "who knows if the good scent stirs the attraction of the air and causes these ethers to enter the nostrils?" More important is to avoid company and to sequester the sick at home, ideally with a well-paid nurse so you can remove yourself to safety without abandoning someone in need.[78] The fabric of social ties must not be rent: Flight from disease does not justify flight from responsibility.

Both Catalano and Massarani maneuver in a world that is spatially partitioned, but one in which they are indivisibly Paduan and Mantuan as well as Jews. Plague and politics are stressors on identity but do not cause rupture or inversion. In this context, the resemblance between Catalano's narrative and the *successo della peste* narratives treated by Cohn is evident. Certainly the features Cohn says are new and defining for the genre are identifiable in the *'Olam Hafukh*: the chronological account of the plague from its purported "Patient Zero" origin to its spread, wane, reignition, and conclusion; the institutional responses of health boards and personnel; the recording of mortality and recovery statistics; religious processions and prayers; vignettes of plague-related trauma; the official end of the plague and ceremonies of thanksgiving. At the same time I have claimed that a hallmark concern of Catalano's narrative is equally to construct its author, and the *'Olam Hafukh* is arguably organized to facilitate that goal. The impulse to self-construction in an ego document is not surprising, but Catalano's narrative suggests the ways that plague pressed on normative conventions of self-representation. In the immediate aftermath of a horrifying mortality event for whose outcome Catalano felt personal responsibility, the need for self-definition—personal and public—must have been urgent. Whether this is a feature of the genre overall needs to be assessed.[79]

And yet the point of this chapter is not just to add another item or quali-fication to Cohn's list. Rather, I am insisting that narratives like Catalano's are deliberately constructed and so is the figure of the narrator who unfurls them. One of the consequences of taking these writers seriously as writers is that we see them engaged with projecting a public persona that displays deeply cher-ished social ideals. At the same time the construction of this "public man," as I am calling him, also betrays a complex subjectivity not to be confused with the public subjectivity of our own time and place. For Catalano, Massarani, Cristofano, and their peers, the public man crystalized in the heat of opposition and great worry. These two elements were essential to how they saw themselves and how they wished to project themselves into public space and memory. Nor can Catalano's role in the domestic sphere be disentangled from his public persona; it is not entirely "private" in the modern sense. We recall that Carlo Cipolla also identified this blend of bureaucratic efficiency, civic zeal, and chronic anxiety in Cristofano di Ceffini in Prato; Cipolla's reading suggests that this dimension of subjectivity was shared by a similar class of Jewish and Christian men of means and responsibility.[80]

Massarani's chronicle, which enlists some of the same conventions of self-representation, reinforces my claims. Significantly, despite the overlap with the Christian paradigm, we should note the frustration and fear that cohere with tension on the borders of what separates Christian and Jew. In negotia-tions with Christian authorities, or in moments of powerlessness before Christian violence or intractability, the retreat to confessional identity and interests is clear. At times it is accompanied by echoes of betrayal, testifying to the sharpening of confessional divides in times of crisis. And yet no one Massarani depicts among the Mantuan exiles ceases to think of himself as Mantuan, even starving in a field outside San Martino. Nor does Massarani himself default on this identity in Regensburg, where his sense of obligation to community and family embroils him in negotiations with the duke; like the refugees, he returns to Mantua having lost family members, a home, and pos-sessions. While neither Massarani's nor Catalano's accounts suggest a collapse of personal identity, they preserve an uneasy and pressing need to articulate that identity against the bedrock of institutions, networks, and responsibilities from "before," now reconfigured in an "upside-down world."

As suggested by the dramatic episode with Norsa, Massarani is alert to the same conventions of public selfhood enlisted by Catalano: The jostling for situational and narrative control tracks the emergence of a particular kind of subjectivity formed in response to resistance from others. It is an intrinsically public form of subjectivity.[81] The choice of vignettes and their meaning are authorial decisions, ultimately one man's version of events. We cannot extrapolate from them to the feelings or behavior of famished beggars, wives or mothers, gravediggers, or children. Nor can we say anything about the villagers, peasants, looting German soldiers, local lords, and Jewish go-betweens who populate Massarani's narrative, or the poor Jews, disgruntled Jews, sick Jews, convalescents, health officers and Christians who populate Catalano's. There is no reason to assume that they share the authors' sense of themselves or relationship to the collective. What we can say is that this plenitude of humanity serves a narrative purpose, and that reinforces the authors' sense of what happened and what it all meant.

In Catalano's case, this process is clear. The persona Catalano constructs for himself also constitutes the public identity he seeks to convey; it is an identity that is defined by exertions to master opposition, to assert authority and impose order while being continuously challenged by outside forces at home, in the ghetto, and beyond. This representation of a "self" in constant danger of usurpation is at once more intersubjective than the modern Western self, with its insistence on interiority and separateness, and more public than the private and personal selfhood that emerged in the modern West. Both now and then, self is a social as much as a psychological ideal; the premodern version is more deeply imbricated in relationship to community. "Community," like "self," is not a stable category. Its shifts in meaning reflect stress on lines of class as well as religion, gender, and family; its borders are also a product of intellectual temperament and training as well as faith. Both Catalano and Massarini's narratives depict communal dissolution and crisis: The projection of public selfhood also tracks a parallel, collective, reconstitution.

In sum, Catalano's chronicle is important for several reasons. It is a fascinating record of the elaborate procedures and protocols enlisted by state and ghetto during a severe epidemic, with a post-hoc assessment of successes and failures; it is also a vivid depiction of the intricate maneuvering between state and ghetto, through their respective health officials, and the porous, sometimes shifting boundaries that separated the ghetto and its inhabitants from the Christian city. But as this chapter's focus illustrates, Catalano's plague narrative can equally serve as a window onto the relatively unexplored terrain of Jewish subjectivity in premodern settings, in this case one of the wealthier and culturally dominant ghetto communities of northern Italy. Rather than constrain treatment of Catalano's plague narrative to an examination of early modern Jewish-Christian interactions, I have in essence asked what it means to *be* Abraham Catalano in a specific setting of historical crisis. To answer this question, I have enlisted Abraham Catalano's narrative construction of himself, which is dependent on and inextricable from his representations of other people, collectivities, spaces, and institutions. It is a subjectivity built on a learned language of inside and outside, us and them, justice and compassion, responsibility and obedience, authority defined against submission or resistance. It may be a much more complex kind of subjectivity—a more complex kind of "self"—than we inhabit today, much more "intersubjective," constructed out of other voices as much as the author's, some harmonizing and some dissident, some personal and some institutional or communal, some affirming professional, class, or confessional affiliations and others resisting them.

Alternatively, it may be that we recognize this subjectivity because we see aspects of it in ourselves. *Dor dor ve-dorshav*, each age and its seekers, each age and its questions. The questions we ask as we search the debris of the past are shaped by our own reality and conditions, institutions and ideological forces, conventions of genre and the media through which we express them, the crucible in which biography—subjectivity—meets history and the world.[82] It is no surprise that we respond to those aspects of a seventeenth-century narrative that reflect our own concerns back to us. Were they then less central to Abraham Catalano? I do not know. I can compare them to the writings of his contemporaries and see that certain motifs have recurring strength. Catalano and Massarani, like Cristofano di Ceffini, thought about themselves in terms of service for the common good.[83] This did not erode their sense of personal entitlement or belief in the rightness of the class, gender, or confessional divisions that defined their societies. They also measured their dedication in direct proportion to its frustrations. As Cipolla noted of the Prato bureaucrat Cristofano, he was challenged constantly by factors beyond his control: "powerful vested interests" in the form of merchants and landowners and clerics; lower-ranking workers, patients, and fellow Jews; critical underfunding and lack of resources.[84] Likewise, all three men depicted themselves as struggling to balance amid a storm of competing pressures with integrity, firmness, and compassion; clearly, this was a topos that resounded deeply for them.[85] Theirs is a risky strategy of representation, unfolding in the disclosure of contesting selves and voices. The accounts are ultimately the author's, but they still originate in real moments of defiance, illuminating other perspectives and other subjectivities that escape the boundaries of the narrative and live outside in the world.

In the end, the storyteller and her story are not so easy to tease apart. Like Catalano, I have offered a narrative that emphasizes moments of dissonance in a way that highlights my own authorial subjectivity. Abraham Catalano, Massarani, and their peers conveyed themselves as dedicated Jews and proud Paduans, Mantuans, or inhabitants of whatever city they made their home. They were men born to privilege but understood privilege as inextricable from the exercise of responsibility for others; exertions on behalf of a greater community gave meaning to their sense of self. They had survived a pandemic crisis that made those responsibilities difficult if not impossible to fulfill. No wonder that they worried. No wonder, too, that these traits possess a certain luminosity when viewed from our own present moment. We worry, too, and have yearned for public men and women dedicated to the common good, even if their efforts may be doomed to defeat.

Chapter 3

Interpolated Poetry
When Prose Is Not Enough

The previous chapter treated two Hebrew prose accounts of the 1630 plague in northern Italy as it affected the Jewish communities of Padua and Mantua. But Abraham Catalano's plague narrative for the Paduan ghetto and Abraham Massarani's expulsion chronicle of the Mantuan ghetto were not exclusively written in prose. Both compositions selectively incorporate poetry, although they do so in different ways and to different effect. Massarani interrupts his account of the return of Mantua's surviving exiles to the ravaged ghetto with a long lament that encapsulates major moments detailed in his chronicle; Catalano embeds a terse poetic lament for his wife in his plague narrative, which also concludes with sixteen short poems written by his son, Moses, offering plague advice.[1] In part this chapter builds on the claim of Chapter 2 that the conventions utilized by Abraham Catalano belonged to a repertoire shared by a like-minded emotional and textual community.[2] Locating some of the same conventions in Massarani's expulsion chronicle, in many respects a different type of record with its own agenda, allowed me to demonstrate that claim. This chapter asks why each man might have wanted to enlist the enhancement of verse, what models he might have drawn on, and how the poetic insertions join the prose texts to constitute a mixed-genre whole. How did poems change the meaning of the prose narratives in which they were embedded? And what did poetry contribute to the construction of public memory of plague?

The conventional answers to these queries are problematic: If we say that poetry enhances the affective reach of these texts, that would be true for the two laments but not for Moses Catalano's appended poems, which are chiefly didactic. If we say that these authors enlist poetry to condense the highlights of the prose, that would be true to some degree of Massarani's text, but not entirely; Massarani's lament does offer a summary of the events related in his chronicle, but a selective one that compresses or suppresses some aspects of the prose narrative while elevating others. The claim would not be true at all for Abraham Catalano's lament for Sarah Catalano and only partially true for Moses's didactic poems, whose emphases can diverge from and even contradict his father's narrative message. A less obvious claim is that insight into the role of the poetic insertions sheds light as well on the intended use of the prose—a claim I pursue here. In Catalano's case, the Italian version of his narrative, apparently a kind of journal record of the events subsequently reformulated in literary Hebrew, utterly lacks poetic insertions; neither the brief lament for Sarah Catalano nor the didactic poems penned by Abraham and Sarah's son, Moses, appear in the vernacular copy. The decision to incorporate them testifies to conscious deliberation and Abraham's desire to add or say something in the Hebrew text that could not be expressed in pure prose.

Mixed-genre works were not unknown to the Catalanos or to Abraham Massarani. The Hebrew Bible is one notable exemplar, not only in its juxtaposition of prose and poetic genres represented by distinct books (the largely prose Numbers or 1 Samuel, say, compared to Isaiah or Psalms) but in mixed-genre sections where poetic utterance interrupts prose narrative. Thus, for instance, the "Song of the Sea" follows and echoes the prose account of the Israelites' escape from Egypt (Ex. 15), Deborah's song of victory recaps a prose account of battle (Jud. 5), Hannah's jubilant song of praise (echoed in Luke's "Magnificat") interrupts the prose story of Samuel's birth to a previously barren woman (1 Sam. 2). Jonah sings to God from inside the belly of the whale, and the prophetic books frequently alternate prose passages with the rhythmic cadences of prophecy. Biblical scholars have wrestled with this phenomenon from a variety of perspectives—source-critical, form-critical, redactive, structuralist, poststructuralist, resumptive. Since the 1980s they have likewise debated the significance of narrative prose in Hebrew Scriptures, reminding us that sacred history did not "naturally" require prose expression.[3] Yet very few have dedicated studies to the specific phenomenon of poetic insertions into prose narrative.[4]

A relative dearth of scholarly interest also characterizes the Hebrew literature of later periods, even though Hebrew genres offer many examples of poetry mixed with prose. Readers familiar with medieval Hebrew literature from Islamic lands and Christian Spain will recognize the insertion of poetic texts as a characteristic feature of the rhymed prose narratives called *maqāmāt*; as the name suggests, the Hebrew *maqāma* owed its origins to Arabic models (and they to Persian and Sanskrit) that also alternated prose and poetry. Jewish grammatical works, lexicons, commentaries, legal responsa, and medical texts often began with poetic preludes, or with rhymed prose preludes that gave way to discursive prose.[5] In a very different mode, liturgical texts alternated prose and verse, as did compound liturgical verse forms like the *yotzer* or *qedushta*. The last chronicle of Jewish persecutions during the First Crusade, composed by Eliezer ben Nathan (the "Raban"), also alternated liturgical verse hymns and prose narrative; the format may indicate its intended use in a liturgical setting.[6] In the Raban's case, I would argue that the poetic laments affectively amplify the prose, but to contain its pathos as well as heighten it. These martyrological hymns produce communal memory that resolidifies shattered communities and institutions, making sense of the violence and destruction unfolding in the prose by framing trauma and loss in familiar liturgical terms.

Poems embedded in medical texts served a different purpose, unconcerned with emotional affect but interested in the mnemonic function of poetry as a means for retaining clinical knowledge. Maud Kozodoy's categorization of the aims behind the versification of medical knowledge is useful. She derives her categories from classical Greek and Latin works that influence later Hebrew production; one purpose is mnemonic, a second enlists verse to protect a text from copyists' elisions or other forms of textual corruption, and a third is aesthetic, what she calls "delight."[7] This technical use of poetry could inspire the versification of entire works, as in Solomon Falaquera's *Iggeret Hanhagat haGuf vehaNefesh*, a verse regimen, but it could apply to embedded verse, too.[8] The use of poetry as summary or digest of prose exposition is illustrated in the medical compendium by Gershom ben Hezekiah, writing from prison in Orange in the late fourteenth century. Similarly, and closer to our authors in time, a gorgeously illuminated medical manuscript from northern Italy prefaces an Italian-language (in Hebrew characters) treatise on urine with an Italian sonnet summarizing diagnostic criteria.[9]

According to Kozodoy, "delight" plays a shrinking role in later compositions, although, as she notes, this attribute too can enhance memory.[10] And while the audience for medical poetry was frequently medical students and practitioners, some of the more prominent exemplars are noteworthy for lacking the kind of precision this audience would seek. Kozodoy suggests that the authors either assumed a learned audience for whom such detail was unnecessary or an unprofessional set of readers who were drawn to these poems, men "thirsting for secular knowledge" in a Hebrew language they could understand.[11] As we shall see, Moses Catalano's poems fall into this second category, offering medical advice without specifics to nonmedical readers who could implement general recommendations but would need a physician for the salves, incense, and diets he exhorted them to try.

Religious and secular exemplars of interpolated poetry are also not lacking among non-Jewish writers. Maureen Boulton thought this stylistic form was mostly limited to French romance texts composed between the thirteenth and fifteenth centuries, but there are many more examples, some of them Italian.[12] Boethius, whose famous *Consolation of Philosophy* was tackled by multiple Hebrew translators from the thirteenth century on, also counterposed hymns and prose, as did Alain de Lille, Boccaccio, Machaut, and Dante. Boulton considered Jean Renart's early thirteenth-century romance, *Guillaume de Dole*, an important precedent.[13] As she notes, the multiple genres and contexts that exhibit this practice resist a single interpretation. Significantly, Boulton's examples are literary texts, not historical ones, and how prose and verse might interact distinctively in the latter is not a question she asks. She does, however, suggest several useful ways of thinking about mixed-genre texts. For Boulton, poetic insertions serve a disruptive function, sometimes arresting the narrative to intensify or subvert it, sometimes marking divisions between prose sections.[14] Poetry and prose also enlist competing models of temporality: Boulton characterizes her prose romances as "linear," in contrast to the "circular" and "atemporal" chronotopes of their poetic interpolations.[15] Jacqueline Cerquiglini, in contrast, focuses more on the poetic speaker and his intended audience.[16] As we will see, both Massarani's and Catalano's lament poems suspend linear temporality but do so by lifting their subject matter above human chronology to align with sacred time and history. The contemporary Hebrew plague lament written by Joseph Concio in the Piedmont also projects into eternity, a scope denied prose accounts.[17] Moses Catalano's didactic verses, on the other hand, neither progress sequentially nor cohere around a central point. Like any series of health-related guidelines (we have seen enough of them lately for the coronavirus), they rely less on hierarchical order and more on didactic clarity. Sometimes information disclosed in prose has been deliberately omitted in the poetic inserts, or, conversely, the poems add information that the prose ignores. Thus, for instance, the emphasis on nuclear family ties, so marked in Joseph Concio's double lament, fares differently in Massarani's and Catalano's compositions. It is also useful to ask, in Boulton's words, how the inserted poetry has "altered the meaning of the narrative."[18] That question, too, has different weight for historical genres than it does for romance fiction: What does the addition of poetry mean for a historical narrative, and what kind of history do the mixed-genre narratives tell?

Significantly, while there are many examples of plague compositions in verse, and from the sixteenth century on, Italian medical and lay writers produced an abundance of *successo della peste* accounts in prose, the mixing of poetry and prose in plague writing does not seem to feature among them. I have not found a single example, although others may be more successful. The question of model, then, is perplexing, until we consider other kinds of nonplague literature. Those other kinds of literature were known to Catalano and Massarani from Jewish sources, like the Hebrew chronicles of persecutions, which had quasiliturgical status among early modern communities. Consciously or not, deferring to these models added a stamp of legitimacy to otherwise "secular" historical accounts. I will return to this point below.

My claim is twofold. First, and unremarkably, the mixing of prose and poetry serves different purposes for these two authors, who also write in different genres. Second, the role played by poetic insertions in these two works sheds light on the intended role of the narratives and suggests why they are, first, different from each other, and second, why they do or do not have analogues in Christian plague literature. Abraham Massarani's *Sefer haGalut vehaPedut*, as its name implies, was written as a historical chronicle, but one designed to serve the collective memory of the Mantuan ghetto and encourage its institutional recovery. It proved more successful in terms of the former goal than the latter, as the ghetto never recovered—economically or culturally—from the blows of that terrible year.[19] Annalistic and theological impulses do not invariably harmonize in this work.[20] In Massarani's telling, disaster strikes as divine chastisement, while relief from disaster testifies to the restoration of God's favor. Massarani's poetic lament, inserted at the pivotal point in his narrative between exile and return, encapsulates these theological premises. At the same time, the poem reflects an elite assumption that religious and secular authorities are the optimal guarantors of communal well-being. The chronicle and its poetic embellishment thus reinforce traditional institutions and values in a time of communal stress. In contrast, the poetic components of Catalano's *'Olam Hafukh* represent a more innovative

attempt to negotiate boundaries that are reflected in the prose narrative—
boundaries between public and private, lay and expert, rich and poor, individuals and institutions. Let us see how this looks in greater detail.

Abraham Massarani: "Oh, What Is This Sound of Weeping?" (*Oy Mah qol ha-bekhiyya*)

Massarani's chronicle begins with the war of Mantuan succession (1628–31),
detailing the siege and sack of the city and ghetto by imperial forces, the
expulsion of the ghetto's twenty-five hundred inhabitants, their wanderings
and tribulations over the next year, and the eventual return of approximately fifteen hundred survivors.[21] The plague features as a collateral tribulation, weakening the ducal army defending the city and compounding the
difficulties of the expelled Jews and their search for shelter. The chronicle
opens with a call to readers to ponder the horrifying fate of Mantua's proud
Jewish community. The introductory sentences are heavy and rhythmic, unfolding in a drumbeat reinforced by grammatical rhyme. I transliterate the
rhyming phrases for readers unfamiliar with Hebrew, emphasizing the rhymes
in bold font:

> Hearken to this, O House of Jacob, [those who are] far and near
> [*haqerovim veharehoqim*], know and see [*ude'u na ure'u*] if there has
> been anything like this since our Sanctuary and glory and majestic
> Dwelling [*qodsheinu ve-tifarteinu uge'on me'oneinu*] turned to ruin
> in an instant, holy souls [*nefashot qedoshot*] finished and annihi-
> lated [*safu tamu*] in great upheaval [*bivehalot 'atzumot*].[22]

Quickly, this summons shifts into rhymed prose descriptions that alternate with unrhymed first-person commentary. Rhymed prose describes the
devastation of the community and the mourning of survivors; in his unrhymed interjections, Massarani grieves that he was not present to eulogize
the community. In rhymed prose, he describes his return to Mantua, where
he discovers that his mother has died and his house is occupied by German
soldiers. In unrhymed prose, he adds his personal grief and the sorrowful state
of his fellow Jews; he shifts back to rhyme to point to the pitiful survivors and
their differing interpretations of their fate, which inspires Massarani to chronicle the community's fall. The prefatory section concludes with an unrhymed

account of his sources, reliable survivors from whose testimony he selectively constructed his narrative. Thus the prelude to his chronicle already illustrates the author distinguishing between language registers, specifically between unrhymed and rhymed prose, the latter characterized by rhetorical, aural, and intertextual features associated with poetry.[23] The divisions are not totally clean but more or less assign intensified poetic language to generic topoi of collective destruction and punishment, reserving unadorned prose for individual experience. The exception also constitutes the moment where the speaker's personal despair metonymically expresses communal loss. Bereft of his mother, dispossessed of his home, he helplessly ponders his losses, then notices that they are shared by a community that has suffered from "War, upheaval, terror, violence, hunger, pestilence and plunder that have raged against them in battle, / leaving the fruitful vine [exposed] to [their] wrath. / One says, alas, Israel has been given over to rebuke / and another that God's hand was outstretched and His sword drawn / to turn the land to a stumbling block / This made me long to know what had happened."[24]

Massarani's distinction between communal and personal voice offers a hint for reading the poetic lament inserted toward the conclusion of his chronicle. The "exile" portion of the chronicle concludes with the story of several hundred Jews imprisoned in Mirandola by order of the duke and subsequently ransomed by Jewish benefactors in Verona. Crushed by debts owed the duke, local peasants, and the departing Germans, the surviving exiles straggle forth from prison to return to Mantua.[25] The chronicle's "redemption" section resumes the narrative with a focus on Massarani's personal role in the negotiations leading to their return. Massarani backtracks to explain that a Jewish delegation from Bologna with news from hostages in Mantua had set off for Regensburg to petition the emperor for help; at the time Massarani happened to be staying there with his uncle, where he first learned of the terrible events he would later relate.[26] Negotiations for assistance to the exiles and the ceremonial reentry of Carlo Gonzaga to the city conclude the account.

Massarani inserts his lament between these two narratives of exile (*galut*) and return (the title's *pedut* means "redemption" or "ransom"). Because the tribulations that befell the community defy enumeration, "this is the lament I constructed on the most memorable catastrophes, which I keened in great mourning." An acrostic pun on his name follows, and then the lament, which begins במחנה העברים / אוי מה קול הבכייה (Oh, what is this sound of weeping from the Israelite camp?). The rhyme is aa bb cc, and so forth. My translation follows:[27]

1 Oh, what is this sound of weeping from the Israelite camp?

2 Hear the sigh of those who roar and fearfully lift their voices.[28]

3 Behold, an evil תֹהוּ from within has betrayed Israel.[29]

4 Everyone shall shriek and wail and carry on in great grief.[30]

5 Zion and the Sanctuary have become a desolate ruin.[31]

6 My tower of strength is destroyed by Duma's overflowing
   wrath.[32]

7 The golden utensils are gone, and the language of prophetic
   seers.[33]

8 Joy and delight have vanished: I no longer feel them.

9 God has removed the daily offering

10 That atones for my soul, and draped the sun in mourning.[34]

11 Ah, I shall sit alone and shed tears.[35]

12 I shall weep day and night, my heart shuddering.

13 Exile, wandering, and bondage among all the nations!

14 My sins delivered me to tribulations and upheaval.

15 This day was meant for evil; the bitter coil was wound snugly.[36]

16 It has finished off Babel, Seir, and Gomer.[37]

17 It has destroyed and totally plundered,[38] it has put an end to
   the city's delight.[39]

18 It has weighed down "Man-tova," [city of] nectar and honey,
   with mourning.[40]

19 Hunger, sword, and captivity—and evil pestilence![41]

20 Everyone is frightened and confounded at every single
   moment.

21 They have moved on, expelled and banished, to a distant land.

22 Elders, youths and aged, rich and penniless[42]

23 The mighty chieftains—and Rabbi Isaac HaLevi!—[43]

24 Were extinguished and finished off. Woe to me, my radiance
   has departed![44]

25 I shall pour out my thoughts about him; I shall sit bereaved in
   mourning.[45]

26 Woe, my hands slacken with the extinction of the angel's
   power

27 To revive.[46] [The angel] was a balm, oasis, nectar, and honey[47]

28 To me in exile, like a crown on my head.

29 In the year "let us journey and laugh" [=1628], two words
   combined,[48]

30 The people of exile ran like fattened calves[49]

31 They were struck with parching and heat, they wandered afar
for dry bread[50]

32 All were nearly annihilated and brought to their graves.

33 Alas, who has heard of such a thing? Devastation and ruin,
devastation and ruin.[51]

34 Both sheep and shepherd [set out] to disgrace and captivity.

35 The poor stretched out their hands, and there was no one to
hold them.

36 They raised their voices in grief when there was no bread to eat.[52]

37 Pestilence broke out among the people, spreading great famine.[53]

38 Some of the people expelled were also taken captive.[54]

39 Ransom was demanded for their leaders from impoverished
people.[55]

40 The price for their lives was costly, and a heavy tax was
imposed.[56]

41 O God, will You not take note of this and have mercy?

42 Rebuild Zion's wall, have mercy on her mourners.

43 Protect Your congregation, which dwells in the shelter of the
Most High.[57]

44 Purify Your people's transgressions and be a shield to them.

45 Hasten the end of days, speed salvation.

46 Please bring the son of David to put an end to [our] clamor.[58]

"Oh, what is this sound of weeping" conforms to the genre of historical
laments Massarani would have known from penitential liturgies utilized on
the Ninth of Av, Yom Kippur, traditional fast days, and more recently instituted, local fast-day liturgies commemorating historical and natural disasters. In fact, it was intended to be recited on the Ninth of Av. The lament
consists of forty-six verses of eleven syllables each, six in the first hemistich
and five in the second. As promised by the prose incipit, it covers the highlights of the period between the sack of the ghetto and city and the return of
the Jews from expulsion. One of its conventional strategies is to blur the
distance between present events and sacred history, first by enfolding contemporary into biblical catastrophe, depicting current events as an echo of
biblical destruction and return. The reason for the "sound of weeping" the
speaker overhears at the poem's beginning is identified in verse 5 as the destruction of Zion and the biblical Sanctuary, which lie in ruins. But even the

explicit mention of Temple implements (the engraved golden buds of the utensils, the daily sacrificial offering, the prophets' warnings) does not prevent Massarani's readers (or listeners) from connecting this scene of sacred ruin to the one they have just experienced. After all, their city too has been laid waste, their elegant synagogues plundered. A premodern Jew did not need prompting to encourage this kind of connotative overlay. The fabulous gilt ark that had graced the Great Synagogue in Mantua for nearly a century also featured elaborate carvings of blossoms and acanthus vines, further encouraging the fusion of past and present through visual analogy.[59] Massarani deliberately conflates current events with sacred history: Sorrow and suffering have befallen the speaker and his community as a consequence of their sins, culminating in "exile, wandering and bondage among the nations" (v. 13). The nations are invoked as biblical toponyms: Babel for the East, Seir for Italy ("Rome"), Gomer for Ashkenaz (Germany) (v. 16). Catastrophe has been universal, indiscriminately sweeping the nations with warfare, famine, and pestilence (vv. 17–19) and making no distinction between young and old, or rich and poor (v. 22). Massarani pauses his catalog of woes to single out Rabbi Isaac HaLevi, whose death occurred early in the prose narrative but is located centrally in the poetic lament. The speaker's grief overwhelms him.

The hymn's second half refers specifically to the experiences of Mantuan Jews, on the one hand "filling in the blanks" by going beyond the earlier biblical tropes, on the other implying that recent experience has outstripped the capacity of generic language. "Who has heard of such a thing?" he asks (v. 33), despite having constructed his account as an echo of earlier history. The expression of disbelief allows the visceral memory of suffering to overflow its typological frame. In similar language, the poets who crafted commemorative laments in the wake of medieval anti-Jewish violence tapped biblical precedents and then wearily acknowledged their inadequacy. Massarani, too, invokes the cyclicity of mythic history but implies that experience escapes its boundaries. This, of course, is also a trope, and one that sets cyclic and linear history in tension. Boulton's observation that poetic insertions pit "circular" (what I am calling cyclic) time against the linearity of prose narrative does not accurately describe the Hebrew historical lament, which engages both cyclical and linear elements, sometimes allowing one to dominate, sometimes leaving them in tension.

Boulton's observation is, however, accurate in part for the Hebrew text. Like many Hebrew laments, even those commemorating historical tragedies, Massarani's obeys a chiastic or ringlike structure that pivots about a core moment, in this case the death of Isaac HaLevi. The chiastic arrangement weights the rabbi's death as the magnetic core of the text.[60] According to the prose narrative, HaLevi was old and perhaps sick when the Jews began their exodus from the city. The frantic Jews split into two groups, whose fates Massarani treats sequentially: One headed down the Po River toward nearby villages, and the other set off on foot toward San Martino.[61] Rabbi Isaac HaLevi was in the latter group, which rented or purchased two wagons from local peasants to carry some of the sickest and frailest Jews, including the rabbi. Not long into their journey, the wagon carrying the rabbi overturned while fording a river, drowning eight passengers, including HaLevi. The prose narrative is full of such terrible incidents, yet HaLevi's fate is singled out for mention in the poetic text. Indeed, he is the only Mantuan Jew named in the lament; moreover, his death appears in verse 23, precisely halfway through the poem. The effect is to sublimate the individual and collective experiences of Mantuan Jews in the figure of the holy rabbi. This, too, was a tactic honed in Hebrew laments from the mid-twelfth century on. By elevating men of rabbinic scholarship and piety as idealized representations of entire communities, poets from medieval and later periods commemorated a threat to religious and communal identity while reinforcing the centrality of religious authorities and institutions.[62] In conforming his lament to this model, Massarani fulfills an objective that would be more elusive for the prose, obligated as it was to record events large and small, and likewise the sufferings of all sorts of individuals.

In this context it is striking that Massarani's lament chooses not to invoke the topoi of family ties rent in expulsion and sickness, a theme emphasized by Joseph Concio in his lament for the plague dead of Turin and Chieri, and by Abraham Catalano in his prose plague narrative.[63] Family units find scarce mention throughout Massarani's prose chronicle, despite frequent references to unattached women who fall prey to kidnappers and extortionists. Curiously, these female figures are almost always described as young and unmarried or alternatively as elderly widows. The remarkable elision of family vignettes is suspended only in the preface, where it is invoked in negation: Massarani returns home to discover his mother has died in exile, and that he and his brothers have lost their home. Does his disinterest in family reflect a personal quirk or Massarani's belief that women and children were incidental to his tale? It is impossible to know.[64]

The lament's ring structure is reinforced by other poetic elements. It is roughly echoed in the distribution of open and closed rhymes.[65] It is also reflected in the alternation of first-person interjections and third-person descriptions of catastrophe. Thus verses 1–10 describe the sound of weeping and mourning, identified with the destruction of Jerusalem and the Temple. Then, in verses 11–14, the first-person speaker proclaims his grief and links his fate to his people's. Verse 15 links past and present, invoking "this day" as the commemoration of the evil decreed for the Mantuan ghetto, whose woes are catalogued in verses 19–22. Since the community was expelled on the Ninth of Av, in July–August 1630, "this day" joins commemoration of this tragedy to the long list of other disasters (including the Temple's destruction) marked on the Ninth of Av.

Verse 23, announcing the death of R. Isaac HaLevi, is the lament's fulcrum. It is followed by another first-person interlude, spanning verses 24–28, in which the speaker declares that he will mourn the rabbi's death. The poetic narrative returns to the succession struggle and the fate of the exiles wandering without divine protection (vv. 29–40). Verses 41–46 comprise a peroration in the form of an appeal to God to pay heed to His suffering people, rebuild "Zion" (presumably also Mantua), and hasten the coming of the Messiah and redemption. Again, the structure is classically chiastic. Two first-person interjections frame the central image of the "martyred" rabbi. They in turn are framed concentrically by accounts of biblical and historical expulsion, and these segments are embraced by the introductory and concluding verses. The introductory verses address the speaker's fellow Jews, who are summoned to join in communal mourning, but the concluding verses address God. Here, too, we see that "circular" structures can tolerate and even demand some forward movement, as Massarani moves his listeners from contemplation of their plight to a restored focus on God—from downward ruin to the security of heaven. Poetic time arches forward in messianic anticipation, projecting beyond the human history spanned by the prose.

Finally, Massarani's lament begins on the outside looking in (actually, overhearing). The speaker asks, as if from a distance, what is the meaning of the weeping he hears? The initial answer is that the weeping is for the biblical destruction, which the lament translates to an Italian setting. By the end of the lament, there is no outside view. The speaker speaks from inside the tragedy he relates as the voice of his community (his "I" has become their "we"), as the singular destruction of the Mantuan ghetto is conflated with the mythic destruction of Jerusalem. Consequently, Massarani's poetic lament does change the meaning of the prose in which it was embedded. Minus the lament, his prose chronicle would have operated very differently, laying out a chronological narrative of the War of Succession from the perspective of Mantua's expelled Jews and culminating in political efforts to return an impoverished group of survivors. The lament, inserted at a pivotal point in the prose, tips the chronology of exile toward return. It alludes only vaguely to the details of wandering and tribulation, along with individual benefactors, villains, and victims. These myriad adventures are compressed into a theologically recognizable, easily digestible, story: Mythic history does prove capacious enough for historical catastrophe, and the saintly rabbi emblematizes the collective suffering of a pious community. With this reframing, the concluding narrative fulfills the promise of restoration. So, too, does the lament extend its force field backward, reshaping the first half of the narrative by offering readers a way to assimilate the exhausting details of siege, plague, expulsion, and wandering as echoes of sacred history. To those who had suffered by living that experience, this kind of reframing may have offered consolation. To readers removed in time or geography, the reconfiguration of living experience in the language of divine chastisement and restitution could still teach a lesson, quelling doubts that "history" escaped God's domain.

Massarani surely had reasons for wanting to communicate such reassurance. Mantuan Jewry before the expulsion was renowned for its cultural excellence, but also for its piety. The marriage of cultural and pietistic excellence was not a contradictory one. The deep investment of Mantuan Jews in the artistic, literary, musical, and scientific pursuits of the Gonzaga period paid dividends in the invigoration of the forms of religious life. The lavish furnishings and architecture of their many synagogues, the profusion of liturgies and synagogue music, the production of luxury prayer books, the multiplication of confraternities and charitable institutions, the paraliturgical ceremonies around weddings, circumcisions, and mourning, the works of ethics and the popularity of Kabbalah—all of these reflect a synthesis of tastes, interests, and ideas circulating in the wider world. But for all its dazzle and sophistication, the Mantuan ghetto spoke with many voices, some more conservative than others. When Mantua's celebrated Jewish composer Salamone Rossi tried to introduce polyphonic hymns into the synagogue, he met with stiff rebellion; Rossi was forced to round up supportive rabbis to write on his behalf. The sheer dominance of ethics, prayer, and Kabbalah among the surviving manuscripts produced in the Mantuan ghetto over the sixteenth and early seventeenth centuries testifies to the weight of religious meaning in Jewish life. Meaning, certainly, could range in valence from deeply held beliefs and behaviors, cherished rituals of synagogue and home, charitable

bequests and fears for salvation, to more spectacular choreographies of piety. Each in its own way contributed to the self-image of a proud community that blazed like a glorious star among the Jewish communities of
northern Italy.

That star had fallen, and the sin of pride remained a ready explanation.
Was Massarani—child of wealth and privilege, raised amid the music, theater, and poetry of the Gonzaga court—unsure how his chronicle would be
received? Was "secular" history too prideful a medium for Jewish catastrophe?
Or did he feel a personal need to bend history toward the familiar curve of
theological reassurance? Either way his lament shifts the tenor of his prose
account off the tracks of "objective" historical reportage and into the realm of
consolation and promise, restitution and return. Did restitution and return
work out that easily? According to modern historians, hardly. But that is the
point: This is a historical chronicle that is asked to take a bow as liturgy. To
the extent that it succeeds, Massarani's lament serves its purpose. To the extent that it fails, historians will continue to scour it for names and dates.

Abraham Catalano: The Poems of 'Olam Hafukh

As illustrated in the preceding chapter, Abraham Catalano's plague narrative differs radically from Massarani's. Its stated concern is to provide an
eyewitness account of the plague outbreak in the Paduan ghetto, as befits
what Samuel Cohn, Jr., has called the *successo della peste* narratives. Accordingly, Catalano begins with preparations for the plague's anticipated arrival,
then tracks the swell and peak of the epidemic, the ebbing of sickness, and
the release of the ghetto from closure. The narrative concludes with a list of
helpful plague-related tips for "future generations for whatever tribulations,
may they not befall you!"[66] The last of those tips is directed to ghetto leaders,
but the others speak to individual (male) householders who have families and
possessions to protect.

Abraham Catalano's recommendations are founded in the bitter experience he records. They are not, however, the last word in the 'Olam Hafukh, an
honor Abraham reserved for his son, Moses, whose sixteen didactic poems
conclude the work. Like Joseph Concio in Chieri, Moses had a reputation
as an occasional poet, some of whose compositions survive.[67] A rhetorically
ambitious stylist, Moses sometimes experimented with macaronic verse; one
extant example is a wedding poem for his little sister, Perla, the only one of

Abraham's children with him in Padua who survived the plague.[68] Moses's plague poems, in contrast, are formally simple and served readers less interested in rhetorical play.

Before discussing these poems, however, we should note that there is one place where Abraham himself composed and embedded a poem directly into his Hebrew narrative. This poem, a eulogy for his wife, Sarah, consists of four terse verses in Aramaic. The rhyme scheme is abab, and each verse divides into two hemistichs, where each hemistich is composed of only two words.

Catalano's switch to Aramaic, which occurs nowhere else in his narrative, is noteworthy. His verses allude to a Talmudic passage describing the pious labors of Rabbi Bena'a, who marked the underground limits of ancient Jewish burial caves so that passersby, and especially Jewish priests (kohanim), would not be defiled by proximity to the dead. When he approached the Cave of Machpelah, the burial cave of Abraham and Sarah, Rabbi Bena'a encountered the biblical patriarch's loyal servant, Eliezer, standing at the entrance. Eliezer permitted Bena'a to enter the cave, where he discovered Abraham lying with his head cradled by Sarah. Eliezer assures Bena'a that he has not stumbled upon a scene of sexual play, for nothing so crude corrupts love in eternity.[69] Commentators on this passage parsed it as a representation of idealized (living!) love.[70] Abraham Catalano's last verse directly cites the Talmudic passage, comparing his long marriage to *his* Sarah to that of the biblical Abraham and Sarah: loving and discreet in its intimacy, forged by bonds that transcended physical desire.

Intriguingly, the switch of language, which occurs nowhere else in the narrative, imbues it with sanctity as well as a degree of opacity. Abraham's intellectual cohort was familiar with scientific, ethical, and historical texts in Hebrew, Italian, perhaps even Latin, but their associations with Aramaic would be through religious literature and law.[71] The veil of Aramaic performs linguistically what the cave does for Bena'a: it creates a charged and private space we enter from "outside," tentatively stepping out of public (Hebrew) space to confront an intimate scene of love and mourning. But that is not all: Catalano embeds this delicate poem in a fraught account of mounting casualties in the ghetto and without. His beloved Sarah is only one of the mostly nameless fatalities he dutifully records. The wearying catalog is disrupted first by the list of Sarah Catalano's attributes and then by the poem itself, after which the litany of death and detail resumes. The layout of the manuscript copies illustrates the pause like a musical fermata, isolating the tiny poem in space, removed from the prose narrative and surrounded by

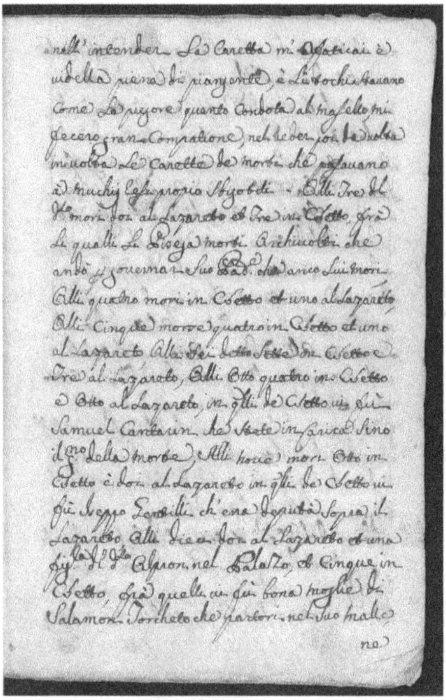

Figure 3. Abraham Catalan[o]. *Libro della Peste che fu in Padova nel anno 5391*, MS
General 308, 1631, https://clio.columbia.edu/catalog/14267149. Rare Book and
Manuscript Library, Columbia University, New York City, scan 38.
Figure 4. Abraham Catalan[o]. *'Olam Hafukh*, MS X 893 Ab8, seventeenth
century, https://clio.columbia.edu/catalog/ht102485676. Rare Book and
Manuscript Library, Columbia University, New York City, scan 21.

white blankness. The flow of the narrative is visually and temporally arrested by the poem suspended in space. In contrast, the Italian version that
provided the scaffolding for the Hebrew account folds Sarah's death into a
monotonous litany of mortality, pausing not at all to let the author or reader
absorb the pain of her death. Clearly, the decision to rework this passage
and arrest the chronology was deliberate:

> Then my wife, the pious, modest Sarah, was struck—the wife of my
> youth, my wedded love, the daughter of the mighty one, the honor
> able great teacher and rabbi Nathan Judah Heilpron[72] of Cittadella—
> and my heart died inside me. Then on the eleventh [of Tammuz] two
> died in the lazaretto and ten in the ghetto, among them the honor-

able David Delia who had joined us to replace the fourth member [of the committee] overseeing health matters.[73] On the twelfth, three in the ghetto and two in the lazaretto, and on the thirteenth, eight in the ghetto and six in the lazaretto. On the fourteenth, three died in the ghetto and one in the lazaretto, and my righteous wife in that aforementioned house, after twenty-one years we had been together. Then Abraham came to eulogize Sarah, saying:

> Precious among women, modest and beautiful
> I pray to come be near you always
> As Bena'a, the marker of burial caves, seeing
> Abraham cradled in Sarah's arms.[74]

At that time the [health] minister appointed over us, Signor Ettore Sala, was struck and died, and the Children of Israel sighed: From that time forward, we knew no peace. On the fifteenth, two died in the lazaretto and two in the ghetto, among them Pinchas Di Negri of the community elders. On Sunday [?] the minister Alvise Valaresso arrived and the ministers in Venice appointed him *provveditore* to replace the Pisani.[75]

As suggested in the preceding chapter, this wrenching passage validates Catalano's representation of himself selflessly dedicated to household and community even as personal tragedy befalls him. It is not a false representation: Abraham Catalano suffers from the plague like his fellow Jews, and for that matter like his fellow Christians. His personal losses include four children as well as his wife, and the strain of managing the ghetto as conditions deteriorate is evident from his account. If he pauses his task of recording the plague's toll to grieve for his beloved wife, that pause opens a window onto private agonies that qualify him to speak on behalf of others who grieve also. At the same time, that window opens then shuts: The private life of Abraham Catalano and, even more so, the private life of his modest Sarah, are shielded from undue exposure. The tableau emblematizes private suffering that was multiplied many times over in scenes we cannot know; the resumption of business and death in the outside world tells us that the grieving Abraham was stunned but did not shirk his duties. Not a day is missing in his tally, and the unfortunate death of the friendly *provveditore*, the arrival of a less sympathetic replacement, and Catalano's brief reference to the harried Jews' attempts to gauge the new man's "heart" while coping with a bread shortage (all the bakers have died) reminds us that he has not stopped working.

Catalano's brief poetic eulogy is anticipated by his prose interjection—"my wife, the pious, modest Sarah"—suspending his factual reportage of casualties. The poem reformulates what he stuttered to say in prose, relocating grief to a lyric space of time-stopping pain. More than the other examples treated in this chapter, this tiny poem corresponds to the lyric insertion type that Cerquiglini called "montage," a category where the poetic "I" is identical to the "I" of the prose and where the poetic utterance could not be assigned to anyone else.[76] The prose anticipates and prepares for the poetic rupture, but the poetry, as Boulton claimed, nonetheless changes the prose. In this case poetry salvages some measure of equilibrium that Abraham's prose, struggling to balance private and public spheres, could not find. In four brief lines and sixteen words, a poem testifies that, for a day that felt like eternity, private pain conquered a public man. But the discreet record of that moment is then reabsorbed into a narrative representation of unflagging public service.[77]

Moses Catalano's poems are a very different kind of insertion and yield correspondingly different answers to our questions about the relationship of prose to verse in these narratives. Technically, they are not inserted but appended, and with one exception, extant copies locate them at the conclusion to the 'Olam Hafukh. The exception is a seventeenth-century anthology of philosophical and ethical tracts, in which Moses's poems are freestanding.[78] Moses, we remember, was not present with his father in Padua during the period described in Abraham's narrative. He was among the handful of Jews who fled the city with his family early in the epidemic, finding shelter in Corte until the epidemic ended. The father describes a scare not long after his return as an example of the continuing bouts of illness that followed the official end of the outbreak, when people continued to fall sick with all kinds of fevers they feared would be diagnosed as plague. Moses Catalano was one of them:

> After returning to the ghetto, my son, Moses, also went to the village of Corte to the home of a townsman named Leandro Porcellin[o]. He stayed there several days and fell ill with a fever then came home. The city guards did not realize he was sick, and after many days he recovered. This incident proved that tender children were more susceptible to this sickness, and after them young men and women—but not the elderly. Nearly all the pregnant women died, and many of those who fell ill and recovered continued to suffer

from tertian and quartain fevers for many days. There was not a household in the ghetto where someone had not fallen ill or died, except for two widows . . . which was a miracle because they were surrounded by afflicted households.[79]

According to the incipit (which varies slightly from copy to copy), Moses wrote his plague poems while he was still in Corte. If that is the case, he must have seen at least part of his father's composition before returning to Padua, and, indeed, some of his phrasing echoes Abraham's. Elsewhere, the poems contest the advice offered in the prose. Perhaps the entire narrative did not make its way to Corte, or Moses disagreed with its conclusions, or did not read it. Certainly, his focus is the prose narrative's final page, which includes Abraham's summative conclusion and suggestions for the future.

As Abraham Catalano noted, he chose not to include any medical advice in his narrative, despite his medical training: "Although I have a medical degree and know what physicians say concerning this subject, I did not see fit to write a thing about the preservative measures in their books. I will only write a history suitable for generations to come."[80] Nonetheless, his final paragraphs distill his experience into a series of recommendations. All but the final directive address a hypothetical reader in the second-person singular imperative; the last turns to communal leaders. Some of the recommendations are qualified by alternative options for those without the financial or material resources to execute the initial suggestion. For instance, Abraham recommends leaving the city when plague arrives, for a second residence or rental. "But *if you only have the house you live in*," he qualifies, "rent another apartment so that it will go well with you. *And if you are poor*, and cannot afford a[nother] room, partition your house for an afflicted member or flee."[81]

Abraham's recommendations are practical. They may be summarized as follows:

1. Don't believe in prophylactics and especially holding citrus fruits to one's nose.
2. Don't rent out your house; leave it empty when you depart.
3. Rent another house, or if you are too poor, partition your living space.
4. Stock up on provisions so you don't have to go out looking for essentials.

5. Store your possessions in a locked room under Health Office seal.
6. Retain linen garments and change of clothes.
7. If you leave money or valuables with someone else, document this in writing.
8. If there are multiple siblings or adult family members, divide the house in two; in the event sickness strikes one half, the other can assist them.
9. Practice "social distancing."
10. Avoid proximity with household sick, but make sure to delegate another household member or hire an attendant to provide care.

Abraham's concluding recommendation, in contrast, switches to the second-person plural and makes a policy suggestion to the "community" that could only be implemented by a ghetto council or emergency committee such as the one he served on: "And as for you, my community, remember and do not forget! Before the plague arrives, you must definitely send a community representative, a faithful ambassador, to Venice. Be sure to pay him [in advance] so that he can be posted there to help in trouble, or if the ministers speak against us [and] against the law about closing the ghetto or such. Then he will be there to stand in the breach."[82] Notice that Abraham's final warning and suggestion open the spatial confines of the narrative and link the ghetto to Venice and the Christian courts and political currents that embed the Jews in a larger world. In so doing, they are a spatial analogue to the temporal projection found in the concluding verses of his and Massarani's lament poems: just as the laments reached beyond earthly time to the world hereafter, Abraham's practical advice concludes with a stretch beyond the ghetto to the larger political and physical worlds. They are the last words of his plague narrative and are followed directly by the poems penned by his son. Moses's poems are absent from the Italian copy—proof that they were added as an afterthought—and in Hebrew copies they usually begin on a separate folio. The poems sometimes appear as quatrains with hemistichs (rhyming aBa-BaBcC), but sometimes as octets (rhyming abababcc). The quatrain format favored by the Columbia manuscript and most other copies is probably correct.[83] The verses are endecasyllabic and can be stressed either syllabically as iambic or quantitatively to a *shalem* (Arabic *kamil*) meter.[84] My translation follows, and then a look at how Moses's advice does or does not accord with his father's and what we can conclude about their interrelationship:

POEMS

By my son, the wise Reb Moses, may His Rock guard him and grant him life, which he wrote about the pestilence while he was still in Corte where he fled the plague.

I.

If there is pestilence in your city, flee
    Outside the camp to someplace clean.[85]
Make your locks of brass and iron[86]
    Be smart and flee quickly![87]
For if you stay there in your city
    You'll be like a dog rolling in vomit.[88]
If you don't see the light in the morning
    You'll grope in darkness at noon.[89]

2.

But if you can't flee
    The pestilence in your city, stay inside.
And when you see it begin to spread
    Close the doors to your house yourself.
But before you shut them, you must take care
    To prepare supplies to sustain you,
Change of garments to clothe you,
    Food and drink to nourish you.

3.

Dig yourself a well to draw water
    For laundry, cooking, and mixing with wine.
Make yourself a cooking stove[90]
    To bake food when you want.[91]
Buy utensils, gird your loins,
    Make do without a maid or manservant—there are none.
If the pestilence is in your neighborhood, take counsel
    To get an[other] apartment and leave.

4.

Separate the members of your household; stop gathering,
    For there's no denying that this is true pestilence.

An intelligent man will stay to himself
    In such times it is not good for brothers to dwell together![92]
For if one starts shaking
    Fear and dread will befall them.
Therefore, separate yourselves and do not fear—
    And lift your eyes to heaven.

5.

Apply a salve with vinegar to your heart
    And on your temples and hands.
Apply it when you go to bed and when you get up
    And put it into your nostrils with your finger.
Make your food heart-strengthening,
    And with all your heart, call out
To heaven, for He is generous to forgive
    And send healing quickly for the plague.

6.

Fumigate the depths of your house
    With heavily scented smoke.
It will mix with your bad air
    The smoke will repel new [impurity].
Therefore, you shouldn't leave your house
    Believing those who talk about[93]
False protections that have no strength.[94]
    For there is no preservation except in flight.

7.

In truth, there is nothing hidden from Him
    Who dwells in secret and sees all secrets.
So if a man takes no heed of his soul
    And wishes to die like a drunkard
Without order or sense
    Let him say, the Lord is my shield and shelter![95]
Behold, [God] sees and hears[96]
    For he will perish like a fool and an idiot.

8.

Seal up all your precious belongings in your house
    With the seal of the municipal health board.
Leave only your bed where you sleep
    And have no pity on your inner sanctum.
Keep all your linen garments to hand
    Don't seal them up lest they start speaking sweetly[97]
And later get strict.
    Scenting them is no use.

9.

If, however, you've fled, bless your departure
    By giving charity, so that your hand[out] reaches
Those confined. Give generously!
    But before you give, you should know
To seek an IOU on your money.[98]
    Those without sustenance are considered poor.
For what good is a man's wealth when he has no food?[99]
    And who will buy bread and wine for them?

10.

So have pity on them lest they be destroyed.
    Give charity so there is healing in your pockets.[100]
Choose men who will serve
    And bring charity to those who receive it.[101]
Let them send in a physician so they are not cut off[102]
    By this plague without physicians.
For why and for what reason should the poor and destitute
    Have no balm in Gilead, no physician there?[103]

11.

Be mindful of these three things
    And you will not fall to the disease of pestilence:
Pray to the One who is awesome in splendor, working wonders[104]
    That He save you from disaster on disaster.[105]
Flee or confine yourself as if you were in prison
    Lest you die or end up confined to the grave.

For all your life-sustaining provision
    Hope in the Lord and behave prudently.

12.

Do not overexert yourself, for heat is injurious
    Because it makes the body susceptible [to sickness].
And strengthen the heart of your household
    So they aren't afraid of the Destroyer.[106]
This disease also appears in a flash[107]
    And ravages commoner and priest.[108]
[But] know that the wolf does not devour all the sheep
  And the Lord will protect you—[by Himself] not through an angel.[109]

13.

Therefore, if pestilence enters the air
    First of all flee!
Woe to the legs that do not leave,
    Woe to the legs that stay put
Every house and apartment are surely finished,
    And will be left in ruins with no inhabitants.
Fathers will die with their offspring
    Along with their families and clans.[110]

14.

And if you do not gird your loins to flee
    But stay put because you can't leave
Close every window at twilight
    And do not open them until dawn.
Close them in the afternoon also.
    If the sun doesn't shine.
When it's windy or rainy
    Keep away from the doorway and windows.

15.

Before you open your windows
    Burn something scented in your house
And fumigate your clothing.

Afterward, if it's sunny, then open [the windows]
And pray to the Lord your God.
    Plead with Him loudly[111]
To remove in His mercy what is bad from the air
    As the sun rises through His might.

16.

Anoint your heart morning and evening
    With a heart-strengthening ointment. This is well known.
Eat a lot of heart-strengthening food.
    Hot and moist food is bad.
Before the One who discerns the organs inside us,[112]
    May your heart be rent—but not your garments!
For in vain the watchman keeps vigil over great and small
    If God does not guard the city.[113]

With respect to form, several observations are in order. The language of
the verses is simple, nontechnical Hebrew, although it assumes some knowledge of medical concepts found in discussions of humoral medicine, the six
non-naturals, and their application in times of epidemic fevers. Moses apparently did not reject current medical opinion as roundly as his father did. By
contemporary standards his medical suggestions are largely practical; the references to salves, overexertion, fumigation, and a preventive dietary regimen
omit specifics and would have required consultation with a medical professional. The poems are all addressed to a second-person singular audience, "you."
This also diverges from Abraham's pattern, as his advice ends with a turn to
communal institutions and leaders. The speaker of Moses's poems, however,
is an impersonal source of knowledge who could be anyone with advice to
offer about coping with plague. This is not the case with Abraham's plague
narrative, and certainly not for the tiny lament for his wife, both of which can
only be "spoken" by the projected figure of Abraham. This distinction, which
drives Cerquiglini's taxonomy, does make a difference here, shifting the personal voice of the prose account to an impersonal (and more optimistic) lay
authority. The speaker of Moses's poems never defers to personal experience
or anecdote, whereas Abraham's narrative stakes its claims to authenticity
and authority precisely on those criteria.

    The predominance of imperative verbs underscores the poems' practical
function. We know from Moses's other, high-flying, rhetorical forays that

he admired complex verse. In contrast, the medical poems he penned for the *'Olam Hafukh* were not intended to be "beautiful" but to offer concise and easily retained information. Another sign of his practical concerns are the conditional clauses offering alternatives to a recommendation the reader might find impossible to follow: Do X, but if you can't, do Y. Moses's repeated injunctions to flee at the first sign of plague, for instance, are first sounded in poem 1, then immediately qualified in the beginning of poem 2: "But if you can't flee / the pestilence in your city, stay inside" (2:2), followed by a list of stay-at-home, precautionary measures over the next few poems. Similarly, poem 14 tells the reader: "And if you do not gird your loins to flee / but stay put because you can't leave," you should open the windows to let in the sun. But if it's windy or pouring, stay away from the windows (14:4). Many of Moses's suggestions are drawn from his father's concluding suggestions. The overlap is evident from my earlier summary of Abraham's recommendations, as are the divergences. Moses, who endorses some of the prophylactics his father scorns, does not reproduce Abraham's assertion that prophylactics are worthless. Rather, he recommends the use of a salve applied to temples, chest, and nostrils, "heart-healthy" foods, sunny air, and fumigations (poems 5, 6, 15, 16). Abraham's second, third, and fourth recommendations concern living space: safeguarding your home by not renting it when you leave, renting a second domicile, or partitioning your home to create an isolation zone. Living quarters preoccupied Abraham; his narrative recounts his early designation of an isolation room within his house and then his (ultimately futile) attempt to move his own family outside the ghetto. Moses, however, emphasizes flight, not retrofitting living spaces; poems 1, 9, and 13 all reflect *his* experience in fleeing plague-stricken Padua. As we have also seen, Moses and his family survived; Abraham lost his wife and four of the five children with him in the ghetto. Perhaps Moses was unwilling to relinquish his conviction that flight was the better option.

Abraham's fourth counsel was to stock provisions for anticipated shortages, a crisis the ghetto encountered despite early attempts to order foodstuffs in advance. Moses anticipates this counsel in his second poem, verse 3 ("prepare supplies to sustain you"), and details it further in poem 3 with suggestions to dig a well, buy a stove, and prepare to get along without servants. He also advances Abraham's coming suggestion to store some clean clothing, which Abraham saved for his next recommendation to lock up valuable possessions in a room sealed by the Health Office, retaining linen garments and a change of clothes. Moses restates this two-part advice in poem 8.[114] Abraham spoke from bitter experience when he recommended documenting in writing whatever pledges or valuables were left with someone else. As a consequence of the high mortality rates throughout the region, communities struggled with problems arising from unclaimed or contested property found in the houses of the dead. Moses slightly altered this recommendation so that it closely followed his exhortation to those who fled to donate charity to the "poor," defining "poor" as those who had no access to food and not just those who had no money.[115] Moses added the counsel to document monies stored elsewhere prior to flight, explicitly linking the act of deposit with flight.

Abraham's next two recommendations are rolled into Moses's fourth poem. Abraham advised a large family (with multiple adults, either siblings or adult children with parents) to partition their living space into two domiciles. If illness should befall someone in one half, the other half would be able to help; this would also make it possible for a home-based workshop to continue operating, a challenge for merchants whose shops and living spaces were not clearly divided.[116] He uses the Hebrew phrase כי ישבו אחים או אב ובנים יחדיו ("if brothers or a father and son dwell together"), similarly wording his next suggestion, אל ישבו שניים יחדיו ("two should not sit together"). His phrasing echoes Psalm 133.1, מה טוב ונעים שבת אחים גם יחד ("how good and pleasant for brothers to sit/dwell together"), but the verse is invoked in Moses's poem 4 to underline that it is definitely *not* good for brothers to sit together. Curiously, Moses does not indicate this is for fear of contagion but for fear of fear—that is, that the dread felt by one brother will be communicated to the other. Abraham's final suggestion to his lay reader was not to abandon sick household members; he recommended that the healthy keep a distance from the sick, but not before delegating another family member or a hired attendant to care for them. Moses does not repeat this suggestion.

However, Moses included other advice that we find nowhere in Abraham's conclusion. One is at least implied in the prose narrative, and that is the importance of good air circulation in the house. Abraham mentions this specifically as an attractive feature in the Accademia villa he tried to rent for his family; in Moses's poems, windows should be closed at night and in chilly weather but opened to let in the sun. This idea, humoral in origin, reminds us that miasmic theory did not vanish with the rise of a contagion model.[117] Moses also, as noted, refers to salves, fumigation, scenting linens (which last he does not like), "heart-strengthening" foods, and also the importance of one's mental or emotional state. These prescriptions all defer to the Galenic categories of the six non-naturals, health factors available for medical manipulation.

Finally, in a striking deviation from his father's counsel, in four poems Moses urges his readers to pray (poems 4, 5, 11, 15, and 16), concentrating this theme in the final two poems. Significantly, prayer does not come with the reassurance of eternal life or messianic salvation. Prayer is what the wise embrace knowing that human knowledge is humbled in catastrophe.[118] Moses's poems speak from a human perspective that acknowledges its own limitations and those of human science. Indeed, where Abraham concludes his list with a political recommendation to the community to install a ghetto advocate in Venice, Moses concludes that all medical efforts are useless if God does not endorse them. "Therefore, may your heart be rent—but not your garments," he declares, for precautions are futile "if God does not guard the city." The shift to the fate of the collective is there, as in Abraham's conclusion, but now fused to the need for prayer, not vigorous lobbying in Venice.

The order of Abraham's prose suggestions is altered in the poems to conform to the new emphasis on flight, encouraged in the beginning, middle, and close to the end of the cycle (poems 1, 9, 13). Abraham's advice generally follows the arc of the epidemic. First, one must find living quarters, stock provisions, and secure one's valuables—all actions that precede an outbreak or which can be executed in its early stages. The next set of recommendations concerns separating the sick and preventing new infection without abandoning those in need. The final directive, to communal leaders, cycles back to a pre-epidemic time. In contrast, Moses's poems have no chronological progression. Between the first two recommendations for flight, we find directives for stocking provisions, but also for a preemptive partition of living quarters and other prophylactic steps. The order to flee is repeated in poem 9, followed by plans for depositing valuables and giving charity before fleeing, then recommendations to pray, and more preventive advice. The final exhortation to flee is also followed by preventive suggestions, some new, some repeating earlier advice, and concluding once more in the need for prayer. The zigzag of advice unravels Abraham's more logical ordering, leaving us a checklist of items that do not need to be addressed in order. The repeated injunctions to flee and to pray provide a unity of sorts to the sequence. Flight (or preparation for flight) precedes all other actions except prayer, which must be exercised continuously.

How does the addition of Moses's poems change his father's narrative? Abraham's concluding advice occupies only a small portion of a long narrative account, which either Moses did not entirely read or chose to ignore. Even for Abraham, the actual narrative of the plague testifies mostly to wisdom earned in hindsight; much of his story recounts the frustrations and terror of unforeseen challenges, or plans gone awry. These obstacles include the unpredictable resistance of individual Jews, or the maneuvering of different Christian factions against ghetto interests, developments that often catch Catalano and his fellow committee members by surprise. For these situations, planning proved meaningless. Other, more predictable, crises—food shortages, the constant need for gravediggers, or the need to guarantee valuables—demand early action. But the cumulative weight of the narrative hangs heavy over the terse directives at its end. The trauma of mass sickness and death, the disruption of normal life, the numbing crush of personal loss and public responsibility, suggest that the best of ghetto planning proved a flimsy reed. Abraham's narrative also testifies to the uncertainty and grief that lingered after the epidemic's end.

From this perspective Moses's poems do represent an attempt to shift the thrust of his father's narrative, if not his message. The 'Olam Hafukh is a narrative of catastrophe that exquisitely conveys the tension between the flawed but dogged efforts of civic leaders to limit the savagery of a terrible epidemic, and the factional, bureaucratic, and popular resistance they encountered. The narrative portion of Abraham's account concludes with the return of convalescent Jews from quarantine and the reopening of ghetto shops, with daily reports to the Health Office of goods sold and monies sealed in locked rooms.[119] It is a weary nod to resumed "normalcy" quite unlike the joyous tone struck by Massarani at his chronicle's end. But unlike Massarani, who sat out the plague in Regensburg, Abraham Catalano had been through too much. His closing advice was backed by bitter authority, devoid of affect and stripped of optimism or hope. Moses's poems soften some of that starkness while dispensing practical and scientific advice. The poems also reintegrate the language of prayer and faith, reminding readers that God's providence ultimately determined their fate. Prayer still mattered, even as it paid to head out of town and invest in good salves. The lightness Moses's poems bring to the end of a terrible story aimed not only for easy retention but for relief. Did Abraham approve of this poetic alchemy? He let the poems stay there, and he introduced them himself. At the same time his incipit reminds the reader that a chasm of geography, choices, and experience carved an abyss between prose and verse. In the chasm between them lies our answer.

Finally, this chapter has examined closely the use of poetic insertions in two important narratives that treat the impact of the 1630 plague on the ghetto communities of Mantua and Padua. What does this study offer historians less interested in literary readings or poems? Several answers may be offered. First, genre matters. Jewish writers, like their Christian and Muslim counterparts around them and in other places, enlisted multiple genres when they wrote about plague. An abundance of scholarship has addressed examples ranging from prose narrative and prayer to ballad, epic, doggerel, broadsheets, almanacs, medical tracts, and administrative reports. With the exception of the broadsheets, which admixed visual imagery, mortality statistics, and didactic, ethical and medical instruction, most plague writers stuck to a single medium. Nonetheless, as Massarani's and Catalano's texts illustrate, when they did mix genres, they did so deliberately. Second, the decision to insert poetry into a prose narrative tells us something about what the authors felt was missing or inexpressible in prose, a lack that could be satisfied by poetry. Does it also express some ambivalence about secular prose genres that teetered on a fine tightrope between secular and religious meaning? Massarani's case suggests that this might have been a factor in the decision to insert a poetic text that effectively recast the tenor of his historical narrative. Abraham Catalano's personal lament for his wife, in contrast, reinforces his narrative preoccupation with the tension between private and public identity. His son's poems, even as they urge a more optimistic outlook, ultimately do little to negate the sense of trauma that lingers in the prose.

Third, the turn to mixed-genre composition tells us that these writers anticipated the heterogeneity of their audiences, some of whom may have been more accustomed to framing catastrophe in theological tropes, some more interested in a humanist kind of history, and some satisfied with recommendations for smelling scents or opening windows. Abraham Catalano's tiny lament for his wife suggests also that even a narrative of collective catastrophe needed space to be private—a space that simultaneously signaled empathy with the private pain of others. For Massarani, empathy is curiously not a concern, a lack noticeable also in his disinterest in families. Whether this reflects a different understanding of "history" or a quirk of personality is unclear.

Fourth, the insertion of poetry into prose also balances the other perceived instabilities or inadequacies of the latter. Massarani's lament defaults to conventions of typology: the idealized rabbi, the erasure of women and lay Jews, the conflation of biblical with contemporary geography and catastrophe, and the path from sin and chastisement to repentance and redemption. By invoking these conventions, Massarani balances the prose chronicle's more democratic requirements of documentation, which demand the inclusion of actors big and small. The lament also repairs the prose record of the unraveling of Jewish institutional authority to emphasize its centrality to ghetto life, asserted as the weakened community sought to rebuild. For Abraham Catalano, balance was more about public and private worlds, depicted in the tension between the strain of coping with the needs of the ghetto and the crises and deaths that befall his home. But the *'Olam Hafukh* is a highly subtle composition, much more so than the *Sefer haGalut vehaPedut*; Catalano knows that the tensions he experienced personally have also stretched to breaking other inhabitants of the ghetto, men and women who now struggle to return to "normal" life.

Fifth, both authors enlisted poetry to package neatly some aspect of the prose they wanted to be exportable. For Massarani the lament built into his chronicle could be extracted for use in a liturgical setting; it is completely unobjectionable as a penitential hymn and was most likely designed for use on the Ninth of Av. For Abraham Catalano the appended didactic poems by his son condensed some (not all) of the recommendations that conclude his narrative, in an easily memorized and pleasant format. The ironic disjunction between the poems' emphasis on flight and the prose emphasis on surviving plague in place was probably not intentional, but it reminds us of the different ways people experienced these outbreaks, and how irreconcilable their perspectives might be.

Sixth, these texts can teach historians that poetic insertions, when they occur, are not to be skipped over, as they operate in synergy with the prose that surrounds them. In fact they can change the tenor of the prose, which does not have the same meaning read without them. Were prose and historical writing, in fact, the best way to ensure a common touchstone of past experience and meaning? Perhaps not, as anyone who has taught history knows.

Our next chapter turns to a genre at the opposite extreme of the spectrum of options for representing plague. How did people pray during this pandemic? How did they recycle texts and language from the distant past and infuse them with new meaning? We will look at a few examples, focusing our attention on the special place given to recitation of the *Pitum haKetoret*, the liturgical passages referring to preparation of the biblical incense used in the Temple cult.

Chapter 4

Jewish Plague Liturgy from Medieval and Early Modern Italy

Like human beings, every text has a tale: a tale of its words—what they say and how they say it—and a tale of its transmission through time and space as a cultural artifact and material form. In the case of plague writing, recent scholarship has treated a variety of genres—theoretical tracts, practical regimens, municipal ordinances, health office records, historical chronicles, and narrative accounts. Epitaphs, amulets, poetry, sermons, fiction, frescoes, monuments, and motets add to the list. Plague *liturgy* has been less attended, almost not at all for Jewish sources.[1]

The preceding chapters have looked at several Hebrew (and one Aramaic) responses to the Great Italian Plague of 1630–31. These were individual texts in chronicle or verse form; except for Moses Catalano's didactic poems, they were all commemorative. In contrast, this chapter examines two types of liturgical response to plague found in Italian Jewish sources.[2] One type takes the form of individual, freestanding, hymns, and another consists of composite liturgies; both categories shift their meaning and use over time. The first part of this chapter concentrates on three liturgical hymns, or *piyyutim*: a twelfth-century *ge'ulah* by Abraham Ibn Ezra, which acquired a new, plague-themed, stanza in the late fourteenth century; and original plague hymns by Joseph Baruch Urbino and Daniel (Anav) of Montalcino. Composed between the late fourteenth and the sixteenth century, their popularity extended into later periods. The second part of this chapter treats a kabbalistic-themed liturgy that attached itself to the *Pitum haKetoret* passages in the daily liturgy. The *Pitum haKetoret* readings, which refer to the compounding of the incense used in the Temple cult, had long been associated with repelling epidemics; in the late sixteenth and the early seventeenth century, they gained new association with the fumigation practices of plague regimens. Both the individual hymns and the plague litany demonstrate the vitality of liturgical genres that responded to plague, the creative repurposing of canonic texts, and the novel ways they acquired contemporary meaning.

For reasons that fascinate historians of medicine, climate, and environment, central and northern Italy proved welcoming hosts to epidemiological catastrophes from the late fourteenth into the seventeenth century.[3] Political upheaval and near-continuous war spanned the Counter-Reformation, including the grim period of the Thirty Years' War. Climate disaster, with extended seasons of drought or flooding, added to the misery wrought by war, taxation, and commodity shortages. Climate historians have focused keenly on larger shifts in weather and temperature, some kinder to fleas and rodents than they were to humans, some disruptive to insects and rodents in ways that had grim human consequences. Demographers have emphasized the relentless flow of human populations: soldiers, mercenaries, and deserters, refugees fleeing violence or hunger, aristocrats escaping "corrupted" urban air by relocating to country villas, merchants traveling by land or sea, captives, slaves, even students and unemployed scholars were constantly on the move. In their wake came the rats, shrews, and voles, fleas and lice that, like the humans, were desperate for food and lodging. Recent studies of the northern Italian plagues also emphasize their compound character, mixing typhus and bubonic plague to lethal effect.[4] For all these reasons, the early modern plagues in Italy included the worst plague outbreaks in Europe since the Black Death.[5] It is no surprise that people were praying.

How they were praying deserves renewed attention. A variety of texts and genres document Jewish institutional responses to epidemics in Italy, and Jewish collaboration with Christian counterparts across the ghetto walls. As more recent studies emphasize, the Italian ghettos, most of them sixteenth- and seventeenth-century creations, reconfigured interactions between Jewish and Christian spaces and lives, but did not diminish them.[6] By the sixteenth century Jewish leaders mobilized quickly when plague appeared. Reflecting plague measures beyond the walls, intra-ghetto roles during outbreaks were distributed among tiers of elected officials, committees, and confraternities; trustworthy advocates were frequently stationed outside the ghetto as intermediaries. Thus, in 1656, during a particularly brutal plague outbreak in Rome, the Jewish community relocated advocates outside the ghetto for the

duration of the plague. Two men were stationed in Venice to lobby on behalf of the community, while others were responsible for a steady supply of
food, medicine, and other goods.[7] Yet another appointee was lodged inside
the city lazaretto as an advocate for quarantined Jews.[8] In other cities, such
as Padua, the Jewish population was ordered to construct their own lazaretto and fumigation areas, but, as we saw in the preceding chapter, lobby-
ists did relocate outside the ghetto. Each city had a history of different
relationships with its Jewish population, and arrangements varied.

At the same time, ghetto walls proved no hindrance to the lively traffic
of lives, commodities, and tastes across and around Mediterranean and Ottoman borders.[9] The texts treated here add plague and prayer to this circulation of goods and ideas. Let me begin, then, with a well-known medieval
poet, Abraham Ibn Ezra, who lived long before the Second Pandemic and
would have been surprised to earn association with its woes.[10]

Abraham Ibn Ezra and Solomon of Perugia: A Marriage of Misreading

Memorably, the vicissitudes of his own history led Abraham Ibn Ezra
(d. 1167) far afield from his native Iberia; his peregrinations included a sojourn in Italy, where his poetry and prosody left a lasting impact on Italian
Hebrew writers. In a large *piyyut* corpus, one minor exemplar, "El Yisrael
Niqrata Lefanim" (Once You Were Called the God of Israel) caught the attention of a late medieval Jew in Perugia named Solomon, who had survived the
plague of 1374. Of Solomon we know nothing, although history tells us
this outbreak was severe. The hymn that attracted him is called a *ge'ulah*
("redemption"), because it elaborates on the fixed prayer in the liturgy
that sounds God's power to redeem. Like many of Abraham's *piyyutim*,
this *ge'ulah* is short: a four-stanza *shir ezor*, or "girdle poem," a popular
strophic genre alternating independent and recurring rhymes. The recurring rhyme concludes each stanza, "girdling" it according to one interpretation of the genre's strange name. The acrostic *A-V-R-M* identifies the
poet; this truncated form of "Abraham" is the form Ibn Ezra usually enlists
for his liturgical hymns. The meter is corrupt but roughly eight syllables
per line. The final stich of the girdle rhyme, כי גואלנו מעולם שמך ("for You
have forever been called our Redeemer") doubled as a refrain, possibly sung
by the congregation.

The appeal of Ibn Ezra's text lay originally in its description of Jewish suffering in gentile lands.[11] But from a later perspective, it might encourage different echoes. The opening verse taps the story of King Hezekiah on his deathbed, where heartfelt prayer would relieve his skin affliction (Isa. 38:18). For Ibn Ezra, mourning was eased by the redemptive power of prayer, but for later Italian readers, the king's ravaged skin mattered, too, summoning a scene of plague and pious death. The next line cites Isaiah 26:13 to underline Ibn Ezra's theme of foreign dominion. But the full biblical passage sweeps Isaiah's grim vision of a great city humbled, dead who do not rise, and an injunction to "enter your chambers" until God's anger has passed—an apt description of residents confined in a plague-struck city. Ibn Ezra's third verse alludes to Ezekiel 12:7, where the prophet enacts Israel's future exile by packing his bags and tunneling through the city wall. A twelfth-century Iberian Jew might think of a remnant's survival in the wake of destruction. For later plague-weary Jews and Christians, the prooftext might suggest flight from cities under closure, sometimes with bitter consequences for those left behind. In his autobiography the writer Abraham Yagel, whose work we encounter later in this chapter, described the plague-driven flight of his erstwhile banking partner, Rina, from Mantua to Luzzara: Suspected of carrying plague, the fleeing Jewish family nearly caused an anti-Jewish riot. The Paduan Jewish physician Abraham Catalano likewise noted the flight of several prominent members of the community in 1630; among them, his eldest son, Moses, survived by fleeing with his family to nearby Corte.[12]

By the time Ibn Ezra's second stanza opens with 1 Samuel 4:19's plague unleashed on the Israelites, his poem has arguably acquired a new meaning. The new theme competes with the original theme of lost sovereignty but does not entirely suppress it.

The fourth stanza petitions God:

מרי נפש מתי תרפאם   ואם בך מעלו חסדך יבואם

ומשחית קינך למה יניאם   הבנים לקח ולא שלח האם

מהרה חושי משבי הוציאם   טרם תבקשם ולא תמצאם

When will You heal those bitter of soul?
　If they have rebelled against You, have mercy on them.
Why should the Destroyer of Your nest obstruct them?[13]
　He has taken the children without releasing the mother.[14]

Hurry, hasten, bring them out of captivity![15]
Before You seek but cannot find them.[16]

The term *mashkhit* (destroyer), had biblical associations with disease and famine (Ex. 12:13, Ez. 5:9); after the Black Death it routinely referred to plague with associations to the Angel of Death. Alluding to the Deuteronomic prohibition against plundering mother and baby birds together, Ibn Ezra underscored the barbarism of Israel's enemies. In 1374, however, the allusion might remind a grieving survivor of the heavy child mortality that characterized the outbreaks of 1361–62 and the 1370s. Dread lingers with the poet's final warning to God that if He does not relent, there will be no one left to rescue or repent.

It is testimony to the vitality of liturgical thinking that Solomon of Perugia could do what he did next: He added a stanza to the original text. Cleverly, he started it with the letter "H" so that it could slide into penultimate place as the fourth of a five-stanza *piyyut* with the expanded acrostic *A-V-R-**H**-M* (Avraham).[17] In some manuscripts, it appears in this position; in others, it has been tacked to the bottom of the original or added in the margin in a later hand. The new stanza reads:

לחולי עמך אל רחמן רופא	העלה נא ארוכה ומרפא
כלה דבר ומשחית ולא נספה	עצור מגפה מעם לך מצפה
רפאינו ה' ונרפא	ותאמר למלאך ידך הרפה
לבז לחיות	רב לנו להיות
קדר ונביות	אדומיות חתיות
כי גאלנו מעולם שמך	ויבואונו רחמיך

Bring a healing cure to Your people's sickness, O God the Merciful Healer.[18]
Stop the plague among the people who look to You. End the pestilence and Destroying Angel lest we perish.[19]
Tell the angel, "Release your hand." Heal us, O Lord, that we be healed![20]
It is too much for us to live with the contempt[21]
Of the Edomites, Hittites, Kedar, and Nevaioth.[22]
Let Your mercy come to us—*for You have forever been called our Redeemer.*[23]

Solomon's stanza draws on Jeremiah, the prophet of lamentation. First, he alludes to Jeremiah 8:22, where the prophet asks why God has not provided healing for His people. Just before this verse, Jeremiah 8:17 described the "serpents" God will send, whose bites are fatal; by Solomon's time, the iconography of biting serpents was a common metaphor for plague. Rashi (d. 1105) glossed Jeremiah 8's image of unburied corpses, describing the traumatized Israelites as their Chaldean foes unceremoniously removed the Israelite dead from their fine houses. Plague chroniclers frequently described a similar sight. Additional plague prooftexts from Numbers 17 and 2 Samuel 24 patch the new stanza to Ibn Ezra's original theme by invoking hostile gentile nations. The composite text was a hit, surviving in numerous Italian liturgies from the late fourteenth century on, most of them Roman. Thanks to Solomon of Perugia, Ibn Ezra's original meaning was subsumed in a petitionary call for healing.

But repurposing old hymns was not an idea unique to Solomon of Perugia. A Venetian plague liturgy printed in 1630 incorporated medieval hymns from Spain and Provence, testimony to the influence of Sephardic exiles.[24] Preceding a fulsome litany of verses referring to the preparation of the biblical incense, the Venetian liturgy iterates the categories of biblical sacrifice— *oleh, hatat, minha, shelamim*—accompanying each with petitionary verses and a hymn. By 1630 some of the hymns were very old: One is by David b. Bakudah, a Sephardic author of the expulsion period; one is of unknown authorship but found also in a famous Burgundian *mahzor* copied in 1304. Like Ibn Ezra, these long-dead authors would have been surprised to discover their new context and aura. There was nothing they could do about it, and, ironically, the displacement of meaning kept their works alive.

Original Plague Hymns

Recycling old poems was not the only liturgical option Italian liturgies preserve. Original poetic compositions also appear, although they are rarer in the medieval period than the early modern. One late-seventeenth-century example, composed around the 1656 plague outbreak in Rome, survives in a small pamphlet dated that year and copied in Pesaro. The author, Joseph Baruch Urbino, was a noted rabbi, poet and translator. His *Selihot 'al Tzarat haDever shelo tavo* ("Penitential Hymns to Repel the Plague") forms a self-contained liturgy, perhaps for use by a local confraternity.[25] Like the Venetian

liturgy discussed earlier, this one is built on a familiar scaffolding—here, a
list of legendary biblical "shepherds." Each lament is preceded by an assurance that invoking the merits of these biblical exemplars can relieve affliction.[26] The prefatory texts specify a psalm to accompany each hymn (e.g.,
Psalm 89 for the first hymn invoking Abraham and Isaac; Psalm 121 for the
second, invoking Jacob). The preface to the liturgy states that it is intended
for Jews affected by the plague in Rome and by the wars in Germany and
Poland. Accordingly, introductions to each hymn refer to "compound woes,
pestilence and sword, war and harsh sickness" or "the woes of those under
siege, in distress from the warring enemy and struck by pestilence."[27]

  Joseph Urbino's hymns testify to the desire to commemorate victims
and console survivors in traditional liturgical forms. At the same time, as
this small liturgy also illustrates, their intended beneficiaries may extend to
a transnational network of communities within the Roman Jewish author's
frame of concern. Urbino's texts are weighted to descriptions of the virtuous
deeds of the biblical figures whose merit becomes the basis for a plea for
divine mercy. Curiously, with the exception of the hymn for David, which
asks God to notice His people afflicted by pestilence, "shaking and sweat-
ing . . . in their homes," only one extended passage, in the hymn for Jacob,
offers any plague-related detail. This passage enlists a recurring motif of
plague texts, the frightening dissolution of family ties:

צופה ויודע ועין פוקח
הבט לאום נכנע ומשתוחח
הומה בלב נשבר ומר צורח
צועק במכאוב מר ולב לוקח
בראות זמן צורר כמו שוכח
האב וגם הבן כאש קודח
אף טף ונשים יד אני שולח
שורר ומתגבר כמרצח
תוך נחלת האל להסתפח

[God] Who sees and knows with open eye:
Look down upon the people afflicted and bowed
Groaning with broken hearts and bitterly wailing
Shrieking in bitter pain and burning heart
Seeing the Foe's arrival, the father as if the son
Forgets and vice versa. Like a blazing fire

I even strike down women and infants
Gaining strength to reign like an assassin
Attached to God's [holy] portion. (MS BL Or. 10219, fol. 4r)

These hymns, designated for Sabbath eve, are strophic without refrains. How exactly they were used is unclear, but even people confined to their homes could hear, see, and smell the sounds, sights, and fragrances of processional liturgies.[28] If this liturgy was performed by a Jewish confraternity, its recitation was delegated to a group of (sometimes young) adult males, who played their own role in the hierarchy of ghetto functionaries, mimicking parallel structures beyond the ghetto walls. The institution of new liturgies and texts assures us that, for religious authorities and those who found comfort in religious rite, they served a purpose not entirely met by preexisting compositions.

A considerably earlier plague hymn survives in two Roman-rite liturgies, one from the fourteenth and one from the fifteenth century; a few print liturgies contain the text also.[29] The poet, Daniel ben Yehiel (Anav) of Montalcino, authored several extant hymns. One is an epithalamium, which suggests he had some reputation as an occasional poet.[30] By modern standards he was not a great one, but the prestigious Anav family wielded other kinds of influence. *"Derashnukha bekhol lev"* ("We Have Sought You with All Our Hearts") is most interesting not as poetry but for the way it assumes familiarity with a wider liturgy associated with plague.

Daniel b. Yehiel's hymn consists of five mono-rhymed quatrains that embed his name in acrostic. In the first stanza the people petition God; the last stanza hopes their petition will be favorably received. The interior stanzas call on God to heed the pleas of a plague-stricken community. The biblical prooftexts favor Psalms, and many had a familiar place in petitionary prayer. Daniel's poem sounds a recurring chord of desperation, echoed in its use of imperatives. Stanza 2 pleads:

נכאי רוח שבנו ובאנו עדיך בתחנון
מלט מכל מחלה צועקים לפניך בחנון
נא הצילנו מדבר הוות ומברק חרבך השנון
ה' ה' אל רחום וחנון

Broken-spirited, we have returned to come to You in petition.
Remove all sickness from those who cry out pleading before You.

Please save us from the ruinous plague and the flash of Your sharp
   sword!
O Lord O Lord, Merciful and Gracious (vv. 5–8)[31]

Hauntingly, Daniel's text maps a vertical hierarchy in which the human
supplicants are broken, low, raising their eyes to heaven, while God is high,
eternal, in heaven, and on His throne. Speaking for the community, the
poet begs God to respond mercifully to their prayer (stanza 1); stop sickness
and plague, and save them (stanza 2); forgive them, work wonders, end "pestilence, [sword], famine, the Destroying Angel and plague" and save them
(stanza 3); save them and remember their chosenness (stanza 4); see their
suffering from His Throne of Mercy (stanza 5). The poem offers no uplift or
resolution but leaves the people's anguished prayer suspended in a final plea
for clemency.

The simplicity of Daniel's text and its familiar prooftexts lent themselves to antiphonal singing, alternating text and refrain. Several phrases
also echo liturgical verses found in the plague liturgies that will be discussed
later in this chapter, such as the plea for an end to "plague and pestilence
etc." and the invocation of God's throne of mercy. Logically, this hymn
would have accompanied a fuller plague litany, although it is not preserved
as such but with other liturgical hymns. In the fifteenth-century copy, it
appears near the end of the prayerbook, following "*Unetaneh Tokef*" and preceding Abraham Ibn Ezra *ge'ulah* with Solomon of Perugia's added stanza.[32]
This proximity reinforces a claim for their use in a shared setting. Conven-
ing public assemblies in times of plague was not always easy, sometimes
because civic authorities circumscribed gatherings and sometimes because
people feared gathering. In Rome, during the great 1575 plague, ghetto officials had to order Jews to visit the sick and care for the dead. In sixteenth-
and seventeenth-century Padua, authorities had trouble mustering a quorum
of Jewish males in prayer.[33] But in these cities and others, specialized wor-
shipers stepped in to meet this contingency. Confraternities added antiplague prayers to their early morning convocations; as with Joseph Urbino's
liturgy, some of these rites must have been theirs.[34] Sylvie-Anne Goldberg
describes an alternative ritual featuring processions to the Jewish cemetery
in Prague during a late-seventeenth-century outbreak; this does not seem
to have been an Italian Jewish practice.[35]

Although we do not know how these hymns sounded, music played an
important role in the early modern ghettoes, particularly in Mantua and

Venice, and musical tastes were refined.[36] The famous Jewish composer Salamone Rossi spent time in both cities during the early seventeenth century.
Isaac Massarani, a friend and collaborator in Mantua, was a countertenor
who taught ballet and lute at the Gonzaga court. Rossi composed a song for
the marriage of Isaac's son, Abraham—the same Abraham who chronicled
the plague and expulsion of Mantuan Jewry.[37]

But music offered more than aesthetic distractions. It was also a source
of medical relief and theurgic power. In medical understanding, music was
a form of psychosomatic therapy that could to effect changes in human and
celestial bodies.[38] As therapy, music frequently appears in discussions of the
"sixth non-natural," the last of six Galenic categories treated by humoral
medicine. While the first five (air or climate; diet; sleep; exercise; evacua-
tion) are concerned strictly with physiological affect, the sixth non-natural
treats what we might now call emotional or psychological well-being. However, as recent studies by Remi Chiu, Christopher Macklin, and Renata
Pieragostini have demonstrated, mood-altering was not music's loftiest function.[39] Music had an important place in Neoplatonic and Neopythagorean
systems, where, like prayer and magic, it sympathetically connected humans
to celestial bodies.[40] The physics of resonance "proved" music's ability to
align celestial forces with those of the sublunar world, a belief encoded in
plague madrigals and motets: Chiu cites Marsilio Ficino's belief that "if you
cry out, singing and making songs in the style of one of these [planets],
they will seem to answer you right back." Pieragostini cites Boethius's belief
that music might align the "soul with the harmony of the cosmos" ; as she
goes on to show, that belief was extended in late medieval Bologna to make
a connection between the health of the corporate body politic of the commune and the cosmos as well. The commune, like the individual soul, might
benefit from "musico-medical" intervention.[41] Macklin, examining polyphonic Marian chants appealing for protection from plague, also emphasizes
that the intimate connection between human corruption and the miasmic
corruption of the air might be rectified in music that redirected the heavenly forces causing pestilence. *Stella celi*, the hymn Macklin traces through
multiple fifteenth- and sixteenth-century settings, is described by Chiu as
aimed at the "destructive concourse of the stars."[42] Like the *Stella celi*, madrigals and motets to plague saints like Saint Sebastian or Saint Roch were
composed from the late fifteenth through the sixteenth century, some in
response to the terrible outbreak in Milan in 1576–77. They, too, had their
cosmic work cut out for them.

Among Italian Jews these beliefs were if anything more developed than in Christian circles. Moshe Idel has traced an interest in music's magical and theurgic qualities to Jewish writers in Italy beginning in the fifteenth century, corresponding to the renewed fascination with Neoplatonic thought described earlier.[43] Nonetheless, he claimed, men like Isaac Arama, Johanan Alemanno, Isaac Abarbanel, Meir Ibn Gabbai, Judah Moscato, and others believed that the powers of music encompassed theurgic powers that could influence processes within the divinity itself, compelling descent of the divine efflux to the lower realm: These speculative theories thus enlisted the language of sefirotic Kabbalah to construct a dynamic model of divine-human interrelationship.[44] That model often found expression in variations on metaphors of acoustical resonance. Arama, Abarbanel, and Alemanno, for instance, invoked the image of two lutes set side by side, so that plucking a string on one would cause vibration in the other; so, too, could one element in the cosmic system cause movement in another.

Thus music, like medicine, might heal individual, social, and cosmic "bodies." Even a passive listener, confined to her home, was integrated into the corporate whole by her ability to hear, and perhaps sing, from multiple sites in the ghetto and city. Whether they could understand their language or not, Jews could hear Christian music, and Christians could hear the songs of the Jews.[45] The plague hymns discussed earlier do not mention fellow Christian sufferers, nor do Christian liturgies refer to non-Christians. But their sounds would have risen in the same sickened air, along with the sounds of pain and mourning, a frail but shared reminder that the plague struck them all.

In fact the close connections between Jewish musicians and their Christian counterparts outside the ghettos have been amply studied. Jewish musicians like Massarani and Rossi were celebrities in the Venetian and Mantuan courts. The musical tastes of the time did not pass them by, as testified by Rossi's importation of polyphony to the synagogue. Did Jews believe that their plague hymns were medically effective, and how might that have translated into specific musical features? Certainly, early modern Italian Jews were thinking about their sacred music in new ways. Idel traced some of the philosophical and esoteric traditions that support this idea, but there are other sources, also. Abraham Portaleone (d. 1612), the renowned Jewish rabbi, physician, and author, composed his magnum opus on the biblical Temple, *Shiltei ha-Gibborim*, in 1609. Ten of its ninety chapters discussed the music performed by the Levites in the biblical Temple, a discussion that features a digression on the polyphonic art song (*shir maḥshavti*) of his day; Portaleone argued that polyphony had cultic origins as venerable as the tropes of liturgical cantillation. (Unbeknownst to him, the cantillation system was probably medieval.)[46] As Don Harrán has noted, there is no comparable Jewish work extant today that tells us so much about Italian Jewish attitudes toward their own musical traditions and their incorporation of contemporary musical styles. In an introduction to the polyphonic settings of his friend Salamone Rossi, Judah Modena defended the use of polyphony in the synagogue. Another contemporary, Judah Moscato (d. 1593), discussed music in his philosophical *Sefer Nefutzot Yehudah* (Venice, 1589), although Harrán sees his interest as primarily kabbalistic.[47] Portaleone was also a physician who wrestled to reconcile religion and science; a few decades later, Abraham Yagel would heavily cite his work.

The extended plague liturgies suggest that prayer did operate on multiple frequencies. One was occult, linking sickness and sin, body and cosmos in Kabbalistic terms. But plague liturgies were also therapeutic, linking descriptions of the biblical cult and incense to fumigation practices endorsed ubiquitously in the plague regimens. These categories are not cleanly separated: Prayer works against plague by effecting the mystical alignment sought by the kabbalists, while incense redirects astral effluvia to detoxify the air. Let me turn, then, to the incense liturgy, *Pitum haKetoret*, and its use in times of plague.

Pitum haKetoret as Plague Liturgy

The institution of fast days with penitential prayers dates to the Mishnah, where it is detailed in tractate Ta'anit. The sheer repeatability of earthly disasters—famine, drought, earthquakes, floods, not to mention human-generated persecutions, conflict, and expulsions—assured these rituals continuing durability. By the late fourteenth century, plague had joined these disasters as a recurring phenomenon, a familiar if dreaded visitor. In Europe, one Christian response—processional liturgies—found an echo in Jewish communities, although, as Eliott Horowitz has shown, an uneasy ambivalence characterized the adoption of elements associated with Christian rites.[48] Inside Jewish communities, too, varied intellectual and religious commitments colored religious attitudes and rites—science and medicine, certainly, but also Kabbalah, which by the sixteenth century had a pervasive influence far beyond esoteric adherents.[49] Often the wide-ranging interests and readings of early modern Jewish writers blend medical, sacred, traditional, and esoteric concepts liberally; some elements of Kabbalistic terminology and thought had seeped into mainstream thought, where they mixed with traditional or scientific language without raising hackles.[50] Plague liturgies preserve some of this spiraling traffic in ideas and practices. In fact the *Pitum haKetoret* (incense grinding) liturgies are perhaps the dominant examples and survive in dozens of manuscript and print prayerbooks. To my knowledge they have only recently been studied as a new liturgical response to plague.[51]

. We have already seen that not all Jewish plague liturgies from early modern Italy are of the *Pitum haKetoret* type. The pamphlet liturgy used in Rome in 1576–77, mentioned earlier, is one example of an alternative liturgical scaffolding for a prayer litany. Another survives in two versions from seventeenth-century Mantua, where a bitter war of succession drew in armies from France, Germany, and Spain.[52] Most accounts located disease first among these troops; a combination of typhus and plague unleashed a devastating epidemic. After a crippling siege, German troops entered Mantua in August 1630 (the Ninth of Av), sacking the city and the ghetto.[53] Three days later, the Jews were expelled. When they returned at year's end, Mantua's general population had shrunken from approximately 50,000 to 10,000; of an estimated 2,500 Jews in the city and countryside before the war, nearly a thousand were lost to sickness, violence, homelessness, and hunger.[54]

Toward the final days of the siege, the Jews of Mantua gathered in prayer, enlisting a liturgy printed just days before the city was breached.[55] The text alternates timeless tropes of repentance and redemption with local historical markers: One hymn commemorated the siege of Bologna in 1402, also during a plague outbreak,[56] while another marked the recent French assault on Casale Monferrato in 1629.[57] A later version of this liturgy, adapted by the Ashkenazi community, substitutes other touchstones, elevating plague motifs and adding a prayer from the *Pitum haKetoret*.[58] It also added a long "yizkor" section listing more than seventy towns, spanning central Ashkenaz to Poland, whose Jewish communities knew lethal pogroms. At least half of the towns on the list experienced anti-Jewish violence during the Black Death, memorialized here not as an epidemiological event but as the memory of those attacks.[59] This was another liturgical option. The Mantuan text does not seem to have circulated beyond the city, but perhaps similar liturgies were cobbled together elsewhere and lost over time.

To judge from the extant copies, however, another option proved more popular. This liturgy elaborated on liturgical readings describing the preparation of the incense offered twice daily in the biblical Temple. The daily liturgy incorporates these readings into the morning and afternoon service. They include recitation of Exodus 30:34–36 and 30:7–8 describing God's command to Moses to prepare the incense, and a combined passage from Talmud (B. Keritot 6a and Y. Yoma 4:5) describing its composition, preparation, and storage. An early association of incense and plague derived from Numbers 17, where Moses commanded Aaron to prepare incense to halt a plague raging among the Israelites. Troubled by the Bible's failure to indicate the source of Moses's knowledge, the Aramaic *targumim* inserted an angel who mediated the recipe. Later exegetes (Rashbam in twelfth-century France, Obadiah ben Jacob Sforno in sixteenth-century Italy) referred explicitly to the prophylactic power of the incense.

A connection between biblical incense and late medieval or early modern fumigation practices occurs in Christian sources, although it did not receive great emphasis. Studies like Susan Harvey's rich examination of scent as part of a larger religious system of meaning have focused on incense in a sacral context; a recent study by Claire Burridge examines the link between sacred and medical uses of incense and other aromatics in the Carolingian period. For Burridge, incense was a "multipurpose substance" whose religious significance was never entirely erased in medical contexts.[60] Some connection thus shows up in Christian settings, but it does not seem to have been made explicitly by late medieval or early modern writers.

Influenced by Spanish Jewish exiles, early modern Jewish readers took the traditional association between incense and epidemic prophylaxis further than their Christian peers. Some, like Abraham Portaleone, praised Moses's pharmacological expertise.[61] Portaleone's *Shiltei ha-Gibburim*, mentioned earlier, dedicated eleven chapters to biblical incense. His treatment reflected biblical and rabbinic learning, but also his knowledge of Dioscorides, the classical botanical corpus, and what he learned from the "spice grinders and pharmacists in Mantua."[62] Portaleone's medical and botanical interests were shared by contemporary Christian humanists, whose enthusiasm for classical botanical and pharmacological works was renowned, as were the lavish pharmaceutical gardens where they cultivated exotic and medicinal plants.[63] Although Jews were not heavily represented among Italian apothecaries—the pharmaceutical guilds in most cities excluded Jews—traces survive of a few, such as the Leucci dynasty outside Florence or Gonzaga Horatius in Siena.[64] Nonetheless, sixteenth- and early seventeenth-century Italian Jews like Portaleone or his contemporary, the former Jew Amatus Lusitanus, maintained lively contacts with Christian peers who shared their interests and passion for collecting and authenticating botanical specimens.[65] If Portaleone had recourse to local spice merchants and apothecaries, he was not alone in exploiting this living resource. Lusitanus collected botanical specimens across the Balkans and in Portugal, and maintained contacts with "vendadores e compradores" of spices during his time in Antwerp.[66] Indeed, Kalman Cantarini, one of the Jewish physicians who would die in the Paduan ghetto in 1631 during the summer of the Great Plague, had composed an herbal of medicinal plants in local use.[67] Christian humanists, too, had recourse to "semplicisti" who scoured the countryside for specimens, and to apothecaries who compounded them.[68] Interestingly, Melchiorre Guilandino, the director of Padua's splendid university garden in 1575, detested Lusitanus's rival, Mattioli—no proof that he was fond of Lusitanus, but suggesting perhaps that he might be accommodating to this *converso* visitor.[69]

But one did not have to go far to witness the compounding of drugs in early modern Italian cities, especially the most famous drug of all, theriac, which was believed to offer the most potent remedy for plague. Apothecaries could prepare and sell theriac only with a special license.[70] In every city, competing pharmacies promoted their unique variations on classical recipes, recipes that were problematic both because their ingredients were difficult to identify against a local plant repertoire and because the ancient Greek authors were notoriously vague about indicating quantities. Female vipers and opium remained constant ingredients, and in part dictated by the former's availability, theriac production in Italy was generally an annual affair. More importantly, it was one that engaged the general public, as apothecaries were required by law to display their vipers and drugs outside their shops for three days prior to their compounding. The spicers who ground the ingredients also labored in the open, lining up before the stalls with their giant mortars and pestles, pounding and chanting in unison.

It is not hard to imagine that an early modern Italian Jew, whether or not he was as learned as Portaleone, Moscato, or Modena, would have connected this scene to the language of the *Pitum haKetoret* passages he had been reciting since childhood. The Talmudic excerpts include a detailed description of the pounding of the ancient incense, also an annual affair.

Figure 5. Civica Raccolta delle Stampe Achille Bertarelli, Castello Sforzesco, Milano, Italy, Ventole e Ventagli (Cart. p 5-1). Flyer, Venice, end of seventeenth–beginning of eighteenth centuries. In Achille Bertarelli, *Le stampe popolari italiane* (Milan, 1974), 47.

Note how the spice grinders pound rhythmically while a foreman calls out to them:

B. Keritot 6a; Y. Yoma 4:5: The rabbis have taught: How was the compounding of the incense performed? The [annual amount of] incense weighed three hundred and sixty-eight minas: three hundred and sixty-five corresponding to the number of days of the solar year, one mina for each day. . . . The incense was compounded of the following eleven kinds of spices: balm, onycha, galbanum, and frank-incense, seventy minas' weight of each; myrrh, cassia, spikenard, and saffron, sixteen minas' weight of each; twelve minas of costus; three minas of an aromatic bark; and nine minas of cinnamon. [Added to the spices were] nine kabs of Karsina lye, three seahs and three kabs of Cyprus wine—if Cyprus wine could not be obtained, strong white wine might be substituted—a fourth of a kab of Sodom salt [sulfur?] and a minute quantity of a smoke-producing ingredient.

Rabbi Nathan says: while he was grinding, he would say: "grind it finely, finely grind it" because the rhythmic sound is good for the compounding of spices.[71]

For Jewish intellectuals like Portaleone, biblical and rabbinic sources preserved a font of lost knowledge whose rediscovery would add luster to the Jewish nation. The prophylactic properties of the incense offered one more proof that sacred Jewish texts preserved the remnants of scientific expertise once the intellectual property of Jews but plundered by the nations.

For other early modern Jews, the incense liturgy inspired metaphysical exegesis. In the thirteenth century, and drawing on Neoplatonist thought, the Zohar, the foundational text of Kabbalah, had already described biblical incense as a prophylactic against plague. The anonymous author of the mystical *Sefer haMeshiv* understood incense similarly.[72] Judah Moscato interpreted the incense passages symbolically as allusions to spiritual perfection. For Neoplatonist readers the biblical incense attracted and redirected the sympathy of a celestial body or force. The incense *liturgy* combined verbal and performative acts that somehow replicated or substituted for the sacrificial rite. For Johanan Alemanno, the combination of song and sacrifice had once performed this function; for Isaac Abarbanel, the biblical King Solomon had also known how to compose songs to cause the descent of the divine efflux. Idel also cites the anonymous author of a work tellingly called the *Sefer Kaf haKetoret* ("The Book of a Handful of Incense"), who explained that each psalm mysteriously embedded a "segula" (charm; a Name of God). To master recitation of the psalms was therefore to acquire power over all sorts of troublemakers, evildoers, evil eyes, and spirits that might beset him.[73]

Reflecting the popularity of these views, a litany of verses and supplications grew up around the incense readings in the form of a special liturgy.[74] Most claimed the same path of transmission, via Joseph Ibn Shraga (d'Agrigento) and Solomon b. Isaac Marini. Marini was a fascinating personality in the Paduan ghetto, a rabbi, physician, and poet whose writings we will consider later.[75] He was the only one of the ghetto's rabbis to survive the 1630–31 plague, a fact that undoubtedly recommended his liturgy to later generations. Joseph Ibn Shraga, a refugee from the Spanish expulsion in 1492, was long dead, but he had been a respected kabbalist in Italian circles.[76] According to Abraham Catalano in Padua in 1630, the Paduan rabbi Marini possessed a copy of Ibn Shraga's liturgy and had it printed in Venice; Catalano (erroneously) thought it had been composed in Pisa, where it saved the author from plague.[77] This and other versions of the plague *Pitum haKetoret* liturgy share an identical template: The *Pitum haKetoret* passages plus strings of verses are repeated one to three times; most allude to biblical plague narratives or other narratives of deliverance.[78] Prose supplications punctuate the verse litanies and make explicit their substitution for Aaron's sacred incense.[79] The text then continues:

ועמוד מכסא דין ושב על כסא רחמים וחמול עלינו ועל טפינו ועוללינו ויונקינו וגער
בשטן ואל ישטין עלינו ואל תתן המשחית לבא אל בתינו ותגדף ותעצור את המגפה
מעלינו וכן יהי רצון מלפניך ה' אלהינו ואלהי אבותינו לכלות מעלינו ומעל כל עמך
בית ישראל דבר וחרב ורעב ורעה ויגון ואנחה ורעה ומשחית המגפה ויצר הרע ופגע רע
ושטן הרע וכליה רעה וכל תחלואים רשעות רעות מאורעו' המתרגשות לבא בעולם
ושמור צאתנו ובואינו מעתה ועד עולם רפאנו יי' אלהינו ונרפא הושיענו ונושעה
כיתהלתנו אתה יהי רצון מלפניך ה' אלהינו

Stand down from the Throne of Judgment and sit on the Throne of Mercy. Have forgiveness upon us and our babies, toddlers, and nursing infants. Rebuke the "adversary" so he does not prosecute us; do not let the Destroying Angel enter our homes. Rebuke and stop the plague among us. May it be Your will, O Lord our God and the God of our fathers, to end among us and all your people, the House of Israel: pestilence, sword, famine, grief, sighing, evil, the Destroying Angel, the plague, the evil inclination, evil disease, the evil "adversary," evil annihilation, and all wicked, evil diseases that come into the world. Guard our coming and going now and forever. Heal us, O Lord, and we shall be healed. Save us and we shall be saved, for You are our glory. May it be Your will, O Lord our God, etc.[80]

We recall echoes of this text in Daniel b. Yehiel's poetic supplication, which pleaded for an end to "pestilence, famine, the Destroying Angel and plague" and appealed to God on His "throne of mercy"—reinforcing my claim that this hymn was once attached to a larger liturgy. Variations on this text in other manuscript copies suggest tweaking for local conditions. One Sephardic exemplar adds "and do not desire the world's destruction," a terse comment on how things looked at that moment.[81] In rare and usually later instances, prayers for relief may include gentiles. More often, copies insert an unpronounceable angelic Name among the closing litanies.[82] I shall return to this Name shortly, but it is one more indication of the commitments that guide the theurgical aspects of this liturgy.

Kabbalah was an occult science that was not divorced from other intellectual interests that attracted early modern Italian Jews, including medicine. By the sixteenth century, as noted earlier, many of its concepts had splashed beyond the borders of esotericism, permeating (in diluted form) religious and metaphysical disciplines where they provoked no objection. Among Jewish physicians, even when they were not kabbalistically inclined, incense received outsized attention as a plague prophylactic, often by linking the aromatic fumigations of the medical regimens to the incense of the biblical cult. The connection was polemical, as it located the origins of a scientific remedy in Jewish sacred texts, knowledge that was the intellectual property of Jews before it passed into gentile hands. While Christian plague regimens ubiquitously recommend scented fumigations to counteract the air's corruption, they do not elaborate on its benefits in the same way; the scented smoke operates humorally, counteracting venomous toxins. Christian regimens do not treat fumigation scents as mystical essences or as rectifying spiritual corruption.[83]

The Jewish connection is illustrated beautifully in the *Moshiah Hosim*, a 1587 plague regimen by Abraham Yagel, who cites the works of Portaleone and Lusitanus. In many respects Yagel's tract hews to genre. The preventive section addresses diet, exercise, sleep, bleeding, and behavior, concluding with drug recipes. The section on aromatic fumigation is unusually extensive. Yagel explains that the ancient incense was compounded to attract celestial effluvia to sympathetic earthly forms. Properly executed, this redirection of planetary forces could purify the air of the corruption wrought by their misalignment.[84] The Angel of Death transmitted the necessary recipes and recitations to Moses; the rabbis arranged this information and added prophylactic psalms.[85] Yagel's regimen concludes with pill recipes, *segullot*, and a commentary on Psalms 38 that leads inexorably to the *Pitum haKetoret* liturgy attributed to Ibn Shraga.[86] Before the first string of verses Yagel includes an angelic Name that had a long association with plague prevention:

צד נלבש קהס מגת צדנלבש

The first six letters come from the words צרי דבש נכאת לט בטנים שקדים—the "choice produce of the land" that Jacob instructs Judah to take down to Egypt: "some balm and some honey, gum, labdanum, pistachios, and almonds" (Gen. 43:11). The second six letters, like the final six, are derived by advancing one letter from each letter in the first Name.[87] As Moshe Idel has shown, use of this Name as an antiplague adjuration can be traced to Joseph della Reina and a kabbalist named Isaac de Leon, both wonder-working mystics active in Spain prior to the expulsion.[88] A century later this tradition found life in northern Italy, still combating plague but now as cutting-edge medicine.

In sum, a taste for medical pluralism might seep from medicine into the affective realm of prayer.[89] For physicians like Yagel or Portaleone, incense was a biblically sanctioned method for channeling astral effluvia and purifying pestilential air. For other physicians less inclined to mysticism, no outcry against this view survives.[90] For those who were not physicians, prayer bestowed agency denied the medical consumer. Prayer, in the hope that God and the planets would hearken, gave voices to frightened, weary people, who could not know when this plague, this time, would slacken, and who would survive. So, too, did preparing scented fires and bedsheets, like reliance on amulets and angels, engage men and women, learned and less learned, in the work of repelling the Angel of Death. Today it may startle us to read Yagel's theory of sympathetic influence as an argument for starting the morning by sitting open-mouthed in the outhouse for thirty minutes, to inure yourself to putrefaction in the air.[91] But the recommendation was made to men and women tending afflicted family members amid the unbearable stench of plague, or those shut in their homes, where the sounds and smells of sickness did not respect walls. Did the outhouse exercise build immunity to plague? Hardly. Whatever their therapeutic value, neither did music, medicine, or unpronounceable Names. But piecemeal or together, they offered a way of being human that was very much under siege.

Even for those who did not worry about whether our biblical fathers were scientists before Dioscorides or Galen, medical and religious ways of thinking intermingled. In a recent study, Michael Rizhik examined a group of vernacular (Judeo-Italian) women's prayerbooks from the early modern period; these books also included the *Pitum haKetoret* readings.[92] So, when Jewish women encountered the *Pitum haKetoret*, what translation appeared for the Hebrew *tsori*, which is "balm" in the Birnbaum siddur and "stacte"

for Lusitanus and in the JPS translation of the Hebrew Scriptures? The
Judeo-Italian texts have another suggestion: theriac, the potent drug compound famous as an antidote for poison and plague.[93] Theriac, like biblical
incense, was a top-secret compound, its recipes guarded zealously. The use of
the word in a liturgical setting—for women who might be literate but who
were not reading Kabbalah or Galen—assures us that medicine and liturgy
were not strange partners even beyond the elite circles of book-loving men.

The causative agent of bubonic plague, *Yersinia pestis*, was discovered in
1894. Today, caught early, it is treated with common antibiotics. But will
people ever stop praying? It is unlikely. As we have seen all too recently, in
some circles prayer has proven more popular than isolation or vaccines. In
public and private settings of all sorts, there has been no objection to adding prayer to secular or medical recommendations. Certainly by the early
seventeenth century, but arguably much earlier, a willingness to tap all possible options characterized urban responses to plague. A rich menu of possibilities suited the great cities of premodern Italy—possibilities as polyphonic as
the music Jews and Christians composed and admired; as multiethnic and
multilingual as the streets, markets, and places of worship they frequented;
as private and public as their interlocked sense of themselves, their families,
and dynastic networks; as sacred and as profane as life and its attendant
rituals affirmed daily in gusto or in grief. As we have learned, we behave the
same way. And if, God forbid, such catastrophe returns, prayer and medicine will be partners again.

Chapter 5

Plague from the Pulpit
Rabbi Solomon Marini in Padua

When the plague appeared in Verona in 1630, we agreed to
petition [God] on behalf of our brethren. The champion, the
honorable teacher and rabbi, Solomon Marini, may the Merciful
One guard and redeem him, found among his books a lengthy
prayer that had been written long ago in the city of Pisa, a great
city of sages. It pleased us, so he went to Venice to have it printed,
and we decided to recite it on Mondays and Thursdays every week
following the reading from Scripture. Once the plague began, [we
also recited] the *Pitum haKetoret* daily.
                                        —Abraham Catalano, *'Olam Hafukh*

Without abandoning the questions of public and private identity that have
occupied the preceding chapters, this chapter turns in a slightly different
direction to think about the challenges of preaching during the plague, focusing on the much-neglected figure of Solomon b. Isaac Marini in Padua.
Jewish preaching from the late medieval and early modern periods has not
attracted attention as a resource for plague historians. One very simple reason is that the texts do not survive.[1] Marc Saperstein observed years ago
that history has not preserved a single manuscript of a Jewish sermon given
during the Black Death, and the same statistical nothing shows little fluc-
tuation by 1630–31.[2] And yet, for early modern rabbis, especially in Italy,
preaching was a highly developed art, which reached a pinnacle in the sixteenth
and seventeenth centuries, especially in Italy. This period has bequeathed us

many manuscript collections of sermons delivered by great Jewish orators like Judah Moscato, Judah Leone Modena, and, later, Saul Morteira in Amsterdam. These men were in turn indebted to late fifteenth- and sixteenth-century Iberian Jews like Isaac Arama, Abraham Shalom, or Moses Al-Sheikh in Safed, whose highly developed sermon forms were reviewed, appreciated, and modeled for two centuries after the expulsion. Italian Jewish preaching styles owed much also to the contemporary enthusiasm for classical rhetoric found among the Christian humanist circles admired by these Jews. From our perspective, most of these works are stupendously long, circuitous, and arcane; no contemporary scholar has matched Saperstein's appreciation of their artistry and melding of learned sophistication with topical concerns. These were sermons intended to impress their listeners (who counted Christians as well as Jews) with their art but equally to deliver timely social critiques—or consolations—in a setting that amplified the preacher's authority as much as his words.[3]

The sermon texts penned by the great rabbis of early modern Italy cannot be identical to the oral performance they ostensibly record. First and foremost, they are literary Hebrew reconstructions of a sermon delivered orally in the vernacular. In Hebrew, moreover, learned additions likely swelled a message aimed originally at a wider audience. In contrast, written texts frequently eliminated the historical and personal details we moderns would most like to know, counting them as ephemera of little interest to posterity. In some cases, like Al-Sheikh's, exegetical forays that began as sermons metamorphosed in print to extensive commentaries on Scripture. In other cases, a sermon text might be recycled, either because the rabbi felt it was good for another run with some tweaking or because pressures of time or circumstance made it difficult to come up with something new. The latter is Morteira's explanation for why he recycled an earlier sermon during the 1656 plague outbreak in Amsterdam (the same outbreak that inspired one of the sermons treated in the discussion that follows).[4]

In fact, Jewish sermons were rarely fully written before they were delivered, and the written texts represent reconstructions produced afterward from notes made by the preacher or one of his students. Since most preaching was done on the Sabbath or festival days, when writing was prohibited, even a designated note-taker would minimally have had to wait several hours before recording what he thought he had heard. A completely fleshed-out sermon, which Saperstein estimates could have run from thirty minutes to three hours depending on the occasion, can be a formidable challenge to read today.[5] Many more sermons never reached that stage of preservation, surviving only in the preacher's sketchy record of textual prompts, awaiting reconstruction that never came. A skeletal outline of this sort, consisting of abbreviated verses from the Hebrew Bible and classical rabbinic sources, poses other kinds of nightmares; this is probably why, despite the survival of such collections, no one has bothered with them.

Necessity can be a great motivator. In the case of the Great Italian Plague, we have already explored several genres and perspectives on this plague's impact on northern Italian Jewish communities. Both Abraham Catalano in Padua and Abraham Massarani from Mantua describe synagogue life and rabbis as central to communal identity and cohesion.[6] It is important to ask what the rabbis of Padua were saying through this terrible crisis, and how they understood their role in times of plague. If what remains are sermon outlines, that is what we must use, asking what these skimpy notations can tell us if we treat them carefully. The following chapter attempts to do so.

Abraham Catalano's plague narrative, the 'Olam Hafukh, mentions the special prayers and worship arrangements that evolved over the course of the epidemic; Catalano's account, treated in earlier chapters, refers several times to the great "champion" of Padua's twenty-four rabbis, Solomon b. Isaac Marini. As the passage opening this chapter describes, it was Marini who discovered and reproduced the plague liturgy recited by Paduan Jews throughout the epidemic. Catalano underscores the rabbi's stature in the community in two other episodes. In one, as the daily death toll mounted, Jews were dying without reciting the traditional deathbed confession before family and friends. At this dire moment, Rabbi Marini undertook to teach Paduan Jews to recite confession from their doorways before they fell mortally ill, assembling a quorum of ten adult males at a safe distance in the street.[7] To set an example, he publicly performed this adapted ritual himself, then ordered a solemn procession of healthy men carrying two Torah scrolls and blasting shofars from the four ends of the ghetto.[8] Late the following summer, while Catalano himself was still confined to his home after the deaths of two sons, Marini—now the sole remaining rabbi of the ghetto—decreed a public fast in the ghetto. Interestingly, Catalano records that this time his decree was not well received, as "many complained about this matter, saying that God would not want to afflict a man's soul at such a time."[9] Where God actually stood on the matter is uncertain, but unlike his twenty-three rabbinic colleagues in Padua, Solomon Marini had survived this far and would long outlast the plague.[10]

Although Solomon b. Isaac Marini left few traces of his life, he was a notable presence among the circles of northern Italian Jewish intellectuals, rabbis, and physicians who intersect throughout this book. He must have been born before the turn of the century, and he died in 1670. Like many elite and ambitious Paduan Jewish males, he studied medicine, as did his brother Shabtai, at the University of Padua. He does not seem to have practiced, however, and is known chiefly, if at all, for a commentary on Isaiah, *Tikkun 'Olam*, printed in Verona in 1652. The family had its roots in Verona, perhaps influencing the rabbi's desire to marshal the forces of prayer on behalf of Veronese Jewish plague victims.[11] Subsequent generations of Marinis distinguished themselves in medicine and letters, remaining in Padua into the eighteenth century if not beyond. The most illustrious may be one of Solomon's grandsons, Shabtai b. Isaac Marini, who was born ca. 1660–65 and awarded his medical diploma in 1685. In addition to his reputation as a physician esteemed by Christians as well as Jews, Shabtai b. Isaac was a life-long poet. Many of his poems (in Hebrew and Italian) were not discovered until long after his death, when Mordecai Samuel Ghirondi found them among papers passed through generations of his descendants.[12] In addition to a lively correspondence and exchange of poems with two friends from his medical school days, who constituted what Meir Benayahu has called a poets' club or "academy," Shabtai produced a variety of wedding poems, epitaphs, laments, and congratulatory sonnets.[13] He also tried his hand at translation, rendering the Mishnaic tract *Pirqei Avot* into rhymed verse and attempting a Hebrew translation of Ovid's *Metamorphoses*.[14] Shabtai's poems circulated widely in his day, and some of the epithalamia show up as decorative additions to illustrated *ketubbot*.[15] From Ghirondi we learn that Shabtai, like his grandfather, was also renowned as a preacher, but none of his sermons survives.[16] Shabtai died in 1748, a figure so revered that Paduan Jews would prostrate themselves on his grave on the eve of Rosh Hashanah and Yom Kippur. Shabtai's son, Isaac, was also a physician-poet.[17]

The celebrity Shabtai's grandfather, Solomon b. Isaac, did not leave such an extensive trail. It is possible that he is the Solomon Marini who cosigned a 1611 letter with other Paduan notables alerting other communities to a fraudulent beggar circulating in the region. Solomon was a mature man in 1630, or he could not have commanded such stature during the epidemic. Amazingly, he not only survived the deadly plague of 1630–31 but lived several decades more, dying on the eve of the Jewish month of Iyyar 5430, the summer of 1670 by gentile reckoning.[18]

Solomon's preaching comprised an important part of his rabbinic activity. So at least it would appear from the efforts he made to preserve some record of what he preached, which survive in two manuscripts currently held by the Jewish Theological Seminary in New York, both accessible as digital scans on the KTIV database of the Israel National Library.[19] The more battered of the two, MS JTS 843, preserves the earlier records, which are not full sermons but, in the words of the KTIV cataloger, just the רעיונות הדרשות (the "ideas of the sermons").[20] These are sermon outlines, ranging from four to twenty-odd lines of manuscript in wretched and frequently faded script that is the work of multiple hands. The outlines are arranged chronologically to follow the Scriptural portion assigned to each Sabbath of the calendar year, with the year scrawled at the top of each page. Helpfully, many of the entries also indicate when the sermon was delivered (Sabbath morning, afternoon, or conclusion) and in what synagogue, showing us that Marini sometimes preached more than once on a given Sabbath and in different venues. Occasionally a few words connect the sermon to a specific historical moment, such as the one that first caught my eye, given "on the second day of Rosh Hashanah in the Ashkenazi synagogue *after the plague*" (emphasis mine—see the discussion following). Indeed, it is this batch of sermon outlines that covers the year 1631 and some years beyond, and despite its wretched condition, it holds great interest. The three sermon outlines I have selected for attention date from 1631: (1) the Sabbath of *parashat* Bo (the pericope, or Scriptural portion "Bo," spanning Exodus 10–13), delivered in January, before the plague had struck the ghetto but when it was raging fiercely in the Christian city; (2) the second day of Rosh Hashanah, a few weeks after the plague's official end; (3) and Shabbat Shuvah (or Teshuvah), given on the following Sabbath, which falls between Rosh Hashanah and Yom Kippur and is dedicated to themes of repentance.

Marini's plan to expand his outlines into a collected volume of sermons is suggested by the tentative title that MS JTS 843 offers the compendium, *Hesheq Shlomo* ("Solomon's Desire"). In addition to the Sabbath and festival sermon outlines, the manuscript contains Marini's outlines for a number of eulogies and occasional gatherings, some poetry, and the introduction to an unfinished or lost translation of Alessandro Piccolomini's *Teorica*.[21] No wonder Abraham Catalano revered this man, and no wonder he is one of the communal leaders whose activities surface repeatedly in Abraham's narrative. While Abraham's own writings suggest a more temperate personality, both men shared an education in Jewish, secular, and medical subjects, a probing concern with questions of ethics and meaning, and admiration for poetry and language. They also played public roles in the Paduan ghetto, especially but not exclusively during the 1631 plague, and their writing reveals something of what that meant to them.

A second manuscript in a different set of hands preserves a great many more of Solomon Marini's sermon outlines dating from 1641–59; it also includes expanded sketches of eulogies for an all-star list of elite Jewish bankers and intellectuals like Judah Modena, Nathaniel Trabot, and Azariah Figo, but also, and of special interest to us, Abraham Catalano, who died in 1641. This manuscript is bound with two other works not authored by Marini, an ethical treatise by Isaiah Romanin, and a copy of Samuel Archevolti's 'Arugat haBosem. While they might seem to be beyond our purview chronologically, these Marini texts include an outline for Marini's sermon for parashat Noah, given in the fall of 1656, the year of the great plague outbreak in Rome. Sparse as it is, the outline clearly represents Marini's attempt to solicit funds for the Rome ghetto during this bleak period. Marini's eulogy for Abraham Catalano is also of value, not only because it preserves a moving record of personal affection and friendship but for its historical details; the eulogy is treated in the next chapter. All these texts are unknown to scholars.

Before turning to Solomon b. Isaac's sermon outlines, a few words are in order about the actual content of these texts and how I have worked with them. As I have already indicated, these examples are drawn from a much larger corpus representing sermons given between 1630 and 1634 (NY MS JTS 843) and 1641–59 (NY MS JTS 6517). The years run as headers at the top of each folio, and the sermons are listed by parasha, sometimes indicating the synagogue and time of day they were delivered. All these indications are abbreviated in the Hebrew but spelled out in my English transcriptions. The outlines range from three or four lines of text to twenty or so; the longer they are, the more "filler" they contain. In general they are short, usually six to eight lines of text. We know enough about the structure of Italian Jewish sermons in this period to identify their basic components in outline form.[22] Each outline begins with the opening words of a biblical verse from the day's reading, called the nosé or tema. This is followed immediately by the opening words of a rabbinic passage, called the ma'amar, also citing only its opening words. If listed, the source of the ma'amar is also abbreviated; in most cases, I have had no trouble identifying these references, and I spell them out fully in my transcription. The body of the text consists mostly of the preacher's jumping off points or transitions, listing the beginnings of the biblical verses that advanced the theme. Generally, as we shall see, the middle section of the sermon took the form of an apparent digression that was then steered back to the opening *ma'amar* and its relevance to the Scriptural portion.

The structure I am describing is conventional for Italian Jewish sermons of this period, and solidified in the sixteenth century, influenced by the preaching format favored by the great Iberian Jewish rabbis whose written sermons circulated in Italy. Solomon Marini's citations of medieval and more recent authorities confirm his affinity for Iberian writers and ideas. The outlines I examined defer repeatedly to Abraham Ibn Ezra, Bahya ibn Pakuda, Maimonides, Isaac Arama, and Moses Al-Sheikh. Furthermore, the sermons suggested by the outlines cohere around a single theme, a development and style Saperstein associates specifically with the Iberian *derush* of the exile generation.[23] Because we know something about the way this kind of sermon should work, we can decode some of the laconic notations in a Marini outline. The outline for Shabbat Teshuva concludes tersely with the two words *"perush ha-ma'amar"* ("explanation of the *ma'amar*"), telling us that the sermon would have closed by explaining how the preceding analysis shed light on the opening *ma'mar* (from the midrash on Psalms), then looping back to the theme of repentance traditional for this day. Similarly, our first outline, for *parashat* Bo, concludes with a verse from Psalms 29 and the words "as concerns peace, and other interpretations from *Neve-Shalom*."[24] However, it is impossible that Marini would have ended his sermon without returning to the theme and meaning of his *ma'amar*; thus we know that this section is missing entirely from the outline as we see it, but that the preacher would have included it.

How do we know that Solomon b. Isaac was using his biblical and rabbinic scaffolding to talk about current events? There are several ways. The first and easiest is when he or his copyist tells us so, usually in the incipit, saying something like, "This sermon was delivered after the plague," or "I gave this eulogy for Abraham Catalano before he was buried," or "on behalf of the Jewish community in Rome." A second option is when a historical connection is included in the outline, as when Solomon pleads for assistance for the Jews of Rome or says that he had wished to preach about something else but is compelled to address "violence and robbery due to the plague." In these cases, it would be lovely if we knew whether the outlines were the work of a student or auditor, or whether they were Marini's. If the former, the inclusion of lines like these suggests that they made an impression on the listener and that he felt they were significant to the message; if the latter, the lines may be more of a mnemonic aid. The third way we can situate Solomon's spare prooftexts in a contemporary setting is by studying their biblical context and how it was understood by the rabbis whose readings Marini cites and admires. This third strategy may strike some readers as overly speculative, but I hope that in execution these doubts will be assuaged. The range of associations I am excavating is hardly random but indicated by Marini himself; it is more a matter of joining puzzle pieces than inventing my own puzzle. Fourth, we have the invaluable resource of Abraham Catalano's plague narrative, which offers a detailed chronological record of unfolding events in the ghetto, and which can be matched by date to the sermon in question. And finally, when I am not certain about how Marini was using his prooftexts, I say so. The proof is in the proverbial pudding: I have stayed as close to Marini's signposts as I could, but readers may wish to emend and improve these readings.

What I am trying to do is to show that a genre of writing that has been entirely ignored does in fact yield valuable meaning. It is not an easy exercise, but if I am right, these minimalist outlines can contribute to a larger picture of what it meant to represent religious authority in a time of communal crisis—in this case plague—what kinds of messages a religious leader thought it important to convey, and, by extension, how he represented himself conveying them. The results also permit us to assess whether, given what we know of actual conditions in the plague-stricken ghetto of Padua, the rabbis' messages resonated with their flock or not.

Parashat Bo (Exodus 10:1–13:16) 5391 (January 1631)
NY MS JTS 843, fol. 14a.

My first example is the brief outline of Marini's sermon for *parashat* Bo in the Jewish calendar year 5391, which would have fallen near or in January 1631. The Scriptural reading for *parashat* Bo is Exodus 10:1–13:16, the story of the "plagues" (*makkot*) that befell Pharaoh and the Egyptians, including the dreadful tenth and final plague that results in the death of the Egyptian firstborn males. Marini will develop his sermon to comment on the sparing of the ghetto from plague, an unforeseen benefit of its closure. The sermon was delivered at the end of the Sabbath and was probably shorter than a full-blown Sabbath morning sermon. The text covers seven lines in the manuscript and is translated below. Biblical citations are indicated in bold font, rabbinic citations in italics, with the sources for both in brackets. Occasionally, I have added a few connecting words, also in brackets. Line numbers correspond to the line count in the manuscript. I have tried to convey as much as possible the minimalist nature of the text. My transcription of the Hebrew text appears in Appendix 1.

Motzei Shabbat[25]

1. **"And the Lord will pass over the doorway"** [Ex. 12:23]. *Ma'amar*: **"I shall pass through the land of Egypt, I and not an angel"** [Exod. 12:12] [. . .] the *Guide* part III, where the philosopher said

2. [unclear] The meaning of **"Have You eyes of flesh?"** [Job 10:4]. The meaning of the *ma'amar* [concerns] God's knowledge of earthly events

3. **"I and not an angel"** [Haggadah on Ex. 12:23].[26] This is to say that the cause[s] of the striking of firstborn was corruption of the air resulting from the preceding plagues. **"And not**

4. **A seraph"** [Haggadah on Ex. 12:23]. For I have distinguished between [the language of?] firstborn. **"And not a messenger"** [Haggadah]—that He passed judgment on [their god?]

5. Secondly, the meaning of the verse **"And it was in the middle of the night"** [Ex. 12:29]. Third, **"And the Gadites went and returned"** [Josh. 22:9, Jud. 21:23].

6. Fourth, the verse **"The Israelites sent Pinchas to the Reuvenites and Gadites"** [Josh. 22:13]. Fifth, the psalm **"Ascribe to the Lord"** [Ps. 29:1] according to Al-Sheikh.

7. Sixth, **"The Lord will grant strength unto His people"** [Ps. 29:11], concerning peace and other interpretations from *Neve Shalom*.

Marini's sermon opens with Exodus 12:23 ("And the Lord will pass over the doorway"): God has instructed Moses to have the Israelite slaves kill a lamb and smear its blood on their doorposts, so that He passes over their homes and slays only the firstborn of the Egyptians. The abbreviated verse is followed immediately by Marini's *ma'amar*, the rabbinic treatment of an earlier verse in the chapter, Exodus 12:12, emphasizing that God's intervention is direct and unmediated. Marini may be exploiting the discussion in the midrash Mekhilta I, 97, which also links Exodus 12:12 to Exodus 12:29, or the formulation in the Passover Haggadah.[27] He then refers us to Maimonides' *Guide for the Perplexed*, III:46, a discussion of the rationale for the biblical sacrifices and specifically the Paschal lamb, which Maimonides understands as one of a group of rituals that God commanded to reinforce Israelite identity by means of practices abhorrent to their neighbors. Marini could have stressed the importance of ritual observance, but that is not his primary interest here, because he needs to connect Maimonides' words to God's statement in Exodus 12:12. The associative link is the Paschal lamb, but the thematic link comes further in Maimonides' discussion: The Hebrew slaves have lived long among the "false beliefs" of the Egyptians, including the belief that the lamb is sacred. The "cure" for this false belief is the radically antithetical institution of animal sacrifice, which initially appeared to be taboo. For Maimonides, the command to violate the taboo against sheep slaughter was in fact salvific for the Jews.

So, too, Marini will argue, the enforced closure of the ghetto, a command that had seemed life-threatening, had ironically saved Jewish lives. Plague had been viciously active in the Christian city for months, with grim mortality, but in the winter of January 1631, it had yet to appear in the ghetto.[28] Marini's fellow Jews are wondering why they have been spared, and he gets their attention with the tempting explanation that the disparate fates of Christian and Jew reflect God's preferential protection of the Jews. More popular scientific explanations for the plague (biblical and medical) ignore divine causation; Marini shows also that "firstborn" need not be taken literally but can apply to the indiscriminate deaths of Christians. This reading fits his prooftexts for another reason. True, plague has thus far spared the ghetto, but despite the absence of sickness, the ghetto has been closed. As Abraham Catalano tells us in his plague narrative, the Committee of Four on which he played a major role had preemptively ordered foodstuffs and arranged for medical personnel, gravediggers, and housing for the sick, but the decree of total closure was unwelcome. Closure dealt a crippling economic blow to the ghetto and hindered or blocked the import of essential goods. Marini could therefore argue, as Maimonides claimed, that what had looked like it could kill them (closure) had paradoxically been their salvation, a sign of Jewish merit and gentile sin.[29]

But that message would go too easy on his audience. The next prooftext, from Job 10:4, stresses God's direct responsibility for events that we perceive as either catastrophic or lucky (including, supposedly, Egyptian/ Christian mortality and Israelite/Jewish exemption). As I understand its use, the Job verse permits Marini to remind his audience that human perception is limited, especially when it comes to what appears to be unjustified suffering; we must accept that God is directly responsible for good and bad. Marini applies current medical theory to all ten biblical "plagues." The tenth "plague" that brought death to Egypt's firstborn was not a response to a discrete cause but the cumulative result of the preceding nine "plagues" of ecological, zoological, and climate disasters, which corrupted the air and caused mass death. Marini and his audience, like their Christian counterparts, were connecting recent years of drought, bad harvests, and unrest to the outbreak, but Marini argues that these preceding factors were also divinely ordained. The limitations of human knowledge thus pertain to scientific understandings of the plague as well as to the Jews' perception of the ghetto's closure.

The sermon then makes a surprising turn with prooftexts (mis-cited) from Joshua 22, referring to the men of the tribes of Gad and Reuven (and technically, half of Manasseh) who fought alongside their fellow Israelites and then cross the Jordan to claim the territory allocated to them.[30] Joshua 22 describes the Gadites and Reuvenites building an altar on their side of the river, which is perceived as an act of political rebellion (against the full confederacy of the twelve tribes) and religious heresy (against the prohibition on sacrifice beyond the borders of God's domain). The Israelites compared the perceived transgression of the Gadites and Reuvenites to that of Pe'or (Num. 25, Josh. 22:17), whose idolatry triggered a plague. A delegation to the alleged rebels headed by Pinchas ben Elazar quelled the threat of intertribal violence when the Gadites and Reuvenites assured Pinchas that the new altar was not a repudiation of Israelite authority but a reminder of their connection to their kinsmen. Since most of the commentaries on Joshua 22 dwell on the indiscriminate punishment of innocent and wicked, this set of prooftexts might seem ill-suited to expound on the differential fates of Jew and Christian in 1631. Therefore Marini must be focused on another aspect of the Joshua story, namely the righteous outrage of the Israelites, the accused's insistence that they and their accusers shared a common destiny, and the averted threat of internecine conflict.

What might inspire this analogy? Again, Abraham Catalano's narrative suggests an answer. Around the time this sermon would have been given, Abraham's narrative mentions the tensions caused by the flight of a handful of Jews exploiting previously acquired health passes.[31] Elsewhere Abraham refers approvingly to Haim Luria, another ghetto physician who fled the city but donated his wine cellar to the poor and sent money from his place of refuge.[32] Similarly, Abraham's son, Moses, whose didactic plague poems conclude his father's narrative, recommends that those who flee should "bless [their] departure / by giving charity" to support those confined at home.[33] Interestingly, a number of commentaries on the Joshua 22 episode focus on the spoil that the departing tribes wished to share with those they left behind, underlining their sense of collective responsibility. Al-Sheikh's commentary on the Joshua passage—a commentary Marini specifically invokes in his next prooftext—is instructive also. According to Al-Sheikh, wicked people with distinct agendas will join forces if collaboration advances their respective goals; in contrast, the righteous share a common goal but often differ on the way to get there. This is what happened in the case of the Gadites, Reuvenites, and half of the tribe of Manasseh, who strove for the same end as the Israelites but had a different approach to realizing it.

How might Marini have constructed a narrative that moved along these textual signposts? He might have exploited his Joshua 22 prooftexts to discuss communal responsibility. Invoking the common good, he could have encouraged compliance with directives from ghetto officials and the Health Office, care and support for the vulnerable and needy. But the theme of shared spoils lent itself nicely to the crisis posed by Jews who had escaped the ghetto and refused to return. If Marini followed the readings of his favorite glossators, he could have claimed that the appearance of betrayal was misleading: Those who had fled did not break faith with their brethren, but they should prove it by contributing to the survival of those left behind.

Marini swivels to Psalm 29 in conclusion, citing commentaries by Moses Al-Sheikh and Abraham Shalom.[34] If my reading is correct, he begins by luring his congregation into a self-satisfied sense of immunity—the evil Christians are being punished by God while they are exempt. His next step was to undermine their smugness by pointing to the internal strife and conflicts that threatened the ghetto. As Al-Sheikh wrote in his commentary to Psalms 29:11, Marini's prooftext, the "main reason for our troubles in this exile" is the absence of peace. Moreover, Al-Sheikh's reading of Psalm 29:1, which Marini cites, includes the Iberian exile's observation that too much "glory and might" (Ps. 29.1) inclines people to pick fights with each other, causing communal woes. The poor, he notes in contrast, have no such need to squabble. And that is the message Marini's squirming listeners would have to take home. In conclusion, a return to his opening *ma'amar* from Exodus (or the Mekhilta) reminded his listeners of the Almighty's reach into every aspect of their lives: chosen by God they might be, but not exempt from His ongoing scrutiny.

Rosh Hashanah, Second Day, 5392 (September 1631)
NY MS JTS 843, fol. 16a

I have moved through my first example in detail to demonstrate the method I am using to reconstruct Marini's sermon argument from his (or his recorder's) parsimonious outlines. The next few examples follow the same method. Most of the sermon outlines for the weeks between *parashat* Bo and the rise and fall of the plague in the Paduan ghetto are faded so badly that it is difficult to read them, but toward the Jewish New Year of 5392, which fell in September 1631, the script grows easier to decipher. Two of Marini's sermons from that period—recorded for the second day of Rosh Hashanah and the following Sabbath—refer explicitly to the recent plague. The first was notated with atypical detail, consuming twenty-two lines of text and including a fair amount of explanatory ligature between prooftexts. This was an important sermon for Marini, and one whose crafting reflected considerable thought. According to Abraham Catalano, the plague was officially declared over in the ghetto on the thirteenth of Elul; this sermon was delivered less than three weeks later, when the stunning devastation of the ghetto population—421 dead out of 721 residents—still overshadowed questions of rebuilding.[35]

Marini again emphasizes the all-powerful hand of God in tragedy and blessing. His sermon is not simple, but it asserts divine providence is demonstrable through God's inherent "exaltedness," an all-encompassing metaphor of height, might, and grandeur that is beyond human perception or understanding. The equation of "exaltedness" with divine providence guides the following argument. God's exaltedness (providence) is evidenced on earth through His actions, as God Himself is unknowable to human beings. Turning to philosophy or science to explain catastrophic events has led Jews to doubt God's responsibility for the plague, but this belief, a consequence of their admiration for gentile learning, merely reflects the limitations of human knowledge. Moreover, God's providential vigilance assures the reward of the righteous and punishment of the wicked. For humans, these judgments (a New Year's theme) are not always clear, but we should accept God's chastisement, which responds to (bad) choices we make in free will. With his final set of prooftexts, Marini exhorts his listeners to trust in God's providence, now equated with "shelter." God's "shelter" is manifest in divine reward and punishment, on the one hand, and divine exaltedness, on the other, returning Marini to his opening *ma'amar* by extending the reach of divine providence to three encompassing social classes that are also symbolized by the three types of shofar blasts heard at the New Year.

The comparatively full exposition of this sermon in note form illustrates several useful points. The Jewish New Year liturgy was shaped by themes of divine judgment and human repentance, as well as the call to take stock of shortcomings iterated in litanies of public confession. Marini's audience would have been expecting a sermon of some length and complexity on these themes. His concern is suited to the holy day, but at the same time confronts directly the exhausted and traumatized community before him, ravaged by plague and surely wondering what they might have done to deserve it. Marini's answer echoes God's reply to Job, which is that we humans cannot understand God's intentions and should simply trust in their ultimate justice. That was not an easy message to deliver in 1631, when (as he disapprovingly acknowledges) other explanations were available. Nonetheless, much as we saw with his earlier sermon, delivered before the plague had taken a single Jewish life, Marini was willing to hold God's line. His sermon for the following week, as we shall see below, will directly criticize unethical activity in the ghetto. For now let me note the rabbi's willingness to challenge some of the intellectual affiliations percolating in the ghetto and to condemn more brazen attempts to capitalize on the chaos ensuing the plague. While the license to criticize his flock came with the pulpit, he could have coated his rebuke more sweetly. The traces of a public persona enacted in scenes of contested authority lightly echo Abraham Catalano's and Abraham Massarani's self-representations in their very different plague accounts. In the pulpit Marini seems very much a public man in the style of his contemporaries.

My translation follows, and then my reading. The Hebrew transcription may be found in Appendix 1:[36]

5392

I gave this sermon on the second day of Rosh Hashanah after the plague,
in the Ashkenazi synagogue.

1. **"The Lord will be seen"** [Gen. 22:14]. In Midrash Tilim, **"In You, O Lord, I seek refuge"** [Ps. 7:2] you find that God will save anyone who trusts in Him. Since the Holy One Blessed Be He[37]

2. Is hidden with respect to His substance, He must be known through His deeds, and since He is immaterial, He cannot be apprehended by the senses.

3. **"I [am the Lord Your God]"** and **"You shall have no [other gods]"** [Ex. 20:2, 20:3]. From the greatness of the sign, we hear that where you find God's[38] exaltedness, there you

4. Find [Him]. This means that[39] because God is exalted over all material things, this is proof that His providence is everywhere. However, when

5. human beings forgot Him and attributed everything to their own power and strength, He had to make His Name known in the world by His evil [*sic!*]

6. Judgments. Another thing: **"The Lord of Hosts is exalted by judgment"** [Isa. 5:16]. Whenever the Holy One Blessed Be He[40] exacts judgment on the wicked, His Name is made greater in the world,

7. To tell us who we are and what are our lives. **"So is humankind like grass"** [Isa. 40:7]. And generally,[41] people attribute all this to the natural order

8. But [ה"א ?][42] Israel learned from them, hence **"Tell the one my soul loves"** **"by the flocks of your companions"** [Song of Songs 1:7]. And **"they mixed among the nations"** [Ps. 106:35]. The meaning[43] of Isaiah's

9. **"The deaf have heard"** [Isa. 42:8], first from a kabbalistic perspective and then from the perspective of[44] speculative knowledge to clarify the verses that follow and that treat the subject of providence.

10. **"And the righteous clings to his faith"** [cf. Hab. 2:4] [meaning that] when he sees the evil of the [natural] order, he acts as if he did not see or hear it. That is **"who is deaf if not**

11. My servant" [Isa. 42:19], *ma'amar* on the verse[45] "**Attribute to God, O *b'nei elim***" [Ps. 29:1] because they should have replied but didn't. The meaning of the Thirteen Attributes according to which He

12. Conducts Himself with His creatures. For instance,[46] "**there is none Holy [like the Lord]**" [1Sam. 2:2], which enlists negative attributes. As for His deeds, "**Do not speak too much**" [1 Sam 2:3], "**for the Lord is a God of knowledge**" [1 Sam. 2:3]—great knowledge

13. In that he rewards and punishes according to the Thirteen Attributes. And that is "**and deeds are not accounted**" [1 Sam. 2:3]: The verse is written ["not accounted"] with an *alef*, meaning that from a human perspective they appear

14. As if they are not "corrected." But you must read the verse with a *vav*, for in God's perspective they are corrected, and this is "**seeing much, you give no heed**" [Isa. 42:20] and "**The Lord desires [Israel's vindication]**" [Isa. 42:21].

15. So that we are left with free will. The interpretation of "**the sentence for evil is not executed swiftly**" [Eccl. 8:11]. Interpreting the verse through "**he paid no heed**" [Isa. 42:25].

16. The interpretation of the psalm, "**who dwell in the shelter of the Most High**" [Ps. 91:1] as a matter of trust and providence. The righteous man "dwells in the shelter of the Most High"— he knows the foundation of his being.

17. But "**abide in the protection of Shaddai**" refers to His deeds, which He advances with respect to punishment and to exaltedness. The first can be divided

18. Into two [parts], punishment in this world and in the world to come. For the former, it says, "**for He will save you**," and for the latter, "**For You are God, my shelter**" [Ps. 91:9]. For the third [category], which is

19. Exaltedness, "**For He has desired me**" [Ps. 91:14]. Explain the *ma'amar*, "all who trust [in the Lord] shall be saved"—in the world to come if not presently.

20. [This is] because providence adheres to three [categories of people]: the king, the righteous, and the multitude. "**He does not withdraw His eye from the righteous**" [Job 36:7]; "**The Lord of Hosts . . .**" [Isa. 44:6?]

21. **"When you multiply prayers"** [Isa. 1:15]. Another interpretation for the third category is [in the types of shofar blasts]: *teqi'ah, shevarim, teru'ah*, which apply to the three verses. **"Happy is the people**
22. **Who know joyful shouting"** [Ps. 89:16]. Thus concludes the *ma'amar*, and so it says, **"Israel was saved by God for eternal salvation"** [Isa. 45:17].

The Scriptural portion for the second day of Rosh Hashanah is Genesis 22, the story of the near-sacrifice of Isaac as God's test of Abraham. Solomon Marini's prooftext for his sermon was the problematic expression in Genesis 22:14: After the angel's command to sacrifice a ram instead of his son, Abraham names the place of this encounter "Adonai-yireh," literally, "the Lord will see" (reinterpreted in the Torah itself as "the Lord will be seen" to avoid anthropomorphism). The verse has a venerable exegetical history, which Marini tunes to the theme of providence. His *ma'amar*, from the Midrash on Psalm 7:2, cites the psalm's second verse, "In You, O Lord, I seek refuge." The juxtaposition of the Torah and psalm verses hints at Marini's concerns, as the Genesis verse concludes a tale of near-extinction while the Psalms verse is an affirmation of faith. In the wake of their own near-annihilation, how should Marini's listeners find a renewed sense that God acts meaningfully in their lives?

The Midrash *Tehilim* on Psalm 7:2 confirms Marini's focus on questions of plague and theodicy, but also on the nature of reward and punishment, the importance of repentance and trust in God's power to save. The midrashic commentary discusses the inadvertent sins of King David, associating the psalm with David's pursuit of Saul in 1 Samuel 26, where David trapped Saul in a cave but refused to kill him. David argued that one of three outcomes would befall Saul: Either God would "strike" him (which the commentary reads to refer to plague), he would die in battle, or he would die of some other cause. With poetic symmetry, David himself would confront all three options when he angered God by conducting a census and was compelled to choose among three punishments. David chose plague, unleashing massive casualties among the people that are finally arrested by prayer. Thus the plague backdrop is clear, as is God's dislike of censuses, a point worth noting.

Marini turns to God's unknowability. God cannot be apprehended by human senses, but human beings see evidence of His presence through His actions. Unfortunately, when humans prefer explanations for earthly events that stress other factors, God must remind them of their error. Marini links

God's immateriality to His *romemut*, or "exaltedness," which he equates
with providence: From His high, or "exalted" status over the material world,
God sees everything and everywhere. This means that suffering, too, is
meted out as God's way of demonstrating His might. But who should suffer? Marini knows that is the first objection his audience could make: It is
fine if God metes out suffering to the wicked, but why the innocent too?
Marini links God's exalted nature to His judgment of good and evil (Isa.
5:16, in line 6), insisting that God's judgments are just and purposeful. The
same idea runs through the commentaries on Isaiah 5:16, Marini's prooftext: the Midrash *Tehilim* 3:1 says, "the righteous will rejoice when He exe-
cutes judgment because He is exalted in the world"; and the same Midrash
on Psalms 8:6 states, "When is the Holy One Blessed Be He 'high'? When
He exacts judgment on the nations." The Midrash *Tanhuma* to Judges 15:1
expresses the same idea: "The Holy One Blessed Be He is exalted in the
world only through judgment." So, too, Leviticus Rabbah 24:1: "When is
the Name of the Holy One Blessed Be He made great in His world? When
He exercises the principle of judgment against the wicked," and more. Both
the Talmud (Berakhot 12) and the Italian exegete Recanati (par. Emor 19),
link Isaiah 5:16 to the Ten Days of Repentance between Rosh Hashanah
and Yom Kippur, another association Marini can tap. These subsidiary associations undergird the argument that reward and punishment demonstrate God's watchful supervision of human lives and are a category of
action through which divine providence (exaltedness) is manifest in the
world.

Marini's dismissal of alternative explanations for disasters alludes to the
secular interests of Paduan Jews whose love of philosophy and science has led
them to neglect their faith (lines 7–8). Isaiah 42:8 and 42:19 (lines 9–11) provide the enigmatic metaphor of deafness, in the second case misquoting the
verse, which reads "blind" and not "deaf." (Hab. 2:4 is also mis-cited in line
10 in a manner suggesting it has been confused with 1 Sam. 26:23, an uncon-
scious interference from that plague narrative.) Marini will return to this
motif in his next week's sermon. He seems to be saying that even though
catastrophes cause the suffering of innocent people, good Jews will not question God's intention in creating them. The commentators on Isaiah 42:18–19
helpfully invoke the Akkedah story that provides the sermon's opening text
(Gen. 22). The biblical Abraham had good reason to complain to God when
ordered to "offer up" his son Isaac. Instead he remained silent, and his faith

created a credit account for future generations to draw on when requesting clemency. Again human knowledge is limited, a claim now buttressed by Maimonides' assertion that anything we posit about God would be ridiculously limiting; all we can safely say with human language is what God is not—the famous "negative attributes" invoked in line 12. So too do the so-called Thirteen Attributes, recited on Rosh Hashanah, Yom Kippur, Sukkot, Passover, and Shavuot, guarantee God's forgiveness, but for Maimonides also prove that God is ultimately unknowable to the human mind. Similarly, we are unable to gauge the weight given to our actions (line 13, where Marini puns on the distinction between deeds that are "weighed" or "counted" [metukhanim] and deeds that are repaired or corrected [metuqanim]). He is still circling the question of divine justice that from human eyes has gone awry, which is a distortion of human perception.

Marini returns to Isaiah 42 and the servant's "blindness" and "deafness" to God's intended purpose for him. God must weigh human deeds and punish bad choices. Marini cannot evade the objection that plenty of evil goes unpunished. One of his favorite commentators, Moses Al-Sheikh, dwells at length on this problem in his interpretation of Ecclesiastes 8:11 (Marini's prooftext in line 15), probing a list of possible explanations for the deferral of judgment on the wicked, eliminating each option to conclude that the question is beyond human comprehension. This is exactly what Marini is saying. Moreover, even justice deferred is ultimately enacted and testifies to God's meticulous account-keeping. The shift to Psalm 91 brings Marini squarely back to a plague context, as this psalm was (and still is) cited routinely in plague liturgies used by Jews and Christians. Plague, a form of punishment, is also an invitation to repent.

Marini begins to swing back to his opening ma'amar and the need to trust in God as our "refuge" (or "shelter"—line 18). The term "shelter" is equated with two manifestations of God's presence, judgment (reward and punishment), and exaltedness. The opening section of the sermon has demonstrated that exaltedness manifests providence, and the middle section that reward and punishment likewise demonstrate God's action in the world. A concluding string of prooftexts from Job 36:7, Isaiah 44:6, and Isaiah 1:15 associates exaltedness and judgment with three categories of people: kings, the righteous, and the rest of us, all summoned by Isaiah 1:15's call to amplify prayer. Marini adds a holiday-themed interpretation of the three categories, associating each with one kind of shofar blast heard on Rosh Hashanah, converging his themes of providence, plague, and holy day into one. For those who will trust in God, salvation is assured if not imminent, and present suffering should not let them falter on the path—or express doubt in the power and willingness of an unknowable deity to settle accounts.

Shabbat Teshuvah 5392 (1631)
NY MS JTS 843, fol. 16a

The surviving notes for Marini's sermon for the Sabbath following Rosh Hashanah are spare, covering six lines of text immediately below the grand sermon we have just examined. This may reflect the fact that it was a direct and topical sermon, welding the traditional theme of repentance associated with this Sabbath to a critique of specific ethical lapses. Other illustrations of this genre of reproof survive in the printed sermons of Marini's Jewish and Christian contemporaries, and we have some idea of the behaviors they condemned. A near-obsessive concern with women's clothing (immodest in cut or ostentatious in display), or the evils of tennis-playing, gambling, sexual license, or disregard for synagogue attendance, are not the focus of this sermon, however. Rather, as I reconstruct it, Solomon Marini condemns predatory legal or financial actions and real estate transactions that have sprung up in the wake of the plague. This sermon therefore offers a startling window onto the disarray that ensued with the deaths of more than half the ghetto inhabitants and the destabilization of existing mechanisms of self-government. Despite its minimalism, its thrust emerges by following Marini's prooftexts.

The traditional Scriptural portion for what the manuscript labels "Shabbat Shuvah" (more commonly referred to as "Shabbat Teshuvah"), the "Sabbath of Repentance" that falls between Rosh Hashanah and Yom Kippur, is from Deuteronomy 32:1–52, God's call to Israel to accept His covenant and the blessings that derive from it, or the curses that will follow disobedience. Marini's prooftext is Deuteronomy 32:46, which reads in full, "Pay attention to all the words I enjoin upon you this day." His *ma'amar* again draws on Midrash *Tehilim*, here on Psalm 17:8, where David (the putative author of the psalm) beseeches God to "guard me like the pupil of Your eye." The Midrash recycles a familiar scenario from Marini's *ma'amar* the previous week. King David has taken a census of the people, and an angry God forces him to choose among three punishments—death, war, or plague. He picks plague. The Midrash associates this story with David's pursuit of Saul in 1 Samuel 26, another tale of plague as chastisement.

Well-studied by Marini, Arama's *'Akedat Yitzhak* (97:1:4) read Deuteronomy 32:46 on multiple levels, referring not just to the collective well-being of Israelite society but to individual physical and spiritual "health" too. War, disease of the body politic, is caused by material conflict; physical illness is caused by an analogous "war" of humors in a state of imbalance; and spiritual sickness appears when our wicked impulses rebel against "the king." This last sickness is like a "fever in the bones," curable only by God. One of Marini's subsequent prooftexts suggests he exploited this analogy to refer to a trifecta of social disorder, plague, and sin. The *ma'amar* leads first to a theme developed on Rosh Hashanah: What we perceive as misfortune or catastrophe has been divinely ordained as a punishment or a trial. Terrible events like plague, whether biblical or Paduan, do not mean God has abandoned His care for us (as the "pupil of His eye") but instead are a consequence of sins against God and sins against fellow Jews. Marini will develop both categories, stressing neglect of synagogue ritual and prayer for the former, and predatory greed in the legal vacuum left by the plague for the latter. The pitiful condition of the ghetto offers fuel to Christian claims that God has ceased to favor them, but God is not to blame. The current suffering of the Jews is instead a direct result of "violence and robbery due to the plague" (line 4). The climax of his sermon is introduced with the familiar Mishnaic metaphor of the world standing on "three pillars" of Torah, worship, and righteous deeds. All three categories of "pillar" are collapsing as a result of Jewish neglect of the prayer house, unethical real estate transactions, and "evil writs." Having delivered this condemnation, Marini would have cycled back to his opening *ma'amar* to exhort his listeners to repent and seek God's mercy.

My translation follows. The Hebrew transcription may be found in Appendix 1.

Shabbat Teshuvah

1. **"Pay attention to all the words"** [Deut. 32:46]. In the Midr[ash] Tilim, [it says] **"David said to the Holy One Blessed Be He, 'guard me like the pupil of Your eye'"** [Ps. 17:8]. The Holy One [unclear?][47]

2. **[Three?] The third judgment**[48] of the [people of?] Israel. When he saw them he complained, for as it says, "God's word caused me

mockery and contempt" [Ps. 44:14, Jer. 20:8]. "I said, I will not
mention Him" [Jer. 20:9].

3. Furthermore, I have wanted for several years to speak on this
   Sabbath about matters related to God's holiness and the atonement of sins. But what can I do

4. When "the land has been filled with violence" [Gen. 6:11] and
   robbery due to the plague. And the matter of the fall of "the three
   pillars of the world" refers to "Torah, worship, and righteous
   deeds" [Mishnah Avot 1, 2].[49]

5. "The pillars of heaven tremble" [Job 26:11]. "And every wall will
   fall to the earth." [Ezek. 38:20]. As for robbery, the verse[50] "woe
   to those who join house to house" [Isa. 5:8]. "Woe to those who
   make evil writs" [Isa. 10:1].

6. Worship refers to matters of the synagogue and Torah. Righteous deeds [to] neglect of Torah. Explain the ma'amar.[51]

Marini's opening prooftext from Deuteronomy is glossed variously
in the sources. However, Arama's analogy to social, physical, and spiritual "warfare" is attractive because we know that Marini is going to
posit a connection between the unethical behavior of individuals that
imperils the plague-struck community. His listeners already expect this
to be a sermon about repentance, and the ma'amar from Midrash Tehilim
directly returns us to plague as divine punishment, a theme developed
in the Rosh Hashanah sermon Marini had delivered several days earlier.
The story of David's plea to be safeguarded "like the pupil of [God's]
eye" permits Marini to elaborate on the two categories of sin—against
God and against humans—for which the holy day season asks Jews to
atone.

The motif of the census as the catalyst of God's wrath is intriguing. A
census was in fact taken in the ghetto the previous spring, by order of the
Paduan Sanità (Health Office), before plague had erupted in the ghetto
but when it was already active in the Christian city. According to Abraham
Catalano, the census was ordered in Adar, and the Jews were distressed by
it, eventually complying by collecting a coin from each person and donating
it to charity.[52] The first case of plague did not appear in the ghetto until
months later, in Elul, almost a year before this sermon was given. However,
at the end of the epidemic, Abraham Catalano records new tallies of how
many Jews survived, how many recovered, how many escaped sickness, and

how many fled the ghetto. He breaks down the mortality statistics by gender and marital status as well.[53] It is possible, therefore, that a second tally had recently taken place and that Marini or some element of his constituency was concerned about the census as a violation of religious taboo.[54]

With the next two prooftexts, paraphrasing Jerermiah 20:8–9 (corrupted by echoes of Ps. 44:14), Marini points to the abject state of the ghetto, which is evident to the "nations." This might seem like a poor reward for their fidelity to God. The full verse from Jeremiah 20:9, elided in the outline, reads "I said, I will not mention Him, I will speak His Name no more—but in my heart it burned like fire, shut up in my bones."[55] This image is echoed in Arama's commentary on Deuteronomy 32:46 (Marini's opening prooftext), where Arama described spiritual illness as a "fever in the bones" curable only by God. Through these prooftexts Marini verbalizes the emotional exhaustion, bafflement, and anger that must have characterized the survivors sitting before him. Marini insists that divine protection still shields them. At the same time, as in his previous sermon (and in good prophetic tradition), he encourages a false sense of security in his audience by praising their loyalty in the face of external derision.

Deflation comes swiftly. The outline preserves the transition. "For several years," Marini (or his recorder) wrote, he has wanted to talk about sanctity and atonement on the Sabbath of Repentance, but "what can I do when 'the land has been filled with violence' [Gen. 6:11] and robbery due to the plague?" The allusion to the biblical Flood reminds Marini's audience that widespread violence led to global destruction once before. Marini has no desire to stay safely in the realm of the generic, though; the next set of prooftexts levels a critique against predatory greed in the ghetto and the emboldened ruthlessness of men with power. He begins with the familiar citation from *Pirke Avot* that the world stands on the three pillars of Torah, worship, and righteous deeds. Alas, all three pillars have fallen. Marini links each one to biblical verses, moving from celestial to terrestrial to local images of structural collapse. Job 26:11 describes celestial pillars shaking, and Ezekiel 38:20 foresees toppling mountains and walls on earth. Isaiah 5:8 describes the greed of those who "join house to house," presumably displacing the original tenants, perhaps knocking down walls. Rashi glossed the "evil writs" of Isaiah 10:1 to refer to forged documents, and Radaq (David Kimhi) thought the verse alluded to corrupt judges and notaries. Marini is pointing a finger at individuals who have taken advantage of vacant housing or housing whose inhabitants cannot defend their right to the space, while others have twisted the law to dishonest gain.

Abraham Catalano again suggests what some of this finger-pointing meant. Immediately following his statistical breakdown of survivors, Catalano describes the "many" households left with one survivor, sometimes an infant or minor. Among Moses Grasseto's household, for instance, eleven family members died, leaving only one grandson "who had no share or portion in their inheritance, but inherited everything." Catalano continues: "And there were many similar cases. The inheritances revolved from house to house, this one inherited the property of the master of the household, that one the dowry of his wife, and still others who lived elsewhere gained inheritances. As I have said, I saw an upside-down world."[56] Marini's use of Isaiah 5:18, then, does not refer to the physical knocking down of walls to expand houses but to the "joining" (consolidation) of properties in the chaos of post-plague opportunity. To make matters worse, on the fifth of Tishre, a large group of Jews who had been convalescing outside the ghetto returned to be enclosed at home for an additional eight days. If their absentee property had been unjustly claimed by new owners, or if the disputed lodgings were the "revolving" inheritances of the dead, we do not know, but the strain on ghetto housing was great.

It is worth reflecting on how the rabbi's attack was received. True, he was the rabbi—and the ghetto's only rabbi now, with the deaths of all the others—but this critique is bold. Catalano's plague narrative preserved at least one instance where Marini's attempt to dictate to the community met with dissent; this was when he tried to impose a public fast in the thick of the epidemic. Sermons of rebuke were familiar to Marini's listeners, but generic chiding of the sort they had heard on Rosh Hashanah was more palatable than a pointed attack. Notably, Marini's contemporary farther south, the famous physician, rabbi, and preacher Jacob Zahalon, cautioned against broadside attacks from the pulpit in his preachers' manual, the *Or haDarshanim*.[57] Zahalon wrote:

> Part 10, sect. 2: When reproving [the people], he should indicate to them that he is . . . chastising himself. He ought to speak with respect for the people, never in a contemptuous or insulting manner. . . .

Part 10, sect. 3: He should be extremely careful to avoid preaching in such a way as to rebuke or shame others—God forbid—for it is not right "to make unworthy use of the crown" of Torah (M. Avot 1:13) to take vengeance against one's enemies. Rather, in his reproofs [the preacher] should speak pleasantly and not in a harsh manner . . . as a father who is [lovingly] chastising his own children.[58]

In Amsterdam, Saul Levi Morteira delivered his own sermon of rebuke on the same Sabbath day that Solomon Marini turned his wrath on his fellow Paduan Jews. Confirming the ubiquity of themes of repentance and providence for this Sabbath, Morteira aimed his critique at his *converso* audience; yet, in Saperstein's words, his strong "reprimands" referred only to generic misdeeds, and "the overall impression left is upbeat."[59]

As Padua's last living rabbi, Solomon Marini may not have worried about losing his job. But he may have also been temperamentally comfortable with direct confrontation from the pulpit; his audience may also have heard the language of rebuke issued from that perch as part of his domain. In this regard it is telling that when the rabbi tried to extend his influence to matters outside the walls of the synagogue, "many people" rebelled. Had we access to Marini's full sermon text as he wished it to be remembered, we would know more. Still, even the outlines suggest that the public persona of the preacher gained wattage from positioned opposition, quite in contradistinction to Zahalon's advice. If that is the case, then Solomon Marini shared with Abraham Catalano, Abraham Massarani, Judah Modena, and other contemporaries of the northern Italian ghettos a penchant for self-fashioning that intensified with resistance. In other words, a sermon, too, can convey public identity—the rabbi's and his congregation's. For the latter, these sermons limn an audience whose preacher thought in need of deeper Jewish learning, but also sharper boundaries between Jew and non-Jew, between real and ideal behavior, between the harsh challenges of an "upside-down world" and the desire to live decently and well. For the preacher, the sermon projected a persona who had the moral authority of God's proxy, while simultaneously embodying his flock and all their foibles. Like all public identities, as I have argued in the preceding chapters, the preacher's public persona could also sink roots in its maker and shape the way he thought of himself. Marini in the pulpit had to coexist somehow with Marini in the market or at the dinner table. How much did one identity permeate the other? Ask a few preachers what they think.

Parashat Noah, 5417 (1656)
NY MS JTS 6517 (Rab. 432), fol. 58r

My final example is Marini's sermon outline for *parashat* Noah, delivered in Padua in 1656. Just as the plague of 1630–31 had ravaged northern Italy but ignored the rest of the peninsula, the outbreak of 1656 was horrendous in central Italy but left the north unscathed. In the Paduan ghetto, twenty-six years after the traumatic events of 1630–31, Solomon Marini was still alive and preaching. His friend Abraham Catalano had died in 1641, and by 1656 so had many other survivors of the 1631 plague. Marini himself was seventy or older when conditions in the Roman ghetto brought him to plead with Paduan Jews to send aid to their plague-stricken brethren. The Scriptural portion Noah fell in mid-October, a few weeks into the New Year. Marini took Genesis 8:11 as his prooftext; the verse refers to the dove Noah sent out from the ark to seek dry land. On the first foray the dove returned empty-"handed" but on the second try carrying an olive leaf or twig, a sign that dry land and foliage were beginning to reemerge. For his *ma'amar*, Marini turns to a Talmudic fable (B. Eruvin 18b) in which the dove declares that she would rather eat bitter olive leaves knowing that they were provided by God than be dependent on humans for finer fare. The sermon threads together a series of prooftexts that illustrate the need for compassion, counterpointed by examples of failure to care for those in need. Marini returns to his *ma'amar* to urge his listeners to help the suffering Jews in Rome: The dove represents an ideal of unadulterated reliance on God, but Marini underscores that we are still responsible for each other.

Information about the Rome ghetto during the 1656 plague comes to us from several sources, among them the writings of Jacob Zahalon. I have already mentioned Zahalon's preaching manual, but he has left us a wealth of writings in traditional and scientific genres.[60] His medical compendium, the *Otzar haHayim* ("Treasury of Life") is a comprehensive blend of theory and empirical observation, incorporating a number of anecdotes illustrating medical principles or conditions.[61] The *Otzar*'s section on epidemic fevers includes an account of Zahalon's experience treating plague patients in Rome in 1656, beginning with a familiar portrait of an urban landscape thrust into disorder and fear. A vivid illustration of plague delirium describes a sick woman who escaped her sickbed and tried to throw herself in the Tiber. In the ghetto itself, Zahalon recounts an incident in which his diagnosis of a patient was challenged by a Christian physician. After the patient's death, much to Zahalon's relief, an autopsy confirmed his diagnosis.[62] The richly detailed account of medical protocols in the ghetto also conveys the overwhelmed state of the ghetto and the calamitous conditions that were known as far away as Padua, inspiring the sermon whose remains I treat below.[63]

My translation follows. The Hebrew transcription appears in Appendix 1.

The Holy Sabbath, *Parashat* Noah, on the Needs of the Jewish Community in Rome

MS JTS 6517 (Rab. 432), fol. 58r

1. **"And the dove came to him"** [Gen. 8:11]. In Eruvin, the dove said, **"Let my sustenance"** [B. Eruvin 18b]. The Mishnah says, **"You shall love your neighbor as yourself"** is the encompassing rule of the whole Torah [B. Shabbat 31a]

2. Not just [unclear?] but also to benefit the collective and the individual [in need]. That is the purpose of Creation and the created. [Maimonides] was not correct in what he said

3. In the Guide, part III, section 13. [To benefit his property?] he offered his life. As it says, **"And if not, wipe me out"** [Ex. 32:32]. As Jonah said,

4. **"Take my life"** [Jonah 4:3]. As Job said, **"Have I not wept for those in hardship?"** [Job 30:25] As David said, **"And when they were sick, I [prayed]"** [Ps. 35:13]. All who feel pain

5. For the suffering of the collective. For the suffering of the faithful community of Rome, shut in and impoverished by the plague. [?] Jonah's words

6. Allude to [. . .] mission. The raven was cruel and did not feel sorry [for Noah]. Ham violated his father's bed and saw his disgrace,

7. and he did not feel sorry [for him]. The interpretation of "let my sustenance": May Israel not need to support one another or another

8. people, but [eat] from the table of their Father in Heaven.

Marini's prooftext comes from Genesis 8:11 and the story of the Flood.
In Genesis 8:11 the dove released by Noah returns to the ark with a torn olive
leaf or twig, indicating that the waters are finally receding. The *ma'amar*
comes from a Talmudic legend in which the dove prefers the bitter olive leaf
provided by God to the finer food she might merit as a pet. Marini takes
this fable in an interesting direction by immediately tagging it to the famous "Golden Rule" of Leviticus 19:18, here embedded in its own rabbinic
legend of the potential convert who came to Rabbis Shammai (the strict)
and Hillel (the gentle) and asked to be taught the whole Torah "on one foot."[64]
Shammai replied that this was impossible, but Hillel recited the Golden
Rule's dictum to "love your neighbor as yourself," adding that this was the
encompassing principle of all the Torah. What does this story have to do
with the dove and her bitter leaf of independence? The second line is not
entirely legible, but logically Marini's next step is to connect love of one's
"neighbor" (*re'akha*) to designate both individuals and collectives. If this is
the essence of Torah, it follows that Marini thinks that Maimonides erred
in his treatment of the purpose of Creation. In the passage alluded to in
outline, Maimonides distinguished between Aristotelian and Jewish views.
For Aristotle the purpose of Creation is the perfection of received form. For
Jews this answer is inadequate. Since God was never "created," He has no
need of a purpose, and gains nothing by our efforts to perfect ourselves. The
work of perfection must therefore be for us, not God, but why? For Jews,
Maimonides says, the purpose of humanity is to worship God. Marini rejects
this argument because it is fundamentally asocial; he seeks to restore the
ethical and social dimensions of "Torah" to a sense of our core purpose in life.
He proceeds to develop this idea with four examples of biblical figures who
were willing to risk or forfeit their lives on behalf of others, and then two
examples of biblical figures who failed to show compassion.

The prooftexts from, respectively, Exodus 32:32, Jonah 4:3, Job 30:25, and
Psalms 35:13 are the positive examples. Upon descending from the mountain
with the tablets of the Law, Moses discovered the Israelites worshiping a
golden calf. The Israelites are punished, first with a plague and then with an
attack by their fellow Levites, leaving thousands dead. Moses pleaded with
God to forgive the survivors or "if not, wipe me out from Your book" (Ex. 32:32).
The verse has a rich commentary tradition but with considerable overlap of
understanding. Particularly for Nahmanides (Ramban) and Ovadiah ben Jacob
Sforno, Moses' plea must be read as his offer to substitute himself for the guilty
Israelites, either by letting his merits count on their behalf or by offering his

life in vicarious atonement. Like Marini, several midrashic texts associate this scene with Jonah's cry to God to "take my life" (Jonah 4:3)—a spin on Jonah's words that runs counter to how we read them today. For modern readers, Jonah's irritation with the penitent people of Nineveh, who make him look silly for his prophecy of doom, is contrasted with the compassion he feels for the withered gourd tree that had provided him with shade. For earlier readers Jonah's statement was linked to his previous command to the sailors to throw him overboard to save themselves and their ship; thus both Jonah and Moses were willing to risk their lives on behalf of the collective.[65]

Marini adds Job to his list, citing Job's bitter recrimination to God, "Did I not weep for the unfortunate, or grieve for the needy?" (Job 30:25). Again, in context, Job's words challenge God: His question is rhetorical, a righteous assertion that his care for others makes his own suffering even more inexplicable. Moses Al-Sheikh, one of Marini's go-to commentators, read Job's words differently, asking if perhaps Job felt sorry for the poor and unfortunate in his heart ("soul") but did not take physical action on their behalf. "Feeling bad" is not good enough. Al-Sheikh taints poor Job's character more than the text demands, but it is the kind of reading Marini would like in this context and may have exploited. King David, for his part, reminded God that he had prayed for his enemies when they were sick (Ps. 35:13). This verse, too, generated considerable discussion over the centuries. Among Marini's reading favorites, we find the Zohar explaining that we are commanded to pray for the wicked to repent; in fact, it is forbidden to pray for the destruction of the wicked because there is no knowing what future worthy might never come to exist. If God had destroyed the idolator Terah, his son Abraham would not have been born, and so on. God will destroy what is totally and irrevocably evil, but not if there is a chance for evil to change to good or produce future good. This argument goes some way to responding to the familiar question of why God lets the wicked prosper, but the psalm also lets Marini point to David as someone who was willing to pray even for groups of people who had meant him harm.

Marini draws together his examples to conclude that God rewards those who feel compassion for collective suffering—he invokes the expression *tzarat ha-tzibbur* much as his contemporaries would invoke the "common good." He then drives his point home: Today's suffering collective is the Jewish community in Rome, "shut in and impoverished by the plague" (line 5). Noah's dove suggests his first counter-example of indifference to suffering, the "cruel" raven who preceded her and never returned to the ark. So, too,

Noah's son Ham had contempt for his father and felt no sorrow on his father's behalf.

It is not clear to me how Marini maneuvered from this position back to his *ma'amar* and the dove with her bitter leaf. Certainly he has argued that God rewards those who express compassion for the suffering of others and disapproves of those who fail to show compassion. He returns to the dove and the wish that we could simply trust in God to provide. We can speculate that he would have then concluded that for now, nonetheless, we depend on each other, and should donate to those in need.

Taken together, Marini's sermon outlines suggest several conclusions. Even among these four examples, the first three spanning nine months and the last delivered decades later, certain themes recur. If Marini's concerns were justified, they imply that people expressed doubt about the meaning of the plague. Each of the 1631 sermons in its own way addresses questions of shattered or shaky belief, sometimes under the umbrella assumption that rational science is to blame. That target is also worth noting. Indirectly or directly, Marini's preoccupation in these plague-themed sermons with the dangers of secular learning testifies to the interests of a class of Paduan Jews whose intellectual and professional interests owed much to education and contacts in the Christian world—despite the fact of the ghetto. Marini emphasizes the inadequacy, even danger, of philosophy and natural science as ways of explaining the world. How much of his audience was characterized by this tendency is hard to say, but certainly these are interests that were shared by the ghetto's learned elite, and in some diluted form by the bankers and merchants who were second-tier consumers of secular knowledge. It is also true that "philosophy" or physics could serve as strawmen for a more general, plague-driven crisis of faith. Bereaved men and women who had lost family members, neighbors, and friends, like Jews who were dispossessed or financially devastated, were not necessarily rejecting belief in divine providence in favor of Aristotle or Galen. Marini targets the instability of faith in the wake of the plague in the language of faith versus science. Whether that binary was itself a trope for wider social dismay remains to be discovered.

Solomon Marini also reflects a generation of preachers who took pride in preaching and who brought to their sermons a deep knowledge of Jewish sacred texts and their vast commentary tradition, including works of philosophy and Kabbalah. And yet at the same time we see from these examples that Marini also returned to the biblical psalms, familiar to a general audience, and to the Midrash *Tehilim*, if not also familiar at least engaging to those without philosophical or Talmudic training. He spoke to a diverse audience and exploited a range of techniques to keep them attentive. A comparatively complex sermon, like the one represented by the outline for the second day of Rosh Hashanah, would have been expected as keeping with the solemnity of the day. A fundraising pitch demanded another strategy, combining a colorful fable with a rendering of a community's distress and the obligation to help them.

Each of these outlines tells us something about a rabbinic response to the plague of 1630–31, but also about the conditions in the ghetto that this particular rabbi sought to address. Sometimes he does so indirectly, marshaling Jewish texts and alluding to contemporary fallacies to make a general critique of what he saw as laxity in faith, overinvestment in secular rationales for disaster, suffering, or disease. The outline for the sermon delivered for *Parashat* Bo cleverly exploits the Jews' willingness to believe that the plague has spared them as a sign of God's favor by developing this theme into a closer look at intra-Jewish tensions and the dangers they portend. The direct critique of unethical behavior in the ghetto at the heart of the sermon for Shabbat Teshuvah is remarkable, especially when we turn to Abraham Catalano's plague narrative for a more explicit sense of the behavior involved. Here we glimpse not only the disarray of the institutional and legal arrangements that have been stressed to breaking by an epidemic that left more than half of the ghetto's inhabitants dead, but also the moral outrage the rabbi was determined to summon in a confrontation with his fellow Jews.

That moment of tension and confrontation is fascinating when considered with the literary examples of public men testing lines of identity in challenges from above or below. The sermon, it is true, can lend itself to this kind of opposition. But, as Jacob Zahalon (and most homiletics professors) would remind us, the sermon of rebuke that pits preacher against audience is not ideal for selling a message, nor is it a recipe for making friends. It says something about the urgency of the moment that Solomon Marini broke form with earlier sermons and said what he had to say. Twenty-six years later, when plague brought suffering and death to the ghetto of Rome, Marini also spoke directly to his purpose. A context of plague, then, might heighten the recourse to oppositional self-presentation, but it is a heightening of conventions that predated these epidemics. Oppositional preaching is not successful as a stratagem unless an audience is also conditioned to its forms and understands the conventions that underlie it; the willingness to tolerate rebuke testifies to an accepted social idiom. When the forms of that idiom are breached, the rebuke can go awry. I do wonder how Marini's audience received his sermon for Shabbat Teshuvah in 1631. My guess is that not everyone was pleased.

"Few issues of significance escaped the scrutiny and judgment of the clergy," Saperstein wrote, which is one reason that these outlines—especially in the absence of full sermons—are valuable historical witnesses to us now.[66] Still, medieval and early modern preachers were not just preaching for history or professional advancement. As Saperstein also notes, they wanted people to change. Were they successful? According to Saperstein, "Not a few confessed their doubts."[67] Did property and inheritance controversies diminish after Marini's sermon? If only the Paduan communal registers survived for this period—but they do not, additional testimony to the disruptions wrought by plague.

The next and last chapter returns to my personal favorite of the men whose public identities and private shadows have occupied this work. In 1641, when Abraham Catalano was buried, his old friend and rabbi, Solomon b. Isaac Marini, gave his eulogy. Two other compositions also mark Abraham's death: a lament by his son, Moses, the author of the didactic plague poems treated in Chapter 3, and the long epitaph that graces his grave in the Jewish cemetery in Padua. I have been asking how men like Abraham Catalano wished to be seen as public figures, and how they used their writing to project a public identity that reciprocally illuminates bits of the private man. My final chapter asks how other men did see Abraham Catalano, and what the interplay of identities crafted by their owners and crafted for them by others can tell us.

Chapter 6

Eulogies, Laments, and Epitaphs
The Death of the Narrator

Abraham Catalano, whose account of the 1631 plague in the Paduan ghetto has figured so prominently in this book, died in Padua on 12 Tishre 5402—by the Christian calendar, September 6, 1641. The physician, philosopher, and public servant had outlasted the terrible plague by a decade, continuing to burnish a reputation for public service, philanthropy, and dedication to study. I have tried to demonstrate how much Abraham's public persona, exemplified in his plague narrative, contributed to his sense of himself as a private individual. This last chapter shifts perspective to ask how others saw Abraham Catalano: What relationship did Abraham's self-presentation have to the ways he was seen by others, and how should that harmony or dissonance inform our reading of the plague testimonies he and his contemporaries left behind? Indeed, how large did the devastating plague of 1631 loom in what others remembered of Abraham Catalano and what was passed down as public memory?

The texts that might answer these questions come from a variety of commemorative genres, each with its own conventions, agendas, and intended audience. Specifically, two rabbinic eulogies, one poetic lament, and a gravestone epitaph leave some record of Abraham's life as those around him wished it remembered.[1] They are not innocent documents. The sermonic eulogies were written and delivered by Abraham's old friend and colleague Solomon Marini, whose plague sermons were treated in the previous chapter. The poetic lament is by Moses Catalano, Abraham's sole surviving son, whose didactic plague poems concluded his father's narrative. Neither Solomon nor Moses saw Abraham dispassionately—how could they?—and touches of personal emotion, as well as a degree of self-investment, may be sensed in their commemorative texts. The epitaph shapes Abraham's legacy for posterity in stone, not paper; presumably, Moses and other friends and family members had some say in its wording, but its author is unknown. Curiously, it is the only commemorative text for Abraham that mentions plague at all, and I want to ask why its presentation of Abraham's life diverges from that of the eulogies or lament.

Why does it matter how these authors saw Abraham Catalano? The answer is not just a claim to insight into the ever-fascinating tension between how others may see us and how we fashion ourselves for their seeing. It bears also on the entire collection of plague-related testimonies discussed in this book, and how we read them. Whatever spillover audience they acquired, the eulogies and lament sustain a dialogue among peers whose shared learning and values crystallize in the depiction of their kinsman and friend. Allusions to familiar texts and cultural debates echo in these texts, enlisting the grief of mourners to reinforce their claims. If public self-presentation was important to men like Abraham Catalano, these commemorative efforts further demonstrate that public identity was performative, a vehicle for communicating values, behaviors, and ideals to communities who took this staging of identity seriously. By extension, contemporary plague narratives, chronicles, or communal laments also reveal a highly imbricated construct of public and private identity distinct from our own and not entirely amenable to the same assumptions. This difference has implications for how we gauge individual and social responses to plague beyond the written or printed page.

When Abraham Catalano died—and we do not know how—he may have been in his late fifties to early sixties. He tells us in his plague narrative, the *'Olam Hafukh*, that he had been married for twenty years when his beloved Sarah died of plague in 1631. It is unlikely he would have married before finishing his medical studies in Padua, and marriage trends among northern Italian Jews in the seventeenth century favored mature grooms.[2] If he was twenty when he married, he would have been fifty-one at his death, but he was probably some years older. He had been through a lot. The plague of 1631 had taken his wife and four children; before and throughout the epidemic, he held enormous responsibility as one of the Committee of Four managing plague policy for the ghetto. After the epidemic we find his name on a variety of documents ranging from financial and legal decisions to marriage contracts, where he shows up as a witness.[3] Three of the four testimonies discussed in what follows refer to his involvement in a school for boys, not mentioned elsewhere. He did not remarry, and Moses and a much younger daughter, Perla, were his sole surviving children. By the time of his father's death, Moses himself was a father to several daughters, two of whom predeceased him.[4] Perla married into the Gans family of Prague and may have relocated there.[5]

The twelfth of Tishre, the day of Abraham's death, fell between the great Jewish Day of Atonement, Yom Kippur, and the harvest festival, Sukkot. During this period petitionary *tahanun* are not recited, and apparently in Abraham's Padua, eulogies were also prohibited until after the end of Sukkot (which lasts eight days).[6] This delay explains why Solomon Marini's sermon outlines for this period include two eulogy texts, one a small graveside eulogy and one a much fuller text delivered approximately three weeks later in the synagogue; both eulogies allude to the deferral of public commemoration for a cherished leader and friend. The shorter outline takes up only seven lines and suggests a simple homage—a place marker for the bereaved until a public eulogy was permitted. In contrast, the longer outline, for a eulogy delivered in the Italian synagogue for the Sabbath of *parashat* (pericope) Lekh Lekha (Gen. 12–17), testifies to a formal composition; it takes up two dozen lines of text in the manuscript and has a complex, showy argument that enlists rather than suppresses the rabbi's personal grief to validate his authority among the mourners.

Let us examine these texts in chronological order, beginning with the short outline for the graveside remarks Marini delivered the day after Abraham's death, and then the public eulogy. I follow the format developed in the preceding chapter: first, a summary of how I reconstitute the sermon from the outline; second, a translation of the outline from the Hebrew; third, a more detailed commentary and analysis.

Marini's burial homily must have been brief; the mourners would have anticipated that expanded remarks would be deferred for a public commemoration. Despite the skimpy notation, it is possible to reconstruct a deeper web of associations and allusions that link the recorded prooftexts. Some of the verses and imagery are tethered to the figure of Eleazar ben Pedat, a third-century rabbi who utters several of Marini's Talmudic prooftexts. Marini enumerates several rationales for the custom of eulogizing the dead, dismissing each one as irrelevant in the present case and including himself among the mourners who grieve Abraham's death. The homily ends with a philosophical twist.

Bold print identifies a biblical citation, italics a rabbinic citation, and underlined italics mark a biblical citation embedded in a rabbinic one. Occasionally, I have added a word or two in brackets to clarify the meaning. The Hebrew transcription may be found in Appendix 2.

NY MS JTS 6517, fol. 7v

On Tuesday 13 Tishre, eulogy for the honorable teacher Reb Abraham Catalano z"l, before the burial:

1. **"To His right *esh dat* for them—surely a lover of the people"** [Deut. 33:2]. "*When R. Pedat died, 'today is a hard day for Israel, <u>like sunset at noon</u>'*" [b. Mo'ed Qatan 25b, citing Amos 8:9].[7] If mourning and eulogizing are supposed to arouse

2. Weeping, this [eulogy] would be superfluous, **"for our eyes pour forth water"** [Jer. 9:17]. And if to proclaim his praises, the same [holds] for they are evident to all. And if for the feeling of loss, also.

3. Even so, it is impossible to [find] help in words, who can. The first eulogy given in the world was by the Creator for Adam, because of "AYYEKA"—"AYKA"

4. Written with a[n extra] *yud*.[8] Because what is permitted has been forbidden,[9] there is no place to say this is it. **"And you look at his place and today he is no more"** [Ps. 37:10]. When loss did not touch

5. Him [?][10] at all, and was all for the one eulogized. David for Saul. Because others suffered the loss, like Israel. But this loss touches us

6. The meaning of "*today is a hard day for Israel.*" Meaning of **"And I will bring the sunset"** [Amos 8:9] and **"I will turn your holidays to mourning"** [Amos 8:10]. A stern prophecy from two aspects: What is beneficial is separated from the natural order, that is from the providential. "Your holidays" alludes to providential benefits that He multiplies to benefit the natural ones

Marini's *nosé*, from Deuteronomy 33:2, is an enigmatic verse that describes God with an *esh dat* to His right; in modern English-language Bibles, the expression is often translated as a "fiery flame" or some such term, but traditional Jewish exegesis understood it to mean "Torah." God's love for His people is thus intimately connected to the gift of Torah and its laws.

Marini dares an analogy between God and Abraham Catalano, whose life also was characterized by his love for his people and obedience to God's law. Abarbanel's commentary on Deuteronomy 33:2–3, with its invocation of Moses' death (and perfection), offers a delicate support for the divine-human analogy in the "perfect" figure of Moses, whose blessings were likewise "perfect" or "whole." One proof of Moses' perfection was that he uttered these blessings just prior to his death, "for at the moment the soul of the 'perfected' ones takes leave of its body, they reach an even higher state." The *ma'amar* is from the Talmudic tractate Mo'ed Katan 25b.[11] The passage in Mo'ed Katan discusses eulogies given for early rabbis. One case is Eleazar ben Pedat (in some versions, Rabbi Yohanan), the legendary amoraic scholar who directed the academy in Tiberias. Eleazar was known for his love of scholarship, dedication to his students, and selfless charity. He serves as Abraham Catalano's avatar in Marini's eulogy. According to one Talmudic passage (b. Berakhot 5b), only one of Eleazar's children survived him—another link to Abraham, whose wife and four children died in the 1631 plague. We remember that Moses, his eldest son, survived by fleeing the city with his own young family; his youngest daughter, Perla, was in the ghetto with her father and survived.[12]

According to legend, when Rabbi Eleazar ben Pedat died, Rabbi Isaac ben Elazar came to eulogize him, saying, "Today is a hard day for Israel, like the sunset [arriving] at noon." Marini will have to build his remarks to tie this line to the opening prooftext from Deuteronomy 33:2–3, and he quickly establishes the themes that he will develop: the delayed eulogy and the inexpressible grief of the mourners, including himself. Marini lists three justifications for eulogies, none of which applies to present circumstances. First, eulogies rouse the mourners to weep; this is a therapeutic explanation, according to which grief-numbed mourners are prodded to express their pain. But this cannot be the case with Abraham's death, because the mourners have already poured forth copious tears (citing Jer. 9:17). A second possibility is that eulogies publicize the virtues of the deceased—but this, too, cannot apply to Abraham, because his virtues were evident to all. A third possibility is that the eulogy concentrates listeners on the fact of bereavement. Marini notes that God Himself delivered the first eulogy when He confronted Adam and Eve hiding in the Garden of Eden. This idea derives from God's problematic query to Adam, "Where are you?" (Gen. 3:9), something God should have known without asking. The midrash resolved this quandary by reading God's "*ayyeka*" (איכה—"where are you?") as "*aykha*" (איכה), meaning "how" but linked to the anaphoric repetitions opening Lamentations: "How lonely sits the city etc." The deliberate misreading is found in Genesis Rabbah, where God says, "I put the first human/Adam into the Garden of Eden and commanded him only to have him disobey My commandment, I sentenced him to banishment and exile, and lamented 'aykha' over him."

Marini enlists this midrash to legitimate the use of eulogies: God Himself set the precedent. Nonetheless, now it is forbidden to eulogize Abraham because of the timing of his death. Marini describes the shock of his absence: "you look at his place and today he is no more," a perfect description of sudden loss. The source, Psalm 37:10, is nonetheless jarring, as it refers to the impermanence of evildoers. However, one of the rabbi's favorite commentaries, Isaac Arama's *'Akedat Yitzhak*, launches from this verse to discuss the immortality of the soul, something we cannot prove or perceive with scientific knowledge. Indeed, it is the Torah, not science, that enables the individual soul to transcend physical death. The relative inadequacy of scientific to religious truth is a recurring Marini theme. Thus, shockingly, Abraham is gone, but by implication he has earned immortality because of his dedication to Jewish (not secular) learning.

Solomon transitions to another set of examples that further illustrates how much Abraham's death has been a terrible blow. Marini observes that mourners need consoling more than the deceased. This claim is found in his *ma'amar*; Mo'ed Katan 25b also tells us בכו לאבלים ולא לאבדה—"weep for the mourners and not for the deceased—for he is at rest but we are grieving." Marini distinguishes between a situation where the eulogizer is not among the mourners and those instances where he is. He offers David lamenting for Saul an example of the former; in the case of Abraham Catalano, however, "we" are the ones touched by grief.

Marini returns to the verses from Amos 8:9–10 embedded in the *ma'amar*, breaking his citation into three parts and explicating each in summary. "Today is a hard day for Israel," the first phrase, links the death of the Talmudic Eleazer b. Pedat to the death of Abraham Catalano. The second phrase, God's threat to cause the sun to set at noon, turning daylight into darkness, refers to God's power to suspend natural law. The third phrase, God's threat to turn Israel's festivals to mourning, Marini associates with the realm of providence. The festivals represent "providential benefits" that are subsumed into the natural order. The binary categories of natural order (הנהגה טבעית) and "miraculous" or providential order (הנהגה נסית, הנהגה השגחתית) are developed throughout Arama's *'Akedat Yitzhak*, and Marini, who leaned frequently on Arama's work, drew on Arama's distinction here as well. For Arama, things subjected to the natural order—the planets, for instance, or natural phenomena on earth—follow the rules of nature; they have no "will" to deviate from the patterns that govern their behavior. When God suspends the laws of nature to permit a deviation in the movement of a planet, the parting of the sea, the unconsumed burning of a bush, these are signs of providential interventions, sometimes called miracles, sometimes "personal providence." God will engineer these deviations to get humanity's attention, usually because they have gone astray.[13]

What is Solomon Marini trying to say by summoning this philosophical argument into his concluding remarks? He turns to hyperbole to convey the magnitude of loss felt by Abraham's surviving family, friends, community, and himself. It is loss so great that both the natural world and the human, social world have been wrenched out of order. At the same time, it is undeniable that one manifestation of order—the calendar—cannot be budged: This festival period prohibits formal, liturgical, mourning. Thus, God has suspended an ordained festival period to become a day of mourning—commemorated formally or not—reminding God's people of His unceasing surveillance of their lives and deeds, ironically testifying to the hand of providence in the death of a kinsman and friend. Technically, although this is not indicated in the outline, Marini should have looped back to his opening verse from Deuteronomy 33:2–3; he could do this by returning to the exemplary Abraham, the brilliance of Torah to his right, and the life of public service and love it illuminated. This good man's death was a very hard day for Israel.

Approximately three weeks later, on the Sabbath of *Parashat* Lekh Lekha (Gen. 12–17), Rabbi Marini mounted the pulpit in the great Italian synagogue in Padua to mourn his friend formally. The outline for this sermon, as noted earlier, was preserved in some detail, and we can see that its structure and artistry were meant to impress. The Scriptural portion described the early career of the biblical Abram (not yet called Abraham), a coincidence Marini exploited to pick his *nosé*, which straddled two verses from Gen. 13:2–3: "Abram was rich in cattle" (Gen. 13:2) and "He went on his travels" (Gen. 13:3).[14] The *ma'amar,* from *Pirke Avot,* describes the man who possesses "moderation, prudence, and humility" as worthy of being "among the students of our father Abraham."[15] Marini will begin by referring again to the deferred commemoration of Catalano's death, then develop the theme of Catalano's exemplary righteousness and humility, recycling

one of his hallmark critiques of secular knowledge. His subtexts include
the fragility of human life, and the immortality of the soul. As an embodi-
ment of *Pirke Avot*'s catalog of ideal virtues, Abraham Catalano belongs
"among the students of our father Abraham," his dedication to learning,
public service, and philanthropy unmarred by pride. Marini concluded
the formal eulogy with a poetic lament composed for his deceased friend,
then added some remarks on Catalano's support for a boys' school and the
synagogue—implying, no doubt, that the listeners might want to pledge a
donation.

My translation follows; for the Hebrew transcription, see Appendix 2.

NY MS JTS 6517, fol. 7v

The eulogy for MHR"R Abraham Catalano, *parashat* Lekh lekha [?] in the
Italian Synagogue.

1. **"And Abraham was rich in cattle"** [Gen. 13:2]. **"And he went on
   his journeys"** [Gen. 13:3]. *"He who possesses these three things is considered a student of our father Abraham"* [Avot 5:19]. With all our
   people's worry

2. When they went in captivity to Babylon, after they left [and] the
   Temple was destroyed, the worst thing was that they were un-
   able to weep until they reached the rivers of Babylon (Ps. 137:1).
   Meaning: The day that this rabbi

3. Died embittered our souls, even more so because of the post-
   poned eulogy for lack of time. Which meant that it has been
   somewhat hidden and a bit forgotten, and the feeling of loss.
   Three benefits

4. We receive from the righteous one.[16] According to the 'Akedat
   Yitzhak, par. Shemini, three for weeping.[17] [They are] the three
   wonders:[18] **"For the earth grew angry"** [Joel 2:10, Ps. 77:19]—the
   three pillars collapse.[19] The meaning of **"From the end of the
   earth**

5. **we hear singing: Glory to the righteous!"** [Isa. 24:16] say the ones
   on high [who] rejoice in the righteous soul, but [for] the ones
   below, **"The earth is wholly tottering"** [Isa. 24:19]. The Holy
   One will investigate

6. Human deeds. Even when they appear great, they are mostly weak, because even the good [deeds] are mixed with pride and foreign purpose. What are we and what are

7. Our lives. The meaning of **"there is no righteous man on earth"** [Eccl. 7:20]. **"For they sin to you"** (1 Kings 8:46).[20] That is why it didn't say *if* they sin, because it is certain [they will]. The meaning of **"Their webs will not serve as a garment"** [Isa. 59:6]. The meaning of **"We have**

8. **all become like an unclean thing"** [Isa. 64:5]. Also, through speculative knowledge most wisdom grows foolish, and thus in philosophy one [argument] contradicts another. Solomon testified, **"I said I shall become wise"** [Eccl. 7:23]. The meaning of **"Dead flies cause**

9. **Stink"** [Eccl. 10:1]. These are foreign purposes and pride, which spoil the exalted acts that are compared to perfumer's ointment. **"A little folly outweighs massive wisdom"** [Eccl. 10:1].

10. He should always think he has not attained full wisdom, which would be foolishness. The meaning of "And I am to see your face" [?], like **"But where can wisdom be found"** [Job 28:12]. That is, when he thinks

11. That it is beyond his grasp and he has not attained [wisdom] or knowledge. This is about investigative wisdom.[21] **"Then where does wisdom come from?"** [Job 28:20], that is the wisdom of Torah, which comes from Kabbalah. **"God**

12. **understood the way to her"** [Job 28:23].[22] *"Everyone who boasts that he is a prophet"*[23] [B. Pesahim 66b].[24] Deborah, Samuel, David, Moses, Hillel. The meaning of **"I have seen evil . . ."** [Eccl. 10:5]. **"Folly was set on lofty heights"** [Eccl. 10:6]. Intelligence when it comes

13. With the knowledge of one's ignorance and defects. **"[While] rich men sat in low estate"** [Eccl. 10:6]. That is, those who think themselves rich in speculative knowledge and deeds. **"One man pretends to be rich and has nothing"** [Prov. 13:7].

14. **"One who pretends to be poor"** [Prov. 13:7][25] thinks he has not attained this. *"When he saw a crowd following him, he said 'though his excellency ascends to heaven* [Job 20:6–7][26] *. . . R. Zutra [said] for power is not forever'* [Prov. 27:24]."

15. The meaning of "*he who possesses these three things is considered a student of our Father Abraham*:" This is the highest, most prized relationship. "**And I am dust and ashes**" [Gen. 18:27] and "**what are we?**" [Ex. 16:7]. "**And I am a worm**" [Ps. 22:7].

16. The deceased rabbi was great in Torah, wise in learning, endowed, a leader of his congregation. And with all that, "*there was not a trace of arrogance or pride in him*" [b. Sukkah 26b]. "**And Abraham**

17. **was rich in cattle**" [Gen. 13:2], he would shepherd his congregation with silver and gold, learning and deed. "**And he went on his travels**" [Gen. 13:3]—first to his "tent," and now he has built himself a house for his soul[27]

18. With the merit of his Torah. The meaning of "**Annihilation and Death [said], our ears [have only heard of it]**" [Job 28:22].[28] For as death draws near, "**their spirit is gathered**" [Ps. 104:29] and they begin to understand mysteries. Then I made this lament for him:

19. Mourn him, community of the Living God! Raise a lament! / For your precious light has been gathered up from you. / A champion, righteous and great in every way, / he took care of your needs [. . .]

20. Wise, he knew where to find understanding. / His writing instructed, he found his way. / He was a very humble man and earned his [good] name. / Alas! Who shall stand up on our behalf?

21. He was sought and went to his [heavenly] house of study. / We sigh in shame. / He said to his soul, come and lodge! / Come back to your Tabernacle and dwelling.

22. Afterward I spoke about the school and the children's teachers who cannot [teach] for free those without knowledge [?], for the deceased rabbi dedicated his life to this. And that is [the meaning of] "**for the Lord desires you**" [Isa. 62:4].

23. Not in buildings or silver utensils. [As it is] said, "for wealth [. . . ?] Those who walk in the synagogue [. . . ?] Soul." Meaning, "**no longer shall you need the sun**" [Isa. 60:20].[29]

This was an ambitious eulogy, and it is not always easy to follow Marini's argument. The density of rabbinic and exegetical allusions advertises the preacher's learnedness; it also signals to a core of literate listeners among a larger audience responding more to thematic and nontextual cues. If the eulogy was delivered in Italian (as it most likely was), the heavy incorporation of rabbinic prooftexts may have been a later addition, or it was understated in oral form. The written Hebrew outline spans seventeen lines of text; it is followed by Marini's short poetic lament, and then a notation referring to Marini's plea for donations to a boys' school that Abraham Catalano had supported. I consider these three components in order. Even where the outline is not entirely clear, Marini's remarks hover over concerns familiar from earlier and later sermons. Dominant among them is the idea that secular learning, with all its prestige and dazzle, is inferior to "Torah." Despite Solomon's recurring invocation of this polemic, there does not seem to have been a rush among young Paduan Jews to jettison traditional Jewish study on the way to the university and foreign knowledge; I have suggested in the preceding chapter that the trope of "foreign knowledge," identified specifically in this eulogy with philosophy, may have been a strawman for a more widespread laxity (from the rabbi's perspective) and disengagement from religious life. Abraham Catalano, certainly, represented a level of high achievement in both realms: He was a graduate of the University of Padua's medical school and well-read in humanist texts, but he was also deeply literate in classical Jewish texts, as his exquisite and resonant Hebrew attests. For the rabbi, therefore, it is essential to portray Abraham as having valued his Jewish learning more than his secular studies, a point reiterated in the poetic lament composed by Abraham's son. The other familiar theme recurring in this eulogy is Abraham's humility and a corollary condemnation of arrogance and pride.

The first three lines of text constitute a prologue, in which Solomon Marini introduces his biblical and rabbinic prooftexts, then addresses the deferred commemoration of Abraham's death. When the ancient Israelites were exiled from their land, the "worst thing" was that they could not take time to mourn until they reached the rivers of Babylon (Ps. 137:1), where they wept. The analogy between this cataclysmic national disaster and Abraham's death casts him immediately as a figure of communal importance, whose death reverberates among a public. Marini transitions from the frustrations of delayed observance to the laws of mourning, then a triad of verses, two describing terrestrial upheaval and one a joyous clamor in heaven. The heavens rejoice to welcome Abraham's soul, but the earth and its inhabitants are distraught. The eulogy shifts focus to elaborate on the puniness of human achievements, even (perhaps especially) when to humans they look significant. Even good deeds are not as worthy as they seem because they are diminished by self-aggrandizement or "foreign purpose." Marini might have chosen among several Hebrew words for self-aggrandizement or pride but he opted for the Aramaic *yohara*, anticipating the citation in line 16 from b. Sukkah 26b. Even righteous men inevitably sin (Eccl. 7:20 and 1 Kings 8:46). As glossed by the commentators, their sins can arise from good intentions (Al-Sheikh) or be on the order of indiscriminate generosity that does not distinguish between the truly and less needy (Kohelet Rabbah 7:20:1, Midrash Lekah Tov to Eccl. 7:20).[30] Abraham Catalano's renowned generosity may have been in this category. Hypocrisy will not cover up our sins, Marini continues, and all of us are guilty (of something; Isa. 59:6, Isa. 64:5). Wisdom has gotten a bad name because of its associations with secular knowledge, where one argument foolishly contradicts another. Indeed, no one can know everything, even King Solomon (Eccl. 7:23 and back to Eccl. 10:1): Several commentaries to Eccl. 7:23 note that Solomon, though wise, could not fathom the red heifer ritual. For Arama the point is that we should not try to know what is beyond human understanding (*'Akedat Yitzhak*, 79:1:4).

Attacking secular knowledge is a favorite theme for Marini. Although the argument of the next few lines is not entirely clear, Marini identifies secular knowledge with "folly," drawing on the contrast of folly and wisdom in Ecclesiastes 7, 8, and 10. Job's two linked queries, "where can wisdom be found?" (Job 28:12) and "then where does wisdom come from?" (Job 28:20), bolster the juxtaposition when Marini interprets the first query to refer to secular or speculative learning and the second to Torah. It is all too easy to confuse the acquisition of secular knowledge with "wisdom" when in fact, it is not always wise. It is easy, too, to feel inferior for lacking this false knowledge (lines 10–11). Solomon returns to the theme of false pride, now in the guise of men who assert that "wisdom" is meaningless. Marini cites another Talmudic proof for this claim, from b. Pesahim 66b, which describes a series of biblical and rabbinic figures whose boastfulness or anger was punished by suspension of their prophetic gifts.. The argument is clinched again with Ecclesiastes 10:5–6.

The eulogy turns to its final synthesis by citing b. Yoma 87a, where a pious sage observes a crowd following him in the street and wisely refuses to let his popularity go to his head. No matter how "high" his reputation is, he will end up like dung; power never endures forever. From here, Marini can reclaim his opening *ma'amar* and *nosé*. To merit being "a student of our father Abraham" is the highest praise. Nonetheless, true humility demands that the recipient of this praise respond as if he is unworthy. Marini draws upon Midrash *Tehilim* 22:15, where his three self-deprecating citations are linked respectively to Abraham, Moses and Aaron, and David.[31] Now it is possible to return to the Paduan Abraham, who like R. Zutra in b. Yoma 87a, was utterly lacking in pride. The Genesis verse calling Abram "rich in cattle" refers to the deceased Abraham's generosity to his community, "shepherding" them with "silver and gold, learning and deed" (line 17). As for Gen.3:3's description of the biblical Abram going on his "journeys," Marini concludes by reading this phrase to describe Abraham Catalano's journey to the grave and then beyond: "first to his 'tent' and now he has built himself a house for his soul." For the mourners packing the synagogue that Sabbath, their weeping was no longer deferred.

But Solomon Marini was not done with them. He had a personal relationship to Abraham Catalano, and he offered an additional tribute in the form of a poetic lament. The copyist recorded the text as three long verses, each subdivided into four parts rhyming abab / cbcb / dbdb. (It is equally possible to read this lament as three stanzas of two bipartite lines, or three stanzas of four decasyllabic verses.) The recurring rhyme (the "b" rhyme) is -*rekh*, with some wobble; it forms a second-person possessive in three out of six rhyme words, turning the force of mourning and grief to the listeners. I suggest that the first decasyllabic verse (or hemistich, or quarter-verse) served as a refrain; the recurring rhyme would have encouraged listeners to add their voices to the solo voice at the conclusion of each stanza.

The speaker addresses the Jewish community collectively, and in the imperative, commanding them to mourn their lost leader and benefactor. The verses reiterate the characteristics developed by the eulogy: Abraham was a leader who tended to his community's needs; he was learned and wise yet humble. Marini alludes to Abraham's writings, most likely the *Mitzaref haSekhel*, Abraham's ethical treatise, but perhaps other writings elicited in more detail in Moses' lament. Now Abraham has journeyed to the heavenly house of study where he shall dwell forevermore. Marini's brief lament concluded the formal eulogy but not his words. He kept speaking, reminding his listeners of a school for children that Abraham Catalano had supported and its need for funds. Abraham's epitaph also refers to this school. No such endeavor is mentioned in Abraham's plague narrative, and it is tempting to speculate that the school and pupils were a byproduct of the 1631 plague. Not only did that disaster leave many orphans while decimating the ranks of teachers, it also deprived Abraham of four of his own children; the two boys, Leon and Judah, may have been students, whose deaths motivated their bereaved father to invest in the schooling of others.[32] Dedicating himself to this kind of charity would suit the man we have come to know so well in his own words and now see through the eyes of others.

Strikingly, Solomon Marini's eulogy reflects many of the same attributes that characterize Abraham's depiction of himself—minus his work during the great plague of 1631. Equally strikingly, while richly testifying to Abraham's public identity and presence, Marini avoids any direct mention of family or private affairs. Nonetheless, a trace of private life hides in Marini's introductory reference to Arama's 'Akedat Yitzhak on the laws of mourning and the "three benefits" we derive from the righteous. According to Arama, one benefit was the unification of aspects or parts of the soul that had hitherto been distinct. Arama's analogy invoked the rabbinic legend of R. Bena'a entering the Cave of Machpelah to see Abraham lying in Sarah's arms, united beyond mortal desire. For Arama, Abraham and Sarah represented the separate components of the soul. But we know that Abraham exploited this same legend in his lament for his beloved wife, Sarah, whom he rejoins now in death. Was Solomon Marini thinking of Abraham's lament, and a plague loss that had never healed? If so, he had either seen the Hebrew reworking of Abraham's original Italian narrative or the two old friends had shared thoughts about the story prior to Abraham's writing. The first option implies that the Hebrew plague narrative had found some circulation in the decade following the epidemic; the second reminds us that not all ideas pass through books.[33] Either way I do not think the allusion is pure coincidence. Alluding discreetly to Sarah Catalano's death during the Great Pestilence, Marini's words whisper to those who most loved the husband, father, and civic leader who had survived his wife by a decade, so softly that his long-ago grief is protected to the end.

Moses Catalano, Abraham's surviving son, had a reputation as an occasional poet; he also composed the sixteen stanzas of didactic plague advice that concluded his father's account of the 1631 plague. As noted in Chapter 3, Moses' plague poems were atypical for him, composed in straightforward Hebrew whose intertextual allusions did not need deciphering for the poems' practical advice. His other extant poetry will find fewer admirers today than it did in seventeenth-century Padua. A few of the examples, like the wedding poem he wrote for his little sister, Perla, were written to read simultaneously in Hebrew or Italian, depending on the word division. The bilingual scansion does not lend itself to great poetry.[34] Moses also drafted a "translation" of the Book of Lamentations into rhymed verse, apparently when he was very young.[35] These demonstrations of rhetorical wizardry held aesthetic appeal among his contemporaries, and when Moses decided to compose a lament to commemorate his father's death, he hewed to this stylistic range. His eight-stanza lament is constructed as a series of tercets with the opening hemistich serving as a refrain. The -*me* rhyme is open and suitably wailing.[36] The final hemistich of the poem recycles the opening (and refrain). Once again the depiction of Abraham's character and achievements is confined to his public life and elides family or the domestic sphere. The son memorializes his father as learned and valuing religious over secular study despite his excellence in both; he refers to Abraham as a homilist or preacher, a detail not mentioned in other sources, also as someone sought out for advice on religious matters.[37] Abraham authored a philosophical essay, Talmudic novelties, and compendia that arranged Jewish legal principles in alphabetical order for easy consultation. In all these efforts, Abraham demonstrated his selfless dedication to the physical and spiritual well-being of his community, who mourn his loss. His son's personal grief remains his private affair.

A translation follows. Aramaic phrases are indicated by italics; the Hebrew-Aramaic transcription may be found in Appendix 2. I am indebted to my former colleague, Stephen A. Kaufman, for his help with the text.[38]

NY JTS Adler 833 = F 30090, scan 5
See also: UCLA USA MS 779 box 9.4 = F 32395[39]

1. Alas, for the earth has been struck / with blindness![40] Alas, for it has been left blind!
2. Woe, for when the ark was to set out[41] / *a precious, priceless, pearl,*
3. A day of destruction confronting the death [destruction][42] of the Gaon / *when the most fortunate of scholars went down.*[43]
4. Alas, for etc.

5. He was a philosopher and physician. But what did / their crown[44] mean to him compared
6. To the crown of Torah, a stronghold[45] / of the Rock, for there He deposited[46]

7. The broken tablets placed in the ark / to study, investigate, leg-
islate or the like.

8. Alas, for etc.

9. Joyous song[47] ended with Joshua. / Daily one sings lamentation
and moans.

10. He [Abraham Catalano] uttered allegories and fine prose / as
tales of moral truths,[48] for there is none that is like them.

11. *Mitzaref haSekhel*[49]—describing the defects [?]

12. Alas, for etc.

13. [When] asked to preach, he did so without anger, / warning his
people about purity and impurity.

14. Anyone who sought advice he answered without charging a fee.
/ He rendered his judgment *firmly, without doubt.*

15. And he arranged his sermons and judgments / for posterity for
them or anyone who thirsts [for them].

16. Alas, for etc.

17. He cared for the honor of the Talmud and effortlessly[50] / dis-
mantled the arguments of his mockers in spoken language.[51]

18. His novel readings of Qiddushin were skilled. / *Everyone said*
that he uprooted mountains.

19. If only Aaron the elder had had his qualities! / "A good name is
better than fragrant oil"[52] for they are incomparable.

20. Alas, for etc.

21. He elaborated [his] explanation for someone seeking knowledge. / From the knowledge of every legal scholar, he drew [the]
water

22. Of wisdom on property law, and with great skill / made night
like day.[53]

23. Because he arranged them alphabetically and by memory, / *he
resolved the contradictions between cases.*

24. Alas, for etc.

25. He is Abraham, and like the one buried in Hebron / *a PROHI-
BITION was also in effect*[54]

26. [For] from various sayings he composed / an ANTHOLOGY, a guardrail for the blind.[55]
27. And bringing them to light is a disaster for me / for by God, a blind man has nothing to say![56]
28. Alas, for etc.

29. He lives like the ones buried in the cave of Efron.[57] / Moreover, his body was buried without reed.
30. His soul ascended to METATRON.[58] / What remains with us is *flesh and bone.*
31. To ask why, we shall sit on the ground like / sheep, and bitterly lament. I shall respond and ask why,[59]
32. Not for him, but because the earth / has been struck with blindness, alas, it has been left blind.

Abraham Catalano's selfless dedication to the welfare of others and to Jewish institutions and learning is highlighted in his son's lament. These are aspects of his life that meant a great deal to him, and both Solomon Marini and Moses Catalano are anxious to convey this. At the same time, the echoing of the same achievements equally confirms their esteem in other eyes. Abraham was doubly learned. His medical diploma ("crown") testified to his acquisition of secular wisdom, but this—another point hammered by Solomon—meant less to him than the "crown" of Torah. Moses carefully distinguishes between his father's scholarly acumen, expressed in his philosophical essay and Talmudic novelties, and the unselfish pedagogy that motivated his homilies and other time-consuming writings destined for use by less learned but needy audiences.

The motif of blindness runs through this lament, beginning with the opening line, which also served as a refrain. The inhabited earth has been struck with blindness—plunged into darkness—by Abraham's death, an image that summons Solomon Marini's depiction of Abraham, like God or Moses, with the blazing illumination of Torah (*esh dat*) to his right. In verse 22, Abraham's mastery of property law illuminated the "night" of obscurity surrounding its rulings. In verse 26, Moses refers to an anthology or compendium that his father arranged to make it easier for unlearned ("blind") people to avoid sin, and in the following verse, he exclaims in despair that "bringing . . . to light" these humble labors is daunting for him, relatively "blind" in insight compared to their author. The final verse of the lament recycles the opening image of the inhabited world struck with prolonged blindness. The insistence that the speaker (Moses) voices his mourning on behalf of "the earth" and not for his dead father reminds us of Marini's eulogy again; Marini had already made a similar distinction, based on Arama's elaboration of a Talmudic directive to "mourn not for the deceased but for the mourners, as the deceased has gone to his rest but the mourners are grieving" (b. Mo'ed Katan 25b).

On the one hand, metaphors of light and darkness, blindness and sight, are conventional. On the other, I wonder if Moses gestures to some biographical reality that the conventions of idealized memorialization obscure. Perhaps Abraham's final sickness included a loss of vision, a misfortune Moses converts into one of dazzling reversal, so that the sighted are "blind" in their ignorance with a (sightless?) Abraham as their source of light. Marini's invocation of the *esh dat* to Abraham's right would join these subtle hints that a physical disability may be implied. Notably, Moses makes no mention of his father's service to the ghetto during the plague epidemic of 1631. Nor does he mention his mother or an anticipated reunion of husband and wife—and four of his siblings—in the world to come. Indeed, his only mention of the afterlife is to yield his father's soul to the great ruler of the angels, Metatron, leaving the mourners on the darkened earth with nothing but "flesh and bone." Moses appended this lament to a copy of his father's philosophical essay, the *Mitzaref haSekhel*, underlining Moses' decision to focus on the fate of Abraham's soul and teachings. It is not what we would expect as a son's testimony today, but like all these records, Moses' lament projects itself into the space of a familiar theater. The verse memorial summons the highlights of Abraham Catalano's public life and stabilizes a public portrait, at the same time situating the son in a shared sphere of a social and literary elite. Moses is present as much in his technique as he is by his personal absence. Unlike his father, or his father's friend, Rabbi Marini—or, for that matter, Abraham Massarani in Mantua or Joseph Concio in Chieri—he rejected the option of invoking his personal loss to validate his claim to speak for others. Like the rabbi, however, he has suppressed Abraham's role in the plague epidemic a decade earlier. Strangely, only the anonymous epitaph remembered this, and spoke more passionately.

Without David Malkiel's exhaustive study of the Padua Jewish gravestones and the epitaphs they preserve, our final text could not be presented.[60] For the last extant words dedicated to Abraham Catalano, we must follow Professor Malkiel to the Wiel cemetery, the oldest of Padua's three

Jewish burial grounds, where Abraham's impressive tombstone still stands. According to Malkiel, Abraham's epitaph is the longest of all the Wiel inscriptions. The inscription fills the rectangular field beneath Abraham's name and date of death; a floral emblem enclosed in a shield floats across the border separating the heading from the epitaph, a lengthy inscription that "trumpets its own importance" among the surrounding graves.[61] Malkiel observes that the epitaphs of Padua's (many) Jewish physicians often downplayed their medical activity in favor of other accolades; in this respect, it is noteworthy that, of all the commemorative testimonials to Catalano treated here, only the epitaph honors his labors on behalf of the ghetto in 1631.[62] The tombstone inscription also refers to the school that Abraham promoted and whose students he seems to have taught; the writing he produced in the wee hours of the night (not detracting from his daytime responsibilities); and the son he raised. The stern rebuke to mourners weeping "as if you were at the rivers of Babylon" should remind us of Marini's synagogue eulogy, perhaps intentionally. The Hebrew adheres to a pattern of endecasyllabic verses alternating *piano* and *troco* forms (11 and 10 syllables) with corresponding alternating rhyme syllables -*ver* and -*vel*.[63] Like the eulogies and lament, the text alludes to rabbinic and biblical sources. Malkiel's Hebrew edition is complemented by Roth's and the photographic image of the gravestone. His English translation, in *Stones Speak*, differs slightly from my own; I have indicated where we differ in the notes, below:

12 Tishre 5402 The sage, physician and genius, the honorable teacher and rabbi
Abraham Catalan z"tz"l
Passed from this world

1. O earthly inhabitants, you would not believe[64]
2. That I am [set as] a memorial over the man
3. Raised as a leader among men[65]
4. To fulfill "I am with him" in destruction and devastation.[66]
5. In his school, he was like Shem and Ever[67]
6. To his suffering students.
7. He grew close to the pen and quill
8. He would dip [in ink] at night.
9. And so, too, for the one he raised with much effort,
10. Nurturing him who bears his image and likeness.[68]

11. He should unanimously be remembered as a leader.[69]
12. Let his name live on forever everywhere!
13. I note this on your day of mourning:
14. When you feel regret for overt and covert sins,[70]
15. If you cry out here to God with broken hope[71]
16. As if you were at the rivers of Babylon[72]
17. This man will cry out with you, with no accompaniment![73]
18. By the merit of his lips murmuring in the grave,[74]
19. He will hasten redemption and the final Jubilee,[75]
20. [when] those who sleep in the mire will grow new wings.[76]

Epitaph poetry was well-developed among Sephardic and Italian Jews.[77] In contrast, as Malkiel observes, gravestone poetry was not common among Christians in Italy, and the Jewish custom does not derive directly from a Christian analogue. Among Iberian Jews, poetry adorned the stones of medieval Jewish graves found in Toledo and continued to thrive in the Spanish diaspora from Amsterdam to the New World. Among extant examples it is not uncommon to find the stone itself address mourners or passersby, as happens in Abraham's epitaph. The great stone marvels, as should onlookers, that it marks the resting place of a great man, offering an allusive, highly condensed list of Abraham's singular achievements: He selflessly served his people during the plague; he was a dedicated teacher and author; he raised a son. Again, this is the only one of our commemorative texts that underlines Abraham's efforts during the plague of 1631.[78] This episode in Abraham's life also leads the list, either because it was chronologically earliest or because it mattered most to the writer. If the latter, his perspective is doubly noteworthy. Abraham's dedication as a teacher comes next. The comparison of his school to the legendary Torah school of Shem and Ever makes clear that the subject of instruction was religious, not secular. His achievements as an author come third, with an image of Abraham writing through the night—meaning that he did not shortchange his students for the sake of personal fame but sacrificed his sleep instead.

The fourth accomplishment for which Abraham should be remembered is the work he invested in raising his son. That, at least, is what Malkiel makes of the two-line description, and I see no other way to read them. As we have seen, Abraham's family life has not been invoked before in either eulogies or lament. By the time of his death, his son Moses was a mature man whose name appears as witness on several communal documents, implying he had stature in the community in addition to his reputation as a poet. He was not a physician like his father and did not leave us any sign of involvement in pious institutions (schools, synagogues, confraternities) or authorship of works on religious themes. He had a wife and daughters, some of whom would be buried in Padua in subsequent decades. He was already married when the plague arrived in Padua in 1631, and his mother was still alive when he fled with his young family for nearby Corte. Thus Abraham never raised Moses on his own, and it is not clear why the epitaph would imply that. Moreover, Moses had a younger sister, Perla, who survived the plague with her father in the ghetto, and to whom Moses would later dedicate a macaronic wedding poem. If Abraham is to be remembered for his labors as a father, why not mention Perla, too? She, in fact, was the child raised without a mother. In short, I am not sure this verse means what we think it does; however, I do not have an alternative hypothesis.

Having listed Abraham's chief attributes, the epitaph's speaker (the stone) turns its attention again to the gathered mourners. The final section of the epitaph notes their grief and urges them to seek the dead Abraham's intercession on their behalf. Malkiel reads this section of the text as rebuking Abraham's kin for unknown sins. I am less sure an assault on their virtue is intended. What seems to me more fitting is that the stone acknowledges the custom of visiting graves to seek intercession and assumes this is part of what motivates the mourners at Abraham's grave.[79] The allusion to Psalm 137 and the rivers of Babylon takes us back to Marini's eulogy, delivered a year earlier and referring to the painful deferral of mourning to honor the festival period. The epitaph also alludes to the Talmudic discussion of the "moving lips" of the dead beneath the earth when their names are recalled; here the dead Abraham is calling out to heaven to intercede on behalf of those weeping penitently at his grave. He does so because their voices call his into being, much as the metaphor of two lutes in resonance was used by exegetes like Arama and Abarbanel to explain sympathetic influence between earth and cosmos.[80] Finally, the merit of the righteous—including Abraham—speeds the longed-for final redemption and resurrection of the dead, as illustrated by the eagles of Isaiah 40 who "will grow new wings." This is no mere act of molting; biblical exegetes refer to the eagle's custom of falling into the sea to die then rise to life again, a fate reflected among the righteous who fly about for one thousand years and then are "renewed" (Radaq, *Ein Ya'akov* to Sanh. 11:16). Thus Abraham's epitaph concludes with a promise of resurrection, especially for those who cling to the teachings of Torah.

Jewish tradition prescribes a year's interval between burial and the dedication of a tombstone. The passage of time may partially explain why Abraham's epitaph diverges in some of its emphases from the eulogies and lament that date closer to the time of his death. One of the most curious of those divergences is the absence in the earlier texts of any direct mention of Abraham's role during the 1631 plague. True, by 1641 a decade had passed with no subsequent outbreak in the community; the terrible plague epidemic of 1656 still lay in the future and would leave northern Italy unscathed. Plague may not have been high on the list of things people were remembering—and yet, given the horrifying losses suffered by Paduan Jews and their social, intellectual, religious, and economic reverberations over the next few years, it is surprising that neither Solomon Marini nor Moses Catalano thought to invoke Abraham's devotion to his community—or his own personal losses— during the 1631 plague. A year after Abraham's death, a more thoughtful reckoning of his life may have emerged, and with it the memory of his activity during the epidemic and in its aftermath. None of the commemorative texts, for that matter, mentions the 'Olam Hafukh, Abraham's plague narrative, which circulated among family members and then the wider community over the years.[81] Ironically, if we know Abraham for any of his writings now, it is for this work. Moreover, if we are to believe Abraham's representation of his own role in the ghetto in 1631, the devastating epidemic was formative for his sense of himself and how he wished to be seen.

Nonetheless, recalling Abraham's role in the crisis of 1631 was not paramount for either his good friend Solomon Marini or his son, Moses (who wrote the didactic poems that concluded the 'Olam Hafukh). I am not sure why. It may be that these epidemics, even when they were terrible, did not play a constitutive role in collective Jewish memory in the way political or religious catastrophes (with human enemies) did. Marini's distinction between events that belong to the natural order and those that belong to the social order may hint that, like other deviations from nature's ordained state of harmony, plague was relegated to the realm of natural disaster—even when it came to punishing human sin. As Nükhet Varlik describes for the Ottoman Empire, plague became naturalized; it too was part of the natural order of things.[82] The linkage of plague and sin in the liturgies, sermons, and laments treated in the preceding chapters may reflect theological and genre conventions more than convictions held by ordinary people once they left the house of prayer. Perhaps, too, in the intervening period, Abraham's plague narrative spoke on behalf of the significance of this moment in his life story. I have no compelling explanation: The erasure of references to the plague—a catastrophe that had taken the lives of more than half the inhabitants of the Paduan ghetto—is simply puzzling. It is one of many silences that accompany this story.

The absence of references to Abraham's family and domestic life are easier to understand. Such details could have been included in oral delivery and subsequently elided in writing.[83] What we call "private life" mattered in public memory most in its potential for validating manifestations of public character valued by a community. The chronicle texts composed by Abraham Catalano and Abraham Massarani and their embedded laments, like the lament of Joseph Concio, included vivid and sometimes searing vignettes of personal anguish and loss, or of domestic scenes of turbulence, conflict, or play. I have argued that these vignettes function to validate corporate memory and to ratify or condemn displays of behavior that reflect communal ideals or a failure to emulate them. The thinness of family references in the texts commemorating Abraham's death is thus striking, even if we assume that the eulogies were delivered to an audience including Abraham's living children and kin. If Abraham's epitaph, for that matter, alludes to his son Moses, why was his daughter Perla, the child spared death in the ghetto, elided? And yet when weighed against the dramatic use of personal vignette in the plague accounts, the suppression of Abraham's "private life" in commemoration of him as an individual reinforces my claims for its emblematic use in genres that represent communal catastrophe. These accounts narrate collective trauma, embedding shards of private life, emotions, and experience into a larger story; when they describe the author's personal encounters, conflicts, or tragedies, they legitimate his claim to speak on behalf of a grieving community.

At the same time, as I have claimed of the prose accounts especially, vignettes of conflict and contested authority are central to the construction of the narrator's persona. These scenes of contest define an early modern identity attested in other genres and settings, and to a great extent shared by Christians and Jews. Scenes of challenge constitute moral and public character, evolving in a continual drama of tested boundaries. This public sense of "self," performed in the public sphere, informs a personal sense of character, too. Where it may be distinguished from, say, Erwin Goffman's classic study of the performative nature of self-presentation is that the selves I have been discussing throughout this book are not living and walking around in public space and encounters; they are on paper, preserved as literary

projections of those spaces and encounters for readers to recognize, decipher, and assess for themselves.[84]

All four of these commemorative texts—the two eulogies, the lament,
and the epitaph—remind us how much the "memory" they prepared for
posterity was largely characterized by public meaning and service. This is of
course precisely how Abraham wished to be seen, and the consensus of his
posthumous depictions confirms that this way of seeing and being seen was
shared by a larger community.

Solomon Marini, Moses Catalano, and perhaps the anonymous epitaph
author also knew each other in private life; they shared ideas and values as
well as their writings. The four texts discussed in this chapter are in dialogue with each other even as they refer to other writings of their own
authorship and from a common textual repertoire reflecting the eclectic
philosophical, scientific, and esoteric interests of the northern Italian Jewish elite. The plague accounts treated in the preceding chapters likewise
demonstrate familiarity with a shared set of idioms, learning, and ideas;
each author also seeks to balance traditional ways of understanding collective catastrophe with newer understandings of disease and health.[85] The force
of these personal networks should not be underestimated: Joseph Concio
highlights the deaths of friends, neighbors, and in-laws in his catalog of
mortalities in Turin and Chieri. Abraham Catalano invokes Solomon Marini
in his plague narrative, and Solomon's sermons for that year dovetail with
Abraham's perspective on events. Moses Catalano flees to Corte, but the plague
poems he penned for his father's narrative demonstrate a lively engagement
and sometimes disagreement with his father's recommendations for future
preparedness. Moses' lament further echoes the portrait of his father crafted
by Solomon Marini in his eulogies, and the anonymous author of the epitaph seems to have known—and modified—them both. When we read these
texts today, we too easily forget that they were written for a small group of
men who knew and meant something to each other. Personal intimacy informs the shape and content of their writing. At the same time, these carefully crafted works testify to a desire to create a more permanent and public
record for readers they will never know.

We are those unknown readers. For us, then, the task of reading these
works demands awareness of the factors I have tried to elicit and emphasize
throughout these chapters: not just whatever historical and social context is
retrievable from corroborating sources, but the deliberate choices each writer
made to enlist a specific genre with its unique strengths and limitations, as

well as the ways he might creatively manipulate them. So, too, the force of individual personality comes to us filtered through the fruitful play of conventions for self-fashioning—what I have called an idiom shared by social and intellectual peers. Reciprocally, I have argued, the same idiom these authors engaged to construct a public image shone inward to shape very private conceptions of "self." The commemorative texts treated in this chapter suggest that, in the case of Abraham Catalano, the delicate interplay of public and private self was legible to his friends and son, even as they in turn negotiated their own needs to highlight some of its features while guarding others from public view. The fact that Abraham himself did not leave us any written commentary or narrative from the last decade of his life is in its own way a testimony, too. His signature on a variety of documents attests to his ongoing concern for poor brides and those on the lower end of the economic ladder. His dedication to a school for Jewish boys that focused on Jewish learning suggests where some of his energy shifted, just as his failure to remarry and his friend Solomon's subtle evocation of his devoted marriage to Sarah hint at the long cost of loss and trauma that followed a terrible plague. The silence of plague, which surfaces only in the epitaph, may tell us something about greater social memory and what it could or could not bear.

Conclusion

Throughout this book, I have tried to show that these authors and their writings are far more complex than we give them credit for when we read them to learn "what happened in the 1631 plague." We are not reading "what happened," but rather a studied representation of events that includes and excludes strategically, evocatively, and often by means of a sophisticated manipulation of a background scrim of resonant traditional texts. Nor are we reading what a specific author "felt" or even "did" in his narrative, because those descriptions, too, are strategically embedded to legitimate larger narrative claims. These men lived and breathed in a society of Jews and Christians who saw public responsibility as inextricable from personal privilege. It is no use trying to untangle the strands to conform to the highly individualized emphasis of our own social context or the severance from communal bonds that defines postmodern "self." The imbrication of private and public self, or individual and collective identity, is partly what gave medieval and early modern communities resilience. But it is also a fluid recipe for identity, whose components interact dynamically, and we would do well to exercise caution before casually applying a model characteristic of one place and time to another.

Strikingly, the three actual accounts of the Great Italian Plague—Abraham Catalano's prose narrative, Abraham Massarani's chronicle, and Joseph Concio's double poetic lament—are deeply pessimistic despite their formulaic expressions of gratitude for God's deliverance. Composed close to the events they describe, they embody its terrors, and trauma reverberates in their vignettes, descriptions, and painful litanies of death. Of the three writers, Abraham least capitulates to convention as he concludes not with gratitude to God but with a weary catalog of suggestions for, God forbid, the plague to come. Ironically, as his narrative details, he and his colleagues had tried to implement most of them, but to no avail. Abraham's unflagging labors in 1631 testify to his commitment to family and community despite the impossibility of saving either one. In 1348, when the medical faculty of the University of Paris concluded that the Black Death was not a "natural" disease but an act of God, they also concluded that this did not exempt physicians from treating the sick, or rulers from initiating measures to protect the defenseless. Three hundred years later, Abraham's moral compass pointed in the same direction. Despair had nothing to do with it.

Finally, this book has asked about the written records of Jewish experience during the great plague that befell northern Italy in 1631. Those records sample multiple genres to illustrate how we write about plagues and collective catastrophe, but also how we include ourselves in the story, how that story is inextricably bound to who we think we are and how we want to be seen and remembered. Notably, all these texts rely on the shared touchstone of Hebrew to shape speaker and story, and their richly evocative Hebrew gave them a common idiom for forging meaning and consolation from biblical, rabbinic, and liturgical texts that Jews had not abandoned even with their rush to be "crowned" in medicine. One of the benefits of traditional language was its capacious embrace of new suffering under the canopy of old meaning. Another was its ability to adapt to new forms of identity in an early modern context invested deeply in the complexities of public versus private self-fashioning.

The religious framing of plague, with its cyclic alternations of prosperity and destruction, focused on the cost of human sin, but it could ride alongside more scientifically formulated theories. In the more recent historical past, we have witnessed a sharper severance of religious and secular responses to pandemic, but closer scrutiny reveals that this coexisting duality still survives, albeit in secular garb: The attribution of pandemics and climate crisis to our singular stupidity and greed is just an alternative version of the sin-and-punishment template. It does not preclude respect for scientific expertise, or a loss of faith in it. Faith responses, too, have assumed a broad spectrum of manifestations, most of which do not spurn science. With respect to our assumption of guilt for injury to the earth and its (re) emergent pathogens, we witness daily that the earth is far from a passive recipient of abuse; it too has agency and acts, and neither human sin nor human repentance takes center stage when we are merely one player in a multispecies and interlocking system of life forms on a planet with some agency of its own.[86] We will have to find a new way to speak about meaning. But to do so, we must learn from the past and these voices. Somehow, from the midst of mass death and despair, they spoke—wearily, even wretchedly—of healing and a future. Somehow, they retained a sense of belonging to a story greater, and longer, than themselves. They wrote for their friends and families, but they wrote for us, too—and they took pains to leave traces of themselves for future readers in what they wrote. We will do the same.

Appendix 1

Sermon Outlines by Solomon Marini

Marini, Solomon b. Isaac

דרושים, קובץ

NY MS JTS 843 (IMHM microfilm F 23951), fol. 14r.

השצ"א [early to mid-January 1631]

מש"ק פ' בא

1   ופסח ה' על הפתח¹ מא' ועברתי בארץ מצרים אני ולא מלאך² הקד' מורה ח"ג³ שדברו הפלוסופי'

2   __סרה על ה' ח¹ קשה שערתַ? פ' העיני בשר לך⁴ פ' המא' שידיעת ה' בתחתונים

3   [א]ני ולא מלאך ר"ל סבות למכת בכורות מעפוש האויר מסבות המכות הקודמ' ולא

4   [ש]רף⁵ שהבחנתי בין שפה [של?] בכור? ולא שליח שעשה דין באלק[ן?]ה'

5   ויו ב' פ' הפסו' עד ויהי בחצי הלילה ⁶ ויו ג' וילכו וישובו בני גד⁷

6   ויו ד' פסו' וישלחו בני ישראל לבני ראובן ובני גד⁸ את פנחס ⁹ ויו ה' מזמו' הבו לה¹⁰ ע'פ' אלשיך

7   ויו ו' פ' ה' עוז לעמו יתן¹¹ כענין השלום ופ' אחרות מנוה שלום

NY MS JTS 843 = F 23951, fol. 16a.

Rosh HaShanah, Second day, 1631.

דרשתי יום ב' של ראש השנה אחרי המגפה בב"ה אשכנזים

1   ה' יראה כמד' תלים בך ה' חסיתי¹² ית' אתה מוצא כל מי שבוטח בהקב"ה הוא מצילו ט הקד' ה' ית'

2   עם היותו נסתר מצד מהותו הוא נודע מצד פעולותיו ולפי שאינו גשמי אינו מושג ברגש

3   אנכי ולא יהיה לך¹³ מפי גבורת המופת שמענו [?] כל מקום שאתה מוצא רוממותו של הקב"ה שם אתה

4   מוצא׳ ר״ל בהיותו מרומם מכל דבר גשמי זהו ראיה שהוא משגיח בכל מקום, אמנם כאשר

5   קרה שבני אדם שכחוהו ויחסו הכל לכחם ועוצם ידם הוצרך להודיע שמו בעולם בשפטיו

6   הרעים דבר *ויגבה ה׳ צבאות במשפט*[14], כל ממקום שהקב״ה עושה דין ברשעים שמו מתגדל בעולם

7   להודיע מה אנו מה חיינו אכן חציר העם[15] <u>*וכ״ם*</u>?? רוב האנשים מיחסים כל זה אל הסדר הטבעי

8   ואלו א״ה וישראל למדו מהם פ׳ [ה]*גידה לו שאהבה נפ[שי]*[16] על *עדרי חבריך*[17] ויתערבו בגוים[18] פ׳ ישעיה

9   *החרשים שמעו*[19] ׳ תחלה על צד הקבלה ואח״כ ע״צ החקירה יבאר הפסוקי / הנמש־ כים בעניין ההשגחה

10   *וצדיק חיזק באמונתו*[20] עם היותו רואה רוע הסדר יעשה כאלו לא יראה ולא ישמע. וזהו *מי חרש כי אם*

11   *עבדי*[21] מאמ׳ על פסו׳ *הבו לה׳ בני אלים*[22] שהיה להם להשיב ולא השיבו / פ׳ הי׳ ג׳ מדות שבהם נוהג

12   עם בריויתיו כג׳ *אין קדוש*[23] בתוארים שולים ובעניין פעולותיו *אל תרבו תדברו*[24] כי *אל דעות ה׳*[25] דעות

13   הרבה בהיותו משכיר ומעניש פי הי׳ג מדות וזהו *ולא נתכנו עלילות*[26] כתיב בא׳[27]— ר״ל בפ׳ בני אדם יראה[28]

14   כאלו אינם מתוקנים תקרי ב־ו׳[29] כי לפניו ית׳ הם מתוקנים וזה ראות רבות ולא תש־ מור[30] *ה׳ חפץ*[31] ר״ל כדי

15   שישאר הבחירה׳ חפשית פ׳ *על אשר לא נעשה פתגם הרעה*[32] פ׳ הפסו׳ *עד ולא ישים על לב*[33]

16   פ׳ מזמור *יושב בסתר עליון*[34] בעניין הבטחון וההשגחה *יושב בסתר עליון הצדיק* יודע היות יסוד מהותו

17   אמנם *בצל שדי יתלונן*[35] מצד פעולותיו יקדים בעבודה מצד העונש ומצד הרוממות והא׳[36] יחלק

18   לשנים עונש העולם הזה והעולם הבא ולא׳[37] אמ׳ *כי הוא יצילך*[38] ולב׳[39] *כי אתה ה׳ מחסי*[40] ולג׳[41] שהוא

19   מצד הרוממות *כי בי חשק*[42] פ׳ המא׳ *כל מי שבוטח מצילו לעתיד לבא*[43] עם שאינו מיד

20   שהההשגחה דבקה בג׳ והם המלך והצדיק והרבים פ׳ *לא יגרע מצדיק עיניו*[44] ג׳ פ׳ *ה׳ צבאות*

21   ג׳ תרבו בתפלות ד״ה ג׳[45] תקיעה שברים תרועה מורים לאלו הג׳ פסו׳[קים] *אשרי העם*

22   *יודעי תרועה*[46] סיום המא׳ וכן הוא אומר ישראל נושע בה׳ *תשועת עולמים*.[47]

NY MS JTS 843 = F 23951, fol. 16a
Shabbat Teshuvah, fall 1631.

שבת תשובה

1 שימו לבבכם לכל הדברי[ם].⁴⁸ במד' תילים אמר דוד לפני הקב"ה ר' של עולם **שמרני כאישון בת עין.**⁴⁹ הקד' ירמיה

2 <u>שלש דין</u> ג' של <u>עם</u>? ישראל ראה אותם כבחזותם ' נתרעם כשאמר כי היה ל[הם] דבר ה' ללעג ולקלס.⁵⁰ ואומר **לא אזכרנו.**⁵¹

3 גם אני היה רצוני זה כמה שנים לדבר בשבת זה בעניני קדושת ה' ובכפרת העונות. אמנם מה אעשה

4 כי מלאה הארץ חמס וגזל מפני המגפה ' ודבר בנפול הג' *עמודי עולם פ' התורה וע־בודה וג'ח*⁵² עמודי

5 שמים ירופפו.⁵³ וכל חומה לארץ תפול.⁵⁴ בענין הגזל פס' **אוי מגיעי בית בבית**⁵⁵. אוי החוקקים חקקי און.⁵⁶

6 עבודה בעניני ב'ה ותורה ג"ח על בטול תורה פרוש המאמר

MS JTS Rab. 432 (MS 6517), no microfilm number, fol. 58a
Parashat Noah (Gen. 4–7), approx. September 1656

התי"ז
שק' פ' נח על צרכי ק"ק רומא

1 **ותבא אליו היונה**⁵⁷ ערובין אמרה יונה יהיו *מזונותי*⁵⁸ מא' **ואהבת לרעך כמוך**⁵⁹ כלל כולל התורה כולה

2 לא בלבד <u>דעלך סני</u>? ' כי גם להועיל לכלל ולפרט ' וזהו תכלית הבריאה והנברא ולא נכונו' דברי

3 המורה בח"ג פ' יג' ולהועיל בממונו וימסור נפשו מאמ' **ואם אין מחני נא'**⁶⁰ מאמ' יונה

4 קח נפשי⁶¹ מאמ' איוב **אם לא בכיתי לקשה-יום**⁶² מאמ' דוד **ואני בחלותם'**⁶³ כל המצר

5 בצרת צבור' על צרת אמיני ק"ק רומא סגורים מעני המגפה ח"ו כב' המאמ'

6 היונה רמז לכי'' שליחות העורב אכזרי לא היה מצטער' שמש מטתו גם חם ראה בזיון

7 אביו⁶⁴ ולא נצטער' פ' *יהיו מזונותי'*⁶⁵ שלא יצטרכו ישראל לפרנסה זה לזה ולא לעם

8 אחר אלה משלחנו של אביהם שבשמים

Appendix 2

Burial and Poetic Eulogies for Abraham Catalano by Solomon Marini and Moses Catalano

Solomon Marini, burial eulogy for Abraham Catalano
NY JTS 517 fol. 7v
13 Tishre 5402

ביום ג' יג' תשרי הספד על כמוה"ר אברהם קאטאלנו ז"ל קודם הקבורה

1   מימינו אש דת למו אף חובב עמים[1] ' <u>יכד</u> דמת ר' פדת *היום קשה לישראל כיום בא השמש בצהרים*[2] אם האבל וההספד לעורר

2   הבכי היה זה אך למותר כי *תרדנה עינינו מים*[3] ' ואם לפרסם שבחיו כמו כן כי הם גלוים לכל ואם להרגש האבידה ג"כ

3   ועכ"ז א'א' לעזור במילין מי יוכל ' ההספד הראשון שנעשה בעולם עשהו הבורא כי על האדם <u>בשל</u> איכה איכה

4   כתיב בי'[4] כיון שנמסר למיתר[5]—אין לו מקום שיאמר כי הוא זה ' והתבוננת על מקומו ואיננו[6] היום כאן ' עם לא היה מגיע

5   לו ית' דבר וכל האבדה היה בנספד ' דוד על שאול[7] ' על שאבדו אחרים כגון ישראל ' אם זה האבידה מגיע לנו

6   פ' *היום קשה לישראל* ופ' *והבאתי את השמש*[8] *והפכתי חגיכם לאבל*[9] נבואה קשה מב' פנים יחלק הטוב הן מן ההנהגה

7   הטבעית הן מן ההשגחיות חגיכם רמז לטובות השגחיות שירבם לטובת הטבעיות

Solomon Marini, second eulogy for Abraham Catalano
Par. Lekh lekha 5402 = 1641
NY MS 6517; JTS Rab. 432, fol. 7v

ההספד מהר"ר אברהם קאטאלנו פ' לך לך לא ב^ ב"ה לועזים

1 ואברם כבד מאד במקנה¹⁰ ' וילך למסעיו¹¹ ' אבות פ' ה' כל מי שיש בו ג' דברים כללו
    מתלמידיו של א"א¹² עם כל דאגת אומתנו בלכתה

2 בשביה בלבל אחר שעזבה המקדש חרב' היותר קשה שלא היו יכולין לבכות ' עד הגיעו
    על נהרו' בבל ופ' הפ' יום פטירת

3 זה הרב המר רוחנו ויותר על שנתעכב הספד מבלי פנאי מה שיהיה כעת בסתר קצת
    שכחית והרגש האבדה ג' תועליות

4 היינו מקבלים מן הצדיק ע"ק פ' שמיני ג' לבכי¹³ הן הג^ הפלאות[?] כי רגזה ארץ'¹⁴
    מתמוטטים הג' עמודים פ' מכנף הארץ

5 זמירות שמענו צבי לצדיק¹⁵ אומרים העליונים ושמחים בנפש הצדיק אך התחתונים
    רעה התרועעה ארץ'¹⁶ הקד' לדרוש

6 פעולות האדם עם שנראות גדולות הנה הן חלושות על הרב כי גם בטובות יתערב בהם
    יוהרא¹⁷ ותכלית מחוץ מה אנו מה

7 חיינו פי אין אדם צדיק בארץ¹⁸ כי יחטאו לך¹⁹ וע"כ לא אמר אם יחטאו כי הוא ודאי '
    פ' קוריהם לא יהיו לבגד²⁰ פ' ונהי

8 בטמא כלנו²¹ גם ב[ח?] לק העיון יסכל רוב החכמה וכן א' מבפלוסופי' סותרת דברי
    אחרת עדות שלמה אמרתי אחכמה²² פ' זבובי

9 מות יבאיש²³ הן התכליות הזרות והיוהרא מפסידות הפעולות המעולות הנמשלות '
    בשמן טוב ' יקר מחכמה ומכבוד סכלות מעט²⁴

10 שיחשוב לעולם שלא השיג חכמה שהוא מלא בסכלות פ' ופניך אני לראות פ' והחכמה
    מאין תמצא²⁵ ' היינו מהיותו חושב

11 שאין בידו ולא השיג מה ידע' זהו על החכמה המחקרית והחכמה מאין תבא²⁶ ' זהו
    חכמת התורה שתבא בקבלה אלקים

12 הבין דרכה²⁷ ' כל המתיהר אם נביא הוא²⁸ דבורה שמואל דוד משה הלל ' פ' יש רעה'
    נתן הסכל במרומים²⁹ השכל כשהוא

13 עם ידיעת סכלותו וחסרונו' ועשירים בשפל³⁰ היינו החושבים עצמם עשירים בעיון
    ומעשה יש מתעושר ואין כל

14 מתרושש³¹ שחושב שלא השיג זה כי הוי³² חזי אמבואה³³ אמר אם יעלה לשמי' שיאו
    ר' זוטרא כי לא לעולם חוסן³⁴

15 פ' כל שיש בו ג' דברים הללו מתלמיד' של א"א שהוא ראש היחס והוא סגולה ואנכי
    עפר ואפר³⁵ ' ונחנו מה.³⁶ ואנכי תולעת³⁷

16 הרב הנפטר היה גדול בתורה חכם בחכמות מושפע מנהיג קהלו וע'כז *לא היה בו שום גדולה ויהדרא*38 **ואברם**

17 **כבד מאד במקנה'** שהיה רועה קהלו בכסף ובזהב עיון ומעשה וילך למסעיו ' אהלה בתחלה ועתה בית בנה לנפשו

18 בזכות תורתו' ג' **אבדון ומות באזנינו**39. כי בקרב מיתתן **מתוסף רוחם**40 ומתחילין להשיג סודות וזה קוננתי עליו:

19 ספדי עדת אל חי **שאי קינה**41 / כי נאסף ממך יקר אורך / אלוף ישר גדול בכל פינה / עוסק בצרכייך ג. . . . .ך

20 חכם ויודע **מקום בינה**42 / הורה בחבורו מצא דרך / האיש מאד ענו בשם קנה / אוי מי תמורתנו יהי עורך

21 בוקש במדרשו והוא פנה / **נחם באנחה**43 בלב מובך / אמר לנפשו נא לינה / **שובי למשכנך**44 ומדורך

22 ואחר דברתי על ת"ת ומלמדי תינוקות שלא יכלו לחנם בבלי דעת' כי הרב הנפטר היה מוסר נפשו על זה וזהו **חפץ ה'**45

23 ולא בבנינים ולא כלים של כסף מאמ' כי הון מטיילי בבי כנשתא כמה נפשתא' פ' **לא יבא עוד שמשך**46

Moses Catalano, lament for Abraham (Catalano) NY JTS Adler 833 (F 30090)[47]

#		
1	הוכה תבל אוי כי נשאר סומא	אוי כי בסנורים ובעורון[48]
2	מרגניתא טבא לית בה טימי[50]	ווי היא ויהי בנסוע הארון[49]
3	כד דמך טוביינא דחכימי[51]	לפני שבר גאון יום שברון
		אוי כי
4	אליו כתרם כי לא יחשב במה	הוא פילוסוף רופא אף מה יתרון
5	היה לצור כי הניח שמה	אל מול כתר תורה בו בצרון
6	לחקור לדרוש לפסוק או כמדומה	שברי לוחות מונחים בארון
		אוי כי
7	מידי יום יום ישיר קינה יהמה	ביהושע כלו שירה ירון~[52]
8	כדעות במדות כי לא ידמה	ובמשל ומליצה פתח גרון
9	שוב העולם כמדומה	מצרף השכל~[53] מהגיד חסרון
		אוי כי
10	הזהיר עמו טהר כל איש טמא	נדרש לדרוש דרש לבלי חרון
11	פסק דינו בריא מאין שמא	אל כל שואל הורה בלתי דורון
12	סדר הלכו להם או כל צמא	ודרושיו ופסקיו~ אל דור אחרון
		אוי כי

הוריד טענות בוזיו בלשון אומי	13 חס לכבוד~ התלמוד <u>וכבמודרון</u>[?]
עקר הרים ויאמרו כל פומי	14 ובחדושי~ קדושין כשרון
טוב שם משמן טוב⁵⁴ כי לא נדמה	15 לו על פי מדותיו הזקן אהרון
	אוי כי
על דעות כל פוסק דלה כל מי	16 במבקש דעת הרחיב הפתרון
השים עליו לילות כיממי	17 חכמות דיני ממון וברוב כשרון
תמיד דינא אדינא קארמי	18 כי סדרם אלף בית ובזכרון
	אוי כי
קיים עירובי תבשילין~⁵⁵ נמי	19 הוא אברהם וכקבור תוך חברון
ערוב פרשיות~ ערוב סמי	20 כי מדברים שונים עשה חברון
באלקים חי כי לית מלתא לסמי	21 ולהוציאם לאור לי שברון⁵⁶
	אוי כי
גם כי קברו גופו בלא גמא	22 חי הוא כקבורם במערת עפרון⁵⁷
נשאר אתנו בשרא עם גרמי⁵⁸	23 עלה רוח נשמתו למט - - טרון
ארצה ונקונן מר אשיב עלמה	24 ולשאול מה נשב כבני מרון
הוכה תבל אוי כי נשאר סמא	25 לא עליו רק על כי בעורון

Notes

INTRODUCTION

1. Susan L. Einbinder, *After the Black Death: Plague and Commemoration Among Iberian Jews* (Philadelphia: University of Pennsylvania Press, 2018).

2. See Columbia's catalog description. Also, email exchange, Dr. Edward Reichman, July 10, 2020. For Cantarini, see entry 165 in Asher Salah, *La République des lettres: Rabbins, écrivains et médecins juifs en Italie au XVIII siècle* (Leiden: Brill, 2007), 120–24.

3. Almost all of these studies are new. The opening chapter, on Joseph Concio's double lament for the Jews of Turin and Chieri, substantially revises and recontextualizes about one-third of a previously published essay. I thank Professor Haviva Yishai and the Ben Gurion University Press for permission to incorporate part of this essay. See Susan Einbinder, "Poetry, Prose and Pestilence: Joseph Concio and Jewish Responses to the 1630 Italian Plague," in *Shirat Dvora: Essays in Honor of Dvora Bregman*, ed. Haviva Yishai (Be'er Sheva: Ben Gurion University and Mossad Bialik, 2018), *73–*101.

4. By the seventeenth century, Italian physicians and municipal officials were trained to think of plague as having a differential impact on different population groups—one way of noting that, by the early modern period, plague had become a disease associated with the urban poor. This observation justified aggressive policies of quarantine and confinement that may have had some effect in containing outbreaks but undoubtedly made them worse within confined spaces like the lazarettos and the ghettoes. Ann G. Carmichael, "Plague Legislation in the Italian Renaissance," *Bulletin of the History of Medicine* 57.4 (1983): 508–25; John Henderson, *Florence Under Siege: Surviving Plague in an Early Modern City* (New Haven, CT: Yale University Press, 2019); Brian S. Pullan, *Rich and Poor in Renaissance Venice* (Oxford: Oxford and Blackwell, 1971); Michelle Anne Laughran, "The Body, Public Health and Social Control in Sixteenth-Century Venice" (PhD diss., University of Connecticut, 1998); Samuel K. Cohn, *Cultures of Plague: Medical Thinking at the End of the Renaissance* (Oxford: Oxford University Press, 2009); Jane Crawshaw, *Plague Hospitals: Public Health for the City in Early Modern Venice* (Hampshire, UK: Ashgate Publishing, 2012, reissued by Routledge in 2016). For the ghettos, policies of containment had their own repercussions, although Catalano's account from Padua illustrates how porous the boundaries of the ghetto could be. The ghettos of Mantua, Padua, Florence, and Venice were all relatively recent creations, and their impact on policy and the experience of physical and social space had little analogue in medieval settings. Whatever they felt about the practices of quarantine and confinement, or the lockdown of the ghetto, Jewish physicians are not on record opposing containment policies. Nonetheless, in practice one finds them trying to locate temporary housing outside ghetto walls—for instance in Padua, where Abraham Catalano secured

lodging for his family in a villa outside the ghetto but then was forced by furious ghetto residents to return.

5. Renate Segre, *The Jews in Piedmont*, 3 vols. (Jerusalem: Israel Academy of Sciences & Humanities and Tel Aviv University, 1988); Luciano Allegra, "Mestierie e famiglie del ghetto," in *Una lunga presenza: studi sulla popolazione ebraica italiana*, ed. L. Allegra (Turin: Sylvio Zamorani, 2009): 167–97; P. L. Bruzzone, "Les juifs au Piémont," *Revue des Etudes Juives* 19 (1889): 141–46; [No author; L.S.?], "Alcuni appunti sul ghetto di Chieri," *Il Vessillo Israelitico* 49 (1901): 127–29, 169–71; D. Colombo and G. Tedesco, "Il Ghetto di Chieri," *La Rassegna Mensile di Israel* 27.2 (1961): 63–66; Michaël Gasperoni, "Inheritance and Wealth Among Jewish Women in the Ghettos of North-Central Italy (Seventeenth–Eighteenth Century)," *Moyen Âge* 130.1 (2018):183–97.

6. The argument for Jewish immunity to plague has been experiencing some revival among geneticists who have recently posited that (much) earlier Jewish exposure to Familial Mediterranean Fever (FMF) may have favored genetic mutations that conferred greater immunity to plague. To date they have not offered one shred of historical evidence to back this theory, which reanimates absurd ethnocentric tropes of the past. See Joshua Teplitzky, "Hygiene and Historiography: Medieval Myths and Modern Mis-receptions of the Jews and the Black Death," *AJS Review* (forthcoming, Winter 2021). I intend to address this topic in a future study.

7. The manuscript was brought to my attention by Michelle Chesner, who oversees the Hebrew manuscript collection at Columbia University and only recently purchased the Italian copy. For detailed catalog information, see NY Columbia University MS General 308, "Libro della peste che fu in Padova nel anno 5391," at https://clio.columbia.edu/catalog /14267149 and for the digitized manuscript, https://archive.org/details/ldpd_15468929_000, both sites last accessed on December 30, 2021. A recent dissertation discusses the Italian narrative; see Rebecca Locci, "La gestione della peste del 1631 nel ghetto di Padova attraverso la cronaca di Avraham Catalano," M.A. dissertation, University of Padua, 2021. My thanks to Dr. Edward Reichman for this reference.

8. Shlomo Simonsohn, *History of the Jews in the Duchy of Mantua* (Jerusalem: Kiryath Sepher, 1977).

9. The shared "systems of feeling" among what Barbara Rosenwein has defined as "emotional communities" offer a parallel phenomenon. Massarani exploits some of the same idioms of self-representation as Catalano because they are part of a shared "system" of meaning. The vocabulary of this system—for which I use the term "idiom"—highlights private and public expressions of pathos, conflict, anxiety, and responsibility. See Barbara Rosenwein, "Problems and Methods in the History of the Emotions," *Passions in Context* 1 (2010): 2–32.

10. Another contemporary account of this plague from Venice, Judah Modena's autobiography, offers its own worthy contrasts. It is not a work this book treats, partly because it is so well known, but it, too, illustrates a cultural preoccupation with self-representation in public and private realms. Judah's persona is, of course, the dominant force of his autobiography. His account of the plague in Venice lets us see the approaching disaster through the eyes of a man with a thousand other preoccupations; it is initially an inconvenience "out there," then looming closer and closer. See Mark Cohen, trans. and ed., *The Autobiography of a Seventeenth-Century Venetian Rabbi: Leon Modena's Life of Judah* (Princeton, NJ: Princeton University Press, 1988). Modena describes the advent of the plague in late May 1630, when he

notes it has begun to "spread throughout Italy," decimating the communities of Mantua, Verona, and Modena before reaching Venice in June. Among the Jews, plague breaks out in the Ghetto Vecchio and then subsides, returning with a vengeance mid-June. Modena notes that, during the lull, the Christian city continued to be harshly afflicted. See pp. 134–36.

11. David Malkiel, *Stones Speak—Hebrew Tombstones from Padua, 1529–1862* (Leiden: Brill, 2013).

12. Stephen Greenblatt, *Renaissance Self-Fashioning: From More to Shakespeare* (Chicago: University of Chicago Press, 1980). Even earlier, how we construct the personas we present to the outside world (albeit in life, not writing) was the topic of Erving Goffman's *The Presentation of Self in Everyday Life* (New York: Anchor Doubleday, 1959). The more recent bibliography is ample.

13. As I was finishing this manuscript, I encountered a review of Sebastian Sobecki's *Last Words: The Public Self and the Social Author in Late Medieval England* (Oxford: Oxford University Press, 2019), reviewed by Robert E. Edwards in *Speculum* 96.3 (2021): 889–90. Sobecki seems to be raising similar questions to some of mine.

14. See Carol Lansing, *Passion and Order: Restraint of Grief in the Medieval Italian Communes* (Ithaca, NY: Cornell University Press, 2008); Barbara Rosenwein, *Emotional Communities in the Early Middle Ages* (Ithaca, NY: Cornell University Press, 2007); Rosenwein, "Problems and Methods in the History of the Emotions," *Passions in Context* 1 (2010): 2–32.

15. Shona Kelly Wray, *Communities in Crisis: Bologna During the Black Death* (Leiden: Brill, 2009); James Amelang, trans. and ed., *Journal of a Plague Year: The Diary of the Barcelona Tanner Miquel Parets, 1651* (Oxford: Oxford University Press, 1991).

16. Cohn, *Cultures of Plague*.

17. Daily mortality accounts proved a riveting component of the cheap broadsides discussed by Mark Jenner and others. There, too, however, the columns of tallies were surrounded on the page by homiletical exhortations, biblical historiolae, and illustrations that represented plague topoi in richly symbolic or metaphoric images. See Mark Jenner, "Plague on a Page: Lord Have Mercy Upon Us in Early Modern London," *Seventeenth Century* 27.3 (2012): 255–86; S. Greenberg, "Plague, the Printing Press, and Public Health in Seventeenth-Century London," *Huntington Library Quarterly* 67 (2004): 508–27. Some of us likewise have been addicted to the daily charts and graphs tracking COVID-19 cases locally, regionally, and worldwide. I am not deriding the comfort extended by mathematical tabulations and models; I am saying that literature rarely just replicates statistical or chronological progressions, but rather condenses, attenuates, inverts, omits, subverts them.

18. See Jens Brockmeier, "Socializing the Narrative Mind," *Style* 45.2 (2011): 259–64; Brockmeier, *Beyond the Archive: Memory, Narrative, and the Autobiographical Process* (Oxford: Oxford University Press, 2015); Matthew Clark, *Narrative Structures and the Language of the Self* (Columbus: Ohio State University Press, 2010); James Phelan, *Somebody Telling Somebody Else: Toward a Rhetorical Poetics of Narrative* (Columbus: Ohio State University Press, 2017); and many others.

19. Again, Jens Brockmeier, "Memory, Narrative, and the Consequences," *Topics in Cognitive Science* 11 (2019): 821–24 at 822.

20. Jenner, "Plague on a Page," 261, and see also 266.

21. The early twentieth-century account of Edgardo Morpurgo called it "la più terribile pestilenza che la storia moderna ricordi." See Edgardo Morpurgo, *Lo studio di Padova, le epidemie ed i contagi durante il governo della repubblica veneta (1405–1797)* (Padua: La Garangola,

1922). For more recent treatments, see, e.g., Guido Alfani and Marco Boneti, "A Survival Analysis of the Last Great European Plagues: The Case of Nonantola (Northern Italy) in 1630," *Population Studies* 73.1 (2018): 101–18; Guido Alfani and Samuel Cohn, Jr., "Nonantola 1630: Anatomia di una pestilenza e meccanismi del contagio," *SIDeS: Popolazione e historia 2* (2007): 99–138; Stephen R. Ell, "Three Days in October of 1630: Detailed Examination of Mortality During an Early Modern Plague Epidemic in Venice," *Reviews of Infectious Diseases* 11.1 (1989): 128–39; Carlo Cipolla, *Faith, Reason and the Plague in Seventeenth-Century Tuscany* (New York: Norton, 1979) and Cipolla, *Cristofano and the Plague: A Study in the History of Public Health in the Age of Galileo* (Berkeley: University of California Press, 1973); Henderson, *Florence Under Siege*; Ann Carmichael, *Plague and the Poor in Renaissance Florence* (Cambridge: Cambridge University Press, 1986); Michelle A. Laughran, "The Body, Public Health and Social Control in Sixteenth-Century Venice"; M. Manfredini et al., "The Plague of 1630 in the Territory of Parma: Outbreak and Effects of a Crisis," *International Journal of Anthropology* 17.1 (2002): 41–57; Richard Palmer, "The Control of Plague in Venice and Northern Italy: 1348–1600" (PhD diss., University of Kent at Canterbury, 1978).

22. Henderson, *Florence Under Siege*, 23–24.

23. Morpurgo dates the onset of plague in the city proper to September 1630, based on ordinances issued that month and a print announcement from the *protomedici* and physicians from the Health Office and lazaretto. Morpurgo, *Lo studio di Padova*, 156–57.

24. Cohen, *Autobiography of a Seventeenth-Century Venetian Rabbi*, 135–36.

25. A few recent examples will have to suffice. For plague, we have recent studies of the Kazakhstan region and the disruption of the local ecosystem, where the plague bacillus survives without a carrier in the soil. Not coincidentally, this region is thought to have been a source of the outbreak that reached Crimea and its Genoan outpost in 1347, spreading to Europe as the Black Death. See Michelle Ziegler's entry in her Contagions blog: https://contagions.wordpress.com/2017/12/18/ancient-plague-strains-in-kyrgyzstan/#more-18555, last accessed November 22, 2021. Another type of study looks at the distribution of rodents carrying *Y. pestis* in agricultural versus conserved land; see Douglas J. McCauley et al., "Effects of Land Use on Plague (*Yersinia pestis*): Activity of Rodents in Tanzania," *American Journal of Tropical Medicine and Hygiene* 92.4 (2015): 776–83; my thanks to Ann Carmichael for the reference. Finally, while COVID-19 is an extremely contagious virus, and therefore not transmitted like bubonic plague, one can observe the same movement of disease from, e.g., Israeli cities and towns via Palestinian workers who export the virus back to their villages, or from wealthy, globetrotting Brazilian households via servants who export COVID-19 back to the favelas. See, e.g., Hana Saleh, "Palestinian Workers in Israel Face More Restrictions Amid Coronavirus Outbreak," *Al-Monitor*, April 3, 2020, https://www.al-monitor.com/pulse/originals/2020/04/palestinian-restrictions-workers-return-israel-coronavirus.html; Mohammed Najib and David Halbfinger, "Palestinians Fear a Coming Coronavirus Storm," *New York Times*, April 9, 2020, https://www.nytimes.com/2020/04/09/world/middleeast/coronavirus-palestinians-israel-gaza-west-bank.html; last accessed November 22, 2021.

26. Cipolla, *Faith, Reason and the Plague*, 20; and see the recent study by Alfonsina D'Amato et al., "Of Mice and Men: Traces of Life in the Death Registries of the 1630 Plague in Milano," *Journal of Proteomics* 180 (2018): 128–37; Henderson, *Florence Under Siege*, 24.

27. Enzo Lucchetti, Matteo Manfredini, and Sergio de Iasio, "La peste de 1630 dans la ville et dans le territoire de Parme (Italie)," *Bulletins et mémoires de la Société d'anthropologie de Paris*, n.s. 10.3–4 (1998): 411–24; M. Manfredini, "The Plague of 1630 in the Territory of

Parma," 41. The authors describe the 1630 outbreak as "perhaps the most important demographic event in seventeenth-century Italy" ("Plague of 1630," 56). Very recent studies have seized upon urban death registries as new sources for quantifying mortalities; for a related approach, see, e.g., Alfonsina D'Amato, G. Zilberstein, S. Zilberstein, B. Compagnoni, P. Righetti, "Of Mice and Men: Traces of Life in the Death Registries of the 1630 Plague in Milano," *Journal of Proteomics* 180 (2018): 128–37; Mirko Traversari et al., "The Plague of 1630 in Modena (Italy) Through the Study of Parish Registers," *Medicina Historica* 3.3 (2019): 139–48; Guido Alfani and Samuel K. Cohn, "Nonantola 1630: Anatomia di una pestilenza e meccanismi del contagio." Some of these data-crunching studies are more persuasive than others.

28. Manfredini et al., "The Plague of 1630." Henderson, *Florence Under Siege*, 24, cites mortality rates of 61 percent for Parma and Verona, whose total pre-outbreak populations are estimated at 30,000 and 54,000, respectively. Ann Carmichael estimates 60 percent mortality, citing census figures of 53,285 and 20,630 for 1627 and 1631, respectively. Carmichael, "Pest House Imaginaries" (pre-published ms.), 8, with my thanks to the author for a copy of the essay.

29. Simonsohn, *History of the Jews in the Duchy of Mantua*; and Simonsohn, "Savants and Scholars in Jewish Mantua: A Reassessment," in *Rabbi Judah Moscato and the Jewish Intellectual World of Mantua in the Sixteenth and Seventeenth Centuries*, ed. Giuseppe Veltri and G. Miletto (Leiden: Brill, 2012), 300.

30. For Venice, see Carla Boccato, "Testimonianze ebraiche sulla peste del 1630 a Venezia," *La Rassegna Mensile di Israel*, 3d ser., 41.9–10 (1975), 458. For Padua, the 100,000 figure for the total population comes from Cipolla, *Faith, Reason and the Plague*, 133; see also Morpurgo, *Lo studio di Padova*, 155, for lower overall figures—an estimated total population in Padua of 35,000 in 1630, with 15,000 lost to plague or flight by the next year.

31. See Chapter 2.

32. Thus, Guy Geltner has recently argued that the famous Pistoian ordinances, far from representing innovative strides into "public health," relied heavily on preexisting policies of containment and public sanitation. See Geltner, "The Path to Pistoia: Urban Hygiene Before the Black Death," *Past & Present* 246.1 (2020): 3–33. As for mortality counts, the estimates vary widely but have recently been subject to an upward revision of 50 to 90 percent in Europe; see Monica Green, "Taking 'Pandemic' Seriously: Making the Black Death Global," *Pandemic Disease in the Medieval World: Rethinking the Black Death, The Medieval Globe* 1.1 ed. Monica Green (Kalamazoo, MI: ARC Medieval Press, 2014): 27–62; see also Green's overview and introduction to the webinar panel discussion, "The Mother of All Pandemics: The State of Black Death Research in the Era of Covid-19" (Medieval Academy of America Webinar, recorded May 15, 2020), https://youtu.be/VzqR1S8cbX8, last accessed November 22, 2021.

33. Ann Carmichael, "Plague Legislation in the Italian Renaissance," *Bulletin of the History of Medicine* 57.4 (1983): 508–25.

34. Cohn, *Cultures of Plague*; Henderson, *Florence Under Siege*; Laughran, "The Body, Public Health and Social Control"; Palmer, "The Control of Plague in Venice and Northern Italy"; see also the studies cited throughout.

35. Quoted by Cipolla, *Cristofano and the Plague*, 15–16; Cipolla cites Tadino's *Raguaglio dell'origine et giornali successi della gran peste* (Milan, 1648), pages 13 and 26 respectively. I have modernized Cipolla's English slightly.

36. Morpurgo, *Lo studio di Padova*, 154.

37. Ibid.

38. There was a period in the scholarship when historians represented the contagion model as supplanting older miasma models; it is more commonly recognized now that even medieval plague tracts tended to blend the two, and all the more so early modern writers. See Jon Arrizabalaga, "Facing the Black Death: Perceptions and Reactions of University Medical Practitioners," in *Practical Medicine from Salerno to the Black Death*, ed. Luis García Ballester, Roger French, Jon Arrizabalaga, and Andrew Cunningham (Cambridge: Cambridge University Press, 1994), 237–88; Ann Carmichael, "Plague Persistence in Western Europe: A Hypothesis," in *The Medieval Globe* 1.1 (Pandemic Disease in the Medieval World), ed. Monica Green (Kalamazoo, MI: ARC Medieval Press, 2014), 157–92; Nükhet Varlik, *Plague and Empire in the Early Modern Mediterranean World* (Cambridge: Cambridge University Press, 2015), Justin K. Stearns, *Infectious Ideas: Contagion in Premodern Christian and Islamic Thought in the Western Mediterranean* (Baltimore: Johns Hopkins University Press, 2011).

39. Henderson, *Florence Under Siege*.

40. L. Seifert, et al., "Genotyping *Yersinia pestis* in Historical Plague: Evidence for Long-Term Persistence in Europe from the Fourteenth to the Seventeenth Century," *PLoSOne* 11.1: e0145194 (January 2016). See also K. Bos et al., "Eighteenth-century *Yersinia pestis* Genomes Reveal the Long-Term Persistence of an Historical Plague Focus," *eLife* 5, 17837 (2016); this piece focuses on genome reconstruction from the 1722 Marseille outbreak, a genome that became extinct. The German strain, which was attested in two grave sites more than 500 km apart, falls between nodes N07 and N10 on branch 1 of the phylogenetic tree published first in 2011. See Kirsten Bos et al., "A Draft Genome of *Yersinia pestis* from Victims of the Black Death," *Nature* 478 [7370] (2011): 506–10; Yujun Cui et al., "Historical Variations in Mutation Rate in an Epidemic Pathogen, *Yersinia pestis*," *PNAS* 110.2 (2013): 577–82; Amine Namouchi et al., "Integrative Approach Using *Yersinia pestis* Genomes to Revisit the Historical Landscape of Plague During the Medieval Period," *PNAS* 115.50 (2018): E11790–E11797.

41. I intend to broaden my perspective, however, in forthcoming work.

42. As Molly Andrews has observed, those who record or work with traumatic testimonies tell themselves "that the process of telling will itself be a healing one." Molly Andrews, "Beyond Narrative: The Shape of Traumatic Testimony," in *We Shall Bear Witness: Life Narratives and Human Rights*, ed. Meg Jensen et al. (Madison: University of Wisconsin Press, 2014), 33.

43. Barbara Christian, "Does Theory Play Well in the Classroom?" (1996), repr. in *New Black Feminist Criticism 1985–2000*, ed. Gloria Bowles et al. (Champaign: University of Illinois Press, 2007), 56.

CHAPTER I

Approximately one-third of this chapter incorporates material from my essay, "Poetry, Prose and Pestilence: Joseph Concio and Jewish Responses to the 1630 Italian Plague," in *Shirat Dvora: Essays in Honor of Dvora Bregman*, ed. Haviva Yishai (Be'er Sheva: Ben Gurion University and Mossad Bialik, 2019), *73–*101. I thank the editor and publisher for permission to recycle. As will be evident, the version here makes several corrections to the earlier piece and shifts its interests and conclusions considerably.

1. Paris MS Alliance Universelle Israelite 139 (IMHM F 3207); NY MS JTS 5063 (IMHM F 29860). Curiously, it is mentioned by Giaochino da Montù in his 1830 account of this plague; he claims to have requested and received a transcription made by "Sansone Levi" of a lament by "Giuseppe Conzio, autore e stampatore." Gioachino Montù da Chieri, *Memorie storiche del gran contagio in Piemonte negli anni 1630 e 31 e specialmente del medesimo in Chieri* (Turin: Giacinto Marietti, 1830), 54.

2. Bregman's edition of Moses Zakut (Zacuto)'s poems includes two other examples written in *terza rima*: poem no. 15 (מאור סהר) on p. 100, and poem no. 23 (הן הפרידה בין גופי דודים) on p. 119; Dvora Bregman, *Esa et levavi: Shirim me'et Moshe Zakut* (Jerusalem: Ben Tzvi Institute and Hebrew University, 2009).

3. See, e.g., Stefanie Beth Siegmund, *The Medici State and the Ghetto of Florence: The Construction of an Early Modern Jewish Community* (Palo Alto, CA: Stanford University Press, 2006).

4. In 1886 Steinschneider listed more than sixty of Concio's known poems, many of them occasional. The list is followed by Steinschneider's transcription of a previously unknown poem by Concio in praise of his patron, Duke Charles Emmanuel I. Moritz Steinschneider, "Poems of Joseph Concio from an Unknown Manuscript" [in Hebrew], *He'Assif* 2 (1886): 225–27; see also Nello Pavoncello, "La tipografia ebraica in Piemonte," *La Rassegna Mensile di Israel*, 3d ser., 36.2 (1970): 96–100, at 97; S. Olivetti, "Uno stampatore e poeta ebreo: Giuseppe Conzio," *La Rassegna Mensile di Israel* 25.1 (1959): 22–25. The press produced exactly ten publications, most of them his own. Pavoncello, "La tipografia ebraica," 97–98. A six-part hymn for the counting of the Omer came off the press in 1632, and is the last known sign of the author and printer.

5. *Zokher haNeshamot*, I: 267–76. References to Joseph's Turin lament, which he calls "The First Story," are indicated with the Roman numeral I followed by the stanza number and then, if necessary, the verse, e.g. I:2:iv. Note that my article in the Bregman festschrift cites by verse number, not stanza; Einbinder, "Poetry, Prose, and Pestilence."

6. Numerous accounts describe the callous brutality of the municipal *pizzigamorti*—"body pluckers"—and their fellow grave diggers; see Jane Crawshaw, *Plague Hospitals: Public Health for the City in Early Modern Venice* (Hampshire: Ashgate Publishing, 2012; reissued by Routledge in 2016), chapter 2; and Crawshaw, "The Beasts of Burial: Pizzigamorti and Public Health for the Plague in Early Modern Venice," *Social History of Medicine* 24.3 (2011): 570–82.

7. For a recent analysis and edition of early modern Paduan Jewish examples, see David Malkiel, *Stones Speak—Hebrew Tombstones from Padua, 1529–1862* (Leiden: Brill, 2014), and Malkiel, *Shirei-Shayish: Ketuvot mibatei hahayim shel Padova 1529–1862* (Jerusalem: Ben Zvi Institute, 2013). For other early modern Italian examples, see Dvora Bregman, "'Now you shall be in verses of stone': The Epitaph Poems of Moses Zacuto" [in Hebrew], in *Studies in Arabic and Hebrew Letters in Honor of Raymond P. Scheindlin*, ed. Jonathan Decter and Michael Rand(Piscataway, NJ: Gorgias Press, 2007), Hebrew section, 13–21; Bregman, *Tzror Zehuvim: Sonetim Ivriyim metekufat haRenesans vehaBarok* (Jerusalem: Ben Tzvi Institute and Ben Gurion University, 1997); and the large selection of epitaph poetry included in her edition of Zacuto's verse, *Esa et levavi*. For medieval examples, see my *After the Black Death: Plague and Commemoration Among Iberian Jews* (Philadelphia: University of Pennsylvania Press, 2018), chapter 4; Avriel Bar-Levav, "Another Place: Cemeteries in Jewish Culture" [in Hebrew], *Pe'amim* 98–99 (2002): 5–37.

8. Renata Segre, *The Jews in Piedmont* (Jerusalem: Israel Academy of Sciences and Humanities, and Tel Aviv: Tel Aviv University, 1986–90). The copyist of the Columbia University copy of Abraham Catalano's plague narrative also enlisted this technique, adding marginal notations that identify his kin in the account. The practice suggests that, with time, local memory was not entirely serviceable but that dynastic ties still mattered.

9. Allegra cites a 1702 census that counted 44,574 residents of Turin, among them, 744 Jews, which he considers a considerable undercount. Given the attrition following the 1630 outbreak, it is hard to estimate what the populations might have been just prior to (or after) the plague. Even 700 Jews would constitute a large community, comparable to that of Padua. Luciano Allegra, "A Model of Jewish Devolution: Turin in the Eighteenth Century," *Jewish History* 7.2 (1993): 29–58, at 32–33.

10. Segre, *The Jews in Piedmont*, LXXIV.

11. Bubonic plague, of course, is not contagious from human to human. *Yersinia pestis*, the bacillus that causes plague, is transmitted to humans by fleas (alternatively, by lice) borne by a variety of mostly small mammals. *Rattus rattus*, the black rat, is typically considered the carrier in premodern Europe, but shrews, voles, mice, prairie dogs, and even camels can also carry plague-bearing fleas. The current list of mammals that can transmit plague numbers more than two hundred. Thus the late medieval and renaissance obsession with plague contagion was an error. It was nonetheless a result of keen observation of a link between musty, cramped, and poorly ventilated spaces and disease, or used clothing, granaries and disease. Contagion, however, in our contemporary sense of the word, was relevant to plague only in situations where the bubonic form of the disease mutated to pneumonic or septicemic forms.

12. I:8. See Carlo Cipolla, *Cristofano and the Plague* (Berkeley: University of California Press, 1973), 17.

13. Plague appeared in the Christian city at the end of June, suggesting a slight delay before its emergence in the Jewish community. Da Montù's 1830 account repeats the familiar belief that the plague entered Turin in the spring of 1629 with soldiers coming from France and Germany (he refers also to the plague outbreak in Lyon in 1628). His "Patient Zero" in Turin is Franceschino Lupo Calzolaio, who falls ill with a bubo in January 1630. See Da Montù, *Memorie storiche*, 7–12.

14. Ibid., 16–17.

15. Ann Carmichael, "Pest House Imaginaries," (pre-published ms.), 26–27. Da Montù refers to several specific sites, including a small lazaretto "nella cascina di Vallèro in poca distanza dal loro Convento"; this site was constructed in July 1630. The Capuchin presence in the religious hospitals and lazarettos is noteworthy, as it may have contributed to the fear of the Jews transported to these locations. Da Montù, *Memorie storiche*, 21, 38–42.

16. Some larger Jewish communities, like that of Padua, assumed responsibility for constructing their own lazarettos and convalescent spaces; see the next chapter. In Venice the practice seems to have been to provide Jewish monitors or advocates for Jews who were confined to the Christian facilities.

17. The government health office, or Sanità, regulated policy during epidemics. I capitalize the name, as it is in Italian and as we would do for our "Department of Health." Gasperoni comments that the institution of the ghetto led to a "more developed" infrastructure in the community; Michaël Gasperoni, "Inheritance and Wealth Among Jewish Women in the Ghettos of North-Central Italy (Seventeenth–Eighteenth Century)," *Moyen Âge* 130.1 (2018):183–97. We will see in the next two chapters that the Mantuan and Paduan documents refer constantly to negotiations between ghetto and Christian officials and institutions.

18. Correcting my transcription and reading in "Poetry, Prose and Pestilence," *94.

19. See the example of Judah Segre at II:77.

20. I distinguish between a clear case of a single-parent family, such as "Rachel, Rosa's daughter" (a matrilineal household; see I:29), and descriptions of a single parent's death which imply the other parent survived.

21. Cecil Roth, "L'accademia musicale del Ghetto Veneziano," *La Rassegna Mensile di Israel* 3.4 (1928): 152–62.

22. Ps. 38:18.

23. Job 23:2.

24. Lam. 1:15.

25. 2 Sam. 19:1.

26. Compare Job 18:6.

27. Gen. 27:20.

28. Esther 2:18.

29. Ps. 132:8.

30. Ps. 46:2.

31. Ps. 139:7.

32. Job 6:25; 33:3.

33. Job 9:2.

34. Job 1:21.

35. The oldest example I have seen (so far) was written by Moses Rieti, ca. 1460 (the Bolognese connection again?), for his wife, Cilla; see Ariel Toaff, *Gli Ebrei a Perugia* (Perugia: Arti Grafiche Città di Castello, 1975), appendix, doc. 42, קינה מרב ר' משה מריאטי על פטירת אשתו. The text begins עורה עורה קול שאוני ואעירה אבלי, pp. 18–20. For seventeenth-century examples, see Bregman, *Esa et levavi*.

36. Ps. 38:10.

37. Cf. Ps. 116:3.

38. Ps. 38:23, and cf. also Ps. 40:14, 70:2, 71:12.

39. "Hear my voice," a common expression—but see Ps. 17:7, 64:2 for examples.

40. Ps. 51:14.

41. Cf. Prov. 18:10, Ps. 139:6.

42. Ps. 31:3, 16.

43. The JPS translates: "You are aware of all my entreaties." The sense is that the speaker's yearnings lie open to God.

44. Literally, show me favor/pity, and save me with pity. The redundancy is clunky in English.

45. The loss of children is alluded to at the beginning of the composite work, in the introductory stanzas that precede the Turin lament. "A voice of bitter weeping is heard in Ramah," Joseph says in the second tercet; his listeners or readers would have filled in the rest of the verse, "Rachel weeping for her children; she refuses to be comforted, because they are gone" (I:2.i and see Jer. 31:15).

46. John Henderson, *Florence Under Siege: Surviving Plague in an Early Modern City* (New Haven, CT: Yale University Press, 2019), 33, notes that a contemporary account of the outbreak in Florence, by Rondinelli, cites Dante, but not as a sustained element of his narrative.

47. Da Montù, *Memorie storiche*, 92–99.

48. Using Dartmouth College's Dante Lab translation, vv. 13–15: "Lady, thou art so great, and so prevailing / That he who wishes grace, nor runs to thee, / His aspirations without

wings would fly"; vv. 19–21: "In thee compassion is, in thee is pity, / In thee magnificence; in thee unites / Whate'er of goodness is in any creature." See: http://dantelab.dartmouth.edu /reader?reader%5Bcantica%5D=3&reader%5Bcanto%5D=33, last accessed November 24, 2021.

49. Readers of the original essay on which this chapter draws will note the shift in my conclusion. See Einbinder, "Poetry, Prose and Pestilence."

CHAPTER 2

1. Michelle Chesner, curator of Hebrew manuscripts at Columbia University, in-formed me in an email of June 11, 2021, that the library had recently acquired the Italian copy. As noted in my introduction, NY Columbia University MS General 308 is titled "Libro della peste che fu in Padova nel anno 5391" and was copied in an early seventeenth-century hand. Images can be accessed online in full at https://archive.org/details/ldpd _15468929_000/page/n49/mode/2up, last accessed November 27, 2021. The dealer pro-vided Ms. Chesner with a detailed evaluation, which I thank her for graciously sharing. The Hebrew manuscript copy is NY MS Columbia University X893-Ab8 (IMHM micro-film number F 16558).

2. Samuel K. Cohn, *The Black Death Transformed: Disease and Culture in Renaissance Europe* (London: Bloomsbury Academic, 2010), 66–68, 97.

3. Ibid., 66–68.

4. Barbara Rosenwein has detailed this phenomenon in her work on the history of emotions. See Barbara Rosenwein, "Problems and Methods in the History of the Emotions," *Passions in Context* 1 (2010): 2–32; Rosenwein, *Emotional Communities in the Early Middle Ages* (Ithaca, NY: Cornell University Press, 2007).

5. Marshall Sahlins, "The Return of the Event, Again: With Reflections on the Begin-ning of the Great Fijian War of 1843 to 1845 Between the Kingdoms of Bau and Rewa," in *Culture in Practice: Selected Essays* (New York: Zone Books, 2000), 293–51; Sahlins, *Apologies to Thucydides: Understanding History as Culture and Vice Versa* (Chicago: University of Chi-cago Press, 2004); Lars Rodseth, "Historical Massacres and Mythical Totalities: Reading Marshall Sahlins on Two American Frontiers," in *Anthropologists and Their Traditions Across National Borders*, ed. Regna Darnell and Frederic Gleach (Lincoln: University of Nebraska Press, 2014), 209–48; see also William Sewell, "A Theory of the Event: Marshall Sahlins's Possible Theory of History," in *Logics of History* (Chicago: University of Chicago Press, 2000), 197–224.

6. The other two judges on the *beit din* were the Paduan rabbi Solomon Marini and Qalonymos min haHazanim (Cantarini). Cecil Roth, "Sefer *'Olam Hafukh* by Abraham Catalano," *Qovetz 'al yad* 4.14 (1946): 73–74, note 4. The Committee of Four included Catalano, Aaron Katz, Moses Grassetto, and Azriel Katz; see Roth, "Sefer *'Olam Ha-fukh*," 75.

7. At the epidemic's conclusion Catalano is demanding negotiations over the location of a decontamination site for Jewish goods and which goods will require decontamination, as well as over the return of convalescent Jews to the ghetto. He notes that he represented the ghetto's position "many times" before the *provveditore* and ministers, "for not a single spokesperson remained of the myriad who had already died or fled." Roth, "Sefer *'Olam Hafukh*," 95.

8. He is what Sherry Ortner calls "existentially complex, a being who feels and thinks and reflects, who makes and seeks meaning." Sherry Ortner, "Subjectivity and Social Critique," *Anthropological Theory* 5.1 (2005): 31–52, citing 33. Future comparison of the Hebrew version treated here with the Italian journal that served as its scaffolding would hopefully confirm how carefully Catalano worked in Hebrew to craft the formal account.

9. The Hebrew text was published once, by Cecil Roth, "Sefer *'Olam Hafukh*"; I have relied also on the earliest complete extant copy, NY Columbia University MS X893-Ab8 (IMHM microfilm number F 16558), but will cite page numbers from Roth's more accessible edition. I thank Michelle Chesner, curator of the Hebrew manuscript collection at Columbia, for alerting me to the existence of their copy, which was the initial spur to explore the Jewish textual responses to this epidemic. There are six extant manuscript copies of the text: in addition to Columbia's copy, the others are MSS Montefiore 473 (F 5373), NY JTS 3568 (ENA 1005) (F 29373), Oxford Michael Add. 13 (F 21598), Budapest (Kaufmann) 335 (MSS-D 7837 microfiche), and London British Library 971 (F 5721). The Columbia copy is the oldest. As noted earlier, the Italian Jewish version most likely predates it and served as its model. The "Libro della peste che fu in Padova" was apparently not intended to circulate widely. Whether Catalano knew he was keeping a record that he would later convert into literary Hebrew is a mystery, but it is true that the literary Hebrew of the polished version would have been accessible to a wider readership than the vernacular, which was written in local dialect ("Tuscan" according to the dealer's notes, but significantly not Venetian, which would have been more dominant as a literary medium) and frequently interpolated Hebrew terms in Hebrew script. See note 1.

10. For the fullest English translation to date, which is neither complete nor entirely reliable, see Alan D. Crown, "*The World Overturned*: The Plague Diary of Abraham Catalano," *Midstream* 19.2 (February 1973): 65–76. My thanks to Ann Carmichael for first drawing my attention to this text, and to Magda Teters for a copy.

11. Giulia Calvi, *Histories of a Plague Year: The Social and the Imaginary in Baroque Florence* (Berkeley: University of California Press, 1989). Calvi focuses on the strategic maneuverings of everyday people and officials trying to evade, bend, or selectively enforce plague-related regulations.

12. For additional details, see Daniel Carpi, introd. and ed., *Pinqas va'ad q"q Padova* (Jerusalem: National Sciences Academy of Israel and Central Archive for the History of the Jewish People, 1974), 20–21.

13. Roth, "Sefer *'Olam Hafukh*," 82. Recall that Grasseto and Katz served with Catalano on the ghetto's Committee of Four (see note 6). Grasseto died of plague toward the end of the epidemic; Catalano's interjected "may he rest in peace" signals to the reader that he will not reach the end of the story alive.

14. Roth, "Sefer *'Olam Hafukh*," 82. The (justifiable) fear was that personal property would be impounded and either immolated or destroyed in a later process of "decontamination," which could involve serial rounds of washing, fumigation, and burial.

15. Roth, "Sefer *'Olam Hafukh*," 84–85.

16. There is some evidence that the chronology has been reworked in the Hebrew so that it is not always identical to that in the Italian—something worth future exploration.

17. Thus, for example, where the Hebrew account notes the committee's failure to pre-order wheat, the author interjects, "For we didn't buy the wheat—and if only we had!—because it became expensive." The Italian simply reads "non fù comparator et in tanto s'incari più de Lire trenta il mozo" (scan no. 8, left side, lines 4–5). Similarly, shortly afterward, when

the ghetto fails to rent land at Brentelle, the Hebrew again includes a personal interjection ("if only we had") that is missing in the Italian "e non fosse stata mai tolta [?] le disgratie che vi caterono" (scan no. 8, left side, lines 18–19).

18. All four examples may be found in Roth, "Sefer *'Olam Hafukh*," pp. 76–77. The Brentelle episode is phrased similarly in the Italian, with a tint of hindsight; expressions of foreknowledge are not in the Italian passages that correspond to the other incidents.

19. I treat these poems in the following chapter.

20. Roth, "Sefer *'Olam Hafukh*," 80. Again, compare scans 15 and 16 of the Italian, where the personal interjections do not appear. In the Italian text the episode concludes with Catalano noting that had they not borrowed the money, "molti sarebero morti da necesita." The hindsight is there but not the personalized "God remembered me favorably" or the strong language describing his own intervention.

21. Roth, "Sefer *'Olam Hafukh*," 82.

22. Roth, "Sefer *'Olam Hafukh*," 88.

23. To borrow Clifford Geertz's distinction between rituals (or texts) that constitute a "model *of*" and a "model *for*," Abraham Catalano's account of the 1630 plague in the Paduan ghetto illustrates the latter; see Ortner, "Subjectivity and Social Critique.".

24. As Nükhet Varlik demonstrates for Constantinople, the plague itself naturalizes over time. See her *Plague and Empire in the Early Modern Mediterranean World: The Ottoman Experience, 1347–1600* (Cambridge: Cambridge University Press, 2015).

25. Roth, "Sefer *'Olam Hafukh*," 88.

26. Ibid., 87. Alex Bamji also notes the phenomenon of a "perceived quality of care" in the lazarettos that led some to seek admission; Alex Bamji, "Medical Care in Early Modern Venice," London School of Economics and Political Science, Dept. of Economic History, Working Papers No. 188 (March 2014), 16.

27. Roth, "Sefer *'Olam Hafukh*," 81. Subsequently, after one brother's death, the remaining brother, Leib, refused to work any longer; see p. 86.

28. Ibid., 90.

29. Ibid., 84. For other instances where Catalano locks horns with his three colleagues, see 78, 80, 84, 87, 88. The issues range from their unwillingness to accept the loan terms offered by a Christian nobleman or minister, Giovanni Michel, to their majority vote to force the poor to serve as gravediggers and caretakers or suffer the suspension of their charity stipends, to a failure to purchase spare mattresses and robes for the poor and for the recovered. John Henderson's study of this outbreak in Florence also notes the practice of people praying from doorways and windows, while masses were celebrated in the street. John Henderson, *Florence Under Siege: Surviving Plague in an Early Modern City* (New Haven, CT: Yale University Press, 2019), 165–66.

30. Roth, "Sefer *'Olam Hafukh*," 83.

31. Ibid., 91.

32. The townspeople compel the Jews to brick up the apartment windows. Ibid., 86.

33. Ibid., 84.

34. Ibid., 86, 94.

35. Ibid., 88. A cursory check of the Italian reveals that the interjected "whose names I shall not utter" is not in the original. The Italian notes drily that "miei colega non volse prometer ch'ella vegness" (scan 33, line 13).

36. NY Columbia University MS General 308, scan 38.

37. Ibid.

38. Roth, "Sefer '*Olam Hafukh*," 91.

39. Cipolla confirms the ubiquitousness of this quandary, which he notes also colored arrangements in Prato: "nobles, rich men and merchants could and did manage to save their possessions from the flames. The poor had no power to do so," Carlo Cipolla, *Cristofano and the Plague: A Study in the History of Public Health in the Age of Galileo* (Berkeley: University of California Press, 1973), 91. In Prato, Cipolla says the city policy was to reimburse 50 percent of the value of destroyed goods. If the percentage was similar in Padua, we can see why the wealthy found it easier to burn their possessions than to pay for decontamination and haggle over damages.

40. Roth, "Sefer '*Olam Hafukh*," 95.

41. His tone of frustration and dogged determination to manage the crisis as it is mediated through the bureaucracy of ghetto, city (Padua), duchy (Venice), and Health Office is reminiscent of Carlo Cipolla's Health Office technocrat Cristofano, who was active during the same plague outbreak in Prato. See the discussion that follows.

42. See Carol Lansing, *Passion and Order: Restraint of Grief in the Medieval Italian Communes* (Ithaca, NY: Cornell University Press, 2008); Rosenwein, *Emotional Communities in the Early Middle Ages*.

43. Roth, "Sefer '*Olam Hafukh*," 80.

44. Ibid., 84.

45. Ibid., 87–88.

46. Ibid., 80–81.

47. Ibid., 89.

48. Ibid., 95.

49. Ibid., 84.

50. Ibid., 86. In this instance, they "cried out together to the *provveditore*." A quick check of the Italian version confirms that different terminology characterizes the Christians' behavior. At the same time, there is not a consistent expression that corresponds to the Hebrew צעק מרה. Again, even this cursory comparison confirms how carefully Catalano has constructed the Hebrew account to resonate in specific ways. Scan 28 of the Italian, describing the burghers who thwart the preferred Jewish location for a lazaretto, qualifies its depiction of their actions: "ma quelli d[e]l borgo *che la maggior parte errano Gentill' huomini*, li corsero [alla?] Proveditor'" (emphasis mine). That qualification is also stripped from the Hebrew.

51. Roth, "Sefer '*Olam Hafukh*," 97.

52. As Ross Brann observed, Catalano's use of this expression may also be ironic. Esau's name and figure are associated in rabbinic and medieval literature with Christianity, just as his brother, Jacob, becomes "Israel" and eponymous with the Jews. To link Esau's distress at having been defrauded to the Italian Jewish experience strangely turns the tables on the ghetto. Ross Brann, private email, March 2020.

53. Roth, "Sefer '*Olam Hafukh*," 84.

54. Ibid., 89. The Italian text reads "mi fecero gran compatione," underlining that "compassion" or "pity" is the emotional state Catalano describes; for this specific scene, see Columbia University's MS General 308, scan 19. Cipolla quotes Cardinal Spada on the Bologna lazarettos teeming with suffering, death, and, above all, disorder: "Here you see people lament, others cry, others strip themselves to the skin, others die, others become black and deformed, others lose their minds. Here you are overwhelmed by intolerable smells. Here you cannot walk but among corpses. Here you feel naught but the constant horror of death.

This is the faithful replica of hell since here there is no order and only horror prevails." Cipolla, *Cristofano and the Plague,* 27, citing from Tadino's *Raguaglio dell'origine et giornali successi della gran peste* (Milan, 1648), 11.

55. Roth, "Sefer *'Olam Hafukh,*" 84.

56. Ibid., 88.

57. Ibid., 77.

58. Ibid., 78.

59. Ibid.,, 97.

60. Ibid., 84. The girl is never named, but her father, Moses di Bianci, is. The father comes to tend his daughter and is confined with her.

61. Gen. 45:26.

62. Roth, "Sefer *'Olam Hafukh,*" 88.

63. Cipolla, *Cristofano and the Plague,* 59.

64. Brian Stock, *The Implications of Literacy* (Princeton, NJ: Princeton University Press, 1983); Rosenwein.

65. Massarani *père* had wealth of his own; see Eduard Birnbaum, *Jewish Musicians at the Court of the Mantuan Dukes* (Jerusalem: Tel Aviv University and the Council for Art and Culture, 1978), 16. Abraham Massarani's wife was related to Moses Sulam, with connections to the Sulam banking dynasty in Venice. Moses was the patron of composer Salamone Rossi, and the husband of Sara Copio Sulam (a poet in her own right and mistress of a celebrated salon). See Birnbaum, "Jewish Musicians at the Court of the Mantuan Dukes"; Don Harrán, "Doubly Tainted, Doubly Talented: The Jewish Poet Sara Copio (d. 1641) as a Heroic Singer," in *Musica Franca: Essays in Honor of Frank A. D'Acccone,* ed. Irene Alm, Alyson McLamore, and Colleen Reardon (Stuyvesant, NY: Pendragon Press, 1996), 367–422.

66. Susan Parisi, "The Jewish Community and Carnival Entertainment at the Mantuan Court in the Early Baroque," in *Music in Renaissance Cities and Courts: Studies in Honor of Lewis Lockwood,* ed. Jessie Ann Owens and A. Cummings (Warren, MI: Harmonie Park Press, 1997), 300–301; Don Harrán, *Salamone Rossi: Jewish Musician in Late Renaissance Mantua* (Oxford: Oxford University Press, 2003), 28–29; Don Harrán, "Madama Europa: Jewish Singer in Late Renaissance Mantua," in *Festa Musicologica: Essays in Honor of George Buelow,* ed. Thomas J. Mathieson and B. V. Rivera (Stuyvesant, NY: Pendragon Press, 1995), 204.

67. Abraham Massarani, *Sefer haGalut vehaPedut* (Venice, 1634), repr. with intro. by Daniel Khawalzan (St. Petersburg, L. Rabinovitz ve-Sh. Rappaport for haMelitz, 1894) (henceforth *SGP*).

68. Ibid., 8–9.

69. Ibid., 3.

70. Ibid., 20.

71. Curiously, Massarani makes a point of telling us that when he first arrived in Vienna, he did not speak the language: "Fate had sent me to Vienna, whose inhabitants' language I had not heard." Did he learn some German over a period of weeks or months? How did the officer know? See ibid., 3, 20.

72. Aminadav Fano, Moses Norsa, and Raphael Colorni.

73. Ben Zion Norsa was indeed extraordinarily wealthy, and one of the imperial officers rebuked by the duke, Colonel Colorado, had occupied his home; Shlomo Simonsohn, *History of the Jews in the Duchy of Mantua* (Jerusalem: Kiryath Sepher, 1977), 54, n. 157. Norsa had bailed out the Mantuan community in 1626 and would do so again shortly after the Jews' return in 1631, when he funded a weaving school for poor boys to learn a trade. See Simonsohn,

Jews in the Duchy of Mantua, 168, 588. He apparently also held property in Venice. By 1633 he was trying to recoup some of the money he had loaned the struggling community; Ibid., 63–64, n. 201. Aminadav Fano was also wealthy; when he sought repayment for his generosity to the impoverished Mantuan returnees, the community was forced to sell books and other assets to repay him; ibid. Raphael Colorni must have been related to Abraham Colorni, who translated the *Mafteah Shlomo* (Solomon's Key) from Hebrew for the duke of Mantua; Birnbaum, "Jewish Musicians at the Court of the Mantuan Dukes," 30.

74. Massarani, *SGP*, 23.

75. Roth, "Sefer *'Olam Hafukh,*" 98. Cipolla notes a similar reaction among some Christian authorities.

76. Ibid. Literally, "from pins to laces," i.e., not a thing. The expression comes from Gen. 14:23, where the frustrated Abraham complains about the ingratitude of his followers—an echo Catalano would have intended.

77. Roth, ibid.

78. Ibid., "Sefer *'Olam Hafukh,*" 98.

79. Samuel K. Cohn, *Cultures of Plague* (Oxford: Oxford University Press, 2010), chapter 4, "The Successo della Peste."

80. Cipolla, *Cristofano and the Plague.*

81. I am grateful to Caroline W. Bynum for helping me clarify this piece of my argument.

82. Ortner.

83. Cipolla, *Cristofano and the Plague,* 66.

84. Ibid., 122.

85. Ibid., 65.

CHAPTER 3

1. The Italian version of the text, preserved in NY Columbia University MS General 308, includes neither the lament nor the appended poems. See Chapter 2 and the discussion of the poem below.

2. For the terms, see Barbara Rosenwein, *Emotional Communities in the Early Middle Ages* (Ithaca, NY: Cornell University Press, 2007); Brian Stock, *The Implications of Literacy: Written Language and Models of Interpretation in the Eleventh and Twelfth Centuries* (Princeton, NJ: Princeton University Press, 1983).

3. The flip side of this assumption is that poetic form was more "naturally" suited to sacred messaging, another assumption worth revisiting—not here, however. By 1630 prose narrative was the dominant medium for chronicling (secular) history as well as plague; poetic plague narratives are rarer and elevate aspects of plague experience less focused on historical causation or sequential development. What is intriguing is when these distinctive discourses, or ways of producing meaning, combine in a single text.

4. Exceptions are David Damrosch, *The Narrative Covenant: Transformations of Genre in the Growth of Biblical Literature* (New York: Harper & Row, 1987) (as the title suggests, predominantly concerned with narrative); Stephen Geller, *Sacred Enigmas: Literary Religion in the Hebrew Bible* (New York: Routledge, 1996); and especially Steven Weitzman, *Song and Story in Biblical Narrative* (Bloomington: Indiana University Press, 1997); Robert Alter's *Art of Biblical Narrative* (New York: Basic Books, 1981) and *Art of Biblical Poetry* (New York: Basic

Books, 1985) treated these genres separately and did not address them in combination. On Damrosch, see also Edward Greenstein, "On the Genesis of Biblical Prose Narrative," *Prooftexts* 8.3 (1988): 347–54. Again, the provocative issue for the scholarship has chiefly been the phenomenon of biblical prose narrative and whether it represents a novel development (Alter) or not (Greenstein et al.).

5. Didactic verse preludes have been treated comprehensively by Maud Kozodoy, "Prefatory Verse and the Reception of the *Guide of the Perplexed*," *Jewish Quarterly Review* 106.3 (2016): 257–82, and Kozodoy, "Medieval Hebrew Medical Poetry: Uses and Context," *Aleph: Historical Studies in Science and Judaism* 11.2 (2011): 213–88. See also Rosa Kuhne Brabant, "Algunos aspectos de la literature didáctica entre los medicos árabes," in *Actas de las II Jornadas de Cultura Árabe e Islámica* (Madrid: Instituto Hispano-Árabe de Cultura, 1988), 273–80; Charles Burnett, "Learned Knowledge of Arabic Poetry, Rhymed Prose and Didactic Verse from Petrus Alfonsi to Petrarch," in *Poetry and Philosophy in the Middle Ages*, ed. John Marenbon (Leiden: Brill, 2000), 29–62. The extensive bibliography in Kozodoy, "Prefatory Verse," is an invaluable resource for further exploration of medical poetry in Hebrew. Kozodoy does not discuss the phenomenon of poetry inserted into prose writing.

6. For the Raban's chronicle and a discussion of its relationship to the earlier accounts, see Eva Haverkamp, *Hebräische Berichte über die Judenverfolgungen während des ersten Kreuzzugs* (Hanover: Monumenta Germaniae Historica, Hahnsche Buchhandlung, 2005).

7. Kozodoy, "Medieval Hebrew Medical Poetry," 216–18. In Christian Europe and the university medical context, the ability to memorize medical texts became critical. Writing of Gilles de Corbeil's *De urinis*, a required text of the medieval curriculum, Kozodoy says: "Students not only learned Gilles' medical poems as part of the curriculum from the twelfth through the fifteenth century, they also used informal verse summaries—i.e., mnemonic verse—to remember the contents of prose works." Ibid., 228.

8. Kozodoy discusses several examples, beginning with the medical poems of Abraham Ibn Ezra, Joseph Ibn Zabara, and Judah al-Harizi, as well as Falaquera. She convincingly demonstrates that Falaquera's work is "modeled" largely on Ibn Sina's *Urjūza* with additions from Ibn Rushd and Maimonides. Kozodoy, "Medieval Hebrew Medical Poetry," 242–64.

9. Cambridge University MS Dd. 10.68, fol.37v. This manuscript is currently the focus of a dissertation study by Sivan Gottlieb at the Hebrew University; my thanks to her for showing me the image.

10. Kozodoy, "Medieval Hebrew Medical Poetry," 248. Delight is clearly a factor in the urine sonnet that is inseparable from mnemonic enhancement.

11. Ibid., 263, 279.

12. Maureen Boulton, *The Song in the Story: Lyric Insertions in French Narrative Fiction 1200–1400* (Philadelphia: University of Pennsylvania Press, 1993); James Wimsatt, review of same, in *Studies in the Age of Chaucer* 17 (1995): 178–82.

13. Boulton, *The Song in the Story*, 9 and throughout.

14. Ibid.

15. Boulton, *The Song in the Story*, 272, 284.

16. Jacqueline Cerquiglini, "Pour une typologie de l'insertion," *Perspectives médiévales* 3 (1977): 9–14. Cerquiglini's typology of the poetic insertions in French prose texts distinguishes among collage, montage, and collage-montage texts. In general, studies of poetic insertion cluster in the period between the late 1970s to late 1990s, when structuralist and formalist readings dominated literary critical approaches. However, see the recent study by Eleanora Beck, *Boccaccio and the Invention of Musical Narrative* (Florence: European Press

Academic Publishing, 2018). Beck's study argues a connection between biblical Hebrew accounts and vernacular Italian innovations by Boccaccio and others, but the Hebrew side of the argument is weak.

17. See Chapter 1.

18. Boulton, *The Song in the Story*, 288. Compare her earlier claim that the fourteenth-century French examples provide evidence of poetic insertions that not only interrupt narrative sequence but "determined the narrative content" surrounding them (4). Her concluding formulation raises the stakes further, suggesting that the compound text is not just the sum of poetry and prose narration but something new.

19. S. Simonsohn, *History of the Jews in the Duchy of Mantua* (Jerusalem: Kiryath Sepher, 1977).

20. Yosef Yerushalmi's once classic distinction between the historiographical impulse of early modern Jews and the cyclical or mythical history of their premodern ancestors is no longer credible; see his *Zakhor: Jewish History and Jewish Memory* (Seattle: University of Washington Press, 1982), and David Myers, *The Faith of Fallen Jews: Yosef Hayim Yerushalmi and the Writing of Jewish History* (Waltham, MA: Brandeis University Press, 2013). Both impulses find a place in Massarani's chronicle. The "new" interest in linear chronology and political analysis still attaches itself to a desire to see historical events in a theological frame emphasizing promise followed by fall, and punishment followed by redemption.

21. I rely on the 1894 reprint of the 1630 edition. See Abraham Massarani, *Sefer haGalut ve-haPedut* (henceforth *SGP*) (Venice, 1634; repr. Daniel Khawalzun, ed. [St. Petersburg: L. Rabinovitz and Rappaport, 1894]), 1–24. The lament is on pp. 18–19.

22. *SGP*, 3.

23. The old structuralist distinction is that poetry emphasizes elements that call attention to language, i.e., to the medium itself. This distinction holds here, too, but I add intertextuality as a feature especially resonant in Hebrew.

24. *SGP*, 3, rhyming *beqizfah / liz'ufah / lig'dufah / shelufah / madhefah / nikhsefah*. After "longed" the passage reverts to unrhymed prose. *Madhefah*, translated as "stumbling block," is a *hapax legomenon* found uniquely in Ps. 140:12. The meaning of the word was contested by later readers; Massarani implies that the "land" has become an obstacle to its inhabitants, perhaps that the political territory or entity has turned against the Jews.

25. These approximately three hundred Jews are the remnant of the thousand exiles who set off by boat down the River Po to seek shelter in surrounding villages. Simonsohn, *History of the Jews in the Duchy of Mantua*, 55; *SGP*, 14–15.

26. His uncle was Eliezer Cases. See *SGP*, 20, Simonsohn, *History of the Jews in the Duchy of Mantua*, 58.

27. *SGP*, 18–19.

28. Lit., of him who roars and fearfully, etc.

29. תור רע—this is clearly a pun on תורה, but the meaning is unclear. An evil turn?

30. E.g., Ps. 31:11.

31. Jer. 26:18; Ps. 79:1.

32. Duma—the angel of death or destruction. Overflowing wrath (בשצף) = Isa. 54:8.

33. See the discussion below. The golden "buds" that decorated the Temple implements are also echoed in the lavish altar and cathedrae of the Mantua Great Synagogue. See the discussion below.

34. Isa. 50:3. I have switched the order of the phrases in vv. 9–10 to make more sense in English.

35. Lam. 1:1; 3.38.

36. Eccl. 4:12—והחוט המשולש לא במהרה ינתק. "This day" refers to the Ninth of Av, the day of expulsion decreed for the Mantuan Jews and also the day of the destruction of the First and Second Temples and the expulsion into Babylonia.

37. Babel = the East, Seir = Rome, Gomer (Gen 10:2–3 and 1 Chron 1:5–6) is the son of Yaphet and the father of Ashkenaz, hence Germany.

38. Ezek. 29:19.

39. השבית = put an end to, e.g., Hos. 1:4. משוש קריה = Jer. 49:25.

40. The pun on the city's name, Man-tova, translates as "good manna," compared biblically and in the poem to nectar and honey.

41. Compare Ezek. 14:21 and 2 Chron. 20:9.

42. Penniless—lit., "empty."

43. The death of R. Isaac is described in the prose section of Massarani's chronicle. It occurred when the expelled Jews were leaving the city. See *SGP*, 14, and below.

44. My radiance—i.e., the rabbi.

45. באון אשב גלמוד - Deut. 26.14; גלמוד = barren, which appears four times in the Bible, three in Job (3:7; 15:34; 30:3), once in Isa. 49:21.

46. Power (תוקף)—Esther 9:29, 10:2; Daniel 11:17. The resuscitating angel no longer has power to revive him.

47. Lit., the "column" of the reviving angel, alluding to the column of smoke or fire that guided the Israelites in the wilderness (Ex. 12:21–22, 14:24; Deut. 31:9; and many more). For balm, nectar, and honey, cf. Gen. 43:11; Prov. 16:24, 19:11.

48. Massarani dates the starting point of Mantuan Jews' downfall with the succession war. The year 1628 is indicated by the acrostic "Isaac departed" [נס"ע יצח"ק] (the "two words" of the verse).

49. Jer. 46:21; I follow the translation of NIV.

50. Parching, parched land—Ps. 107:35, Isa. 41:18, and more. לקו—Were struck (with illness); the word is rabbinic.

51. שממה = devastation; see, e.g., Ex. 23:20; Ezek. 33:3. The hendiadys שממה וכליה is not biblical.

52. The wording poses problems. עולל can be grieve (Lam. 3:51), but the idiom is associated with the eye, not voice. Cf. Job 16:15, עולל קרנו, which I am tempted to think was meant here (buried his brow/horn in the dust)—except that הרים does indeed go with "voice." I am uncertain what to do with this expression. In the second stich, the problem is an aural error of transcription: חקו should be חכו. "There is no bread for his palate," which I have translated more idiomatically as "no bread to eat."

53. Spreading—lit., sprinkling מזה, as in the blood of the sacrificial offerings, a technical usage attested in many examples (e.g., Lev 4:6, 4:17; 14:7, 14:16, 14:27, 14:51, etc.; Nu. 19:4, 19:18, 19:19). For דבר פרץ, see Ps. 106:29.

54. The chronicle describes several instances of hostage-taking and ransom; see SGP, 15–17.

55. I believe the allusion here is not to the incidents described earlier but to the handful of wealthy Jews held by the Germans in Mantua when the rest of the community was expelled. The lengthy negotiations for their release are what ultimately bring knowledge of the expulsion to Massarani in Regensburg. See *SGP*, 11, 20.

56. הוקר דמי נפשם—not biblical, but cf. 2 Kgs 1:13–14.

57. Ps. 91:1.

58. Cf. Jer. 8:19, Ps. 40:2, and more.

59. Andreina Contessa, "The Mantua Torah Ark and Lady Consilia Norsa: Jewish Female Patronage in Renaissance Italy," *Ars Judaica: The Bar Ilan University Journal of Jewish Art* 12 (2016): 53–70.

60. *SGP*, 14; Simonsohn, *History of the Jews in the Duchy of Mantua*, 55. Simonsohn notes that the rabbi, Isaac b. Judah Levi, or HaLevi,was ordained in Mantua in 1622; a few fragments of his responsa survive. At the time of the expulsion, he was one of the few remaining rabbis in the community. See ibid., 718.

61. *SGP*, 13; Simonsohn, *History of the Jews in the Duchy of Mantua*, 55. Both groups departed on the twenty-second of Av.

62. See my *Beautiful Death: Jewish Poetry and Martyrdom in Medieval France* (Princeton, NJ: Princeton University Press, 2002). The literary ideal is resolutely masculine and in this text contributes to the erasure of female presence and piety. Nonetheless, as Andreina Contessa has noted, Jewish women played visible and active roles in the ghetto during the period of the Gonzaga dukes. Contessa treats the stunning ark and cathedrae donated to the Great Synagogue (Scola Grande) by Consilia Norsa in 1542. Consilia's name also appears in a colophon to a lavishly illuminated *mahzor*, perhaps a wedding gift, she was gifted in 1520. According to Evie Cohen, the *mahzor* illuminations stress "the prominent appearance of women in scenes of religious observance." See Contessa, "The Mantua Torah Ark," citing Cohen at p. 60.

63. The emphasis on family ties extends to the copyists of Joseph Concio's and Abraham Catalano's texts. The Columbia copy of the *'Olam Hafukh* uniquely contains marginal notations in which the copyist, Cantarini, details his relationship to personages in the text. For example, toward the end of the narrative, when Catalano lists the members of the ghetto who fled and what became of them, marginal notations elaborate more fully on the names of the persons described. One refers to the physician Judah Katz, the brother of some plague victims, who resided in Venice. The marginal notation adds, "He is the brother of my father, may his memory be a blessing." See NY MS Columbia X893 Ab8.

64. See the preceding note. note. Beyond the importance given to nuclear and extended families in the Italian communities, women like Consilia Norsa also consolidated the Jewish banking dynasties in the region through marriage. Interestingly, the confrontation between Ben Zion Norsa, Massarani, and the German officer that takes place in front of the Great Synagogue suggests that this Norsa, like Lady Consilia and her husband, Isaac, came from the Ferrarese branch of the Norsa banking clan. Had they been connected to the Mantuan Norsas, they would have been praying in the Norsas' private synagogue. See Contessa, "The Mantua Torah Ark," 57.

65. Vv. 27–28 do not rhyme, and it is not clear if this is an error of transcription, transmission, or intentional. V. 27 ends with the word *devash* and v. 28 with *roshi*. If we follow *devash* and call this a closed rhyme couplet, then the pattern is even more symmetrical: CC OOOO CCC O C O CCC OOOO CCC O. If we tabulate by *roshi*, the symmetry is lessened.

66. Abraham Catalano, *'Olam Hafukh*. Page numbers refer to the only printed edition, edited by Cecil Roth from the Montefiore manuscript copy; see C. Roth, "Sefer *'Olam Hafukh* by Abraham Catalano," *Qovetz 'al yad* 4.14 (Jerusalem 1946), 67–101. There are, however, six manuscript copies extant; see the list in Chapter 2. For the poetic texts, I have compared

Roth's edition against the earliest copy, NY MS Columbia University X893-Ab8 (IMHM microfilm F 16558); as well as the Montefiore, Guenzburg, and British Library copies, all of which are accessible through the Israel National Library's KTIV website.

67. Roth, "Sefer *'Olam Hafukh*," 70–71.

68. Ibid., 71. The poem for Perla, who married Raphael Gans haLevi of Prague, is one of a few extant efforts by Hebrew poets of its type: The verses can be read either in Hebrew or Italian. This one begins אזן הסות אוינו, or "Hoggi iu atto divino."

69. Talmud Bavli, Baba Batra 58a.

70. See the Steinsaltz edition of the Talmud, Baba Batra (New York: Random House, 1989); Steinsaltz, like other commentators, cites the Maharal here. Stephen Kaufman commented that the expression "I pray to come near to you" also retains earlier semantic echoes of a sexual encounter. Just as physical intimacy has been discarded in rabbinic semantic usage, so too has it been transcended in the couple's relationship. My thanks to Steve Kaufman and Gabriel Wasserman for their invaluable suggestions for translating from the Aramaic. Stephen Kaufman, personal email communication, March 23, 2020.

71. This is ironically the opposite of what we might expect, since Hebrew is usually the language associated with greater sanctity and Aramaic the lesser. But I think that Catalano has deliberately reversed the hierarchy, and it must be because Hebrew, in the *'Olam Hafukh* specifically but also in a larger corpus of "secular" writings, is being used not as a sacred language but as a classical one.

72. Lit., האלוף כמוהר"ר = the mighty one, the honorable and great teacher and rabbi.

73. One had died and been replaced.

74. Professor Kaufman suggests reading the third line more literally, as "as did that tomb-marker Bena'a when he saw . . ." I have translated כנפא as arm, imagining Sarah's arms embrace Abraham to her chest, but it literally should be "bosom."

75. Roth, "Sefer *'Olam Hafukh*," 90.

76. Cerquiglini, "Pour une typologie de l'insertion."

77. See the preceding chapter.

78. Moscow MS Guenzburg 356 (IMHM F 27969), fols. 272b–273b, slightly more than halfway through the codex.

79. Roth, "Sefer *'Olam Hafukh*," 94.

80. Ibid., 98; Columbia X893 Ab8, fol. 10r. The term "crowned as a physician" is used also in Christian diplomas, and shows up in Hebrew dedicatory sonnets, epitaphs, and other sources. We would say "I received my degree."

81. Ibid. Emphasis mine.

82. Ibid. This practice was implemented during the terrible 1655–56 outbreak in Rome, where it is documented in the community regulations (*tikkunim*); see Ya'akov Andrea Lattes, ed., *Pinqas qehillat Roma [5]375–[5]455* (Jerusalem: Ben Zvi Institute, 2012), nos. 676, 677, pp. 172–73.

83. As Maud Kozodoy has demonstrated, medieval Hebrew medical poetry often favored the use of internal rhyme of the *muzdawwaj* type adopted from Arabic models; this term describes the internal, coupletlike rhyme of hemistichs (aA bB cC, etc.). Kozodoy, "Medieval Hebrew Medical Poetry," 219–20. Burnett, "Learned Knowledge of Arabic Poetry," 42, notes the origins of the most common prosodic form found in the Arabic *urjūza* poetry and its Latin spinoffs. This is not the form of Moses's poems, but there is no reason for him to have jettisoned an otherwise conventional adherence to hemistichs. The more polished manuscript copies confirm this.

84. Italian Hebrew sometimes played with double scansion. See Dan Pagis, "The Invention of the Hebrew Iambic and Shifts in Italian Hebrew Prosody" [in Hebrew] *Ha-Sifrut* 4 (1973): 651–712. The *shalem* variant used in the poems is (reading right to left): - - - / - u - - / - u - - // - - - / - u - - / - u - -

85. My thanks to Dr. Edward Reichman for pointing out that Moses alludes to (and reverses!) the Talmudic advice to stay put during an epidemic (see B. Qama 60b); personal email, August 1, 2020. See Edward Reichman, "Precedented Times: The Rabbinic Response to Covid-19 and Pandemics Throughout the Ages" (pre-published copy; cited with thanks to the author); see also Dr. Reichman's essay, "From Cholera to Coronavirus: Recurring Pandemics, Recurring Rabbinic Responses," *Tradition Online*, April 2, 2020: https://traditiononline .org/from-cholera-to-coronavirus-recurring-pandemics-recurring-rabbinic-responses/ (last accessed December 4, 2021).

86. Brass and iron are frequently paired biblically, cf. Gen. 4:22, Jos. 6:19, Jer. 6:38, Ez. 22:18, and others.

87. Lit., flee quickly like someone who knows.

88. Ezek. 16:6, 16:22 with covenantal echoes.

89. Deut. 28:29; Job 5:14.

90. Lev. 11:35.

91. עין לאוות—as your eye desires. The usual expression is אוות-נפש, as your soul desires; cf. Deut. 12:15, 12:20, 12:21; Deut. 18:6; 1 Sam. 23:20.

92. "In such times"—lit., "then." "It is not good"—Ps. 133:1.

93. I think this is another aural error, where the copyist has written יסיחו instead of ישיחו.

94. Job 41:1.

95. Ps. 32:7.

96. Lit., "The eye sees and the ear hears." Cf. Prov. 20:12.

97. "They"—the health officers. Abraham Catalano describes this fight to exempt linen garments from storage and decontamination. See note 114.

98. Lit., "dinars."

99. Prov. 11:4. The point seems to be that people who are not technically "poor" (and entitled to charity) are nonetheless confined to their homes without access to food or provisions. They should be considered as if they were poor and are entitled to help.

100. Lit., sleeves (pockets are a later invention.) The metaphorically capacious sleeves hold alms. We would say "so that your pockets are deep."

101. This was a chronic problem during the 1630 outbreak, as most of the "volunteers" who delivered supplies to the confined became sick and died, until eventually the Committee of Four was forced to hire disreputable men who abused and stole from their clients. See Abraham Catalano's account in Roth, "Sefer *'Olam Hafukh*," 84.

102. The biblical uses are all for Israel's enemies, who will be "cut off"—Isa.11:12, Mic. 5:8, Ps. 37:22, etc.

103. Jer. 8:22. Abraham Catalano also describes the dearth of physicians for the ghetto needy; see Roth, "Sefer *'Olam Hafukh*," 84.

104. Ex. 15:11.

105. Jer. 4:.20.

106. Jer. 23:4, Isa. 54:16. The plague is called "the Destroyer," as it is brought by the Angel of Death (the "destroying" angel).

107. In a flash; cf. Isa. 50:11.

108. Isa. 24:2, Hos.4:9. We might say "lay and elite."

109. Alluding to the Haggadah.

110. Nu. 4:34, 4:36, 4:38, etc.

111. Zeph. 1:14.

112. Compare Jer. 11:20, 17:10, 20:12; Ps. 7:10.

113. Ps. 127:1.

114. Abraham Catalano refers to the contested status of linen garments in detailing the heated argument he and the committee have with the Health Office at the conclusion of the epidemic, when officials decree that all the Jews' clothing must be decontaminated or burned. The Jewish representatives protest that this imposed harsher conditions on the ghetto than on Christian residents, who were permitted to keep linen garments. See Roth, "Sefer 'Olam Hafukh," 95: "And we cried out to him, why should we have to do what the rest of the city doesn't? [For them,] only what was in the room of the afflicted is sent off [to the *sabore*], or the contents of houses where no one remains. Why take our beds out from under us, and why not allow us to keep our white linen garments like everyone else?"

115. The prose narrative describes the flight to Montagnana of a Paduan Jewish physician, Haim Luria, who not only donates his wine cellar and foodstuffs to the poor when he leaves but continues to send assistance from safety. See Roth, "Sefer 'Olam Hafukh," 81.

116. Giulia Calvi, *Histories of a Plague Year: The Social and the Imaginary in Baroque Florence*, trans. Dario Biocca and Bryant Ragan (Berkeley: University of California Press, 1989).

117. Bubonic plague and typhus are not contagious between humans, but that was the model. See Carmichael, *Plague and the Poor in Renaissance Florence* (Cambridge: Cambridge University Press, 1986).

118. We will see the same attitude in Solomon Marini's sermons, which dismiss "scientific" and intellectual knowledge in favor of religious truths. See Chapter 5.

119. Roth, "Sefer 'Olam Hafukh," 97.

CHAPTER 4

1. John Henderson, *Florence Under Siege: Surviving Plague in an Early Modern City* (New Haven, CT: Yale University Press, 2019), 13, notes the generally "undertreated" role of religion in early modern plague outbreaks. Very recently, however, note Dr. Edward Reichman, "Incensed by Coronavirus: Prayer and Ketoret in Times of Epidemic," *Lehrhaus* (June 8, 2021), at https://www.thelehrhaus.com/timely-thoughts/incensed-by-coronavirus-prayer-and-ketoret -in-times-of-epidemic/, accessed December 27, 2021.

2. For Christian plague liturgy, see the piece by William Paden, "An Occitan Prayer Against the Plague and Its Tradition in Italy, France and Catalonia," *Speculum* 89.3 (2014): 670–92, and the older piece by William Shupbach, "A Venetian 'Plague Miracle' in 1474 and 1576," *Medical History* 24.3 (1976): 312–16. Shupbach does not describe the language or form of prayers offered. For the musical liturgies, see more later in this chapter.

3. The bibliography is huge. See, e.g., Bruce Campbell, *The Great Transition: Climate, Disease and Society in the Late Medieval World* (Cambridge: Cambridge University Press, 2016); Ann Carmichael, "Plague Persistence in Western Europe," *Medieval Globe* 1.1 (2014): article 8; and Carmichael, "The Last Past Plague: The Uses of Memory in Renaissance Epidemics," *Journal of the History of Medicine and Allied Sciences* 53.2 (1998): 132–60; Samuel Cohn, *Cultures of Plague: Medical Thinking at the End of the Renaissance* (Oxford: Oxford University

Press, 2009); Guido Alfani and Samuel Cohn, "Nonantola 1630: Anatomia di una pestilenza e meccanismi del contagio," *SID/eS (Popolazione e Storia)* 2 (2007): 99–138; Jane L. Crawshaw, *Plague Hospitals: Public Health for the City in Early Modern Venice* (Hampshire: Ashgate, 2012; reissued by Routledge in 2016); Brian Pullan, "Plague and Perceptions of the Poor in Renaissance Italy," in *Epidemics and Ideas*, ed. T. Ranger and P. Slack (Cambridge: Cambridge University Press, 1992), 101–24.

4. Guido Alfani, "Plague in Seventeenth-Century Europe and the Decline of Italy," *European Review of Economic History* 17.4 (2013): 408–30, see section 2.3. A syndemic of typhus and plague also characterized some sixteenth-century outbreaks, e.g., Venice 1570; see Richard Palmer, "The Control of Plague in Venice and Northern Italy 1348–1600," PhD diss. (University of Kent, 1978), 78–122, 211; and Henderson, *Florence Under Siege*, 47–48. Edgardo Morpurgo's 1922 study of this outbreak in Padua contended that typhus preceded plague in 1630; see my discussion in Chapter 3. Edgardo Morpurgo, *Lo studio di Padova, le epidemie ed i contagi durante il governo della repubblica veneta (1405–1797)* (Padua: La Garangola, 1922).

5. See, for example, Morpurgo, *Lo studio di Padova*, 152, who calls it "la più terribile pestilenza che la storia moderna ricorsi."

6. Serena Di Nepi, "Jews in the Papal States Between Western Sephardic Diasporas and Ghettoization," in *Religious Change and Cultural Transformations in the Early Modern Western Sephardic Communities*, ed. Y. Kaplan (Leiden: Brill, 2019), 292–322; Marina Caffiero and S. Di Nepi, "The Relationship Between Jews and Christians: Toward a Redefinition of the Ghettos," introduction to special issue of *Rivista di storia del Cristianesimo (RSCr)* 14 (2017): 3–10; Bernard Cooperman, "Ethnicity and Institution Building Among Jews in Early Modern Rome," *Association of Jewish Studies Review (AJSR)* 30 (2006): 119–45; Eleazar Gutwirth, "Jewish Bodies and Renaissance Melancholy: Culture and the City in Italy and the Ottoman Empire," in *The Jewish Body*, ed. M. Diemling and G. Veltri (Leiden: Brill 2009), 57–92; Alan Charles Harris, "La demografia del Ghetto in Italia," *La Rassegna Mensile di Israel*, 3d ser., 33.1 (1967): 1–16; David Ruderman, "The Ghetto and Jewish Cultural Formation in Early Modern Europe," in *Jewish Literatures and Cultures*, ed. A. Norich and Y. Eliav (Providence, RI: Brown Judaic Studies no. 349, 2008), 117–27; Stephanie Siegmund, *The Medici State and the Ghetto of Florence: The Construction of an Early Modern Jewish Community* (Palo Alto, CA: Stanford University Press, 2005); Kenneth Stow, *Theater of Acculturation: The Roman Ghetto in the 16th Century* (Seattle: University of Washington Press, 2001). The bibliography is large on this topic, and these citations are only a sampling of works related specifically to Jews. In other academic realms, the emphasis on networks and cross-boundary communication is also thriving. See, e.g., David Abulafia, *A Medieval Emporium: The Catalan Kingdom of Majorca* (Cambridge: Cambridge University Press, 2002); Daniel Hershenzon, *The Captive Sea: Slavery, Communication and Commerce in Early Modern Spain and the Mediterranean* (Philadelphia: University of Pennsylvania Press, 2018); Nükhet Varlik, *Plague and Empire in the Early Modern Mediterranean World* (Cambridge: Cambridge University Press, 2015), for a few relevant examples.

7. Jacob Lattes, ed. and introd., *Pinqas Qehillat Roma 5375–5455 [= 1615–1695]* (Jerusalem: Ben Zvi Institute, 2012), entry 676, p. 172.

8. Ibid., entry 678, p. 173.

9. Again, there is a growing bibliography. See, e.g., Alexander Bamji, "The Control of Space: Dealing with Diversity in Early Modern Venice," *Italian Studies* 62.2 (2013): 175–88; K. Golden, "An Italian Tune in the Synagogue: An Unexplored Contrafactum by Leon Modena," *Revue des Etudes Juives* 177.3–4 (2018): 391–420; Elliott Horowitz, "Procession, Piety, and

Jewish Confraternities," in *Jews of Early Modern Venice*, ed. R. C. David and B. Ravid (Baltimore: Johns Hopkins University Press, 2001), 231–47; Michelle A. Laughran, "The Body, Public Health and Social Control in Sixteenth-Century Venice," PhD. diss. (University of Connecticut, 1988); Paola Lanaro, ed., *At the Centre of the Old World: Trade and Manufacturing in Venice and the Venetian Mainland 1400–1800* (Toronto: Centre for Reformation and Renaissance Studies, 2006); Edwin Seroussi, "Ghetto Soundscapes: Venice and Beyond," in *Shirat Dvora*, ed. Haviva Yishai (Be'er Sheva: Ben Gurion University and Mossad Bialik, 2018), 157*–171*; Varlik, *Plague and Empire*; Tamar Visi, "Plague, Persecution and Philosophy: Avigdor Kara and the Consequences of the Black Death," in *Intricate Interfaith Networks in the Middle Ages*, ed. Ephraim Shoham Steiner (Turnhout: Brepols, 2016), 85–117. For the general context, see Guido Alfani, "Plague in Seventeenth-Century Europe and the Decline of Italy," *European Review of Economic History* 17.4 (2013): 408–30; Guido Alfani and S. Cohn, "Nonantola 1630"; Ann Carmichael, *Plague and the Poor in Renaissance Florence* (Cambridge: Cambridge University Press, 1986); Carlo Cipolla, *Cristofano and the Plague: A Study in the History of Public Health in the Age of Galileo* (Berkeley: University of California Press, 1973); John Henderson, *Florence Under Siege: Surviving Plague in an Early Modern City* (New Haven, CT: Yale University Press, 2019); Matteo Manfredini et al., "The Plague of 1630 in the Territory of Parma: Outbreak and Effects of a Crisis," *International Journal of Anthropology* 17.1 (2002): 41–57.

10. By "Second Pandemic," I refer to the recurring outbreaks of bubonic plague between 1347 in Europe (the Black Death) to roughly the mid-eighteenth century; the Second Pandemic is now believed to have originated in the Mongolian steppes at least a century prior to its appearance in Europe; see Monica Green, "The Mother of All Pandemics: The State of Black Death Research in the Era of Covid-19" (Medieval Academy of America webinar, recorded 15 May 2020): https://youtu.be/VzqR1S8cbX8, last accessed December 28, 2021. The Third Pandemic began at the end of the nineteenth century and continues to the present day.

11. Solomon may have meant his allusion to Jer. 31:9 to refer not just to the special bond between God and Israel but to God's special connection to the biblical King Solomon (2 Chron. 22:9 and 28:6), thus pointing slyly to himself.

12. Abraham Yagel, *Gei Hizayyon*, cited in S. Simonsohn, *History of the Jews in the Duchy of Mantua* (Jerusalem: Kiryath Sepher, 1977), 30, 252–53; C. Roth, "Sefer *'Olam Hafukh* by Abraham Catalano," *Qovetz 'al yad* 4.14 (Jerusalem 1946), 67–101. See Chapter 2 for a treatment of Catalano's narrative. Moses Catalano (unlike his younger siblings) survived the plague by fleeing with his family to nearby Corte. His didactic plague poems are usually appended to his father's plague narrative, and survive independently in one copy, Moscow MS Guenzburg 356 (IMHM F 22969), fols. 272b–273b, a very hastily scribbled copy catalogued as seventeenth-century Italian. See my "Poetry, Prose and Pestilence: Joseph Concio and Jewish Responses to the 1630 Italian Plague," in *Shirat Dvora: Essays in Honor of Dvora Bregman*, ed. H. Yishai (Be'er Sheva: Ben Gurion University and Mossad Bialik, 2018), *73–*101, at page *78, and chapter 1.

13. יניאס—see Nu. 32:7; delay or obstruct, or undo (Ps. 33:10). In medieval poetry, the verb could also have the sense of repelling (an enemy).

14. Deut. 22:6–7.

15. 1 Sam. 20:38.

16. All translations are mine unless otherwise indicated. The text of Abraham Ibn Ezra's poem cited here is based on two manuscripts that include Solomon of Perugia's addition,

Parma MS Biblioteca Palatina 1785 (IMHM microfilm F 13009), MSS D-4673, and Parma MS Biblioteca Palatina 3134 (IMHM microfilm F 52982). Other exemplars were consulted; they are identical.

17. Curiously he seems not to have realized that all of Abraham Ibn Ezra's *piyyutim* use the shorter acrostic AVRM, never AVRHM. See my PhD diss., "Muʿāraḍa as a Key to the Literary Unity of the 'Muwashshah" (Columbia University, 1991).

18. Jer. 8:22, 30:17.

19. Nu. 17:13, 25:8. See also 2 Sam. 24:21, 25. For the "Destroying Angel"—2 Sam. 24:15–16, 1 Chron. 21:15.

20. Jer. 17:14.

21. Gen. 38:23.

22. The full roster of nations does not appear in a single biblical verse. Nevaioth was the eldest son of Ishmael (Gen. 25:13).

23. The italicized final hemistich of the last verse returns as a refrain in each stanza.

24. *Tefillah bi'zman she-lo tavo ha-magefah,* "found" by Solomon b. Isaac Marini (or Marizi) (Venice: Vendramin 1630). My thanks to Jean-Claude Kuperminc, director of the collection at the Alliance Israelite Universelle, for making scans of this liturgy available.

25. *Selihot ʿal Tzarat haDever shelo tavo.* The liturgy is preserved in the British Library, London MS BL Or. 10219 (IMHM microfilm F 7581), henceforth MS BL Or. 10219. It is a small pamphlet of 9 bifolios, dated 1656. I am grateful to Mr. Kedem Golden for alerting me to its existence.

26. The biblical heroes are invoked sequentially: Abraham and Isaac in the first hymn, Jacob and Joseph in the second, David in the third, Moses in the fourth. Oddly, David precedes Moses, and the texts refer to six "shepherds," although the introductory folio refers to seven.

27. MS BL Or. 10219, ff. 3v and 6v respectively.

28. Marie-Louise Leonard, "Healing Communal Wounds: Processions and Plague in Sixteenth-Century Mantua," *Science Museum Group Journal* 11 (Spring 2019), http://dx.doi .org/10.15180/191106, last accessed December 28, 2021.

29. Parma MS Biblioteca Palatina 3529 (IMHM microfilm F 14036), or MSS D 6038, f. 156 (14th c., Italy); and Parma MS Biblioteca Palatina 1785 (IMHM microfilm F 13009), MSS D-4673, ff. 216b–217a (15th c., Italy). According to Israel Davidson's *Thesaurus of Medieval Hebrew Poetry* (New York: KTAV Publishing, 1970), II:380, it was preserved in collections of *selihot* (penitential hymns) from Turin and Rome.

30. Davidson lists all four poems in addition to the one treated here: (1) דר בשמי אולמו, which survived in Turin and Rome liturgies; (2) דשנת בשמן ראשי ושלחן לפני ערכת, which survives in a liturgy from Ferrara; (3) נפש יקרה את אדני הללי, an epithalamium; (4) יהלל אל במינים ועוגב, a *yotzer* for Hanukkah. My thanks to Albert Kohn for pointing to his "strong" presence among collections of Shabbat *zemirot* from the region; personal (email) communication, April 23, 2020. Moses Catalano and Joseph Concio, whose plague poems have been treated in earlier chapters, were also occasional poets.

31. Parma MS Biblioteca Palatina 3539, f. 156 and Parma MS Biblioteca Palatina 1785, ff. 216b–271a. Again, the italicized, final, half-verse will recur as a refrain in each stanza. The verse count is the same in both manuscript copies.

32. Parma MS Biblioteca Palatina 1785, fol. 216b. The ancient prayer "Unetaneh Tokef" ("Let Us Acknowledge") is associated with the New Year liturgy, where its solemn invocation

of God's judgment is a stern summons to repent before the Judge who determines life and death.

33. Daniel Carpi, ed., *Pinqas va'ad q"q Padova, 1578–1603* (Jerusalem: National Sciences Academy of Israel and Central Archive for the History of the Jewish People, 1974), entry 6, pp. 69–70 for 1578. In 1631 the same problem arises; see Roth, "Sefer *'Olam Hafukh,*", 73–74.

34. Horowitz, "Procession, Piety, and Jewish Confraternities," 231–47. The Venice liturgy of 1630 explicitly indicates participation of the confraternity called *Ashmoret haBoker.*

35. Sylvie-Anne Goldberg, *Crossing the Jabbok: Illness and Death in Askenazi Judaism in Sixteenth- Through Nineteenth-Century Prague* (Los Angeles: University of California Press, 1997), chapter 7.

36. Kedem Golden, "An Italian Tune in the Synagogue: An Unexplored Contrafactum by Leon Modena," *Revue des Études Juives* 177.3–4 (2018): 391–420; Stefano Patuzzi, "Music from a Confined Space: Salamone Rossi's *HaShirim asher liShlomo* (1622/23) and the Mantuan Ghetto," *Journal of Synagogue Music* 37 (Fall 2012): 49–58; Cecil Roth, "L'accademia musicale del Ghetto Veneziano," *Rassegna mensile di Israel* 3.4 (1928): 152–62; Seroussi, "Ghetto Soundscapes."

37. Edward Birnbaum, *Jewish Musicians at the Courts of the Mantuan Dukes 1542–1628,* trans. and intro., J. Cohen (Tel Aviv: Tel Aviv University, 1978), 15–16; Don Harrán, *Salamone Rossi: Jewish Musician in Late Renaissance Mantua* (Oxford: Oxford University Press, 2003); Patuzzi, "Music from a Confined Space." On Abraham, see Chapters 2 and 3 of this book.

38. See especially the impressive new work of Remi Chiu, *Plague and Music in the Renaissance* (Cambridge: Cambridge University Press, 2017); Christopher Macklin, "Plague, Performance and the Elusive History of the Stella Celi Extirpavit," *Early Music History* 29 (2010):1–31; Patuzzi, "Music from a Confined Space"; Seroussi, "Ghetto Soundscapes"; and the many studies of Don Harrán.

39. Chiu, *Plague and Music,* 52; Macklin, "Plague, Performance and the Elusive History of the Stella Celi Extirpavit," 2; Renata Pieragostini, "The Healing Power of Music? Documentary Evidence from Late-Fourteenth-Century Bologna," *Speculum* 96.1 (2021): 156–76.

40. Richard Kieckhefer, *Magic in the Middle Ages,* 2d ed. (Cambridge: Cambridge University Press, 1989, repr. 2014), 27.

41. Chiu, *Plague and Music,* 57. Pieragostini, "Healing Power of Music?" 156, 166. As the remainder of this chapter shows, the Jewish sources emphasize the reverse direction: i.e., the use of music as a way of aligning the cosmos with the petitioner.

42. Chiu, *Plague and Music,* 62.

43. Moshe Idel, "Magical and Theurgical Interpretations of Music in Jewish Texts from the Renaissance to the Hasidic Period" [in Hebrew], *Yuval* 4 (1982): 33–64.

44. According to Idel, this model could have no traction among Christian thinkers, for whom "God" was not a dynamic entity. Ibid., 35.

45. As Deborah James has observed, musical performance had the ability to constitute a "class" of listeners that could alternately define itself against another group or transcend existing divisions. Deborah James, "'Music of Origin': Class, Social Category and the Performers and Audience of 'Kiba,'" *Africa: The Journal of the International African Institute* 67.3 (1997): 454–75.

46. Alessandro Guetta, "Can Fundamentalism Be Modern? The Case of Abraham Portaleone (1542–1612)," in *Acculturation and Its Discontents: The Italian-Jewish Experience Between Exclusion and Inclusion,* ed. D. Myers, M. Ciavolella, et al. (Toronto: University of Toronto Press, 2000), 99–115, at 105; Don Harrán, "In Search of the 'Song of Zion': Abraham Porta-

leone on the Music in the Ancient Temple," *European Journal of Jewish Studies* 4.2 (2011): 215–39.

47. Harrán, "In Search of the 'Song of Zion,'" 216.

48. Horowitz, "Procession, Piety, and Jewish Confraternities." For a look at contemporary Christian processional liturgies, see, e.g., Marie-Louise Leonard, "Healing Communal Wounds."

49. Elliott Horowitz, "Speaking of the Dead: The Emergence of the Eulogy Among Italian Jewry of the Sixteenth Century," in *Preachers of the Italian Ghetto*, ed. D. Ruderman (Berkeley: University of California Press, 1992), 137–38, and see Ruderman's introduction, 8.

50. Yossi Chajes, "Magic, Mysticism, and Popular Belief in Jewish Culture (1500–1815)," in *The Cambridge History of Judaism*, vol. 7—*The Early Modern World*, ed. Jonathan Karp and Adam Sutcliffe (Cambridge: Cambridge University Press, 2017), 475–90.

51. Reichman, "Incensed by Coronavirus."

52. Simonsohn, *History of the Jews in the Duchy of Mantua*, 45–49.

53. Ibid., 53–55. The remainder of his account closely follows Abraham Massarani's *Sefer haGalut vehaPedut* (Venice, 1634).

54. Simonsohn, *History of the Jews in the Duchy of Mantua*, 192.

55. The printer was Joshua of Perugia, a printer and bookdealer who had briefly run a book stall in the Mantuan Jewish market. Ibid., 683, and 276, n. 257. One copy survives in the Hebrew Union College Library in Cincinnati, and I am grateful to them for scanned copies.

56. The Bologna *piyyut* testifies also to the practice of recycling hymns deemed to have proven effective in times of similar catastrophes in the past. The preface to the Mantuan liturgy explains:

בקשות ותפלות נתיסדו ונתקנו על פי גאוני וחכמי ישיבת מנטובה בעת מלחמה והיות העיר במצור אין יוצא ואין בא: אוספנו עליהם תפלה אחת מצאנו במחזור ישן כי נוסדה בהיות בולונייא במצור. . . .

Penitential hymns and prayers composed and arranged by the *geonim* and sages of the rabbinic academy in Mantua during [a time of] war when the city was under siege; no one came in or out: We have added to them a prayer that we found in an ancient prayerbook that was composed when Bologna was under siege (*Bakashot u-tefilot nityasdu . . . 'al pi ge'one . . . Mantovah* [Venice, 1630)], title page).

The Bolognese author was Mattityahu ben Isaac. Perhaps not coincidentally, the recent rabbi of Mantua's majority Italian Jewish community, Hananiah Eliakim Rieti, came from a prominent banking family in Bologna. Many of Rieti's compositions found use in local confraternity rites, and his supporters may have nurtured Bolognese memory. Michela Andreatta, "The Printing of Devotion in Seventeenth-Century Italy: Prayer Books Printed for the Shomrim la-Boker Confraternities," in *The Hebrew Book in Early Modern Italy*, ed. Joseph R. Hacker and A. Shear (Philadelphia: University of Pennsylvania Press, 2011), 161.

57. *Bakashot u-tefilot . . . Mantovah*, 8–9. The Casale poem is by Jacob Segre. Another contributor, Mordecai ben Berakhia Reuven, pleaded for help "now when we are poor and wretched, facing siege, distress and the bereaving sword from without, fear and dread from within . . . moreover, famine prevents us from bringing meat to our homes or law to our youth, for there is no one who can presently occupy himself with Torah and study, the din and storm in our hearts grows ever stronger, and we do not know what we shall do." This

prayer is followed by a penitential litany (*avinu malkeinu*) that includes a prayer for the welfare of the soon-to-be-ousted duke (9a). Surely the strangest use of this liturgy occurred the following year: When representatives of the expelled Mantuan Jews in Regensburg sought to communicate with Jewish hostages in Mantua, they sent them a copy of this liturgy, concealing information on negotiations for their release by adding them in box letters disguised to resemble those of the print font. See Abraham Massarani, *Sefer haGalut vehaPedut* (Venice, 1634(, repr. with intro. by Daniel Khawalzun (St. Petersburg, L. Rabinovitz ve-Sh. Rappaport for haMelitz, 1894), 21.

58. According to its title page, it was performed before the Grand Porto synagogue, which was burned in 1610 and not rebuilt until 1645, considerably after the 1630 plague and expulsion. Simonsohn, *History of the Jews in the Duchy of Mantua*, 569.

59. Plague *without* violence has been naturalized by sheer virtue of repetition, while war remained capricious and noteworthy. See Abraham Melamed, "The Perception of Jewish History in Italian Jewish Thought of the Sixteenth and Seventeenth Centuries: A Reexamination," in *Italia Judaica: Atti del II Convegno internazionale* (Rome: Istituto Poligrafico e Zecca dello Stato, 1986), 138–70.

60. Claire Burridge, "Incense in Medicine: An Early Medieval Perspective," *Early Medieval Europe* 28.2 (2020): 219–55; Susan A. Harvey, *Scenting Salvation: Ancient Christianity and the Olfactory Imagination* (Los Angeles: University of California Press, 2006).

61. Andrew Berns, "Judah Moscato, Abraham Portaleone, and Biblical Incense in Late Renaissance Mantua," in *Rabbi Judah Moscato and the Jewish Intellectual World of Mantua in the 16th–17th Centuries*, ed. Giuseppe Veltri and G. Miletto (Leiden: Brill, 2012), 105–19 at 112–117; David S. Farkas, "Because the Sound Is Good for the Spices," *Hakirah* 14 (2012): 148–50.

62. Berns, 116; see also Guetta, "Can Fundamentalism Be Modern?" 102. A close contemporary, the Spanish exile and physician Amatus Lusitanus, also treated botanical terms in depth. Berns, 110–11 with reference to stacte (balm) and aloe wood, both featured in the biblical recipe. On Lusitanus, see António Melo, "Propriedades terapêuticas das plantas aromáticas em Amato Lusitano: o cardamomo," in *Pombalina: Legado clássico no Renascimento e sua recção*, ed. Nair de Nazaré Castro Soares and C. Teixeira (Coimbra: Universidade de Coimbra, 2017), https://doi.org/10.14195/978-989-26-1293-5_14, last accessed December 28, 2021, pp. 241–55; José Maria Valderas, "La polémica en la investigación botánica del siglo XVI. Mattioli contra Lusitano," *Collectanea Botanica* (Barcelona) 25 (2000): 255–304; and José Maria Valderas, "Mattioli contra Lusitano, II. Las 'censuras' y la interpretación de Dioscórides," *Collectanea Botanica* (Barcelona) 26 (2003): 181–225.

63. Crawshaw, *Plague Hospitals*; Richard Palmer, "Pharmacy in the Republic of Venice in the Sixteenth Century," in *The Medical Renaissance of the Sixteenth Century*, ed. A. Wear et al. (Cambridge: Cambridge University Press, 1985), 100–117, Filippo de Vivo, "Pharmacies as Centres of Communication in Early Modern Venice," *Renaissance Studies* 21.4 (2007): 505–21; Stefan Halikowski, "The Physician's Hand: Trends in the Evolution of the Apothecary and His Art Across Europe, 1500–1700," *Nuncius* 24 (2009): 97–125; and n.b., Bruno Kisch, "The History of the Jewish Pharmacy in Prague," *Historia Judaica* 8 (1946): 149–80 (Prague's Jewish pharmacy tradition began with the emigration of two Jewish pharmacists from Venice); Valentina Pugliano, "Pharmacy, Testing and the Language of Truth in Renaissance Italy," *Bulletin of the History of Medicine* 91.2 (2017): 233–73; Barbara Di Gennaro Splendore, "Craft, Money and Mercy: An Apothecary's Self-Portrait in Sixteenth-century Bologna," *Annals of Science* 74.2 (2017): 91–107. For a history of the great university botanical garden in Padua and its direc-

tors, see Alessandro Minelli, ed., *The Botanical Garden of Padua 1545–1995* (Venice: Marsilio, 1995). There has been a flurry of recent writing on the integration of New World plants into the Italian pharmaceutical repertoire. These are fascinating studies but not relevant to this one; plague remedies seem to have been less concerned with innovation than with authentication of classical ingredients, as my cited references suggest.

64. On Leucci and his family, see Stefanie Siegmund, *The Medici State*, 123. One Jewish member of the apothecaries' guild in Florence was a woman. Sarra (the daughter of Agnolo di Zaccharia, also a guild member) was admitted to the guild in 1575; see Siegmund, *The Medici State*, 287. Also for Siena, see Simonsohn, *History of the Jews in the Duchy of Mantua*, 248. Eleazar Gutwirth cites a source describing the pharmacists of Ottoman Turkey as overwhelmingly Jewish; see Eleazar Gutwirth, "Language and Medicine in the Early Modern Ottoman Empire," in *Religious Confessions and the Sciences in the Sixteenth Century*, ed. J. Helm and A. Winkelman (Leiden: Brill, 2001), 87, 90.

65. Pugliano, "Pharmacy, Testing and the Language of Truth," 239: 259–60; Halikowski, "The Physician's Hand"; Valderas, "La polémica," 258.

66. Samuel Kottek, ""Jews between Profane and Sacred Science in Renaissance Italy: The Case of Abraham Portaleone," in *Religious Confessions and the Sciences in the Sixteenth Century,* eds. Jurgen Helm and A, Winkelman (Leiden: Brill, 2001), 108–11; Melo, "Propriedades terapêuticas das plantas aromáticas," 242; Valderas, "La polémica," 263–64.

67. Rebecca Locci, "La gestione della peste del 1631 nel ghetto di Padova attraverso la cronaca di Avraham Catalano," M.A. dissertation, University of Padua, 2021, pp. 80–81. My thanks to Dr. Edward Reichman for sharing this source.

68. Halikowski, "The Physician's Hand," 37.

69. Minelli, ed., *The Botanical Garden of Padua*, 59–60.

70. Marianne Stössl, "Lo spettacolo della Triaca, produzione e promozione della 'Droga Divina' a Venezia dal Cinque al Settento," *Quaderni del Centro Tedesco di Studi Veneziani* 25 (1983): 4–47, at 10–11. Much of the following description draws on Stössl, and Pugliano ("Pharmacy, Testing and the Language of Truth").

71. I have amalgamated the translation of the biblical passages from the JPS Bible and the Talmudic passages as they appear in the Birnbaum daily prayerbook, *HaSiddur Ha-Shalem* (New York: Hebrew Publishing Company, 1977), 30–32. The ellipses are not trivial, but the reader can find them easily; however, I cite the sections relevant for my discussion. The JPS translates "balm" as "stacte," as I note below.

72. Moshe Idel, "Investigations into the Methodology of the Author of *Sefer haMeshiv*" [in Hebrew], *Sefunot* 17 (1983): 185–286. See also Idel, "Magical and Theurgical Interpretations," 33–64.

73. Idel, "Magical and Theurgical Interpretations," 39, 42, 45.

74. The KTIV database includes dozens of examples, and I have relied on six manuscript versions plus another two in print. *Fourteenth–fifteenth century manuscripts:* Parma MS Biblioteca Palatina 1789 (IMHM microfilm F 13013), ff. 43a ff.; Parma MS Biblioteca Palatina 3134 (IMHM microfilm F 52982), ff. 185 ff. *Fifteenth-century manuscripts:* Parma MS Biblioteca Palatina 1811 (IMHM microfilm F 13033), f. 62a ff.; Parma MS Biblioteca Palatina 1917 (IMHM microfilm F 13073), ff. 62 ff; Parma MS Biblioteca Palatina 1784 (IMHM microfilm F 13008), ff.156 ff.; Parma MS Biblioteca Palatina 1751 (IMHM microfilm F 12978), ff. 69b ff. Of this group, only Parma 1917 (F 13073) is a Sephardic rite *siddur*; the others are chiefly Roman rite. *Print versions:* Abraham Yagel, *Moshiah Hosim* (Venice, 1587), and *Tefilah bi'zman ha-magefah she-lo tavo* (Venice, 1630).

75. See Chapter 5.

76. Benjamin Gampel, ed. *Crisis and Creativity in the Sephardic World, 1391–1648* (New York: Columbia University Press, 1997); Moshe Idel, *Kabbalah in Italy, 1280–1510* (New Haven, CT: Yale University Press, 2011).

77. בוירונה היתה המגפה שנת הש"ץ והסכמנו אנחנו פה להעתיר בעד אחינו והאלוף כמוה"ר שלמה מאריני. נר"ו מצא באמתחות ספריו תפלה ארוכה אשר חברה בימי קדם בעיר פיזא . . . וילך האלוף הנ"ל לויניציאה וידפיסנה ונקבעה לאומרה ביום שני ויום חמישי מדי שבוע בשבוע אחר קריאת התורה וגם פטום הקטרת מדי יום ביומו באשר החל הנגף . . . . Roth, "Sefer 'Olam Hafukh," 73–74.

78. Moshe Idel, "Magical and Theurgical Interpretations," 33–64.

79. Parma MS Biblioteca Palatina 1811 (=F 13033); Parma MS Biblioteca Palatina1784, MSS-D 4672 (=F 13008); Parma MS Biblioteca Palatina 3134 (=F 52982).

80. The text is the same in all three manuscripts cited above, n. 78.

81. Parma 1917.

82. The printed Venice edition indicates explicitly that the arrangement of the verse litanies also embeds angelic or divine "Names" forward or backward.

83. See Idel, "Magical and Theurgical Interpretations.' But see Susan A. Harvey, *Scenting Salvation: Ancient Christianity and the Olfactory Imagination* (Los Angeles: University of California Press, 2006). Henderson, *Florence Under Siege*, 31–32, notes the connection early modern Italian physicians and policymakers made between fetid smells and pestilence; the odors "seed" the air with toxic pollution, creating miasmic conditions for disease.

84. Yagel, *Moshiah Hosim* (Venice, 1587), 16r, 27r; my thanks to the Klau Library of the Hebrew Union College in Cincinnati for scans.

85. Ibid., 29v, 30r.

86. Yagel, *Moshiah Hosim*, 32–33; Berns, "Judah Moscato, Abraham Portaleone, and Biblical Incense;" Ruderman, "The Ghetto and Jewish Cultural Formation."

87. See Moses Zacut, *Sefer Shorshei haShemot* (Jerusalem: Nezer Shraga, 1998–99), 123.

88. Idel, "Investigations," 262–66.

89. I use this term, in the sense invoked by David Gentilcore, to refer to the coexistence of "a range of healers and forms of healing." David Gentilcore, *Healers and Healing in Early Modern Italy* (Manchester: Manchester University Press, 1998), x. Pieragostini also refers to "medico-magical" practices that document an eclectic approach to plague responses. Pieragostini, "The Healing Power of Music?" 156–76.

90. In 1629, before the plague had reached Padua, Abraham Catalano noted that religious authorities voted to add Ibn Shraga's *Pitum haKetoret* liturgy to their Monday and Thursday morning prayers on behalf of the afflicted Jews of Verona. When the plague hit home, the *Pitum haKetoret* passages were read daily. Catalano does not report attending these rites but does not dismiss them. As one of the Committee of Four responsible for coordinating the ghetto's plague response, how could he? He himself prayed regularly, even when he was confined to his house after his daughter died of plague. Echoing the recommendation of Cardinal Borromeo in Milan a half-century earlier, he prayed by his window, which opened out to face the Ashkenazi synagogue. On Borromeo, see Chiu, *Plague and Music*, 125–26.

91. Yagel, *Moshiah Hosim*, 27v.

92. Michael Rizhik, "'How do we light' and 'Grinding of the incense' in Italian Vernacular Prayerbooks" [in Hebrew] *Masorot* 13–14 (2006): 181–202.

93. Ibid., 194.

CHAPTER 5

1. The same cannot be said for Christian preaching, where even though texts do survive, they have been minimally treated. John Henderson's recent study of the 1630 plague in Florence devotes an entire chapter to religious responses but mentions sermons only fleetingly. Likewise, Samuel Cohn's *Cultures of Plague* does not dwell much on homiletical genres. The standard anthologies of primary sources for the Black Death in English translation also underrepresent the sermon; the available texts do not pique scholars' interest. See John Henderson, *Florence Under Siege: Surviving Plague in an Early Modern City* (New Haven, CT: Yale University Press 2019), 149–51; Samuel Cohn, Jr., *Cultures of Plague: Medical Thinking at the End of the Renaissance* (Oxford: Oxford University Press, 2009), 230ff. Of interest is Henderson's documentation of mandated sermons in the Duomo with dictated themes linking plague to sin, also that plague processions would begin with a public sermon delivered in open air. In Milan, Cohn notes that Cardinal Borromeo ordered monks to preach during the 1576 plague outbreak and to emphasize themes of moral laxity punished by pestilence. As for the anthologies, John Aberth, *The Black Death: The Great Mortality of 1348–1350, A Brief History with Documents* (Boston: Bedford/St. Martin's, 2005), has a section on "Religious Mentalities" without a single sermon entry; Rosemary Horrox, *The Black Death* (Manchester: Manchester University Press, 1994), also has a solid section on "The Religious Response" totaling twenty-seven entries of which two (nos. 48, 49) are sermon excerpts (possibly also no. 46). Despite its prestige in premodern times, it is not a genre that has attracted modern scholarship.

2. Saperstein treats a sermon delivered by Saul Morteira in Amsterdam in 1656 during a plague outbreak; see Marc Saperstein, *Exile in Amsterdam: Saul Levi Morteira's Sermons to a Congregation of 'New Jews'"* (Cincinnati, OH: Hebrew Union College Press, 2005). For one more plague sermon (that makes no reference to plague beyond a closing prayer to be spared its effects), see Umberto Cassuto, "Un rabbino Florentino del Secolo XV," Appendix 2: "Prediche per la peste di Firenze 1456," *Rivista Israelita* 4 (1907): 33–37. I know of no other examples.

3. As Saperstein points out, this bid for authority could spectacularly fail; audience approval was never a given. See Marc Saperstein, *Jewish Preaching 1200–1800: An Anthology* (New Haven, CT: Yale University Press, 1989), 52–58. But in a setting where a rabbi had amassed a reputation and rapport with his listeners, the synagogue context, like the placement of the sermon in the liturgy, buttressed claims to authority. As is still true today, the more controversial a sermon was, and the less solid the preacher's standing in a community, the riskier his gambit to derive novel or contemporary relevance from sacred traditions and texts.

4. For an overview of the methodological challenges, see Saperstein, *Jewish Preaching 1200–1800*, 18–24. For Morteira's sermons, see Saperstein, *Exile in Amsterdam*, and Saperstein, "Four Kinds of Weeping: Saul Levi Morteira's Application of Biblical Narrative to Contemporary Events," *Studia Rosenthalia* 42/43 (2010–11): 25–41.

5. Saperstein, *Jewish Preaching 1200–1800*, 38.

6. Simonsohn says of the Mantuan ghetto that the "Great Synagogue was the centre of communal life." Shlomo Simonsohn, *History of the Jews in the Duchy of Mantua* (Jerusalem: Tel Aviv University and Kiryath Sepher, 1977), 571.

7. Abraham Catalano, *'Olam Hafukh.* For the reader's convenience, citations are from the only modern edition of the Hebrew text, in C. Roth, "Sefer *'Olam Hafukh* by Abraham

Catalano," *Qovetz 'al yad* 4.14 (Jerusalem, 1946), 67–101, here citing p. 90. Subsequent references will be to Roth, "Sefer *'Olam Hafukh.*"

8. Ibid.

9. Roth, "Sefer *'Olam Hafukh,*" 91.

10. From another perspective, the staggering mortality among the ghetto's rabbis suggests they did not abandon their pastoral responsibilities during the worst of the plague. The Mantuan ghetto also saw the loss of nearly all of its two dozen rabbis; see Simonsohn, *History of the Jews in the Duchy of Mantua,* 575.

11. Morpurgo distinguishes between the Veronese Marinis and another family of the same name attested in Padua during the fifteenth and sixteenth centuries. Steinschneider also did not trace the family back before the early seventeenth century. See A. V. Morpurgo, "Notizie sulle famiglie ebree esistite a Padova nel XVI secolo," *Il corriere israelitico* 47 (1908): 231; Moritz Steinschneider, "La Famiglia Marini," *Il vessilo israelitico* 28 (1879–80): 147–50. These early bibliophiles were convinced that the name "Marini" was originally a place name but were not sure to what it referred.

12. Meir Benayahu, "Abraham Cohen of Zante and the Physicians' and Poets' Club in Padua" [in Hebrew], *Ha-Sifrut* 26 (1978): 108–40, at 110–12. See also Mordecai Samuel Ghirondi, Efrayim Ghirondi, and Hananel Neppi, *Toldot gedolei yisrael u-geonei italiah* (Trieste: Tipografia Marenigh, 1853).

13. Benayahu, "Abraham Cohen of Zante."

14. Benayahu, 112–13. The *Pirke Avot* translation survives in a single manuscript (according to Benayahu, MS Mantua 124). The *Metamorphoses* translation covers only one book and is based on the Italian translation of Giovanni Andrea d'Anguillara; Ghirondi attempted to publish it in 1748 but died as the work got underway. See Laura Bonifacio, "L'episodio di Dafne e Apolo nelle 'Metamorfosi' di Ovidio tradotte da Shabbetay Hayyim Marini," *Henoch* 13.3 (1991): 319–35; Dvora Bregman, "Shabtai Hayyim Marini's Translation of Ovid's Metamorphoses" [in Hebrew], *Dohaq—K'tav 'Et LiSifrut Tovah* 3 (2013): 1–7.

15. On the deluxe illustrated *ketubbot* (wedding contracts) of early modern Italian Jews, see Shimon Sabar, "The Beginnings and Flourishings of Ketubbah Illustration in Italy: A Study in Popular Imagery and Jewish Patronage During the Seventeenth and Eighteenth Centuries," PhD diss. (University of California–Los Angeles, 1987).

16. "חכם גדול בתורה ובקי בחכמות חיצויות ודרשן מפואר, וכל חכמי האומות היו באים לשמוע דרושיו הנפלאים על האמונה ועל המוסר האלדי, עד שרוב דרשניהם היו מזכירים שמו לשבח בדרשותיהם . . ." ("A great Torah sage who was learned in science and a splendid preacher; all the gentile sages would come to hear his wonderful sermons on faith and divine ethics, until most of their preachers would cite him in praise in their sermons"): Mordecai Ghirondi, cited in Benayahu, "Abraham Cohen of Zante," 112.

17. Benayahu, "Abraham Cohen of Zante."

18. Ibid., 110; Steinschneider, "La Famiglia Marini," 148.

19. This chapter was written during the period of our own pandemic confinement, when libraries were shuttered. Without online databases like KTIV, it would have been impossible to continue work on this book. My deep thanks to those who maintain KTIV, as well as to the libraries and private collections worldwide that have made digitized copies of their Hebrew manuscripts available through this centralized source.

20. The KTIV description of the other manuscript, JTS 6517, calls them תמציתם של דרשות, "the essence of the sermons."

21. It is not clear which of Piccolomini's works this title refers to. Alessandro Piccolomini was a sixteenth-century humanist from Siena who studied and later taught at the University of Padua. He authored a number of works on philosophy, astronomy, natural science, etc., and Marini refers elsewhere to his *Sfera del mondo*. See Florindo Cerreta, "Alessandro Piccolomini: Teacher of Moral Philosophy," *Italica* 33.1 (1956): 22–25.

22. I follow Marc Saperstein's description of the early modern terminology and the sermon structure fashionable in this period in Italy. See Saperstein, *Jewish Preaching 1200–1800*, introduction.

23. Ibid., 75–79.

24. For these citation sources and fuller discussion, see the treatment of the texts later in this chapter.

25. For my transcriptions of the original Hebrew, see Appendix 2.

26. See also Sifre Deut. Piska 42.

27. And see Judah Goldin, "Not by means of an angel and not by means of a messenger," in *Religions in Antiquity: Essays in Memory of Erwin Ramsdell Goodenough* (New Haven, CT: Yale University Press, 1968), 412–24. Thank you to Jason Kalman for pointing me to this essay.

28. This lag is detectable in other cities as well. Delays in outbreak are also described in Venetian sources, in Turin and Florence for the 1630 plague, in Milan for the severe epidemic of 1576, etc.

29. Note also the discussion in *HaEmunot ve-haDe'ot* 6:1 where the author explains Ex. 12:29 and the plague arrested by Pinchas in 1 Sam. 26, equating "firstborn" with the wicked and emphasizing that both "plagues" must be read as punishments for sin that are deflected only by the merit of the righteous.

30. The confusion with Judges 21:23 is intriguing. This narrative also touches on the dangers of intertribal discord.

31. Roth, "Sefer 'Olam Hafukh," 77.

32. Roth, "Sefer 'Olam Hafukh," 81.

33. Moses Catalano, poem 9.

34. Moses Al-Sheikh was born in Adrianople ca. 1520 but spent most of his career in Safed, where he produced commentaries on most of the biblical canon. He claimed that his *Torat Moshe* (Constantinople, 1593) began as homilies delivered weekly in Safed, then expanded to full-blown exegetical commentary. See Joseph Hacker, "The Intellectual Activity of the Jews of the Ottoman Empire During the Sixteenth and Seventeenth Centuries," in *Jewish Thought in the Seventeenth Century*, ed. I. Twersky, B. Septimus (Cambridge, MA: Harvard University Press, 1987); Meir Benayahu et al., *Rabbi Moshe Alsheikh* [Hebrew] (Jerusalem: Ben Zvi Institute, 1966); Benjamin Williams, *Commentary on Midrash Rabba in the Sixteenth Century* (Oxford: Oxford University Press, 2016); *Encyclopedia of the Jews in the Islamic World*, ed. Norman Stillman, https://referenceworks.brillonline.com/browse/encyclopedia-of-jews-in-the-islamic-world, consulted June 25, 2020, last accessed December 13, 2021. Abraham Shalom spent his life in Catalonia, where he died in 1492. His major work, the *Neve Shalom*, was published twice, in Constantinople in 1539 and then in Venice in 1594. He was a staunch pro-Maimunist who nonetheless incorporated kabbalistic and Platonic views into his writing. The *Neve Shalom* was arranged in the form of "homilies" on aggadic passages from the Talmudic tractate Berakhot but also integrating philosophical problems and analyses. See Herbert Davidson, *The Philosophy of Abraham Shalom* (Berkeley: University of California Press, 1964); Hava Tirosh Rothschild, "The Political Philosophy in

the Thought of Abraham Shalom" [in Hebrew], in *Jerusalem Studies in Jewish Thought*, special issue in honor of Shlomo Pines, ed. Moses Idel et al., vol. 2 of the festschrift (1990): 407–40; Mauro Zonta, *Hebrew Scholasticism in the Fifteenth Century* (Dordrecht, Netherlands: Springer Nature, 2006), 165–66. I do not know which passages in the *Neve Shalom* Marini was eyeing with regard to "peace," but Tirosh Samuelson probes its contributions to political philosophy. Shalom's affinity for certain Neoplatonic concepts that included the belief that the individual human reflected in microcosm larger social and cosmic formations would lend itself to Marini's desire to draw a connection between individual or local conflict and the common good.

35. Roth, "Sefer *'Olam Hafukh*," 92–93.

36. Again, for the Hebrew transcription, lightly annotated, see Appendix 2.

37. "The Holy One Blessed Be He"—abbreviated הקד' ה' ית'.

38. In the Hebrew, "the Holy One Blessed Be He," now abbreviated with the conventional הקב"ה.

39. "This means that"—abbreviated ר"ל, literally "they meant/wished to say." See also lines 13, 14.

40. הקב"ה

41. I am not sure about the abbreviation עכ"ם, but the sense of the line is clear.

42. Unclear.

43. "The meaning"—abbreviated פי, for פירוש. This abbreviation holds throughout the text.

44. "And then from the perspective of"—abbreviated ואח"כ ע"צ, which I read as "ואחר כך על צד." Marini incorporates Kabbalah and philosophy as proofs, reflecting the wide if popularized dissemination of kabbalistic and philosophical concepts among his audience as well as the casual integration of both methods in the writings of the commentators he admired.

45. Abbreviated מאמ' על פס' for מאמר על פסוק. This signals a secondary *ma'mar* to Ps. 29:1, which we have already seen attract Marini's attention in our previous example.

46. "For instance"—abbreviated כג for כגון.

47. Midrash *Tilim* (*Tehilim*): abbreviated מד' תילים. "The Holy One Blessed Be He": abbreviated הקב"ה. "The Holy One": abbreviated הקד'. The last word of the line is unclear.

48. "Third judgment": written דין ג'.

49. The line includes several abbreviated notations: "three" is ג'; "refers to" (literally, "interpretation" or "meaning"] is פ'; and "righteous deeds," גמילות חסדים, is ג"ח.

50. "Verse" (פסוק), abbreviated פס'.

51. "Synagogue," בית הכנסת *t*, abbreviated ב"ה; "righteous deeds," גמילות חסדים, abbreviated ג"ח.

52. Roth, "Sefer *'Olam Hafukh*," 77.

53. Roth, "Sefer *'Olam Hafukh*," 92–93, for the declaration that the plague has ended, and 94 for the breakdown: The dead include 214 men and 207 women. Catalano breaks down the casualties further, recording that 38 married couples died, 30 widows remained without husbands and 20 widowers without wives; fifteen households were completely wiped out and many counted just one survivor (in some cases a baby or child). The level of detail—which moreover attests to the family-centric values discussed in previous chapters—strongly suggests that a second tally was taken.

54. I asked Lori Jones, who has worked extensively on the Christian plague tracts, if she could recall squeamishness about censuses characterized in any Christian accounts. Dr. Jones noted that the story from 1 Samuel or 2 Kings is cited frequently, but only as proof

that plague is punishment from God. She could think of no examples of resistance to census-taking. My thanks to her for this communication. Personal email exchange, May 25, 2020.

55. The verse also stars in a beloved hymn by Judah HaLevi that Marini easily could have known. In HaLevi's poem a female personification of Israel seeks to understand why her Beloved has turned away. She says, "I said, I will not mention Him, etc." Judah HaLevi, *"Yonat rehoqim"* ("Distant Dove") [Hebrew], with English translation in Raymond Scheindlin, *The Gazelle* (New York: Jewish Publication Society, 1991), 70–71.

56. Roth, "Sefer *'Olam Hafukh,*" 94. For a similar scenario in Mantua, see Simonsohn, *History of the Jews in the Duchy of Mantua*, 53.

57. According to Sosland, the *Or* was begun mid-century, but the first known fully formed manuscript version dates to 1672. The work was banned by the Inquisition in 1693. See Henry Sosland, *A Guide for Preachers on Composing and Delivering Sermons: The* Or ha-Darshanim *of Jacob Zahalon* (New York: Jewish Theological Seminary, 1987), 77ff.

58. Ibid., 148, section 10, 2:3, with the Hebrew on 39*–40*.

59. Saperstein *Exile in* Amsterdam, 186–87; the text of the sermon, "Guarded Him as the Pupil of His Eye," spans pp. 447–88 (giving us some idea of the sermon's duration!).

60. Some cross disciplinary divides, such as the famous prayer he composed for recitation by physicians. For the physicians' prayer, see Samuel Kottek, "La Prière des Médecins de Jacob Zahalon," *Pardes* 15 (1992): 185–93. For Zahalon's plague account and more general career, there are a few old essays in need of updating: Jacob Leibowitz, "Plague in the Roman Ghetto (1656) According to Jacob Zahalon and Cardinal Gastaldi" [in Hebrew], *Korot* 4.3–4 (1967): 155–69, and a later English synopsis in *Korot* 14.3–4 (2000): 165–67; Henry Friedenwald, "Jacob Zahalon of Rome: Medieval Rabbi, Physician, Author and Moralist," *Bulletin of the Medical Library Association* 8.1 (1918): 1–10.

61. *Otzar haHayim* (Venice, 1683).

62. According to Zahalon, the Jewish physician would examine the patient, and if he saw signs of plague, he would call in the Christian physician assigned to the ghetto for further examination. The gentile physician could then order the transfer of the patient (and his bed) to the Jewish lazaretto. In this case Zahalon had dismissed the "bubo" on the patient's groin as a hernia, but the Christian physician disagreed. When the patient died, the body was sent to a second Christian physician to be autopsied; he confirmed Zahalon's diagnosis. The fraught atmosphere is vividly depicted, the subcurrent of religious tension, and the economic stakes—the diagnosis determines whether or not the victim's house shall be shut up. Friedenwald, "Jacob Zahalon of Rome," 3, for the English; *Otzar haHayim* for the Hebrew.

63. I considered a chapter on Zahalon for this book, but decided to limit this study to northern Italy. Zahalon more than deserves new attention, and there are signs it is forthcoming. See Iris Idelson-Shein, "Rabbis of the (Scientific) Revolution: Revealing the Hidden Corpus of Early Modern Translations Produced by Jewish Religious Thinkers," *American Historical Review* 126.1 (March 2021): 54–81; Edward Reichman, "The Physicians of the Rome Plague of 1656, Yaakov Zahalon and Hananiah Modigliano," *Seforim Blog* (https://seforimblog.com), February 19, 2021 entry, last accessed December 14, 2021. Magdelena Janosikova has given several talks on Zahalon and the contemporary Jewish physician, Abraham Wallich, in the last year: "United in Scholarship, Divided in Practice: (Re)Translating Smallpox and Measles for Seventeenth-century Jews" was discussed at the Early Modern Workshop organized by Joshua Teplitzky and Francesca Bregoli (Zoom, Feb. 19, 2021); I was a respondent to this paper.

64. Professor James McIlwain has asked me whose foot was intended, the teacher's or the student's? I find the question complicated by the truth that all feet are not equal. If

Hillel were considerably older than the would-be convert, his lesson would be shorter than the questioner's capacity to listen. If Hillel practiced yoga, he might have balanced for a considerable while. I do not know the answer.

65. See the Midrash *Tanhuma*, Shoftim 5:1; Midrash *Tanhuma* (Buber), Shoftim 4:1; Mekhilta de Rabbi Ishmael 12:1:4.

66. Saperstein, *Jewish Preaching 1200–1800*, 79.

67. Ibid., 61.

CHAPTER 6

1. According to the KTIV database, a seventeenth-century manuscript containing sermons and notes by Judah Modena also includes a lament for Abraham, possibly authored by his son. The manuscript is dated 1632, when Abraham was, however, quite alive. It is also indecipherable, and I have omitted it from my corpus, as either the date or the identification of the text is in error. See the entry for Moscow Russia MS Guenzburg 356 (IMHM microfilm no. 27969).

2. Alan Charles Harris, "La demografia del Ghetto in Italia," *La Rassegna Mensile di Israel*, 3d ser., 33.1 (1967): 1–16; Shalom Sabar, "The Beginnings and Flourishings of Ketubah Illustration in Italy: A Study in Popular Imagery and Jewish Patronage," PhD diss. (University of California, Los Angeles, 1987).

3. For Abraham Catalano as a witness, see the entries in David Carpi, ed. and introd., *Pinqas va'ad q"q Padova* (Jerusalem: National Sciences Academy of Israel and Central Archive for the History of the Jewish People, 1974), and Shlomo Simonsohn, *History of the Jews in the Duchy of Mantua* (Jerusalem: Kiryath Sepher, 1977). The KTIV database includes several *ketubbot* (wedding contracts) with Abraham's signature as witness. The dates document a wave of marriages following the conclusion of the epidemic. See JER NLI MS Heb 901.258=2 for the marriage of Naftali Katz and Bruna bat Jacob di Bianci (1631, 7 Tevat 5092); JER NLI MS Heb 901.1993 for the marriage of David b. Nathan haCohen and Sarah bat Israel Cohen (1633); JER NLI MS Heb 901.263=1 for the marriage of Benzion b. David Tzarfati Ghirondi and Simhah bat Shemaryahu Morpurgo (1634, 14 Shevat); and JER NLI MS Heb 901.20001=2 for the marriage of Maimon Buzir (?) haCohen to Ricca bat Israel haCohen (1641, 9 Iyyar). The bride Ricca must have been the sister of Sarah, whose *ketubbah* Abraham witnessed in 1633; Maimon and Ricca's marriage took place only a few months before Abraham's death and must be the last documentary evidence of his continuing role in ghetto life.

4. David A. Malkiel, *Stones Speak: Hebrew Tombstones from Padua, 1529–1862* (Leiden: Brill, 2014).

5. Joshua Teplitzky tells me that the relevant records in Prague have been destroyed by fire. Personal email communication, September 2–3, 2020.

6. Pinchas Roth, email, May 12, 2020.

7. B. Moed Katan 25b relates the story about the death of R. Yohanan, but elsewhere the deceased is identified as R. Pedat (Eleazar b. Pedat); see, e.g., Jacob ibn Habib's sixteenth-century compendium of Talmudic aggadot, *'Ein Ya'aqov*, Mo'ed Katan (Venice, 1516), 3:26.

8. Eikha Rabba 1,1; see Al-Sheikh to Lam. 1:1.

9. I am forced to emend the text to read: למותר שנאסר כיון. The Hebrew reads כיון שנמסר למיתר, which makes no sense. I believe Marini alludes to b. Sanhedrin 108b, which includes a fabular exchange between Noah and the raven. When Noah sends the raven out to scan for dry land, the raven accuses Noah of wishing to send him to his death—so that Noah can

have sex with the raven's wife (!). Referring to the traditional view that sex was prohibited on the ark, Noah replies that if he is forbidden from having sex with the (human) woman who is ordinarily permitted to him, all the more so would he be prohibited from having sex with a creature with whom sex is ordinarily prohibited: ש"כ לא לי נאסר לי בנאסר לי נאמר במותר רשע לו אמר. This legend preoccupied Marini, as he will also invoke it in his sermon on behalf of the plague-stricken Jews in Rome in 1656. Curiously, an image of the dove with the olive leaf in her mouth became the Marini family emblem. (See the following discussion.) Here what Marini seems to be saying is that if the purpose of a eulogy is to let people express their grief, this too would not apply to the present occasion, as eulogizing, while ordinarily permissible, is prohibited. In other words: למותר שנאסר כיון.

10. There is an abbreviated word here that looks like 'ית, usually יתברך, May He Be Blessed (i.e., God). That reading makes no sense here, and I do not know what could be meant. The idea Marini wants to develop is clearer: When a loss (death) affects only the deceased, or other people around the deceased, it is easier to eulogize than when you are personally touched.

11. It also appears in the 'Ein Ya'aqov.

12. See Chapter 2.

13. This argument does not quite respect Marini's distinction between suspensions of natural law and religious law, but I think the slippage is his. As he reformulates the contrast, even suspensions of natural law come under the category of providence.

14. The burial eulogy's ma'amar also straddles two verses, Amos 8:9–10.

15. I follow the reading of Maimonides. The Hebrew שפלה ונפש ,שפלה ורוח ,טובה עין are not so easy to translate. The English translation in Sefaria reads "a good eye, a humble spirit, and a lowly soul," then interpolates (using Maimonides?) to explain "a good eye" as being content with what one has, "a humble spirit" as "exceeding humility," and "a lowly soul" as "watchfulness and separation from lust." www.sefaria.org.

16. We derive three benefits from burying the dead, as described in the 'Akkedat Yitzhak, par. Shemini: (1) not leaving the dead unburied, (2) not letting the body putrefy, and (3) facilitating the union of the soul components, which Arama analogizes to Abraham and Sarah in the cave of Machpelah when discovered by Bena'a. Since, in fact, Abraham Catalano's wife, Sarah, would have been buried already, the metaphor also depicts the union of husband and wife in death. Whether Sarah was buried beside Abraham, or consigned to a mass burial plot, the meaning is the same.

17. 'Akkedat Yitzhak, par. Shemini, "three days are decreed for weeping" for the dead.

18. Cf. Daniel 12:6 הפלאות קץ, the "end of [these] wonders."

19. If he means the same "three pillars" he referred to in his sermon for Shabbat Teshuvah in 1631, then the reference is to Avot 1:2, where the three pillars that support the world are Torah, worship, and righteous deeds. See Chapter 5.

20. Cf. Al-Sheikh, also Kohelet Rabbah 7:20;1, where the example is someone who gives charity indiscriminately when some recipients are more needy than others.

21. A tentative translation (!). The wording is obscure.

22. "Her" = wisdom.

23. B. Pesahim 66b—everyone who boasts that he is wise loses his wisdom.

24. Those prophets who acted haughtily or boastfully were punished with the suspension of their prophetic gift, and those who acted in anger likewise lose the gift of prophecy. The Talmudic examples are Moses, Deborah, David, and Hillel, as in Marini's list, but not Samuel. The Talmudic example is Eliab, David's brother.

25. Prov. 13:7.

26. With the conclusion of the verse: "though his excellency ascends to heaven, he will die like dung."

27. "Tent," as in Gen. 13:3. Abraham Catalano traveled to the grave and now his soul is properly sent off on its journey.

28. I.e., they (Death and Annihilation) do not know where Wisdom is.

29. "Because God will be your light forever."

30. Similarly, Abraham Ibn Ezra glosses Eccl. 10:1—which Marini cites in lines 8–9—with the statement that even a little sin can damage a very good person: for instance, King Solomon, whose wisdom and righteousness were undercut by his failure to monitor the idolatrous behavior of his wives.

31. See also the *Hovot haLevavot*, Gate 6 on "submission," 7:12—"and he [Abraham] showed only lowliness and humility before God, and honor and goodness to human beings."

32. Cecil Roth, "Sefer *'Olam Hafukh* by Abraham Catalano," *Qovetz 'al yad* 4.14 (Jerusalem, 1946), 67–101, citing p. 91.

33. Recall that the lament is missing in the original Italian. See Chapter 3.

34. Roth, "Sefer *'Olam Hafukh*," 71, prints the Italian/Hebrew epithalamium, beginning אזן הסות אוינו in Hebrew, or "Hoggi in alto divino" in Italian; on the same page, he refers to another exemplar of this type beginning גדי תמול תקנתי or "Già di te molti canti."

35. Roth, "Sefer *'Olam Hafukh*," 70.

36. The phonetic dissonance must be a product of modern pronunciation; the shift from -*ma* to -*me* probably was not noticeable in the Italian dialect Moses spoke, which correspondingly influenced his Hebrew pronunciation as well.

37. One manuscript preserves a homily or sermon written by Abraham, which the KTIV catalog describes as a "philosophical sermon"; The manuscript is housed in Ancona, and according to the copyist, he found it among some of Abraham's papers. See MS Ancona Italy MS 7 (IMHM microfilm F 2532), folio 6b.

38. Stephen A. Kaufman, personal email exchanges throughout August 2020.

39. The UCLA collection has been closed during the pandemic, and I have not been able to see this copy. The manuscript has unfortunately not been digitized.

40. Gen. 19:11, 2 Kgs. 6:18.

41. Num. 10:35.

42. Jer. 17:18.

43. "Most fortunate of scholars"—the expression is used to describe R. Eleazar; see Ket. 40a, Keritot 13b, Gitt. 26b.

44. A pun, as "crown" was used also to refer to a diploma, and the term moved into Hebrew. Abraham Catalano had been "crowned" (graduated) from the University of Padua medical school.

45. Cf. Zech. 9:11—and now a double reward counterpoints the double destruction of v. 3.

46. The Adler copy reads נמה, but I have emended to שמה.

47. Cf. Prov. 29:6.

48. Mishnah Torah 3:43:6—ושני המועדים האלה—רצוני לומר סוכות ופסח—מלמדים דעות ומדות. The passage goes on to describe the benefits we enjoy now as due to the merits of our biblical ancestors, Abraham, Isaac, and Jacob, who were perfect and enlightened (שלמים); Maimonides then criticizes those who read the biblical text metaphorically and not as truth. I think Moses Catalano may have had some echo of this passage in his mind, though it does not dictate his meaning, which suggests that his father did enlist parables as vehicles of "truth."

49. Abraham Catalano's essay, a philosophical-ethical composition.

50. Literally, "as if gliding."

51. In the vernacular? Plainspoken?

52. Eccl. 7:1.

53. Meaning that "he illuminated the obscurity of the rulings and made them clear."

54. M. Beitzah 2, 1; b. Qiddushin 82a. *'Eruv tavshilin* refers to the preparation of food on a holiday (technically forbidden) when it is followed by the Sabbath. I think Moses is referring to the deferral of the commemoration of Abraham's death until the conclusion of the festival season. In other words, the hemistich could be translated "his funeral was delayed." It may be preferable to read the first hemistich as "when he was buried in Hebron" and not "like the one buried in Hebron." Abraham Catalano was buried on 13 Tishre, the day after he died, but Solomon Marini's eulogy in the Italian synagogue was not given until three weeks later, on *par.* Lekh Lekha. The words *tavshilin* in v. 25, *parshiyot* in v. 26, and *Metatron* in v. 30 are all written with curlicued overlining, which I assume is a musical indication. I have put the words in capital letters.

55. Lit., an *'eruv*, or border, for the blind, inside which they could act safely. Stephen Kaufman reads "out of divergent sayings he made a collection of passages, a limit for the blind." Personal email communication, August 10, 2020.

56. Moses refers to himself as "blind," i.e., ignorant, compared to his father, so that arranging his writings is a catastrophic assignment.

57. The owner of the property containing the cave of Machpelah where Abraham and Sarah were buried.

58. The greatest of angels, sometimes also associated with the Angel of Death.

59. A strange simile: sheep do not sit on the ground.

60. David A. Malkiel, *Shirei Shayish: Ketuvot mi-batei ha-hayyim shel Padova 1529–1862* (Jerusalem: Ben Tzvi Institute, 2013); and Malkiel, *Stones Speak*. I had borrowed both books from the Hebrew Union College Klau Library in the spring of 2019, then returned them to the Klau. The pandemic made it impossible to obtain copies again. I am grateful to Professor Malkiel for providing a pdf of the English volume; I had fortunately scanned some of the Hebrew before returning it.

61. Malkiel, *Stones Speak*, 70–71.

62. Ibid., 301. Regarding the "escutcheon" carved on Abraham's stone, Malkiel notes that more typically it would be bordered so as not to overflow into the space allotted for the inscription. Ibid., 193.

63. Malkiel, *Shirei Shayish*, 58. The full inscription with annotation runs from 57 to 59.

64. "Earthly inhabitants"—cf. Ps. 24:1, where Rashi, Ibn Ezra, and Al-Sheikh all distinguish between the psalmist's parallel use of *eretz* and *tevel*, reading the former to refer to the Land of Israel and the latter to the gentile world. If this distinction resonated for northern Italian Jews, it would imply that the tombstone calls out to them reminding them that they live (and die) in exile.

65. 2 Sam. 23:1. "Leader"—literally, captain; cf. Jonah 1:6. Perhaps the author also was thinking of passages like the midrash *Pesikta Rabbati* 47:1, which compares the fate of a ship without a captain to Israel without a leader.

66. "I am with him"—Ps. 91:15; this psalm served Jews and Christians as plague prayer. "Destruction and annihilation"—cf. Isa. 59:7, 60:18; Jer. 48:3, in the epitaph also associated with plague: Abraham did not desert his people in time of plague.

67. See, e.g., Rashi to Gen. 25:22, for reference to Shem and Ever's "Torah school," which the pregnant Rebecca could not pass by without the unborn Jacob kicking in desire to attend, while Esau kicked when she walked past places of idolatry.

68. "Nurturing him" (להשביר שבר). Malkiel translates the line: "Of his having raised and sustained, sparing no pain, the one who bears his image and likeness," *Stones Speak*, 70–71. The phrase להשביר שבר appears in several seventeenth-century epitaph poems from northern Italian Jewish cemeteries treated by Malkiel in "Poems on Tombstone Inscriptions in Northern Italy" [Hebrew] *Pe'amim* 98–99 (2004): 142 (Judah of Ravenna, d. 1606); 147 (Judah Longio, d. 1648, and Shlomo b. Yoav, d.1623, both in Mantua). Malkiel notes the association to Joseph feeding and sustaining his brothers in Egypt (Gen. 42:6).

69. "Unanimously"—*ve'ayn qovel*. Malkiel translates, "remind the Master with one voice," *Stones Speak*, 70–71. For "unanimously" or "one voice," which are synonymic, the use is not as in Esther 4.4 (*ve'ayn qovel*="he wouldn't receive them") but *qovel* as derived from *q-w-l*, or voice. I therefore read the expression as "with no dissent," i.e., unanimously. As with *novel/naval* in v. 17, the elongated vowel seems to reflect a regional pronunciation. I depart from Malkiel's "remind the Master," which I don't think makes sense. It is Abraham who should "be remembered" as a leader among men (*le-resh mata*), for the combination of attributes encapsulated in the verses.

70. "Overt and covert"—lit., "sin in the heart and on the face." Malkiel translates "when with heart and countenance you regret your sins." *Stones Speak*, 70–71.

71. Malkiel, *Stones Speak*, 70–71: "You cry out to God, hoping for succor."

72. Ps. 137:1. See discussion that follows.

73. Malkiel, *Stones Speak*, 70–71, translates, "This man, unceasing, will cry out like you." I prefer to read *belo novel* as *belo navel*, e.g., Ps. 71:22, "I too shall give thanks to You with instruments." I think the idea is that Abraham calls out responsively from the grave without musical accompaniment or catalyst. Recall the "two-lute" imagery developed by Abarbanel, Alemanno, and Arama, treated in Chapter 4, a metaphor for sympathetic influence based on the way a string sounded on one lute will set a nearby instrument into resonance; Moses points in this direction by alluding to the Talmudic dictum that mentioning a deceased, righteous man's name will cause his lips to move in the grave (based on Cant. 7:10). Here, then, the living humans who call out at Abraham's grave cause the dead man to call out in response on their behalf.

74. Bekhorot 31b.

75. Malkiel, *Stones Speak*, 70–71: "And the virtue of his words . . . / will hasten Redemption."

76. Isa. 40:31.

77. The bibliography is now extensive (and growing). For a sampling, see Dvora Bregman, "'Now you shall be housed in stone': The Epitaph Poems of Moses Zacuto" [in Hebrew], in *Studies in Arabic and Hebrew Letters in Honor of Raymond P. Scheindlin*, ed. Jonathan Decter and Michael Rand (Piscataway, NJ: Gorgias Press, 2007), Hebrew sec., 13–21; David Malkiel, "Poems on Tombstone Inscriptions in Northern Italy," 120–54; and Malkiel,, *Shirei Shayish* and *Stones Speak*; Marian Sárraga and Ramón Sárraga, "Early Links Between Amsterdam, Hamburg and Italy: Epitaphs from Hamburg's Old Sephardic Cemetery," *Studia Rosenthaliana* 34 (2000): 23–55; Marian Sárraga and Ramón Sárraga, "Sephardic Epitaphs in Hamburg's Oldest Jewish Cemetery: Poetry, Riddles and Eccentric Texts," *AJS Review* 26 (2002): 53–92; Karlheinz Müller, Simon Schwarzfuchs, and Avraham Reiner, eds., *Die

Gransteine vom jüdischen Friedhof in Würzburg aus der Zeit von dem Schwarzen Tod (Würzburg: Monumenta Germaniae Historica, 2012); and my study of the Toledo Jewish plague epitaphs in *After the Black Death: Plague and Commemoration Among Iberian Jews* (Philadelphia: University of Pennsylvania Press, 2018), chapter 4.

78. Malkiel thinks that Abraham is recalled for treating the sick during the plague, but this is not accurate. Although he was a physician, Abraham did not practice medicine before or during the plague. His narrative account details his committee's efforts to find and replace physicians and less-trained medical personnel during the epidemic, and never once refers to serving in any medical capacity himself.

79. Elliott Horowitz, "Speaking to the Dead: Cemetery Prayer in Medieval and Early Modern Jewry," *Journal of Jewish Thought and Philosophy* 8 (1999): 303–17.

80. See note 72 above and Chapter 4.

81. My thanks to Dr. Edward Reichman for informing me that the precious and earliest copy of the *'Olam Hafukh* at Columbia University was copied by the physician Isaac Hayim Cantarini (d. 1723), another University of Padua graduate; as Reichman notes, many of Cantarini's family members appear in the narrative, and he added marginal notes clarifying their relationship to him; email, July 10, 2020. Several members of the Cantarini family served as physicians in the Paduan ghetto during the plague. See Rebecca Locci, "La gestione della peste del 1631 nel ghetto di Padova attraverso la cronaca di Avraham Catalano," M.A. dissertation, University of Padua, 2021, 79–81.

82. Nükhet Varlik, *Plague and Empire in the Early Modern Mediterranean World* (Cambridge: Cambridge University Press, 2015).

83. Marc Saperstein, *Jewish Preaching 1200–1800: An Anthology* (New Haven, CT: Yale University Press, 1989), 22–23.

84. Erwin Goffman, *The Presentation of Self in Everyday Life* (Edinburgh: University of Edinburgh, 1956). Goffman was also primarily concerned with the enclosed systems of the workplace or political sphere. The ghetto surely constitutes such a space, but it is less homogeneous than Goffman's examples, its power lines and staging grounds dynamically complex. Nonetheless, it is important to underline my distinction between the interactions of living people and the literary record of those interactions by a self-interested author.

85. See Ann Carmichael's "The Last Past Plague: The Uses of Memory in Renaissance Epidemics," *Journal of the History of Medicine* 53 (1993): 132–60. By changing strategies, I refer also to contemporary attempts to reconcile miasmic and contagion theories of plague, and the consequences of those attempts as they were expressed in policies of containment, treatment, and prevention. Sometimes the migratory careers of Jewish physicians prove interesting as they testify to exposure to different theoretical trends; see, for example, the case of the two Jewish physicians who offered their services to the Serenissima in Venice during the 1630–31 outbreak: Carla Boccato, "Testimonianze ebraiche sulla peste del 1630 a Venezia," *La Rassegna Mensile di Israel*, 3d ser., 41.9–10 (1975): 458–67. But it is also possible to track the shift in medical trends in our plague liturgies, too, and their fascination with the prophylactic powers of incense. The effort to balance theological explanations for the lague with medical ones can also be sensed in our texts.

86. See, e.g., Nicholas Evans, "Blaming the Rat? Accounting in Colonial Indian Medicine," *Medicine Anthropology Theory* (MAT), June 25, 2018, http://www.medanthrotheory.org /article/view/4872, last accessed December 23, 2021. S. Eben Kirksey and Stefan Helmreich,

"The Emergence of Multispecies Ethnology," *Cultural Anthropology* 25.4 (2010): 545–76; Mel Salm, "Anthropocene Diseased: A Provocation," in the online COVID-19 FORUM II, April 6, 2020, somatosphere.net/forumpost/Anthropocene-covid-19/, last accessed December 24, 2021.

APPENDIX I

1. שמ' יב:כג
2. שמ' יב:יב
3. מורה חלק ג' סימן מ"ו
4. איוב י:ד
5. שמ' יב:יב
6. שמ' יב: כט
7. בלבול פסוקים. כנראה חשב על יהושע כב:ט. אמנם השווה שופט' כא:כג.
8. השווה יהושע כב:יג
9. יהושע כב:יג
10. תה' כט:א
11. תה' כט:יא
12. תה' ז:א
13. שמ' כ:ב, ג.
14. יש' ה:טז
15. יש' מ:ז
16. שיר השירים א:ז
17. שיר השירים א:ז
18. תה' קו:לה
19. יש' מב:יח
20. השווה חבקוק ב:ז, שמואל א, כו:כג
21. יש' מב:יט—מי עַוֵּר כי אם עבדי
22. תה' כט:א
23. שמואל א, ב:ב
24. שמואל א, ב:ג
25. שמואל א, ב:ג
26. שמואל א, ב:ג
27. הפסוק כתוב "לא נתכנו" באות א".
28. השווה דב' לב:לו
29. לקרוא לפי הקרי ולא לפי הכתיב, "לו נתכנו" ולא "לא נתכנו".
30. יש' מב:כ
31. יש' מב:כא
32. קהלת ח:יא
33. יש' מב:כה
34. תה' צא:א
35. תה' צא:א
36. וה"אלף" = והראשון
37. במשמעות "ולסוג הראשון" [א'].
38. תה' צא:ג

39. זאת אומרת, ולסוג ב'

40. תה' צא: ט

41. לסוג ג'

42. תה' צא:יד

43. השווה חובות הלבבות—ומי שבוטח בזולת ה' מסיר האלהים השגחתו מעליו

44. איוב לו:ז

45. נדמה לי שהוא מתכוון לומר שיש עוד הסבר לסוג ג' והוא בקולות השופר

46. תה' פט:טז

47. יש' מה:יז

48. דב' לב:מו

49. תה' יז:ח

50. תה' מד:יד

51. ירמ' כ:ט

52. משנה אבות א, ב

53. איוב כו:יא

54. יחזק' לח:כ

55. ישע' ה:ח

56. ישע' י:א

57. בר' ח:יא

58. ערובין יח,ב - אמרה יונה לפני הקדב"ה רבונו של עולם יהיו מזונותי מרורין כזית ודורין בידך ואל יהיו מתוקין כדבש ותלויין ביד בשר ודם.

59. ויקרא יט:יח

60. שמ' לב:לב

61. יונה ד:ג

62. איוב ל:כה

63. תה' לה: יג

64. בר' ט:כג ואילך

65. ערובין יח,ב

APPENDIX 2

1. דב' לג:ב, ג

2. יעקב בן שלמה אבן חביב, אגדת עין יעקב, מועד קטן, כרך ב' ע' 285–286

3. ירמ' ט:יז

4. איכה רבה א, א: ויקרא ה' אל האדם (בר' ג:ט) רבי נחמיה אומר אין לשון איכה אלא קינה, הדא מה דאת אמר ויאמר לו איכה, אוי לכה. [וראה אלשייך שאומר שבוכים על העם המגורש ולא על א"י כמו שה' היה קונן על אדם ולא על גן עדן שלא היה נפגע במעשה אדם וחוה וקוראים "איכה" כאילו כתוב "איכה", ולכן ה' מקונן על האדם שימות בגלל חטאו.

5. לתקן "נמסר למיתר" לקרוא "נאסר למותר", לפי סנהדרין קח, ב

6. תה' לז:י – ועוד מעט ואין רשע, והתבוננת על מקומו ואיננו

7. שמואל ב, א:טו ואילך

8. עמוס ח:ט

9. עמוס ח:י

10. בר' יג:ב

11. בר' יג:ג

12. משנה אבות ה,יט—והשלשה הם עין טובה, רוח נמוכה, ונפש שפלה. וראה את הדיון של הרמב"ם הקושר את השלישי לפסוק מבר' יח:כז [אפר ועפר] שיופיע בהמשך הקינה

13. מועד קטן כז, ב—שלושה ימים לבכי וכו' [הלכות אבלות]. ואראמא מביא את הדיון בעקדת יצחק, פרשת שמיני. הג' תועלות הן [1] אל תלין, [2] שהגויה לא תרקב, ו[3] לאפשר ייחוד חלקי הנשמה, הנמשלים ליחוד אברהם ושרה במערת מכפלה.

14. יואל ב:י, תה' עז:יט

15. יש' כד:טז

16. יש' כד:יט

17. תלמוד בבלי, סוכה כו: - אם בא להחמיר על עצמו מחמיר ולית ביה משום יוהרא. וראה שורה 16 למטה

18. קהלת ז:כ

19. מל' א, ח:מו

20. יש' נט:ו

21. יש' סד:ה

22. קהלת ז:כג

23. קהלת י: א

24. קהלת י:א, ושם "שכלות"

25. איוב כח:יב

26. איוב כח:כ

27. איוב כח:כג

28. פסחים סו:

29. קהלת י:ה, וקהלת י:ו

30. קהלת י:ו

31. משלי יג:ז

32. הוה" בכ'"י

33. במקור [יומא פז,א] : אזיל ולולאי שתהא פעאה כיציאה וכי הוי חזי אמבוהא אבתריה אמר [איוב כ:ו] אם יעלה לשמים שיאו

34. משלי כז:כד ץ. אמנם ר' זוטרא מצטט את הפסוק בקטע המוחבר מהתלמוד, יומא פז.

35. בר' יח:כז

36. שמ' טז:זז-ח

37. תה' כב:ז . וכל ג' הפסוקים מצוטטים במדרש תהילים כב:טו: "כך הקב"ה נותן גדולה לצדיקים והם ממעיטים עצמם. אברהם אמר ואנכי עפר ואפר. משה ואהרון אמרו ונחנו מה. דוד אמר ואנכי תולעת ולא איש וכו'." וראה גם חובות הלבבות, שער שישי על הכניעה, ז:יב: ולא הוסיף אלא ענוה ושפלות לפני האלהים וכבד וטובה לבני-אדם כמו שאמר אברהם עת ששבחו הבורא וכו'

38. סוכה כו,ב - אם בא להחמיר על עצמו ולית ביה משום יוהרא [וראה שורה 6 למעלה]

39. איוב כח:כב

40. תה' קד:כט

41. ירמ' ז:כט

42. איוב כח:יב, כ, וראה שורות 10–11

43. השווה תה' עז:ג

44. השווה תה' קטז:זז

45. יש' סב:ד

46. יש' ס:כ

47. A second copy documented in the special collections of the University of California, LA USA MS 779 bx 9.4 (IMHM F 32395), was inaccessible throughout the pandemic.

48. בר, יט:יא, מל' ב, ו:יח

49. במד' י:לה

50. מרגלית טובה ויקרה

51. כריתות יג ע"ב, גיטין כו ע"ב ועד—השמח בין החכמים
52. משלי כט:ו
53. מצרף השכל—ספר שחבר אברהם קאטאלנו
54. קהלת ז:א
55. משנה ביצה ב,א, קידושין פ"ב ע"א—ואולי הוא מרמז לאיחור הטכס
56. שברון—ירמ' יז:יח, יחזק' כא:יא
57. עפרון—בעל מערת מכפלה. בר' כג:י ואילך
58. בשר ועצמות

Bibliography

MANUSCRIPTS

Abraham Catalano

Budapest (Kaufmann) MS 335 (IMHM MSS-D 7837 microfiche)
London MS British Library 971 (IMHM microfilm F 5721)
MS Montefiore 473 (IMHM microfilm F 5373)
NY Jewish Theological Seminary 3568 (ENA 1005) (IMHM microfilm F 29373)
NY MS Columbia University X893-Ab8 (IMHM microfilm F 16558)
Oxford Michael Add. 13 (IMHM microfilm F 21598)

Joseph Concio

NY MS JTS 5063 (IMHM microfilm F 29860)
Paris MS Alliance Universelle Israelite 139 (IMHM microfilm F 3207)

Plague Hymns and Liturgies

London MS British Library Or. 10219 (IMHM microfilm F 7581)
Parma MS Biblioteca Palatina 1751 (IMHM microfilm F 12978)
Parma MS Biblioteca Palatina 1784 (IMHM microfilm F 13008)
Parma MS Biblioteca Palatina 1785 (IMHM microfilm F 13009), MSS D-4673
Parma MS Biblioteca Palatina 1789 (IMHM microfilm F 13013)
Parma MS Biblioteca Palatina 1811 (IMHM microfilm F 13033)
Parma MS Biblioteca Palatina 1917 (IMHM microfilm F 13073)
Parma MS Biblioteca Palatina 3134 (IMHM microfilm F 52982)
Parma MS Biblioteca Palatina 3529 (IMHM microfilm F 14036), MSS D 6038

Solomon Marini

NY MS Jewish Theological Seminary 843 (IMHM microfilm F 23951)
NY MS Jewish Theological Seminary 6517 (no microfilm number)

SECONDARY SOURCES

Aberth, John, *The Black Death: The Great Mortality of 1348–1350, A Brief History with Documents* (Boston: Bedford/St. Martin's, 2005).

Abulafia, David, *A Medieval Emporium: The Catalan Kingdom of Majorca* (Cambridge: University of Cambridge Press, 2002.

Achinstein, Sharon, "Plagues and Publication: Ballads and the Representation of Disease in the English Renaissance," *Criticism* 34.1 (1992): 27–49.

Adler, Israel, "The Rise of Art Music in the Italian Ghetto," in *Jewish Medieval and Renaissance Studies*, ed. Alexander Altmann (Cambridge, MA: Harvard University Press, 1967), 321–64.

Agresta, Abigail, "From Purification to Protection: Plague Responses in Late Medieval Valencia," *Speculum* 95.2 (2020): 371–95.

"Alcuni appunti sul ghetto di Chieri," *Il Vessillo Israelitico* 49 (1901): 127–29, 169–71.

Alfani, Guido, "Plague in Seventeenth-century Europe and the Decline of Italy," *European Review of Economic History* 17.4 (2013): 408–30.

Alfani, Guido, and Marco Boneti, "A Survival Analysis of the Last Great European Plagues: The Case of Nonantola (Northern Italy) in 1630," *Population Studies* 73.1 (2018): 101–18.

Alfani, Guido, and Sam Cohn, Jr., "Nonantola 1630: anatomia di una pestilenza e meccanismi del contagio (con riflessioni a partire dalle epidemie milanesi della prima Età Moderna)," *Popolazione e Storia* 2 (2007): 99–138.

Allegra, Luciano, "Mestieri e famiglie del ghetto," in *Una lunga presenza. Studi sulla popolazione ebraica italiana*, ed. L. Allegra (Turin: Silvio Zamorani, 2009): 167–97.

——, "A Model of Jewish Devolution: Turin in the Eighteenth Century," *Jewish History* 7.2 (1993): 29–58.

Alter, Robert, *Art of Biblical Narrative* (New York: Basic Books, 1981).

Amelang, James, trans. and ed., *Journal of a Plague Year: The Diary of the Barcelona Tanner Miquel Parets, 1651* (Oxford: Oxford University Press, 1991).

Andrade, António Manuel Lopez, "Dióscórides renovado pela mão dos Humanistas: os comentários de Amato Lusitano," in *Espaços do pensamento científico da Antiguidade*, ed. Carmen Soares (Coimbra: Universidade de Coiombra, 2013), 71–90.

Andreatta, Michela, "The Printing of Devotion in Seventeenth-Century Italy: Prayer Books Printed for the Shomrim la-Boker Confraternities," in *The Hebrew Book in Early Modern Italy*, ed. Joseph R. Hacker and A. Shear (Philadelphia: University of Pennsylvania Press, 2011), 156–70.

Andrews, Molly, "Beyond Narrative: The Shape of Traumatic Testimony," in *We Shall Bear Witness: Life Narratives and Human Rights*, ed. Meg Jensen et al. (Madison: University of Wisconsin Press, 2014), 32–47.

Arrizabalaga, Jon, "Facing the Black Death: Perceptions and Reactions of University Medical Practitioners," in *Practical Medicine from Salerno to the Black Death*, ed. Luis García Ballester, Roger French, Jon Arrizabalaga, and Andrew Cunningham (Cambridge: Cambridge University Press, 1994), 237–88.

——, "Problematizing Retrospective Diagnosis in the History of Disease," *Asclepio* 54 (2002): 51–70.

Bakashot u-tefilot nityasdu 'al pi ge'one . . . Mantovah . . . (Mantua: Joshua of Perugia, 1630).

Bamji, Alex, "The Control of Space: Dealing with Diversity in Early Modern Venice," *Italian Studies* 62.2 (2013): 175–88.

———, "Medical Care in Early Modern Venice," London School of Economics and Political Science, Dept. of Economic History, Working Papers No. 188 (March 2014).

Bar-Levav, Avriel, "Another Place: Cemeteries in Jewish Culture" (in Hebrew), *Pe'amim* 98–99 (2002): 5–37.

Beck, Eleanora, *Boccaccio and the Invention of Musical Narrative* (Florence: European Press Academic Publishing, 2018).

Belfanti, Carlo, "Guilds, Patents, and the Circulation of Technical Knowledge in Northern Italy During the Early Modern Age," *Technology and Culture* 45.3 (2004): 569–89.

Benayahu, Meir, "Abraham Cohen of Zante and the Physicians and Poets' Club in Padua" [in Hebrew], *Ha-Sifrut* 26 (1978): 108–40.

Benayahu, Meir, N. Ben Menahem, and Sh. Shalem, *Rabbi Moshe Al-Sheich* [in Hebrew] (Jerusalem: Ben Zvi Institute, 1966).

Benedictow, Ole, "Problems with the Use of Mathematical Epidemiological Models in Plague Research and the Question of Transmission by Human Fleas and Lice," *Canadian Journal of Infectious Diseases and Medical Microbiology* (2019), article ID 1542024. https://doi.org/10.1155/2019/1542024.

Berns, Andrew, "Judah Moscato, Abraham Portaleone, and Biblical Incense in Late Renaissance Mantua," in *Rabbi Judah Moscato and the Jewish Intellectual World of Mantua in the 16th–17th Centuries*, ed. Giuseppe Veltri and G. Miletto (Leiden: Brill, 2012), 105–19.

Birnbaum, Edward, *Jewish Musicians at the Courts of the Mantuan Dukes 1542–1628*, trans. and intro., J. Cohen (Tel Aviv: Tel Aviv University, 1978).

Boccato, Carla, "La mortalità nel Ghetto di Venezia durante la peste del 1630," *Archivio Veneto* 175 (1993): 111–46.

———, "Testimonianze ebraiche sulla peste del 1630 a Venezia," *La Rassegna Mensile di Israel*, 3d ser., 41.9–10 (1975): 458–67.

Bonifacio, Laura, "L'episodio di Dafne e Apollo nelle 'Metamorfosi' di Ovidio tradotte da Shabbetay Hayyim Marini," *Henoch* 13.3 (1991): 319–35.

Bos, Kirsten, et al., "A Draft Genome of *Yersinia pestis* from Victims of the Black Death," *Nature* 478 [7370] (2011): 506–10.

———, "Eighteenth-Century *Yersinia pestis* Genomes Reveal the Long-Term Persistence of an Historical Plague Focus," *eLife* 5, 17837 (2016).

Boulton, Maureen, *The Song in the Story: Lyric Insertions in French Narrative Fiction 1200–1400* (Philadelphia: University of Pennsylvania Press, 1993).

Brabant, Rosa Kuhne, "Algunos aspectos de la literature didáctica entre los medicos árabes," in *Actas de las II Jornadas de Cultura Árabie e Islámica* (Madrid: Instituto Hispano-Árabe de Cultura, 1988), 273–80.

Bregman, Dvora, *Esa et levavi: Shirim me'et Moshe Zakut* (Jerusalem: Makhon ben Tzevi and the Hebrew University, 2009).

———, "'Now You Shall Be in Verses of Stone': The Epitaph Poems of Moses Zacuto" [in Hebrew], in *Studies in Arabic and Hebrew Letters in Honor of Raymond P. Scheindlin*, ed. Jonathan Decter and Michael Rand (Piscataway, NJ: Gorgias Press, 2007), Hebrew section, 13–21.

———, "Shabtai Hayyim Marini's Translation of Ovid's *Metamorphoses*" [in Hebrew], *Dohaq—K'tav 'Et LiSifrut Tovah* 3 (2013): 1–7.

————, *Tzror Zehuvim: Sonetim Ivriyim metekufat haRenesans vehaBarok* (Jerusalem: Makhon Ben Tzvi and Ben-Gurion University, 1997).

Brockmeier, Jens, *Beyond the Archive: Memory, Narrative, and the Autobiographical Process* (Oxford: Oxford University Press, 2015).

————, "Memory, Narrative, and the Consequences," *Topics in Cognitive Science* 11 (2019): 821–24.

————, "Socializing the Narrative Mind," *Style* 45.2 (2011): 259–64.

Bruzzone, P. L., "Les juifs au Piémont," *Revue des Etudes Juives* 19 (1889): 141–46.

Burnett, Charles, "Learned Knowledge of Arabic Poetry, Rhymed Prose and Didactic Verse from Petrus Alfonsi to Petrarch," in *Poetry and Philosophy in the Middle Ages*, ed., John Marenbon (Leiden: Brill 2000), 29–62.

Burridge, Claire, "Incense in Medicine: An Early Medieval Perspective," *Early Medieval Europe* 28.2 (2020): 219–55.

Caffiero, Marina, and S. Di Nepi, "The Relationship Between Jews and Christians: Toward a Redefinition of the Ghettos," introduction to special issue of *Rivista di storia del Cristianesimo (RSCr)* 14 (2017): 3–10.

Calvi, Giulia, *Histories of a Plague Year: The Social and the Imaginary in Baroque Florence* (Berkeley: University of California Press, 1989).

Campbell, Bruce, *The Great Transition: Climate, Disease and Society in the Late Medieval World* (Cambridge: Cambridge University Press, 2016).

Carmichael, Ann. "The Last Past Plague: The Uses of Memory in Renaissance Epidemics," *Journal of the History of Medicine* 53 (1993): 132–60.

————, *Plague and the Poor in Renaissance Florence* (Cambridge: Cambridge University Press, 1986).

————, "Plague Legislation in the Italian Renaissance," *Bulletin of the History of Medicine* 57.4 (1983): 508–25.

————, "Plague Persistence in Western Europe: A Hypothesis," in *The Medieval Globe* 1 (Pandemic Disease in the Medieval World), ed. Monica Green (Kalamazoo, MI: ARC Medieval Press, 2014), 157–92.

Carpi, Daniel, ed. and introd., *Pinqas va'ad q"q Padova* (Jerusalem: National Sciences Academy of Israel and Central Archive for the History of the Jewish People, 1974).

Cassutto, Umberto, "Un rabbino fiorentino del secolo XV," Appendix 2: "Prediche per la peste di Firenze 1456," *Rivista Israelita* 3 (1906): 116–28, 224–28; *Rivista Israelita* 4 (1907): 33–37, 156–61, 225–29.

Cerquiglini, Jacqueline, "Pour une typologie de l'insertion," *Perspectives médiévales* 3 (1977): 9–14.

Cerreta, Florindo, "Alessandro Piccolomini: Teacher of Moral Philosophy," *Italica* 33.1 (1956): 22–25.

Chajes, Yossi, "Magic, Mysticism and Popular Belief in Jewish Culture (1500–1815)," in *The Cambridge History of Judaism*, vol. 7—*The Early Modern World*, ed. Jonathan Karp and Adam Sutcliffe (Cambridge: Cambridge University Press, 2017), 475–90.

Chiu, Remi, *Plague and Music in the Renaissance* (Cambridge: Cambridge University Press, 2017).

Christian, Barbara. "Does Theory Play Well in the Classroom" (1996), repr. in *New Black Feminist Criticism 1985–2000*, ed. Gloria Bowles et al. (Champaign: University of Illinois Press, 2007), 51–67.

Cipolla, Carlo, *Cristofano and the Plague: A Study in the History of Public Health in the Age of Galileo* (Berkeley: University of California Press, 1973.)

———, *Faith, Reason, and the Plague in Seventeenth-Century Tuscany* (New York: Norton, 1979).

Clark, Matthew, *Narrative Structures and the Language of the Self* (Columbus: Ohio State University Press, 2010.

Cohen, Mark, trans. and ed., *The Autobiography of a Seventeenth-Century Venetian Rabbi: Leon Modena's "Life of Judah"* (Princeton, NJ: Princeton University Press, 1988).

Cohn, Samuel K., *The Black Death Transformed: Disease and Culture in Renaissance Europe* (London: Bloomsbury Academic, 2010).

———, *Cultures of Plague: Medical Thinking at the End of the Renaissance* (Oxford: Oxford University Press, 2009).

Colombo, Dino, and Tedesco, Giuseppe, "Il ghetto di Chieri: Alcuni avvenimenti importanti. Suo stato attuale. Parte prima: dalle origini alla fine del 700," *La Rassegna Mensile di Israel*, 27.2 (1961): 63–66.

Contessa, Andreina, "The Mantua Torah Ark and Lady Consilia Norsa: Jewish Female Patronage in Renaissance Italy," *Ars Judaica: The Bar Ilan University Journal of Jewish Art* 12 (2016): 53–70.

Cooperman, Bernard, "Ethnicity and Institution Building Among Jews in Early Modern Rome," *Association of Jewish Studies Review (AJSR)* 30 (2006): 119–45.

Crawshaw, Jane, "The Beasts of Burial: Pizzigamorti and Public Health for the Plague in Early Modern Venice," *Social History of Medicine* 24.3 (2011): 570–82.

———, *Plague Hospitals: Public Health for the City in Early Modern Venice* (Hampshire: Ashgate Publishing, 2012; reissued by Routledge in 2016).

Crown, Alan D., "*The World Overturned*: The Plague Diary of Abraham Catalano," *Midstream* 19.2 (February 1973): 65–76.

Cui, Yujun, et al., "Historical Variations in Mutation Rate in an Epidemic Pathogen, *Yersinia pestis*," *PNAS* 110.2 (2013): 577–82.

D'Amato, Alfonsina, G. Zilberstein, S. Zilberstein, B. Compagnoni, P. Righetti, "Of Mice and Men: Traces of Life in the Death Registries of the 1630 Plague in Milano," *Journal of Proteomics* 180 (2018): 128–37.

Da Montù, Gioachino, *Memorie storiche del gran contagio in Piemonte negli anni 1630 e 31 e specialmente del medesimo in Chieri e ne' suoi contorni* (Turin: Giacinto Marietti, 1830).

Damrosch, David, *The Narrative Covenant: Transformations of Genre in the Growth of Biblical Literature* (New York: Harper & Row, 1987).

Davidson, Herbert, *The Philosophy of Abraham Shalom* (Berkeley: University of California Press, 1964).

de Vivo, Filippo, "Pharmacies as Centres of Communication in Early Modern Venice," *Renaissance Studies* 21.4 (2007): 505–21.

Di Gennaro Splendore, Barbara, "Craft, Money and Mercy: An Apothecary's Self-Portrait in Sixteenth-century Bologna," *Annals of Science* 74.2 (2017): 91–107.

Di Nepi, Serena, "Jews in the Papal States Between Western Sephardic Diasporas and Ghettoization," in *Religious Change and Cultural Transformations in the Early Modern Western Sephardic Communities*, ed. Y. Kaplan (Leiden: Brill, 2019), 292–322.

Eben Kirksey, S., and Stefan Helmreich, "The Emergence of Multispecies Ethnology," *Cultural Anthropology* 25.4 (2010): 545–76.

Edwards, Robert E., Review of Sebastian Sobecki, *Last Words: The Public Self and the Social Author in Late Medieval England* (Oxford: Oxford University Press, 2019), in *Speculum* 96.3 (2021): 889–90.

Einbinder, Susan L., *After the Black Death: Plague and Commemoration Among Iberian Jews* (Philadelphia: University of Pennsylvania Press, 2018).

———, *Beautiful Death: Jewish Poetry and Martyrdom in Medieval France* (Princeton, NJ: Princeton University Press, 2002).

———, "Poetry, Prose and Pestilence: Joseph Concio and Jewish Responses to the 1630 Italian Plague," in *Shirat Dvora: Essays in Honor of Dvora Bregman*, ed. Haviva Yishai (Be'er Sheva: Ben Gurion University and Mossad Bialik, 2018), *73–*101.

Ell, Stephen R., "Three Days in October of 1630: Detailed Examination of Mortality During an Early Modern Plague Epidemic in Venice," *Reviews of Infectious Diseases* 11.1 (1989): 128–39.

Evans, Nicholas, "Blaming the Rat? Accounting in Colonial Indian Medicine," *Medicine Anthropology Theory* (MAT), 25 June 2018, http://www.medanthrotheory.org/article/view/4872.

Farkas, David S., "Because the Sound Is Good for the Spices," *Hakirah* 14 (2012): 148–50.

Friedenwald, Henry, "Jacob Zahalon of Rome: Medieval Rabbi, Physician, Author and Moralist," *Bulletin of the Medical Library Association* 8.1 (1918): 1–10.

Gampel, Benjamin, ed., *Crisis and Creativity in the Sephardic World, 1391–1648* (New York: Columbia University Press, 1997).

Gasperoni, Michaël, "Inheritance and Wealth Among Jewish Women in the Ghettos of North-Central Italy (Seventeenth–Eighteenth Century)," *Moyen Âge* 130.1 (2018):183–97.

Geller, Stephen, *Sacred Enigmas: Literary Religion in the Hebrew Bible* (New York: Routledge, 1996).

Geltner, Guy, "The Path to Pistoia: Urban Hygiene Before the Black Death," *Past & Present* 246.1 (2020): 3–33.

Gentilcore, David, *Healers and Healing in Early Modern Italy* (Manchester: Manchester University Press, 1998).

Ghirondi, Mordecai Samuel, Efrayim Ghirondi, and Hananel Neppi, *Toldot gedolei yisrael u-geonei italiah* (Trieste: Tipografia Marenigh, 1853).

Goffman, Erwin, *The Presentation of Self in Everyday Life* (New York: Anchor Doubleday: 1959).

Goldberg, Sylvie-Anne, *Crossing the Jabbok: Illness and Death in Askenazi Judaism in Sixteenth- Through Nineteenth-Century Prague* (Berkeley: University of California Press, 1997).

Golden, Kedem, "An Italian Tune in the Synagogue: An Unexplored Contrafactum by Leon Modena," *Revue des Études Juives* 177.3–4 (2018): 391–420.

Goldin, Judah, "Not by means of an angel and not by means of a messenger," in *Religions in Antiquity: Essays in Memory of Erwin Ramsdell Goodenough* (New Haven, CT: Yale University Press, 1968), 412–24.

Green, Monica, introduction to online panel discussion, "The Mother of All Pandemics: The State of Black Death Research in the Era of Covid-19" (Medieval Academy of America webinar, recorded 15 May 2020): https://youtu.be/VzqR1S8cbX8.

———, "Taking 'Pandemic' Seriously: Making the Black Death Global," *Pandemic Disease in the Medieval World: Rethinking the Black Death*, *The Medieval Globe* 1.1 (2014): 27–62.

Greenberg, S., "Plague, the Printing Press, and Public Health in Seventeenth-Century London," *Huntington Library Quarterly* 67 (2004): 508–27.

Greenblatt, Stephen, *Renaissance Self-Fashioning: From More to Shakespeare* (Chicago: University of Chicago Press, 1980).

Greenstein, Edward, "On the Genesis of Biblical Prose Narrative," *Prooftexts* 8.3 (1988): 347–54.

Guetta, Alessandro, "Antonio Brucioli and the Jewish-Italian Versions of the Bible," in *Jewish Books and their Readers*, ed. Scott Mandelbrote and J. Weinberg (Leiden: Brill, 2016), 45–71.

———, "Can Fundamentalism Be Modern? The Case of Abraham Portaleone (1542–1612)," in *Acculturation and Its Discontents: The Italian-Jewish Experience Between Exclusion and Inclusion*, ed. D. Myers, M. Ciavolella, et al. (Toronto: University of Toronto Press, 2000), 99–115.

———, *"Erudizione de' confusi* by Yedidya ben Moshe Recanati, a Late Renaissance Italian Translation of Maimonides' Guide of the Perplexed," *Yod: Revue des Études Hébraiques et Juives* 22 (2019): 107–32.

———, "The Italian Translation of the Psalms by Judah Sommo," in *Rabbi Judah Moscato and the Jewish Intellectual World of Mantua in the Sixteenth and Seventeenth Centuries*, ed. Giuseppe Veltri and G. Miletto (Leiden: Brill, 2012), 279–98.

Gutwirth, Eleazar, "Ethical and Poetical Pharmacologies from Medieval Spain," *Revue des Etudes Juives* 170.3–4 (2011): 477–502.

———, "Jewish Bodies and Renaissance Melancholy: Culture and the City in Italy and the Ottoman Empire," in *The Jewish Body*, ed. M. Diemling and G. Veltri (Leiden: Brill 2009), 57–92.

———, "Language and Medicine in the Early Modern Ottoman Empire," in *Religious Confessions and the Sciences*, ed. J. Helm and A. Winkelman (Leiden: Brill, 2001), 79–85.

Hacker, Joseph, "The Intellectual Activity of the Jews of the Ottoman Empire During the Sixteenth and Seventeenth Centuries," in *Jewish Thought in the Seventeenth Century*, ed. I. Twersky, B. Septimus, (Cambridge, MA: Harvard University Press, 1987).

Halikowski, Stefan, "The Physician's Hand: Trends in the Evolution of the Apothecary and His Art Across Europe, 1500–1700," *Nuncius* 24 (2009): 97–125.

Harrán, Don, "Doubly Tainted, Doubly Talented: The Jewish Poet Sara Copio (d. 1641) as a Heroic Singer," in *Musica Franca: Essays in Honor of Frank A. D'Acccone*, ed. Irene Alm, Alyson McLamore, and Colleen Reardon (Stuyvesant, NY: Pendragon Press 1996), 367–422.

———, "In Search of the 'Song of Zion': Abraham Portaleone on Music in the Ancient Temple," *European Journal of Jewish Studies* 4.2 (2011): 215–39.

———, "The Levi Dynasty: Three Generations of Jewish Musicians in Sixteenth-Century Mantua," in *Rabbi Judah Moscato and the Jewish Intellectual World of Mantua in the Sixteenth and Seventeenth Centuries*, ed. Giuseppe Veltri and G. Miletto (Leiden: Brill, 2012), 161–99.

———, *Salamone Rossi: Jewish Musician in Late Renaissance Mantua* (Oxford: Oxford University Press, 2003).

Harris, Alan Charles, "La demografia del Ghetto in Italia (1516–1797 circa)," *La Rassegna Mensile di Israel*, 3d ser., 33.1 (1967): 1–16.

Harvey, Susan A., *Scenting Salvation: Ancient Christianity and the Olfactory Imagination* (Los Angeles: University of California Press, 2006).

Henderson, John, *Florence Under Siege: Surviving Plague in an Early Modern City* (New Haven, CT: Yale University Press, 2019).

Hershenzon, Daniel, *The Captive Sea: Slavery, Communication and Commerce in Early Modern Spain and the Mediterranean* (Philadelphia: University of Pennsylvania Press, 2018).

Horowitz, Elliott, "Procession, Piety, and Jewish Confraternities," in *Jews of Early Modern Venice*, ed. R. C. David and B. Ravid (Baltimore: Johns Hopkins University Press, 2001), 231–47.

———, "Speaking of the Dead: The Emergence of the Eulogy Among Italian Jewry of the Sixteenth Century," in *Preachers of the Italian Ghetto*, ed. D. Ruderman (Berkeley: University of California Press, 1992), 137–38.

———, "Speaking to the Dead: Cemetery Prayer in Medieval and Early Modern Jewry," *Journal of Jewish Thought and Philosophy* 8 (1999): 303–17.

Horrox, Rosemary, *The Black Death* (Manchester: Manchester University Press, 1994.

Idel, Moshe, "Investigations into the Methodology of the Author of *Sefer haMeshiv*" [in Hebrew], *Sefunot* 17 (1983): 185–286.

———, *Kabbalah in Italy, 1280–1510* (New Haven, CT: Yale University Press, 2011).

———, "Magical and Theurgical Interpretations of Music in Jewish Texts from the Renaissance to the Hasidic Period" [in Hebrew], *Yuval* 4 (1982): 33–64.

Idelson-Shein, Iris, "Rabbis of the (Scientific) Revolution: Revealing the Hidden Corpus of Early Modern Translations Produced by Jewish Religious Thinkers," *American Historical Review* 126.1 (March 2021): 54–81.

James, Deborah, "'Music of Origin': Class, Social Category and the Performers and Audience of *Kiba*," *Africa: The Journal of the International African Institute* 67.3 (1997): 454–75.

Janosikova, Magdalena, "United in Scholarship, Divided in Practice: (Re)Translating Smallpox and Measles for Seventeenth-century Jews," Early Modern Workshop hosted by Joshua Teplitzky and Francesca Bregoli (zoom), February 15, 2021.

Jenner, Mark, "Plague on a Page: Lord Have Mercy Upon Us in Early Modern London," *Seventeenth Century* 27.3 (2012): 255–86.

Kieckhefer, Richard, *Magic in the Middle Ages,* 2d ed. (Cambridge: Cambridge University Press, 1989, repr. 2014).

Kinkeldey, Otto, "A Jewish Dancing Master of the Renaissance," in *Studies in Jewish Bibliography and Related Subjects in Memory of Abraham Solomon Freidus*, ed. Daniel Haskell (New York: Alexander Kohut Memorial Foundation, 1929), 329–72.

Kisch, Bruno, "The History of the Jewish Pharmacy in Prague," *Historia Judaica* 8 (1946): 149–80.

Kottek, Samuel, "Jews between Profane and Sacred Science in Renaissance Italy: The Case of Abraham Portaleone," in *Religious Confessions and the Sciences in the Sixteenth Century,* eds. Jurgen Helm and A, Winkelman (Leiden: Brill, 2001), 108–11.

———, "La Prière des Médecins de Jacob Zahalon," *Pardes* 15 (1992): 185–93.

Kozodoy, Maud, "Medieval Hebrew Medical Poetry: Uses and Context," *Aleph: Historical Studies in Science and Judaism* 11.2 (2011): 213–88.

———, "Prefatory Verse and the Reception of the *Guide of the Perplexed*," *Jewish Quarterly Review* 106.3 (2016): 257–82.

Lanaro, Paola, ed., *At the Centre of the Old World: Trade and Manufacturing in Venice and the Venetian Mainland 1400–1800* (Toronto: Centre for Reformation and Renaissance Studies, 2006).

Lansing, Carol, *Passion and Order: Restraint of Grief in the Medieval Italian Communes* (Ithaca, NY: Cornell University Press, 2008).

Lattes, Ya'akov Andrea, ed., *Pinqas q"q qehillat Roma [5]375–[5]455* (Jerusalem: Ben Zvi Institute, 2012).

Laughran, Michelle Anne, "The Body, Public Health and Social Control in Sixteenth-Century Venice," PhD diss., University of Connecticut 1998

Leibowitz, Joshua, "Bubonic Plague in the Ghetto of Rome (1656): Descriptions by Zahalon and Gastaldi," *Korot* 14.3–4 (2000): 65–68.

———, "The Plague in the Rome Ghetto (1656) According to Jacob Zahalon and Cardinal Gastaldi" [in Hebrew], *Korot* 4.3–4 (1967) : 155–69.

Leonard, Marie L., "Healing Communal Wounds: Processions and Plague in Sixteenth-Century Mantua," *Science Museum Group Journal* 11 (Spring 2019), http://dx.doi.org/10.15180/191106

Locci, Rebecca, "La gestione della peste del 1631 nel ghetto di Padova attraverso la cronaca di Avraham Catalano," M.A. dissertation, University of Padua, 2021.

Lucchetti, Enzo, Matteo Manfredini, and Sergio de Iasio, "La peste de 1630 dans la ville et dans le territoire de Parme (Italie)," *Bulletins et mémoires de la Société d'anthropologie de Paris*, n.s. 10.3–4 (1998): 411–24.

Luciano, Allegra, "A Model of Jewish Devolution: Turin in the Eighteenth Century," *Jewish History* 7.2 (1993): 29–58.

Macht, David L., and William Kunkel, "Concerning the Antiseptic Action of Some Aromatic Fumes," *Proceedings of the Society for Experimental Biology and Medicine* (1920): 68–70.

Macklin, Christopher, "Plague, Performance and the Elusive History of the Stella Celi Extirpavit," *Early Music History* 29 (2010):1–31.

———, "Stability and Change in the Composition of a 'Plague Mass' in the Wake of the Black Death," *Plainsong and Medieval Music* 25.2 (2016):167–89.

Maggioni, Giuseppe, and Cappelletti, Elsa Mariella, "Un celebre medicamento composto: la teriaca," in *La spezieria, medicamenti e arte farmaceutica nel Veneto dal Cinquecento ad oggi*, eds. E. Cappelletti, G. Maggioni, and G. Rodighiero (Treviso: Antilia 2002), 15–80.

Malkiel, David. "Poems on Tombstone Inscriptions in Northern Italy" [Hebrew], *Pe'amim* 98–99 (2004): 120–54.

———, *Shirei Shayish: Ketuvot mi-batei ha-hayim shel Padova 1529–1862* (Jerusalem: Ben Zvi Institute, 2013).

———, *Stones Speak—Hebrew Tombstones from Padua, 1529–1862* (Leiden: Brill, 2014).

Manfredini, Matteo, et al., "The Plague of 1630 in the Territory of Parma: Outbreak and Effects of a Crisis," *International Journal of Anthropology* 17.1 (2002): 41–57.

Massarani, Abraham, *Sefer haGalut vehaPedut* (Venice, 1634), repr. with intro. by Daniel Khawalzun (St. Petersburg, L. Rabinovitz ve-Sh. Rappaport for haMelitz, 1894).

McCauley, Douglas J., et al., "Effects of Land Use on Plague (*Yersinia pestis*): Activity of Rodents in Tanzania," *American Journal of Tropical Medicine and Hygiene* 92.4 (2015): 776–83.

Melamed, Abraham, "The Perception of Jewish History in Italian Jewish Thought of the Sixteenth and Seventeenth Centuries: A Re-examination," *Italia Judaica: Atti del II Convegno internazionale* (Rome: Istituto Poligrafico e Zecca dello Stato,1986): 138–70.

Melo, António, "Propriedades terapêuticas das plantas aromáticas em Amato Lusitano: o cardamomo," in *Pombalina: Legado clássico no Renascimento e sua recção*, ed. Nair de Nazaré Castro Soares and C. Teixeira, (Coimbra: University of Coimbra, 2017), 241–55.

Miletto, Gianfranco, "The Human Body as a Musical Instrument in the Sermons of Judah Moscato," in *The Jewish Body: Corporeality, Society, and Identity in the Renaissance and Early Modern Period*, ed. Maria Diemling and G. Veltri (Leiden: Brill, 2008), 377–93.

Minelli, Alessandro, ed., *The Botanical Garden of Padua 1545–1995* (Venice: Marsilio, 1995).

Morpurgo, Edgardo, *Lo studio di Padova, le epidemie ed i contagi durante il governo della repubblica veneta (1405–1797)* (Padua: La Garangola, 1922).

———, *Notizie sulle famiglie ebree esistite a Padova nel XVI secolo* (Udine: Del Bianco, 1909).

———, "Notizie sulle famiglie ebree esistite a Padova nel XVI secolo," *Il corriere israelitico* 47:231 (1908–9).

Müller, Karlheinz, Simon Schwarzfuchs, and Avraham Reinder, eds., *Die Gransteine vom jüdischen Friedhof in Würzburg aus der Zeit von dem Schwarzen Tod* (Würzburg: Monumenta Germaniae Historica, 2012).

Myers, David, *The Faith of Fallen Jews: Yosef Hayim Yerushalmi and the Writing of Jewish History* (Waltham, MA: Brandeis University Press, 2013).

Namouchi, Amine, et al., "Integrative Approach Using *Yersinia pestis* Genomes to Revisit the Historical Landscape of Plague During the Medieval Period," *Proceedings of the National Academy of Sciences* 115.50 (2018): E11790–E11797.

Olivetti, Sergio, "Uno stampatore e poeta ebreo: Giuseppe Conzio," *La Rassegna Mensile di Israel* 25.1 (1959): 22–25.

Ortner, Sherry, "Subjectivity and Social Critique," *Anthropological Theory* 5.1 (2005): 31–52.

Paden, William, "An Occitan Prayer Against the Plague and Its Tradition in Italy, France and Catalonia," *Speculum* 89.3 (2014): 670–92.

Pagis, Dan, "The Invention of the Hebrew Iambic and Shifts in Italian Hebrew Prosody" [in Hebrew], *Ha-Sifrut* 4 (1973): 651–712.

Palmer, Richard, "The Control of Plague in Venice and Northern Italy: 1348–1600," PhD diss., University of Kent at Canterbury, 1978.

———, "In Bad Odour: Smell and Its Significance in Medicine from Antiquity to the Seventeenth Century," in *Medicine and the Five Senses*, ed. W. F. Bynum and Roy Porter (Cambridge: Cambridge University Press, 1993), 61–68.

———, "Pharmacy in the Republic of Venice in the Sixteenth Century," in *The Medical Renaissance of the Sixteenth Century*, ed. A. Wear et al. (Cambridge: Cambridge University Press, 1985), 100–117.

———, "Physicians and Surgeons in Sixteenth-Century Venice," *Medical History* 23 (1979): 451–60.

Parisi, Susan, "The Jewish Community and Carnival Entertainment at the Mantuan Court in the Early Baroque," in *Music in Renaissance Cities and Courts: Studies in Honor of Lewis Lockwood*, ed. Jessie Ann Owens and A. Cummings (Warren, MI: Harmonie Park Press, 1997).

Patuzzi, Stefano, "Music from a Confined Space: Salamone Rossi's *HaShirim asher liShlomo* (1622/23) and the Mantuan Ghetto," *Journal of Synagogue Music* 37 (Fall 2012): 49–58.

Pavoncello, Nello, "La tipografia ebraica in Piemonte," *La Rassegna Mensile di Israel*, 3d ser., 36.2 (1970): 96–100.

Phelan, James, *Somebody Telling Somebody Else: Toward a Rhetorical Poetics of Narrative* (Columbus: Ohio State University Press, 2017).

Pieragostini, Renata, "The Healing Power of Music? Documentary Evidence from Late-Fourteenth-Century Bologna," *Speculum* 96.1 (2021): 156–76.

Pugliano, Valentina, "Pharmacy, Testing and the Language of Truth in Renaissance Italy," *Bulletin of the History of Medicine* 91.2 (2017): 233–73.

Pullan, Brian S., "Plague and Perceptions of the Poor in Renaissance Italy," in *Epidemics and Ideas*, ed. T. Ranger and P. Slack (Cambridge: Cambridge University Press, 1992), 101–24.

———, *Rich and Poor in Renaissance Venice* (Oxford: Oxford and Blackwell, 1971).

Reichman, Edward, "From Cholera to Coronavirus: Recurring Pandemics, Recurring Rabbinic Responses," *Tradition Online*, April 2, 2020: https://traditiononline.org/from -cholera-to-coronavirus-recurring-pandemics-recurring-rabbinic-responses/

———, "Incensed by Coronavirus: Prayer and Ketoret in Times of Epidemic," *Lehrhaus*, Tuesday, June 8, 2021, https://www.thelehrhaus.com/timely-thoughts/incensed-by-corona virus-prayer-and-ketoret-in-times-of-epidemic/

———, "The Physicians of the Rome Plague of 1656, Yaakov Zahalon and Hananiah Modigliano," *Seforim* Blog (https://seforimblog.com), February 19, 2021.

———, "Precedented Times: The Rabbinic Response to Covid-19 and Pandemics Throughout the Ages" (pre-published copy, cited with thanks to the author).

Rizhik, Michael, "'How do we light' and 'Grinding of the Incense' in Italian Vernacular Prayerbooks" [in Hebrew], *Masorot* 13–14 (2006): 181–202.

Rodseth, Lars, "Historical Massacres and Mythical Totalities: Reading Marshall Sahlins on Two American Frontiers," in *Anthropologists and Their Traditions Across National Borders*, ed. Regna Darnell and Frederic Gleach (Lincoln: University of Nebraska Press, 2014), 209–48.

Rosenwein, Barbara, *Emotional Communities in the Early Middle Ages* (Ithaca, NY: Cornell University Press, 2007).

———, "Problems and Methods in the History of the Emotions," *Passions in Context* 1 (2010): 2–32.

Roth, Cecil, "L'accademia musicale del Ghetto Veneziano," *La Rassegna Mensile di Israel* 3.4 (1928): 152–62.

———, "Sefer *'Olam Hafukh* by Abraham Catalano," [in Hebrew] *Qovetz 'al yad* 4.14 (1946): 67–101.

Ruderman, David, "The Ghetto and Jewish Cultural Formation in Early Modern Europe," in *Jewish Literatures and Cultures*, ed. A. Norich and Y. Eliav (Providence, RI: Brown Judaic Studies no. 349, 2008).

———, ed., *Preachers of the Italian Ghetto* (Berkeley: University of California Press, 1992).

Sabar, Shimon, "The Beginnings and Flourishings of Ketubbah Illustration in Italy: A Study in Popular Imagery and Jewish Patronage During the Seventeenth and Eighteenth Centuries," PhD diss., (University of California–Los Angeles, 1987).

Sahlins, Marshall, *Apologies to Thucydides: Understanding History as Culture and Vice Versa* (Chicago: University of Chicago Press, 2004).

———, *Culture in Practice: Selected Essays* (New York: Zone Books, 2000), 293–51;

Salm, Mel, "Anthropocene Diseased: A Provocation," online COVID-19 FORUM II, April 6, 2020: somatosphere.net/forumpost/Anthropocene-covid-19/?format=pdf.

Saperstein, Marc, *Jewish Preaching 1200–1800: An Anthology* (New Haven, CT: Yale University Press, 1989).

———, *Exile in Amsterdam: Saul Levi Morteira's Sermons to a Congregation of 'New Jews'"* (Cincinnati, OH: Hebrew Union College Press, 2005).

———, "Four Kinds of Weeping: Saul Levi Morteira's Application of Biblical Narrative to Contemporary Events," *Studia Rosenthalia* 42/43 (2010–11): 25–41.

Sárraga, Marian, and Ramón Sárraga, "Early Links Between Amsterdam, Hamburg and Italy: Epitaphs from Hamburg's Old Sephardic Cemetery," *Studia Rosenthaliana* 34 (2000): 23–55.

———, "Sephardic Epitaphs in Hamburg's Oldest Jewish Cemetery: Poetry, Riddles and Eccentric Texts," *AJS Review* 26 (2002): 53–92.

Segre, Renate, *The Jews in Piedmont*, 3 vols. (Jerusalem: Israel Academy of Sciences & Humanities and Tel Aviv University, 1988).

Seifert, L., et al., "Genotyping *Yersinia pestis* in Historical Plague: Evidence for Long-Term Persistence of *Y. pestis* in Europe from the Fourteenth to the Seventeenth Century," *PLoSOne* 11.1: e0145194 (January 2016).

Seroussi, Edwin, "Ghetto Soundscapes: Venice and Beyond," in *Shirat Dvora*, ed. H. Yishai (Be'er Sheva, Ben Gurion University and Mossad Bialik, 2018): 157*–171*.

Sewell, William, "A Theory of the Event: Marshall Sahlins's Possible Theory of History," in *Logics of History* (Chicago: University of Chicago Press, 2000), 197–224.

Shupbach, William, "A Venetian 'Plague Miracle' in 1474 and 1576," *Medical History* 24.3 (1976): 312–16.

Siegmund, Stefanie Beth, *The Medici State and the Ghetto of Florence: The Construction of an Early Modern Jewish Community* (Palo Alto, CA: Stanford University Press, 2006).

Simonsohn, Shlomo, *History of the Jews in the Duchy of Mantua* (Jerusalem: Kiryath Sepher, 1977).

———, "Savants and Scholars in Jewish Mantua: A Reassessment," in *Rabbi Judah Moscato and the Jewish Intellectual World of Mantua in the Sixteenth and Seventeenth Centuries*, ed. Giuseppe Veltri and G. Miletto (Leiden: Brill, 2012), 299–319.

Sosland, Henry, *A Guide for Preachers on Composing and Delivering Sermons: The Or ha-Darshanim of Jacob Zahalon* (New York: Jewish Theological Seminary, 1987).

Stearns, Justin K. *Infectious Ideas: Contagion in Premodern Christian and Islamic Thought in the Western Mediterranean* (Baltimore: Johns Hopkins University Press, 2011).

Steinschneider, Moritz, "La Famiglia Marini," *Il vessillo israelitico* 28 (1879–80): 147–50.

———, "Poems of Joseph Concio from an Unknown Manuscript" [in Hebrew], *He'Assif* 2 (1886): 225–27.

Stock, Brian, *The Implications of Literacy: Written Language and Models of Interpretation in the Eleventh and Twelfth Centuries* (Princeton, NJ: Princeton University Press, 1983).

Stössl, Marianne, "Lo spettacolo della Triaca. Produzione e promozione della 'Droga Divina' a Venezia dal Cinque al Settento," *Quaderni del Centro Tedesco di Studi Veneziani* 25 (1983): 4–47.

Stow, Kenneth, *Theater of Acculturation: The Roman Ghetto in the 16th Century* (Seattle: University of Washington Press, 2001).

Tefillah bi'zman she-lo tavo ha-magefah, "found" by Solomon b. Isaac Marini (Venice: Vendramin, 1630).

Teplitzky, Joshua, "Hygiene and Historiography: Medieval Myths and Modern Misreceptions of the Jews and the Black Death," *AJS Review* (forthcoming, Winter 2021).

Teter, Magda, "The Pandemic, Antisemitism, and the Lachrymose Conception of Jewish History," *Jewish Social Studies* 26.1 (Fall 2020): 20–32.

Tirosh Rothschild, Hava, "The Political Philosophy in the Thought of Abraham Shalom" [in Hebrew], in *Jerusalem Studies in Jewish Thought*, special issue in honor of Shlomo Pines, ed. Moshe Idel et al., vol. 2 (1990): 407–40.

Toaff, Ariel, *Gli ebrei a Perugia* (Città di Castello: Arti Grafiche Città di Castello, 1975).

Traversari, Mirko, et al., "The Plague of 1630 in Modena (Italy) Through the Study of Parish Registers," *Medicina Historica* 3.3 (2019): 139–48.

Valderas, José Maria, "Mattioli contra Lusitano, II. Las 'censuras' y la interpretación de Dioscórides," *Collectanea Botanica* (Barcelona) 26 (2003): 181–225.

———, "La polémica en la investigación botánica del siglo XVI. Mattioli contra Lusitano," *Collectanea Botanica* (Barcelona) 25 (2000): 255–304.

Varlik, Nükhet, *Plague and Empire in the Early Modern Mediterranean World* (Cambridge: Cambridge University Press, 2015).

Visi, Tamar, "Plague, Persecution and Philosophy: Avigdor Kara and the Consequences of the Black Death," in *Intricate Interfaith Networks in the Middle Ages*, ed. Ephraim Shoham Steiner (Turnhout: Brepols, 2016), 85–117.

Weitzman, Steven, *Song and Story in Biblical Narrative* (Bloomington: Indiana University Press, 1997).

Williams, Benjamin, *Commentary on Midrash Rabba in the Sixteenth Century* (Oxford: Oxford University Press, 2016).

Wimsatt, James, review of M. Boulton, *The Song in the Story*, in *Studies in the Age of Chaucer* 17 (1995): 178–82.

Wray, Shona Kelly, *Communities in Crisis: Bologna During the Black Death* (Leiden: Brill, 2009).

Yagel, Abraham, *Moshiah Hosim* (Venice, 1587).

Yerushalmi, Yosef, *Zakhor: Jewish History and Jewish Memory* (Seattle: University of Washington Press, 1982).

Zacut, Moses, *Sefer Shorshei haShemot* (Jerusalem: Nezer Shraga, 1998–99).

Zonta, Mauro, *Hebrew Scholasticism in the Fifteenth Century* (Dordrecht, Netherlands: Springer Nature, 2006).

Index

Acknowledgments

Most of this book was written during the first year and a half of the coronavirus pandemic. On the one hand, the combination of travel restrictions, library closures, online teaching, and confinement encouraged a study characterized more by literary than historical methods, although I have tried to balance both. On the other hand, the same obstacles were eased by the generosity of scholars here and abroad who provided copies of articles and sections of books inaccessible via shuttered libraries, and by the continued maintenance of online resources like the National Library of Israel's invaluable KTIV database of digitized Hebrew manuscripts.

I thank David Malkiel and Josh Teplitzky for providing me with copies of their work; Michelle Chesner of Columbia University Library and Yoram Bitton and Jordan Finkin of the Hebrew Union College's Klau Library for scans and assistance; Jean Kuperminc of the Alliance Israelite Française for scans; and Michael Young at UConn's Homer Babbidge Library for help with sources and permissions. Thanks again to Josh Teplitzky and to Eddie Reichman for sharing sources, ideas, and feedback, and to Ann Carmichael, Susan Harvey, Lori Jones, Larry Klein, Andreas Lehnertz, Jim McIlwain, and Yossi Ziegler for ongoing correspondence and conversation. Caroline W. Bynum, Susan Harvey, and Bill Jordan all kindly read drafts of different sections and provided valuable feedback, as did the amazingly thorough anonymous readers for Penn Press. Indeed, I am grateful to all the extra eyes who often saw more than I could. My former colleague, Steve Kaufman, generously assisted with Aramaic, and my students in two iterations of a Black Death course came up with observations and questions that, whether they knew it or not, improved this book.

The Mediterranean Studies Center at the University of Haifa hosted me for a fruitful month in December 2018, and the Mandel School in the Department of Jewish History at Hebrew University provided a visiting faculty fellowship in the fall of 2019; my thanks to Zur Shalev and Gil Gambash in Haifa, and to Elisheva Baumgarten in Jerusalem for these opportunities, which the University of Connecticut graciously allowed me to pursue. Over the course of our protracted lockdown, I gave zoom talks on Jews and the Great Italian Plague for UCLA's Center for Medieval and Renaissance Studies; the University of Minnesota's medieval and Jewish Studies programs; the Center for Jewish Studies at SOAS University of London; Wake Forest College; and Temple University. Thank you to these hosts and to their audiences.

My mother, who has always been my sharpest critic, died in February 2021 after months of illness; despite her failing health, she followed updates on my work with characteristic brilliance and wit. My sister, Jodie Cohen-Tanugi, gamely inherited the job of nonexpert-but-brilliant reader, and the final form of the introduction owes much to her keen comments. Jerry Singerman, who shepherded two of my previous three books to publication, also brought this one to contract. His singular contributions to medieval studies scholarship in general, and to my writing personally, are matched only by his steadfast decency and his loyalty as a friend. I dedicate this book to him.

CPSIA information can be obtained
at www.ICGtesting.com
Printed in the USA
JSHW030917020822
28462JS00001B/1

9 781512 822878